Thomas Merton

and

James Laughlin

Thomas Merton

AND

James Laughlin

/ · /

SELECTED LETTERS

EDITED BY DAVID D. COOPER

W · W · NORTON & COMPANY

NEW YORK   LONDON

The text of this book is composed in 11.5/13 Bembo
with the display set in ITC Garamond Book Condensed
Composition and manufacturing by the Maple-Vail Book Manufacturing Group

Library of Congress Cataloging-in-Publication Data

Merton, Thomas, 1915–1968.
Thomas Merton and James Laughlin : selected letters / edited by
David D. Cooper.
p.   cm.
Includes bibliographical references and index.
ISBN 0-393-04069-0
1. Merton, Thomas, 1915–1968—Correspondence.   2. Poets,
American—20th century—Correspondence.   3. Trappists—United
States—Correspondence. 4. Laughlin, James, 1914–
Correspondence. 5. Publishers and publishing—United States—
Correspondence. 6. Authors and publishers—United States—
History—20th century.   7. Authorship—Moral and ethical aspects.
I. Laughlin, James, 1914–   .   II. Cooper, David D.   III. Title.
PS3525.E7174Z485   1997
818'.5409—dc21

[B]   96-39819
                                                                        CIP

W. W. Norton & Company, Inc., 500 Fifth Avenue, New York, N.Y. 10110
http://www.wwnorton.com

W. W. Norton & Company Ltd., 10 Coptic Street, London WC1A 1PU

1 2 3 4 5 6 7 8 9 0

For
William H. Shannon

It seems to me that the particular configuration of my own life, with all its shortcomings, demands some sort of synthesis of poetry and prayer. I fully realize that I might perhaps aspire to a technically "higher" kind of life if I would try to refuse to be a poet. But I have reason to think that if I made this refusal it would in fact be an act of pride and disobedience. Others will assume, on the other hand, that it is pride for me to continue to be a poet, especially when I am not a very good one. . . . I owe to the Lord my feeble efforts to synthesize, in my own life, the disparate elements that have been given to me. Hence I am to some extent monk, to some extent poet, and so on, and trying to reduce all this to unity. . . . [I]t would be wrong to say I was satisfied. On the contrary, I am more dissatisfied with the results than anyone else, but they are what they are, and they have to be accepted by me. . . .

—TM to Cecilia Corsanego, 31 January 1964

CONTENTS

INTRODUCTION

If making close friends is part of the hard work of becoming a whole person, the friendship of Thomas Merton and James Laughlin reveals a remarkable labor of mutual self-completion. Told in an expansive narrative of nearly eight hundred letters, the story of their friendship begins in the early 1940s when Laughlin inaugurated his New Directions publishing enterprise in Greenwich Village and Merton forsook all worldly enterprise for monastic life at the Abbey of Gethsemani, a Trappist monastery hidden away in rural Kentucky's knob country. Merton and Laughlin continued to write each other's lives in letters until Merton's was cut short by a tragic accident in that bruising year, 1968.

Son of New Zealand–born watercolorist Owen Merton and American art student Ruth Calvert Jenkins, Thomas Merton, born in 1915, would never know the emotional stability or financial security that cushioned James Laughlin's childhood. Laughlin's father, Henry Hughart Laughlin—whose grandfather, along with five uncles, founded the prominent Jones and Laughlin Steel Corporation in 1856, a bulwark of Pittsburgh's booming Gilded Age steel business—sent his son to the finest schools. From his birth in 1914 James Laughlin rode a predictable American trajectory of upper-class status and success. He first attended the private Arnold School in Pittsburgh. In an effort to spare their sons the unpleasantness of the Depression in America, Laughlin's parents sent James and his brother to the exclusive boarding school Le Rosey near Geneva, Switzerland, where his classmate, Muhammad Reza Pahlavi, future Shah of Iran, was whisked off by his bodyguards every Saturday night for amusement in Geneva. Next came terms spent at the Eaglebrook School in Deerfield, Massachusetts. Laughlin's admittance into Harvard University in 1932 was virtually guaranteed by his prep school tenure at the famous Choate School in Wallingford, Connecticut (not far from his wealthy aunt's country estate near Norfolk), where his teacher Dudley Fitts first introduced Laughlin to as yet uncelebrated contemporary authors and poets like Ezra Pound and Gertrude Stein.

Thomas Merton's boyhood is a study in contrasts. On the opening page of *The Seven Storey Mountain* (1948), his best-selling autobiography, Merton chronicled the year of his birth in the chilling and stark imagery of a world war convulsing the French landscape a few hundred kilometers north of his birthplace in Prades, the South of France. He noted the corpses of soldiers strewn among rotting horse carcasses along the river Marne and the French forests denuded by artillery barrages. Faced with chronic money problems and the uncertainties of a violent war being waged in Europe, the Mertons moved to America, launching a long period of geographic instability, financial insecurity, and emotional disruption that would scar Thomas Merton's early years. After his mother died when Merton was only six years old, his father set out on a restless quest for artistic inspiration. On occasion Merton would accompany Owen on painting trips to Bermuda, Provincetown, and back to the South of France. Most of the time the boy was left with maternal grandparents on Long Island or with family friends in France or an uncle and aunt in England.

Merton's boyhood, in a word, was rudderless, without fixed horizon. His early education was frequently and unpredictably disrupted. He bounced from public grade schools on Long Island to a local school on Bermuda where Merton often skipped class, to a French lycée in Montauban where the French boys ruthlessly picked on him because of his big ears, and back to middling boarding schools in England. By the time Merton was seventeen, the last of the weak blocks of familial security had been knocked from beneath him by his father's particularly debilitating death from a malignant brain tumor. "As an orphan," he later confessed poignantly in a letter to Robert Lawrence Williams collected in *The Hidden Ground of Love* (1985), "I went through the business of being passed around from family to family, and being a 'ward,' and an 'object of charitable concern,' etc. etc. I know how inhuman and frustrating that can be—being treated as a thing and not as a person. And reacting against it with dreams that were sometimes shattered in a most inhuman way."

By 1933, when Thomas Merton entered Clare College to begin a short-lived university career at Cambridge, James Laughlin, nineteen years old and in mild rebellion against the commercial ethos of his wealthy family, was on a leave of absence from Harvard. He traveled to Rapallo, Italy where, in August 1933, he met and later studied with Ezra Pound. Pound dashed Laughlin's desire to join the fledgling modernist literary movement when he unceremoniously dismissed Laughlin's poems and told him that he'd never make it as a poet. Instead, Pound encouraged Laughlin to use his family's means to good end and become a publisher. "I thought to myself," Laughlin later reflected calmly, at a distance, in an autobiographical account published in *American Poetry* (Spring 1984), "that if I couldn't be a writer, maybe as a publisher I could hang around with writers and have a good time." While the young student was no doubt shaken by

Pound's snub, the incident at the "Ezuversity" is often overstated. Nevertheless, as Kenneth Rexroth later concluded in the preface to his *American Poetry in the Twentieth Century* (1971), "Laughlin worked day after day, often till far into the night, himself, and hard, to publish writers who often were far less good than himself, year after year, for little thanks. He is an excellent and original poet, and might have been writing his own poems."

In any event, Laughlin listened to Pound's advice. With financial backing from his aunt, Mrs. Leila Carlisle, who also provided an unused stable on her Norfolk estate that housed New Directions' first offices, and a $100,000 graduation present from Henry Hughart Laughlin (which the young graduate promptly used to purchase a ski lodge in Alta, Utah, that would reap enough return on investment to bankroll his publishing company for many years), Laughlin launched the New Directions Publishing Corporation. From the very beginning he published the poets who would spur the modernist literary revolution in America and form a stable of new writers Laughlin would publish for many years to come, including Pound, William Carlos Williams, Kay Boyle, Dylan Thomas, Djuna Barnes, Henry Miller, and Thomas Merton.

While Pound counseled Laughlin in Rapallo on how to spend his money, Thomas Merton, emotionally anguished by the cruel death of his father, set out on his own journey to Italy that, like Laughlin's, would have a lasting impact on his future life course. Merton made a solitary sojourn to Rome in the summer of 1933, where he underwent a wrenching psychotic break in a lonely hotel room one night that he later characterized as a religious conversion experience. Cut to the quick by an intense, sudden, and painful insight into the corruption of his own soul, mysteriously linked to a deep interior peace such as he had never felt before, inspired by the religious art of Rome, the episode became the benchmark of Thomas Merton's religious life. The summer in Rome set Merton upon a course that would establish him as one of the twentieth century's most significant religious personalities and place him among its most prolific writers and poets.

In Italy, in the summer of 1933, Thomas Merton and James Laughlin—unknown to each other at the time and separated by what may seem an unbridgeable chasm of class, family background, education, social privilege, and promise—began what to both of them would be their life work in which each would play formative and prominent roles for the other.

But first, for Merton at least, there would be more searching and more trial. Returning from Rome, he entered Clare College at Cambridge University. Shortly afterwards, he was invited to leave under threat of a palimony suit. The spiritual malaise and moral searching that began in Rome continued to agitate deeply within him. After being received into the Roman Catholic Church in 1938 and not long after graduating Columbia University with a master's degree in English Literature the following year, Merton awakened to a calling to priesthood and the monastic life. He visited a Trappist monastery for the first time on the day after Japan bombed Pearl Harbor. As the world inched toward another conflagration, Thomas Merton had finally arrived home. He imagined a future far different than his past. "[T]here will be no more future," he reflected enthustically in "St. Bonaventure Journal," included as Part III in the journal sequence *Run to the Mountain—The Story of a Vocation* (published recently, 1995), "not in the world, not in geography, not in travel, not in change, not in variety, conversations, new work, new problems in writing, new friends—none of that, but a far better progress, all interior and quiet!!!"

On December 13, 1941, Merton, twenty-six years old, was officially accepted into Gethsemani and issued the robes of a Cistercian oblate. He met the abbot, Dom

Frederic Dunne, who gave Thomas Merton his new name in religious life—"Louis"—thereby completing a transformation from poet and would-be novelist, English professor, erstwhile fellow traveler, and jazz aficionado into a contemplative aching for silence, solitude, wordlessness, and freedom from human suffering and worldly folly. Dom Frederic, the gentle abbot who received Merton as a postulant and later presided over frater Louis's profession of simple and solemn vows, quickly became Thomas Merton's Ezra Pound, guiding and encouraging his literary pursuits. This was a quiet but formative irony that Merton and Laughlin would never fully appreciate in spite of its critical importance to a personal friendship that spanned a quarter century, a literary relationship that spawned more than twenty books, and a commercial partnership that would reap the sort of profits that made it possible for New Directions to publish important but notoriously unprofitable poets.

Merton was less prepared to accept the insistent urgings of Dom Frederic, however, than Laughlin had been to follow Pound's career counseling. Convinced that his literary instincts could only disrupt a life of prayer, Merton's misgivings and ambivalence over his identity as a poet and writer grew intense and divisive upon entering the monastery, a motif that surfaces in both Merton and Laughlin's letters during the 1940s and early 1950s. Dom Frederic's warm support and determined encouragement of Merton's literary talents—cresting early with the phenomenally successful autobiography *The Seven Storey Mountain*—provided emotional shelter from Merton's storms of self-doubt. When Dom Frederic died in 1948, Merton lost an important mentor whose wise guidance helped to quiet the turmoil of Merton's inner divisions. This support was critical during Merton's early years in the monastery, when he was not only wracked by persistent conflict between his literary instincts and his new identity as a monk but had to adjust as well to the formidable rigors of monastic life in the 1940s, a communal life of extreme hardship, sacrifice, and asceticism. Even though the Cistercians are a communitarian or "cenobitic" monastic order, the monks lived in strict silence before the reforms set in motion by the Second Vatican Council in the 1960s. Their lives were punctuated daily by communal prayers, spartan meals and little sleep, reflective study and spiritual reading, and plenty of manual labor in the monastery fields.

Fortunately, James Laughlin stepped into the breach after Dom Frederic's death. From the moment Mark Van Doren, Merton's Columbia University professor, mentor, and thesis adviser, sent Laughlin an uneven collection of Merton's first poems, published as *Thirty Poems* in 1944, New Directions issued a virtual carte blanche to publish just about anything and everything the young monk/poet submitted. It is no exaggeration to say, in fact, that James Laughlin and New Directions *made* Thomas Merton as a poet, and—along with Robert Giroux and Merton's literary agent, Naomi Burton Stone—contributed considerable impetus to Merton's still-swelling reputation as a writer, social critic, autobiographer, ecumenist, spiritual guide, and commentator on our life and times. Laughlin and his staff, for example, routinely brokered Merton's poems to leading literary magazines like the *Saturday Review, The New Yorker,* and *Poetry.* They underwrote some of Merton's most controversial political writing—notably *Breakthrough to Peace* (1962), whose difficult road to publication is mapped in Merton and Laughlin's letters of 1961 and 1962, and the trenchant *Raids on the Unspeakable* (1966). The New Directions office also organized a *samizdat* of influential figures to read Merton's mimeographed essays on peace, nuclear weapons disarmament, and social justice issues during the civil rights movement and the Vietnam War after Merton's Trappist superiors flatly ordered him to stop writing about faith and social witness as they bore directly on the political turbulence and social unrest roiling an anxious and troubled era. Laughlin even made it possible for Merton to set out on his ill-fated Asian trip in 1968 by arranging for his American Express Card and traveler's checks and coaching Merton on the fine arts of foreign travel.

Viewed strictly from a literary vantage point, it may seem odd that Thomas Merton became one of James Laughlin's most favorite New Directions poets. Given his philosophy of publishing, it is even surprising that Laughlin pressed ahead so quickly and unequivocally in publishing Merton's early work. In the lead chapter of *Random Essays* (1989), Laughlin's chronicle of his literary life, he frankly admits that "Merton's early religious poems, except for their color and vigor of imagery, do not particularly interest me. There is something facile about them." Merton's pious early verse ran radically counter to the hallmarks of literary modernism that Laughlin actively sought in the experimental writing of early New Directions poets like Pound, William Carlos Williams, Henri Michaux, George Oppen—and Gertrude Stein, whose *Three Lives,* reprinted by New Directions in 1941, makes Merton's *Thirty Poems* (1944) seem, in comparison, too glib indeed. As a publisher Laughlin was instinctively drawn to experimental poetry that fulfilled the critical injunctions of the new literary modernism: mold-breaking innovations in literary forms and cut-to-the-quick, bare knuckles social commentary leavened with lassitude and angst. He sought out poets who rebelled against "the standardization of language," as he put it in "New Words for Old: Notes on Experimental Writing" (first published in 1936 and later collected in *Random Essays*), poets who searched "with all . . . ingenuity for a solvent to" conventional literary forms. This gave the early New Directions list an obvious house style and an unmistakable feel: unconventional, iconoclastic, nonconformist. Aesthetic experimentation merged with

Laughlin's sense of place in literary history to produce a publishing philosophy he summed up in the preface to *New Directions 15* (1955): "The theory was simply this: Literature, a whole culture in fact, goes dead when there is no experiment, no reaching out, no counter-attack on accepted values. Even if the experiment is a failure, it must exist as a force and be given a showing place."

The religious poetry that dominated Thomas Merton's earliest work, up to and including *The Tears of the Blind Lions,* published by New Directions in 1949, hardly fit the new style, to say the least. Merton was fundamentally a psalmodist. For stylistic inspiration he looked backward to biblical and liturgical prototypes such as the aubade, the canticle, and the hymn. While the social commentary of Merton's religious verse counter-punched accepted values, it was a conservative and reactionary criticism, decidedly retrograde when compared to the social critiques launched by other New Directions authors at the time. Expressing a disdain for worldly living undoubtedly connected to his bohemian youth, tempered by a theological legalism Merton embraced upon entering the monastery, his early poems lashed out at the godlessness and apostasy that he uncritically associated with secular America, making for, quite frankly, some forced and clumsy poetry characterized by severe vacillations between sentimentality, sarcasm, righteousness, and rage.

In addition, there was a moral angle to consider in the publishing relationship. By the early 1950s, as Merton explained in an unpublished letter to his agent dated 27 January 1951, he began considering "a moral question which would confront me if I were found to be actively cooperating in the production of books by other people ([Laughlin's] protégés) who write what might be considered as morally undesirable material." Merton had a good point. At a time when New Directions published the poems of a cloistered religious, it was also publishing Djuna Barnes and Arthur Rimbaud and issuing titles from Henry Miller, whose books were headed to the Supreme Court in a landmark pornography case. The second edition of Kenneth Patchen's *The Journal of Albion Moonlight* appeared under the New Directions imprint the same year Laughlin published Merton's own first volume of poetry. Patchen's journal—a descent, the jacket blurb boasted, into "the far boundaries of love and murder, madness and sex"—flaunted the traditional Christian moral concerns central to Merton's early work.

Nonetheless, Merton remained steadfastly loyal to Laughlin. As their letters indicate, they rarely broached any moral qualms that Merton might have harbored privately over other books New Directions published. In Letter #41, for example, Merton skirts potentially serious questions of moral propriety by camouflaging them as matters of "monastery diplomacy." Merton and Laughlin's literary as well as personal relationship never broke stride over the issue of art and Christian morality. Merton and Henry Miller, largely at Laughlin's instigation, even became fast friends and mutual admirers of each other's writing.

For his part, although Laughlin privately faulted Merton's early poems for lacking range and technical severity, he still found something extremely likable and approachable in Merton's verse from the very beginning, even if the monk's early poems had little resonance in the New Directions canon. Laughlin stuck with him. It is a testament to Laughlin's devotion to Merton and his sharp instincts as an editor that he continued encouraging Merton to write poems even during a fallow period in the early 1950s when the monk swore off poetry writing. It is also a testament to Laughlin's prescience as a reader that Merton, beginning with the publication of *The Strange Islands* in 1957, would blossom into one of New Directions' most experimental poets. From the drafts of new poems Merton began sending him in 1956, Laughlin sensed an important new direction in the writing, the beginning of what he considered the secularization of Merton's poetry. Laughlin applauded, he writes in *Random Essays,* "the new verbal tone, a mixture of satire and irony, fused into black humor, and a structure of depersonalization . . . in which the speaker is much withdrawn from the content of the poem" that began to energize the new poems, cresting in the deadpan prose poem *Original Child Bomb* (1962) and the chilling "Chant to Be Used in Processions Around a Site with Furnaces" (1961), which Laughlin considered Merton's most remarkable poem. Suddenly freed from restraint, Merton combusted into an experimental poet par excellence. He "wrote" found poems. He translated contemporary and ancient poetry from the Greek, Spanish, Portuguese, French, and Chinese. He began exploring the possibilities of an "antipoetry" based on the mass culture criticism of the leftist critic and philosopher Herbert Marcuse and the Chilean poet Nicanor Parra. Other new modes of writing breached from the depths of Merton's creative unconscious: satire and pseudo-comedy, prose poetry, long poems, collage, surrealistic wordplay, mosaic, ethnographic verse, parody, and pseudo-myth. It took a horrible accident in Bangkok to shut off the faucet, leaving behind two volumes of fascinating and multi-layered poetry—*Cables to the Ace* (1968) and *The Geography of Lograire* (1969)—for a new generation of literary critics and Merton scholars to sort out.

Part of the reason for James Laughlin's continued devotion to Merton-the-poet was Laughlin's extraordinary affection for Merton-the-person. Considering the often difficult, frequently volatile, and sometimes outright nasty episodes Laughlin suffered at the hands of other New Directions writers, Thomas Merton must have seemed a real saint. Even the gentle pediatrician could be a pain. Hugh Witemeyer reports in his Introduction to *William Carlos Williams and James Laughlin:*

Selected Letters (1989) that certain tensions trailed through the long relationship between Laughlin and Williams. Frustrated by Laughlin's frequent travels abroad and his domestic ski trips, Witemeyer writes, "the workaholic doctor sometimes envied and resented the globe-trotting . . . jaunts and bachelor freedoms of his wealthy young friend," a resentment that came to a head in 1950 when Williams turned to Random House to publish his poems. Although he eventually returned to the New Directions fold, Laughlin was hurt by what he considered Williams's betrayal, and their relationship became awkward and strained for many years to come. It is painfully clear from *Delmore Schwartz and James Laughlin: Selected Letters* (1993) that Schwartz also resented Laughlin's frequent absences from the Greenwich Village office and his laid-back lifestyle. He even accused Laughlin of conspiring with Nelson Rockefeller to have an affair with Schwartz's second wife. Unhinged from reality, Schwartz's letters, according to Robert Phillips, "developed into dark and obsessive harangues. . . . He accused Laughlin of disaffection, even of cheating him on his royalty statements. . . . [I]t must have been extremely painful to Laughlin to receive such attacks." The mercurial Kenneth Rexroth (whose letters to Laughlin were edited by Rexroth's biographer Lee Bartlett and published in 1991), populist to the core, often pounded Laughlin with invective during fits of impatience, and on occasion he accused Laughlin of being a puppet for New York literati. Henry Miller—chronically broke—habitually complained about his contracts, accusing Laughlin, as George Wickes recounts in his Introduction to *Henry Miller and James Laughlin: Selected Letters* (1996), of taking "unfair advantage of him." And, of course, the deeply complicated Ezra Pound, to whom Laughlin remained steadfastly devoted even while weathering Pound's storms of political rage, forced Laughlin to take strong public stands against the poet's anti-Semitism and pro-Fascist diatribes.

For Laughlin it must have felt like an interpersonal retreat of sorts from the bruising relationships with other New Directions writers when he flew down to Louisville and rented a car for the hour long ride south to Bardstown for annual visits with Thomas Merton at Gethsemani. Laughlin recounts those trips with simple affection in his essay about Merton. That Laughlin selected the piece to lead off *Random Essays* says something about his esteem of and affection for Thomas Merton.

There is perhaps no greater testament to Laughlin's personal affection for Merton and his commitment to Merton's vision and continuing message as a writer than the long and painstaking labor Laughlin devoted to the posthumously published *Asian Journal of Thomas Merton*. When the fragmentary notebooks and journals Merton kept during his Asian travels in 1968—often consisting only of nouns and verbs strung together into lists or cryptic shorthand reminders for entries Merton clearly intended to flesh out for later publication—fell into Laughlin's hands after Merton died, Laughlin was determined to make a book out of them despite a daunting editorial task that would take him the better part of two years. With the help of Naomi Burton Stone and Gethsemani's Brother Patrick Hart, Laughlin pieced together into a seamless narrative the disjointed prose fragments Merton recorded in three separate notebooks. He tracked down the names and addresses of the many people Merton talked to during his two-month travels. He traced arduous bibliographic leads in order to identify exact sources of quotations from Buddhist and Hindu spiritual texts that Merton randomly strewed throughout his notebooks. Laughlin even skillfully and tediously transcribed a poem Merton wrote, in a jiggly hand, into a small pocket notebook amid plane timetables and phone numbers while riding on a train; and he included "Kandy Express" in an eighty-page section of uncollected works he later appended to the massive *Collected Poems of*

Thomas Merton, issued by New Directions in 1977. Due largely to a combination of Laughlin's editorial pertinacity and his continued devotion to a writer/friend, *The Asian Journal* nearly rivaled the critical attention and popular appeal of Merton's first chapter in a long autobiographical opus, the run-away bestseller *Seven Storey Mountain.* Looking back over six productive and ambitious decades in the book business, Laughlin didn't hesitate to rank *The Asian Journal,* as he noted in a letter to me, "one of the most important things I did in publishing."

Throughout their nearly thirty-year friendship, Laughlin and Merton's relationship never strayed from intimacy and mutual understanding, respect and tolerance. From the beginning they shared a search for integrity as writers and as midwives to the voices of others along with a common desire to live meaningfully and fully in a world that often seemed to defy authentic living and real purpose. On a journey of very different life courses, Merton and Laughlin met on the commons of their frequent letters. More so than any other New Directions author with the possible exception of William Carlos Williams, Laughlin always made it a point to go out of his way to visit Merton personally at his remote monastery. Meanwhile, through their letters they invited each other into their moral struggles. They fed each other's moral aspirations. They shared the simple rhythms of their felt worlds. Along the way, Merton nourished Laughlin's nascent spirituality, deepened his ethical commitments as a publisher, and inspired a compassion for social justice in the Harvard-educated son of a wealthy Pittsburgh socialite. For his part, Laughlin, who longed from an early age to be the poet that his mentor, Ezra Pound, discouraged him to become, was largely responsible for Merton becoming the poet he never really wanted to be. Merton had the incredible good fortune, as Robert Coles, a friend of both men, has perceptively written in the inaugural number of the literary journal *Conjunctions,* dedicated to Laughlin, "to work with, to have the continual personal support of a very special person—someone who, maybe it can be said, finds satisfaction in enabling others to have their say . . . someone who . . . has been graced in a most special way, so that his own pride is that of the pastoral person—the one who is forever attentive to the needs of others."

With the literary insight of a good editor, the insistence of a trusted friend, and the savvy of a successful publisher, Laughlin made it possible for Merton to look back later in life over his vocation as a writer and reflect disconcertedly in the Preface to the 1966 Japanese translation of *The Seven Storey Mountain:* "It is possible to doubt whether I have become a monk (a doubt I have to live with), but it is not possible to doubt that I am a writer, that I was born one and will most probably die as one."

—Shell Beach, California
Summer 1996

NOTES ON THE TEXT

The extant correspondence of Thomas Merton and James Laughlin consists of 739 items: 403 letters from Merton to Laughlin (dated 28 September 1945 through 28 November 1968) and 336 from Laughlin (14 May 1945–4 December 1968). Of that corpus I have selected for this edition 176 Merton letters and 40 letters from Laughlin. In addition, I have included one letter from Merton to Robert M. MacGregor, longtime managing editor at New Directions, and a letter from Laughlin to a special friend of Thomas Merton's written after Merton's death and included as an Epilogue.

Thomas Merton's letters to James Laughlin are preserved at the New Directions Archive in the basement of Laughlin's home in Norfolk, Connecticut. Those original letters will eventually be deposited, along with the entire New Directions Archive, in Harvard University's Houghton Library. In the early 1960s Thomas Merton began making single carbons of his letters to Laughlin. Ninety carbons (dated 29 January 1960 to 19 July 1968) are collected in the Thomas Merton Studies Center at Bellarmine College, Louisville, Kentucky. The Bellarmine collection also includes 201 original Laughlin letters to Merton, dated 15 March 1949–4 December 1968.

The balance of Laughlin's letters are filled in by carbons and photocopies from the Norfolk archives.

In selecting letters for the present edition I have tried to link certain narrative lines in Merton and Laughlin's long and fulsome correspondence that shed light on the following: (1) their personal and professional relationship, especially the bearing Merton's strong sense of moral imperative as a writer had on Laughlin's vision of social purpose and ethical accountability as a publisher; (2) the role that Laughlin played in facilitating Merton's development as a poet and writer, including discussions of books Laughlin frequently posted to Gethsemani, the writers he encouraged Merton to read, and the visits Laughlin arranged for Merton with other New Directions authors; (3) critical incidents in their private lives balanced by renderings of their ordinary routines, especially Merton's at the monastery; (4) their comments and reflections on important public events—literary, social, and political; and (5) the genesis and evolution of Merton's books published by New Directions. I have tried to make selections that blend these narrative lines together into a coherent story of two literary lives told in letters.

In doing so, I have had to cut Merton and Laughlin's total extant correspondence by two thirds, and I have also elided some passages within letters. Editorial abridgments are indicated by the standard ellipses. In rare instances when either Laughlin or Merton used an ellipsis in a letter, I follow the ellipsis with a "sic" placed in editorial brackets. For the most part, cut and abridged material pertains to banal business detail, copy editing, dead-end projects, or extreme marginalia. I have also respected James Laughlin's desire that the present volume include, like the others in the Norton series, many more Merton letters than his own.

In preparing these letters for publication, I employ the editorial apparatus designed by Hugh Witemeyer for his edition of *William Carlos Williams and James Laughlin:*

Selected Letters (1989), the first in a uniform seven volume series covering Laughlin's correspondence with principal New Directions writers. Following Witemeyer's guidelines, each letter in the present edition begins with a boldface headnote designating its number, its original form, and the number of pages in manuscript. Epistolary forms are identified by the following abbreviations: TLS (typed letter signed), TL (typed letter unsigned, usually indicating that the letter I am working from is either a carbon or a photocopy), ALS (autograph—handwritten—letter signed), APCS (autograph postcard signed), and APC (autograph postcard unsigned). Holographic additions to typed letters are enclosed in scroll brackets.

Except for rare instances, all of Thomas Merton's letters emanated from the Abbey of Gethsemani in Kentucky; therefore, on Merton's letters I include letterheads and inside addresses *only* on letters not sent from Gethsemani or when the letterhead varied from the standard Gethsemani stationery. I include inside addresses on all Laughlin letters *except* for those posted from the New Directions office in New York City, where most of his letters were transcribed by office staff.

I apply the same standardizations used by Witemeyer, including the uniform positions of dates, salutations, closings, and signatures. Salutations and signatures appear in small caps. The titles of literary works conform to conventional style formats: italics for books, plays, magazines, and long poems; quotation marks enclosing the titles of poems, essays, and short stories. Although both Laughlin and Merton were careful and fastidious letterwriters (the bulk of Laughlin's letters, incidentally, were dictated and later transcribed by typists whose initials I have omitted), I have silently corrected obvious typographical errors, errant grammatical mistakes, and misspellings unless they appear intended and/or serve a stylistic purpose.

The form and punctuation of each salutation and the

date of each letter is reproduced in facsimile. In those instances where I have had to extrapolate the dating of a letter, the extrapolation appears in square brackets. Likewise, all editorial insertions appear in square brackets and include missing words, clarifying information, or completions of truncated titles and names.

Editorial notes identify biographical references, explain bibliographical detail, and clarify contextual ambiguities that may have arisen in the course of cutting or abridgment. In the event that a name is not explained in an editorial endnote, the index may provide a cross-reference. The following abbreviations are used frequently in the annotations: JL (James Laughlin), TM (Thomas Merton), and ND (New Directions). Similarly, works by Thomas Merton cited frequently in the notes are abbreviated as follows: *AJ (The Asian Journal of Thomas Merton), Courage (The Courage for Truth: The Letters of Thomas Merton to Writers), CP (The Collected Poems of Thomas Merton), Ground (The Hidden Ground of Love: The Letters of Thomas Merton on Religious Experience and Social Concerns), LE (The Literary Essays of Thomas Merton), Road (The Road to Joy: The Letters of Thomas Merton to New and Old Friends), RU (Raids on the Unspeakable), SJ (The Sign of Jonas), SSM (The Seven Storey Mountain),* and *Witness (Witness to Freedom: The Letters of Thomas Merton in Times of Crisis).* I have included a primary source bibliography of James Laughlin and Thomas Merton's major books.

ACKNOWLEDGMENTS

I am indebted to the community of scholars, editors, and writers whose books have been my companions during preparation of this volume—in particular the editors of the five previously published volumes of James Laughlin's selected correspondence with New Directions writers: Hugh Witemeyer, *William Carlos Williams and James Laughlin: Selected Letters* (1989); Lee Bartlett, *Kenneth Rexroth and James Laughlin: Selected Letters* (1991); Robert Phillips, *Delmore Schwartz and James Laughlin: Selected Letters* (1993); David M. Gordon, *Ezra Pound and James Laughlin: Selected Letters* (1994); and George Wickes, *Henry Miller and James Laughlin: Selected Letters* (1996). For information about Thomas Merton, I have consulted the following biographies: Monica Furlong, *Merton: A Biography* (San Francisco: Harper & Row, 1981); Michael Mott, *The Seven Mountains of Thomas Merton* (Boston: Houghton Mifflin, 1984); and William H. Shannon, *Silent Lamp: The Thomas Merton Story* (New York: Crossroad, 1992). For tracking bibliographical references, I have relied heavily on *Thomas Merton: A Comprehensive Bibliography. New Edition,* compiled and edited by Marquita E. Breit and Robert E. Daggy (New York: Garland, 1986). I have learned much about the depth, breadth, and richness of Thomas Merton's contribution to twentieth-century thought through discussions, as well as books, articles, and letters by mentors, colleagues, and friends, among them: Christine M. Bochen, Anne Carr, Robert Coles, W. H. Ferry, John Howard Griffin, Robert Inchausti, George Kilcourse, Michael Kiley, Victor Kramer, Ross Labrie, Therese Lentfoehr, Elena Malits, Patrick F. O'Connell, Anthony Padavano, Parker Palmer, Basil Pennington, Brother Paul Quenon, Bonnie B. Thurston, Monica Weis, SSJ, Brother Richard Wilbur, and George Woodcock. I am especially grateful for the counsel, scrutiny, and guidance given to my work over the years by Robert Daggy (Director of the Thomas Merton Studies Center), Brother Patrick Hart (who read the manuscript of the present edition and generously offered clarifications, explanations, corrections, and suggestions for improvement), and Lawrence Cunningham, who has helped train my tin ear for theology. While these individuals are in no way accountable for any of my errors, omissions, or sour notes, they remind me that scholarly work is always an intellectual barn raising of sorts—public works made possible through the labor of countless dedicated and skilled hands.

James Laughlin invited me to edit his correspondence with Thomas Merton. Through Laughlin I have come to know Merton much more intimately, and I have gained insight and perspective into a crucial chapter of modern American literary history that Laughlin has writ large through his New Directions enterprise. I am grateful too for J.'s friendship, for the hospitality that he and his wife Gertrude Huston showered on Christina and me during our visits to Norfolk when everyone happily abandoned me in the New Directions office for afternoon walks in the woods to Tobey Pond, and for the circle of friendships spawned by J. and Gertrude, especially with Harry and Sandra Reese of Turkey Press in Isla Vista, California, publishers of Laughlin's two most recent volumes of poems.

I wish to thank Michigan State University and John Eadie, Dean of the College of Arts and Letters, for research support and sabbatical leave, and also Berea College—where I spent an Appalachian spring teaching and writing—for providing a research assistant, Sarah Zook, who helped organize and index the raw materials for this book. Anne Fairchild, a graduate of Michigan State University's Program in American Studies, typed the manuscript. In preparing the introduction, notes, and texts of letters for the present edition, I have greatly benefited from editors and staff at W. W. Norton, including Amy Cherry, Donald Lamm, Cecil Lyon, Drake McFeely, and especially my editor, Sarah Stewart.

Some of these letters have been previously published. Letter #212 first appeared in *Thomas Merton in Alaska,* edited by Robert E. Daggy (New York: New Directions, 1988). Letters #11, 12, 28, 29, 30, 31, 59, 60, 90, 91, 204, 205, 206, 209, and the Epilogue were first published in *DoubleTake,* 6 (Fall 1996); I am grateful to Liz Phillips and Sue Halpern at *DoubleTake* for their editorial craftsmanship and enthusiasm, and to Robert Coles for encouraging and nurturing my writing. Thomas Merton's letters are published with the permission of the Trustees of the Thomas Merton Legacy Trust. James Laughlin's portrait of Thomas Merton, included as an Appendix, first appeared in *Merton: By Those Who Knew Him Best,* edited by Paul Wilkes (San Francisco: Harper & Row, 1984).

It is an honor for me to dedicate this book and my labor in producing it to the Dean of Thomas Merton Studies, Bill Shannon, my teacher and my friend.

LETTERS

1. T L S - 1   May 27th [1945]

D E A R L A U G H L I N :

I am delighted to hear that you really plan to come here. It is very simple to get here. We are about fifty miles south of Louisville in farming country. You take US 68 out of Bardstown going southwest towards New Haven and fork off when you come to a lot of hills and woods. There will be a big sign. Everybody will be able to tell you where the monastery is. From Louisville to Bardstown you take a big main road the map will tell you so will all the people. I think it is US 150 if I can read the map I have got here.

You can stay at the monastery, that is the best and most comfortable and most restful, unless you hit one of the big week-end retreats (Friday through Monday morning). But in that case you could sleep at the gate house. If your wife is with you she could stay across the road with the wife of the hired man who works for the monastery. That is where everybody's mothers and sisters stay when they come to see the monks. In that case you could stay with her or in the monastery whichever you preferred. She would be able to get up in the visitors' gallery to hear some of the singing in church, but not come in to the monastery itself. But really it is very quiet and nice here and I do want to talk to you about these jobs besides having the pleasure of meeting you. Today is Tuesday and you are already on the road. I hope this will catch you in Colorado but I doubt it!

> In Christo,
> FR. M. LOUIS, O.C.S.O.

{Let us know in advance if your wife is with you so that we can fix up a place for her.}

/ · /

the monastery: The Monastery of Our Lady of Gethsemani, located in central Kentucky on land originally purchased from the Sisters of Loretto. At the invitation of Kentucky Bishop Flaget, the Abbey of Gethsemani was established in 1848 by forty-five founders from Melleray, a Trappist monastery in western France.

In Christo: "In Christ." May also be construed as "In Christ's Name."

fr. M. Louis, O.C.S.O.: M. Louis (pronounced "Lewis") is TM's religious name given to him when he was accepted as a choir monk at Gethsemani on 21 February 1942. TM's religious namesake is the sainted king of France. "M." stands for Mary, an initial carried on the names of all the monks of TM's order as a reminder of their patroness in religious life. Latin for "brother," the lower-case abbreviation "fr." stands for "frater" and is intended as a gesture of humility. OCSO abbreviates the Order of Cistercians of the Strict Observance.

2. TLS-2   Sept. 28th 1945

DEAR MR LAUGHLIN.

It seems to be better to save Mark [Van Doren] a lot of bother, and deal with you directly, especially as there is no real reason why one should not! Anyway, here are, as I think, enough for the book you want. Sorry to have taken so long. I presume you mean to print *30 Poems* at the end. These are arranged in chronological order, and

I think, that way, they are interesting, because of the development they represent—coming here, and all that. The transition to the monastery is marked by "letter to my friends 1941," and the arrangement will make itself clear, only don't you think it would be good to draw the reader's attention to the fact, somewhere? The transition falls just about in the middle. Besides, there are one or two poems that need to be identified as having been written by someone not a monk, just as there are others that make more sense when it is clearly seen that they were written by a monk. Although of course contexts are accidental in each case: but they help some. If you want to throw out any of these, begin with "Man in the Wind" and "Ariadne" perhaps, (suit yourself.) (I mean if you want to discard any on account of space.) If you discard any for other reasons, I don't know if I have got anything fit to replace them. Anyway, I hope these will do. Although the censor doesn't want my Trappist name printed (I just thought it was a rule that it had to be) Rev. Fr. Abbot said that the fact that I am in the monastery should not be left out of the blurb. Mark told you of a notion I had about a liturgical volume, ivth and vth century hymns, prefaces etc. with translations, and I did a little work on it, but I have been frightfully busy with other work—a historical book on our Order, I mean the saints of our Order (Cistercian). If you would let me know what sort of a size, (for the liturgical book) would most appeal to you, it might help—or perhaps it would be best if I got together around twenty or thirty items as a kind of sample and showed them to you, because right now I can't take time to go ahead and finish the thing.

I wrote a dedication, or rather rewrote the same one, so that should be left out (I mean the one that was in *30 Poems*), and we didn't get a whole "Imprimatur" because then the book would have to go to the bishop—and he is just as slow as the censor. But be sure that "Cum permissu superiorum" gets in there somewhere.

So much for all the little details: and I assure you that they are little enough so that no trouble will be caused if you slip up on one or another, so do not worry too much. I hope the book is satisfactory, and look forward to hearing from you about it. If you ever get any ideas on anything I might be capable of doing be sure and let me know. Fr. Abbot is pleased to have one of his monks doing poetry etc. Also, any time you are around this part of the world, drop in to the monastery: Cistercians have always been very hospitable, and I think you would like it.

> In pace et charitate Christi,
> FR. M. LOUIS, O.C.S.O.
> (TOM MERTON)

/ · /

Mark: A distinguished professor of English, dedicated teacher, and Pulitzer Prize-winning poet (1940), Mark Van Doren (1894–1972) was TM's mentor at Columbia University where he studied English literature from 1935 to 1939. When TM entered the monastery in December 1941, he left several manuscripts with Van Doren, who first mentioned TM's work to JL. TM's letters to Van Doren are collected in *Road,* pp. 3–55. TM also discusses his special relationship with Van Doren in the pre-monastic journal *Run to the Mountain: The Story of a Vocation* (1995).

30 Poems at the end: At the urging of Mark Van Doren, ND published TM's first poetry volume, *Thirty Poems,* in 1944, the entire text of which was reprinted as an appendix to TM's second book of poems, *A Man in the Divided Sea* (ND, 1946). See also *CP,* pp. 25–57.

the censor: A cleric—in TM's case, a member of his own order—appointed by a bishop to read a work prior to publication and judge whether it conforms to ecclesiastical standards governing faith and morals. The censorship process is twofold. First, a *Nihil Obstat* signifies the censor's approval that a work is free from doctrinal error. The work is then submitted to the bishop of the diocese where it is to be printed for his Imprimatur, a formal permission to publish. The system of strict censorship that prevailed in the 1940s was largely dismantled following the reforms of the Second Vatican Council in the early 1960s.

Rev. Fr. Abbot: Dom Frederic Dunne (1872–1948), Abbot of Gethsemani, 1935–48. Derived from Aramaic, abbot means "father." The abbot is responsible for the spiritual and physical well-being of the entire monastic community.

a historical book on our Order: Probably the big mimeographed volume *Modern Biographical Sketches of Cistercian Blessed and Saints* (Abbey of Gethsemani, 1945).

Cistercian: A Catholic monastic order based on the Rule of St. Benedict, the Order of Citeaux (*Cistercium* in Latin) was founded in 1098 and named after its first monastery, at Citeaux in Burgundy, France. Reform movements initiated in the sixteenth century eventually led to a reorganization of the order into two "observances" in 1892: the Common Observance, or the Sacred Order of Cistercians (SOCist), and the Order of Cistercians of the Strict Observance (OCSO) whose rigorous insistence on a contemplative life of silence, prayer, austerity, and humility was fashioned after reforms promulgated at La Trappe monastery in France, hence their popular name, Trappists.

"Imprimatur": Latin term meaning "Let it be printed."

"Cum permissu superiorum": "With the permission of the [religious] superior."

In pace et charitate Christi: "In the peace and charity of Christ."

3. TLS-2   Nov. 2nd 1945.

DEAR LAUGHLIN:

Thanks for the letter which, I guess, crossed with the things I sent you last week—including funnily enough a religious anthology. I would like to work up something of the kind, if more than what I sent were needed, or if what is there could be polished up. The selection is not all I would have it: I would like to get things having a more direct bearing on religious *experience*—although most of these already do have that. What do you think of including something not English—like poems of St. John of the Cross for instance, (Spanish—his language is something like Gongora but what he says: terrific.) . . .

About the design of the book: first, *Thirty Poems* is fine, especially the title page. For Cistercian things: our general character has always been the most lapidary simplicity. The best way to get an idea of it is to look at pictures of our twelfth century monasteries, like Pontigny, Fontenay (the best), Tintern, Fountains, Fossanova. Harvard would have plenty of material on that. However, anything in the same general spirit—even Anglo-saxon-

ish. Symbols: our fathers were always making a thousand
rules about every kind of pictorial restraint. The basic
liturgical symbols, as abstractly, as spiritualized as you like:
Cross, chalice, fish (ichthus), anything suggesting bread
and wine, (Eucharist), or, for that matter, the symbolism
in the verse itself is pretty much along these lines, in a
general way. But you and your men will do a swell job, I
am sure.

Finally: yes, I would be glad to get something to read
from New Directions: what do you think would help me
to write better? Especially to keep the vocabulary from
getting stale, or me from getting into ruts, mannerisms,
etc.? I used to like very much Lorca and Dylan Thomas—
but remember that our life here obligates us to steer clear
of even what is merely indifferent to the interior life. In
other words—it is not that we are forced to lock ourselves
up with a pile of pious trash, on some purely *a priori* basis.
But what we read should help us to know God either
directly, in Himself, or through knowledge of people as
He has made them—or by contrast as they have made
themselves. Anyone who has something serious to say
about the ultimate meaning of life or of the world is,
therefore okay: but if it is just good experimental writing,
for its own sake, I guess perhaps not. If this sounds unin-
telligible, it would perhaps be more sensible to give you
the rule in its ordinary formulation: no newspapers, no
magazines, no radio, no movies, no books on stamp-col-
lecting, no fashionable novels, no text-books on astron-
omy. But I notice a lot of the brothers with books on
agriculture, so anything corresponding, in the field of the
craft God has given me to follow . . . verse, would be at
least tolerated. Anyway, thanks, and do send your cata-
logues. Maybe I will receive them, and maybe not.

If you say any prayers, say one for me.

In charitate Christi,
FR. M. LOUIS, O.C.S.O.

/ · /

St. John of the Cross: Spanish founder of the Discalced Carmelites, poet, and ascetic-mystical theologian, St. John of the Cross (1542–1591) is best known for his treatise, *The Ascent of Mount Carmel—The Dark Night of the Soul,* the subject of TM's only full-length theological commentary, *The Ascent to Truth* (1951).

Gongora: Luis de Gongora y Argote (1561–1627) was a controversial poet of Spain's Baroque period, known for his highly experimental poetry and language.

Lorca: Spanish poet, playwright, and martyr for the Republican cause during the Spanish Civil War, Federico García Lorca (1899–1936) was assassinated in Granada by political adversaries. ND published translations of Lorca's work which JL would eventually send TM, including *III Tragedies: Blood Wedding, Yerma, Bernarda Alba,* translated by Richard L. O'Connell and James Graham-Lujan (1947).

Dylan Thomas: JL sent TM a copy of *New Poems* (ND, 1944) by the Welsh poet Dylan Thomas (1914–1953). Although TM was put off by what he felt was Thomas's preoccupation with "incest and witchcraft" (TM to JL, 17 Nov. 1945), Thomas's "integrity as a poet," TM nonetheless noted at the same time in his journal, "makes me very ashamed of the verse I have been writing" (*SJ,* p. 59).

In charitate Christi: "In the charity of Christ."

4. TL-2   January 12th [1946]

DEAR MERTON—

Here at last are some proofs. I think from now on it will go quicker. This chap is a legal printer and has no other literary clients. . . .

Their great victory parade is trumpeting under my window and the streets are mobbed with the happy plebs. It seems to me that the celebration of military "glory" is about the greatest of all sins.

Let us by all means go ahead with the anthology as you suggest. Perhaps your volume might be called *The New Directions Book of Christian Poetry.* Or do you think that sounds too much like *Macomber's Guide to the Prevention of Cavities by Dental Prophylaxis?*

I would like to see you include a few things at least

from most of the languages in which such poems have been written. I am pretty sure we can get friends who know those languages to submit suggestions to you and translations for you to pass on. The bulk of it, of course, should be in the English stuff, but I'm sure the translations from the other sources will add dimension and colour. . . .

Do not worry about the amount of work involved in terms of time. There is no terrible hurry about this at all. You can take your time and make it as good as it can be. If any of the poems you choose are in copyright (Hopkins would be) we will arrange to pay for the permissions out of your royalties. I assume that you wish the royalties to go to the Monastery as is being done with your poems. It would be a straight 10% and I believe such a book would earn a lot of money over the years.

Please let me know what books or what line of books you want me to request for you from the Harvard library. I shall write today to my old professor at Harvard (G. B. Weston) for suggestions about Italian books.

I think Nabokoff will help us find a couple of Russian poems and translate them. For the German there are half a dozen friends who can be queried.

I note your silent period in March and April and we shall try to get the book of poems all wound up before that time.

By all means start on the Liturgical book whenever you want. The idea appeals to me very much and I shan't do much about it except let you follow out your ideas and then work to give them a happy format. I would try to give this the handsomeness of what the trade calls a gift book.

> With best wishes,
> [UNSIGNED CARBON]

/ · /

some proofs: editorial page proofs for *A Man in the Divided Sea* (1946).

Hopkins: Converted to Catholicism in 1866, the English poet Gerard Manley Hopkins (1844–1889), noted for his innovations in poetic techniques, entered the Jesuit Order in 1868. While at Columbia University, TM started doctoral research on Hopkins.

G. B. Weston: George Benson Weston (A.B. Harvard College 1897), book lover, musician, professor of Italian literature and language.

Nabokoff: The Russian-born novelist Vladimir Nabokov (1899–1977) came to the United States and was naturalized as a citizen in 1945. He served on the faculty of Russian literature at Cornell, 1948–59. ND published Nabokov's second novel, *The Real Life of Sebastian Knight,* in 1941. The misspelling is likely a transcription error.

your silent period: "In Advent (Dec. 1 (about) to Christmas) and Lent," TM wrote JL on 17 November 1945, "we cannot receive mail or answer it: but if there is proof to be read, mark 'urgent' all over it, and it will be o.k." TM followed on 6 January 1946 with the following clarification of the monastic calendar: "From March 6th to April 21st we won't be able to receive or write letters, it will be Lent."

5. TLS-1

March 1st, 1946

DEAR LAUGHLIN:

Last couple of days before Ash Wednesday, just time to write and thank you for *Some Natural Things* which I very much enjoyed, best of all, in a way, the fragment about all the Swiss hotels, also the fragments from "America I love you," also "the Mountain and the Hunting Dog" and in fact the whole book. In some respects your poems remind me of the way my (and Mark [Van Doren]'s) good friend Bob Lax writes. As for the Hopkins book I think it is very well done, and find that the Catholic angle was treated with plenty of penetration and understanding.

When the poems come out will you please send three copies to my grandmother in New Zealand, as I also have a lot of aunts out there. It is where my father came from. She is: *"Mrs. G. H. Merton, 35 Cambridge Terrace, W., Christchurch, South Island, N.Z."*

Rev. Father just okayed a new project—creative, more or less poetic prose, autobiographical in its essence, but not pure autobiography, something, as I see it now, like a cross between Dante's Purgatory and Kafka and a Medieval Miracle play, called the *Seven Story Mountain*. It has been brewing for a long, long time, and as soon as I finish the present job I am on I think I might be able to get on to it and finish it fairly fast. How does it sound to you? I don't know how long it is liable to turn out to be, but I would like to keep it down to about a hundred and fifty pages. If it is more prose than poetry it is liable to go much bigger, as I have an awful lot of things to say: but I would rather, if God wills, shut up about most of it. Say a prayer to Our Lady to tell me what to do.

Happy Lent, or, anyway, Happy Easter,

MERTON

/ · /

Some Natural Things: JL's second book of poems, published by ND in 1945.

Bob Lax: TM's close friend from his Columbia University days, Robert Lax (1915–)—poet, writer, editor for *The New Yorker, Jubilee,* and *PAX*—went into self-imposed exile in the Greek islands in 1962. TM collected and edited their twenty-four year correspondence; it was eventually published in 1978 as *A Catch of Antiletters* (Sheed, Andrews & McMeel). ND issued the first comprehensive gathering of Lax's poetry: *33 Poems,* edited by Thomas Kellein (1988).

Dante's Purgatory: TM modeled his popular autobiography *SSM* after the *Purgatorio (Purgatory),* Part II of Dante Alighiere's (1265–1321) *Divine Comedy.* The seven storeys in TM's title allude to the seven sins that Dante allegorizes as he ascends the mountain of Purgatory, or purification: pride, envy, wrath, sloth, avarice, gluttony, and lust.

Kafka: The Prague-born Austrian novelist, Franz Kafka (1883–1924), wrote dreamlike novels that probed ruthlessly the paradox, absurdity, futility, and anxiety of human existence. Kafka's explorations of the ambivalence of family relations and the incomprehensibility of God make him a particularly interesting choice for TM to describe his nascent autobiography.

6. T L S - 2   Aug. 17th, 1946

DEAR LAUGHLIN:

The *[Man in a] divided sea* got to me yesterday. It is fine.
You have given the poems a swell presentation. I certainly
like that electra type. The cover is fine, and grows on one.
I like very much the title page. There was, however, a slip-
up on page 29, when the end of the poem "Dirge" on p.
27 got transferred over and tacked on to the end of the
song there. After ["]all the quiet pianos["] the remaining
lines belong to ["D]irge.["] However, that way it makes
another, curious, poem, and I don't suppose anyone will
be overwhelmed with perplexities.

Would you please let us have some more copies, to
have a few around the house and some to send to other
monasteries—say about ten or a dozen? I want to send
one to the Abbot General of the Order, in Europe.

About the prose—7 *Story Mountain*—it did not turn
out the way I thought it might at first. Therefore, no
fantasy, no Kafka[,] no miracle play. It is straight [auto]bi-
ography with a lot of comment and reflection, and is
turning into the mountain that the title says. I cannot
make it in less than 650 typewritten pages. It seems to me
that you do not usually risk printing such big fat books as
this, and perhaps it would not be your dish, but I will
certainly let you have the first look at it. If God wills, I
shall get it finished in a month or so from now, and you
can have it then.

. . . The anthology business needs some discussion,
because as I see it, it is almost a moral impossibility for
me to handle the whole thing out here. I could make a
partial selection, and let somebody else do the rest: if you
like, I'd go over the whole thing when it was complete,
but it seems that the business of mailing books back and
forth would get into great complexities.

The Liturgy [book] presents no difficulties, and I

would like to get on with that late next spring or in the summer. After finishing the mountain I shall have to spend the winter on a book about Contemplative Prayer that I have been waiting to get at for a long time, and something always turns up to interfere with it.

I have sent for some books from Europe for our library that will give me material for some work on Duns Scotus, which I am very keen on doing: but that will be a couple of years off, and a ticklish job. How do you feel about a book, some 150 pages long, on Scotus? There is practically nothing about him available, especially in English.

Meanwhile, I have now got ready another group of poems about as long as *thirty poems* (I mean it would make a book that size). How do you feel about that? Would you rather consider the possibility of a longer book, or should I send you these, as they are? Personally I am all for another short, dollar book if the paper situation permits it. In any case, it would take some time for it to go through the censors. From now on, since I got into minor orders this summer, everything must go to the bishop, according to canon law. I wish the *[Man in a] divided sea* had gone to him: there was time, but we didn't send it to him, thinking it would save some time. The office of a diocesan censor is always lamentably slow, because it is a big bottle-neck, choked up with books that have the poor man going blind like Hopkins.

Finally, I thought the other day I might do some pen and ink sketches that might serve here and there as tail-pieces etc. How is your reaction to the idea in general? If you think there is any point to it, I might try a few: but there isn't much time for it.

But anyway, if you come down, we will be able to discuss all this at leisure. My big job now is to finish the *7 story mountain.*

In charitate Christi,
MERTON

Duns Scotus: John Duns Scotus (1270–1308), Scottish Franciscan, Scholastic theologian and writer.

7. TLS-1   Easter, 1947

DEAR LAUGHLIN:

Thanks very much for your letter and the check. As they both arrived in Lent I could not acknowledge them sooner.

I am sorry we got crossed up on the autobiography, but it was definitely not a book for you and I explained that in a letter. So when you made no special reference to it in replying I took it for granted that you agreed with me. You know I write a pile of stuff varying from poems and things you are interested in, on down to lives of obscure members of our Order, with footnotes and whatnot, which nobody but the abbey would ever print. So you see I naturally think in terms of a whole graded series of different publishers. I assure you that you have first claim on poems and, of course, on the kind of thing we were talking about before, including the Liturgy anthology which, by some kind of miracle, I trust to be able to do before the end of this year, but please don't hold me to a time limit.

Naomi Burton understands all this and has the interests of New Directions at heart. I want her to handle all the stuff I write for the general, that is non-Catholic public because I simply can't keep track of business matters by myself. She will keep everything straight.

Have you looked over the *Journal of my Escape from the Nazis?* I don't know if you can do anything with it, and I tremble to think what the bishops will make of it, with the doubletalk that is there. In any case I would have to go over it. I admit that it needs a whole job of rewriting and building up, but frankly I don't think I would be able to do the first thing in that direction. I wrote that draft six years ago, and now that I am in the monastery you can imagine that I am in a completely different frame of mind. I couldn't get myself back into that mood, nor would I want to.

You have by now a ms of some new poems, and I enclose two more. "The Poet to his Book" goes at the end, but you can slip the other in anywhere you see fit. I think, if you are willing, that it would be best to call it a day on this volume with this material, and send it as it now stands to the bishop for censorship. Please let me know at once if you agree, and also tell me in what diocese (the city will do!) you intend to get it printed and I will send it to the proper bishop. Censor takes time and it is best to get started now if you want to bring the thing out by next year.

I wish you some of the tremendous things there are in Easter and which the new-hat people will never find out about until they get cleaned out inside—and I wish you some of the things that the merely pious people will never find out about until they get rebuilt inside by the process that they secretly fear. In fact I wish you the things that I wish for myself and which I will have to get turned inside out before I will really get.

Incidentally some time this year there ought to be a new Trappist monastery in—you'll laugh—Utah. We are making a foundation there, and will start living on some farm in some kind of a camp of army huts or something in a couple of months. I don't know where exactly but I think it is near Ogden or wherever things grow. The Latter Day Saints will not raise much of a smile, I expect.

> In Christo Regnate.
> FR. LOUIS

P.S. The Abbot General of the Order likes the poems and the idea of my wri{ting such things.}

/ · /

Naomi Burton: TM's friend and literary agent at the Curtis Brown Agency, Naomi Burton (Mrs. Melville E. Stone), later became an editor at Doubleday. She was born in England, came to the United States in 1939, and was naturalized as a U.S. citizen in 1945. Along with JL and Tommie O'Callaghan, she served as Trustee of the Thomas Merton Legacy Trust. She also co-edited, with JL and Brother Patrick Hart, *AJ* and *Love and Living* (1979). Ms. Burton Stone wrote about her friendship and literary relationship with TM in her autobiography, *More Than Sentinels* (Doubleday, 1964). TM's writings on the spiritual life provided the impetus for Ms. Burton Stone's eventual conversion to Catholicism.

Journal of my Escape from the Nazis: An experimental autobiographical novel TM wrote while teaching at St. Bonaventure University, before entering the Abbey of Gethsemani. It was eventually published, shortly after TM's death, under the title *My Argument with the Gestapo: A Macaronic Journal* (Doubleday, 1969). ND issued a paperback edition in 1975.

a ms of some new poems: Figures for an Apocalypse (ND, 1948).

In Christo Regnate: "In Christ's Royal Kingship."

8. TL-2

April 25th [1947]
692 Wisconsin Street
San Francisco, California

DEAR MERTON—

Many thanks for your two letters and for the poems to be added to the script of the new book. I have shown the new poems to quite a few of the poets out here and the comments have been most enthusiastic. [Kenneth] Rexroth is especially impressed with them, and sends you his greetings.

I think that we would do best to print the book with the same chap who did the last one—Dudley Kimball of Parsippany, New Jersey. He is dreadfully slow, and it may take him a year to get it out, but he likes you and your poetry very much, and particularly asked me if he couldn't do the next book of yours.

Will you send a copy of the script to the censor in that district? I assume that it is quite safe for us to proceed with the composition, is it not? I mean, the censor is not likely to land on any of these poems? I can't see how he could, since they are so deeply religious in feeling.

Would you like to have me send out some of the single poems for possible appearance in magazines pending the publication of the volume? Or does Miss Burton do this for you? All the agents I know won't bother with single poems because the fees are so small. But I think it is good to send them around because it builds up toward the book, and also gets the poems read by more people. Let me know.

I note what you say about the *Journal [of My Escape from the Nazis]*. I haven't had a moment to read it yet—have been deep in proofs and correspondence and copy writing—but I hope that some day we can do a prose book for you that will reach a large audience.

The situation for New Directions becomes more and more difficult as the inflation proceeds unabated. Production costs have now almost exactly doubled since the time we started in business. Of course, we sell a lot more books now, but the wages that have to be paid to office help and warehouse help are fabulous. Each year I must dig down deeper into my principal to keep the business going. This does not bother me too much, but it simply enrages my wife, who says that I will leave my children nothing—which is probably true—but I wonder whether that will really be much harm to them. My experience of the life of the "upper class" in the USA is not such as to make me convinced that that is the milieu in which one is most likely to find peace of heart and accomplishment of soul.

Nevertheless, I do feel obligated to try to be as business-like as possible about the press, which involves embarrassing you with requests such as this: to try to publish as much with New Directions as you feel you can. Probably you would disapprove of a good many of the books we issue, but I imagine you do agree with the basic premise back of our work—that a non-commercial channel should be kept open for the writers who wish to create literature regardless of its appeal to a debased public taste.

That sounds rather pompous doesn't it?

I am now trying to buttress up the edifice by getting us quite a number of volumes of important foreign authors who are not in print here. There should be a steady sale for those. I also hope to start doing some of my printing in Italy, and selling in England as well as in the US. There is a lively interest there in advance guard writing.

Our London agent had an enquiry for an English edition of your book there, and I enclose a copy of what I wrote him. I hope this meets with your approval.

It is fine that you hope to go on working on the Liturgical book. And don't forget the anthology either. What about a little short anthology—say 160 pages—to go in The New Classics series at [$]1.50—the *New Directions Book of Catholic Verse?* I think that would have quite a public and be most useful.

/ · /

Rexroth: Prolific poet, essayist, critic, and central figure of the San Francisco Renaissance, Kenneth Rexroth (1905–1982) published several books with ND, including *The Phoenix and the Tortoise* (1944) and the highly respected translations *One Hundred Poems from the Japanese* (1956). See Lee Bartlett, ed., *Kenneth Rexroth and James Laughlin: Selected Letters* (Norton, 1991).

Dudley Kimball: Printer at Blue Ridge Mountain Press and one-time mayor of Boonton, New Jersey, Kimball printed many books for ND, including Delmore Schwartz's collection of short stories, *The World Is a Wedding* (1948), and William Carlos Williams's *A Dream of Love* (1948).

9. TLS-1   June 17th, 1947

DEAR LAUGHLIN:

Here are two poems I wanted to give you, with corrections.

A magazine called '47 wrote asking for poems—will
you send them one or two? The letter was from Clifton
Fadiman. They are at 68 W.45th St. NYC. If you dig up
anything by the poet Supervielle maybe I could look it
over for the anthology.

I think I really need to read some verse, I am getting
stale. The fact is I have hardly read a line of poetry as
poetry—i.e. from a literary point of view, since I came
here, with a few rare exceptions.

It was really swell that you came down here. I hope
there was nothing about the place to upset you. It is a
rough sort of a life and you must not expect too much of
us. It is essential to our vocation to be living like the
people on the economic fringe, like the untouchables,
and we find our peace through poverty and the rest of it.
In fact if we try to *be* something we get upset right away.

Anyway, I say it again, come back when you can stay a
while.

> Dominus tecum.
> FR. M. LOUIS, O.C.S.O.

{P.S. Since the bishop sent that imprimatur you can send
any poem from *Figures [for an Apocalypse]* to any magazine
but watch out for the ones already printed.}

/ · /

Clifton Fadiman: Editor-in-chief of Simon & Schuster and later editor with
the Book-of-the-Month Club, Clifton Fadiman was an influential literary
force during the 1940s. Married to the novelist Helen MacInnes, Fadiman
was MC of the popular radio quiz show *Information Please*.

Supervielle: Jules Supervielle (1884–1960), a Uruguayan-born French poet.
TM was drawn to Supervielle's poetry because of its simplicity and preoccu-

pation with myth and dream. JL eventually sent TM a copy of Supervielle's *Gravitations* (1925). ND published a selection of Supervielle in 1967.

Dominus tecum: "The Lord be with you."

10. TLS-2   July 2nd, 1947

DEAR LAUGHLIN:

Thanks so much for both your letters. About the books you send, we will send back everything that you don't tell us to keep. Talking about the beautiful covers—I thought I had an idea for *Figures [for an Apocalypse]* but I hadn't either. But I think it does call for some color.

I am delighted at your offer to help out with the little book on the monastery and be sure we shall take you up on it. I haven't spoken to Rev. Father about Marbridge yet, but his usual reaction is: "Are they Catholics?" If you know of a first rate printer who has a Catholic in the house somewhere it would be a selling point for Rev. Father. But it is not essential!

The Utah colony was chosen the other day, minus me. They leave next Monday. It can become something very wonderful. If only they could just copy Senanque! A lot of us in the house are working for that sort of thing for all we are worth, and the brother who is busy on the plans has the pictures in front of him all the time: but in the end I know it will be far from Senanque and much more like Gethsemani.

Sometime I want to talk about that idea you spoke of—the notion you like in [D. H.] Lawrence, about the sacramental character of human love. If only I knew offhand of some one book that would give you a quick introduction to Christian mysticism on that point! From St. Augustine and people like that I myself have built up a certain ideology on the point but I haven't time to write a whole book on it. But the thing is definitely this. The union between

man and wife is designed by God as a means of sanctification and a way to mystical union with Himself, an incor-
poration in, an identification with Him in the work of His
creation. Marriage should be consummated in a fire of
love which is not merely natural but Divine: but for it to
have that sacramental character it must be absolutely purified of all *selfishness.* Marriage is a Sacrament which the
man and wife minister to one another: but a Sacrament is
ordered to God. The trouble with Lawrence's idea is that
it ends not in God but in the depths of one's own physical
being, and is ultimately nothing but the deification of
one's own satisfaction, which turns out to be just the
opposite from what it should be. Ultimately it turns love
from a blessing into a curse that withers up and blasts a
man's capacity for true happiness which must be in the
spirit, and to which the body can only contribute by complete subordination to the spirit.

I thought you ought to know this much. If I were you
I would pray once in a while in a simple way, whichever
way suits you best, and ask God to give you some light
about all the things that are for the real peace and happiness of men. You are not at all made for the misery of the
cannibal world you have to live in, out there, and I do
wish you everything that will help you to get free of it in
so far as you can.

It will be some time before we get around to the picture book.

I am even busier than usual. Anyway God bless you
and your wife and everybody you are concerned with. If
you see Mark [Van Doren] tell him I have been meaning
to write and may get around to it some day.

In Corde Christi,
FR. M. LOUIS, O.C.S.O.

/ · /

the little book on the monastery: *Gethsemani Magnificat: Centenary of Gethsemani Abbey* (Abbey of Gethsemani, 1949), produced by Marbridge, a commercial printing firm that JL frequently used for ND work.

Senanque: Cistercian monastery at Senanque, France.

Lawrence: D. H. Lawrence (1885–1930), English novelist, poet, and critic. Lawrence's views on human sexuality were well known from the erotic novel *Lady Chatterley's Lover* (1932). Other works on sexuality include his *Fantasia of the Unconscious* (1922) and *Pornography and Obscenity* (1929).

St. Augustine: (354–430), Catholic bishop, theologian, and doctor of the Church. Augustine's approach to understanding spiritual reality put great emphasis on interior experience and divine transcendence—the two pillars of Christian tradition that mark him as the founder of Christian theology. TM refers to Augustine's principal influence on Church instruction or catechism. Augustine's *City of God* and *Confessions* echo strongly in TM's early poetry and *SSM*.

the picture book: Later, on 6 November 1947, TM solicited JL's help on "an 'official souvenir' booklet—pictures of bishops and benefactors as well as a lot of pictures of the house etc. And I have that to take care of also. It will be almost all pictures, 64 pages, larger format (is 8 1/2 × 11 possible?) and a little more showy and my headache is to keep it from looking like a High school yearbook and at the same time not offend everybody and give them something handsome"—*Cistercian Contemplatives: A Guide to Trappist Life* (Abbey of Gethsemani, 1948).

In Corde Christi: "In the heart of Christ."

11. TL-2

July 12th [1947]
Norfolk, Conn

DEAR MERTON—

I am very pleased that you approved of the idea of reprinting your essay in the next annual. It will surely make some people think. I suppose the type of poet we have so many of—the ones for whom poetry is simply a means for building up the ego at any price—will react with a total negative. But there should be many to whom it will cause real inner trouble, and for their ultimate good. I'll make the corrections which you note. . . .

What you wrote about the sacrament of marriage is very clear and very right, and ideal to strive for. The curious thing about Lawrence is that he always gave me the feeling that underneath he realized that the matter didn't end in the bodily celebration but that there was some tick in his make-up that prevented his getting through to the right conclusion. I suppose he was really limited in some ways by his background.

I would be most grateful if you would suggest to me some books which might put me in the way of furthering my desire to increase the spiritual component in my life. I have a weakness for "color" and there is a danger of my approach being sentimental—as you point out in your essay—but I think I am an essentially religious person. I do feel most constantly a wish to lead a less material and frivolous life. I am not good with people—I mean them well, but the ready and empty word does not come easily to me—so that I think my bent is probably more toward meditation than social work.

I was brought up in a very superficial religious environment. All the older men of my family were elders in the Presbyterian churches of Pittsburgh. There was an enormous amount of Bible reading and catechism learning but no inside religious *feeling*. When I go to church with my mother I feel as though I were attending a social rather than a religious feeling. My reaction was quite normal. In school, I was fairly anti-religious, though never militantly so. I have also been through a long road of cultivating the senses, often without much regard for the feelings of the victims. In the last few years I have grown very close to my father's elder sister, a remarkable woman of great spiritual intensity. She practices the beliefs of a group called "Unity" and has achieved a great power to direct her spiritual force by concentration in meditation. The metaphysics of her group I find pretty weak, but I like some of their results. Their "constructive thinking" can clear a great deal of nonsense out of the mind. My aunt has also branched out into communication with the departed, and through a dear old lady in New York, who is certainly not a charlatan, she receives messages from the beyond. These are vague in character, generally hortatory, and reflecting the beliefs of the Unity group. Through this contact a number of messages have come for me from my father, to whom I was much attached. They are simply messages of encouragement and affection, very vaguely expressed, and not in his characteristic idiom. Whether they are authentic seems to me beside the point.

What seems important is my faith that his being did not dissolve with his death here and my continuing love for him and hope to be re-united with him.

Well, I bore you with all this just to give you a little of the picture, hoping that it will help you to advise me with some reading with which I can grow.

I wonder if you have not already been assisting me with your prayers, because in the days since I visited you I have so often felt a new kind of opening toward simple communication with God. A great many times my mind has suddenly emptied of whatever I was doing or think-ing and a sort of glow has entered in which is identified with the Idea of God. I have not really known what to do or say except to enjoy the feeling and recognize its nature and be grateful for it.

My office here is situated in fields at the edge of a forest, and in the forest there is a grove of pines which I have tended for many years, cutting out the dead branches and cleaning up the undergrowth. I work there a little every day and at these times I try to bring my thoughts into connection with God in this surrounding of peace and quiet.

Really I do not know what to say to Him because all the intellectual paraphernalia seems so completely foreign to the spirit of such occasions. To reason seems quite futile because it cannot be reasoned about. So I have gone no further than removing all thoughts from my mind and making it empty to receive the emotion of happiness that comes to me at such times.

I am hoping that the regular exercise of this calming process will, like the training of the muscles, produce a more habitual calm in my whole life so that I will, in contact with other people, less often do things which are the product of nervous unrest and personal instability.

But enough of that for now. I am going to Utah for a week in September and will try to visit your brothers in their new home. Then I can bring you word about them.

[UNSIGNED CARBON]

/ · /

reprinting your essay: "Poetry and the Contemplative Life" had just appeared in *Commonweal,* 46 (4 July 1947). Included as an appendix in *Figures for an Apocalypse ND, 1948), the essay would never appear in an ND annual.*

12. TLS-2   July 17th. [1947]

DEAR LAUGHLIN:

Thanks for the proofs which I return with a few alterations, and above all thanks for your long letter. . . .

I am happy that you confirmed my guesses about your interior life. You are a very gifted person and much more gifted than you realize, and I do hope you will be able to turn all these gifts to the great use for which they are intended: and you will become a tremendously happy and fruitful person in the supernatural order.

And so I presume permission to give you what I can in the way of advice.

Your way is the way of simplicity and integrity. God will guide you, directly and through people and through events and you should prepare yourself now to be ready for His guidance—that means to be simple and be yourself with Him all the time and realize by faith how much He is with you and how much He is doing for you and how much He is concerned with you.

Therefore, first of all, cultivate all you can your gift of the sense of His presence. Cultivate it by faith (which is all that it is) and by recollection. You do not have to get too mixed up with all those people. You like the mountains—stay there! At least as much as you can without ruining your material interests. For since you are married they are a duty and therefore a means of union with God.

Otherwise be with God. And remember to recollect yourself even in the times when it is not the good glow you have got now, but even when it is dry and empty and God does not seem to be there. Practice the same simplicity.

On the other hand, if you will permit me, I would suggest that the thought of communication with souls is something you ought to avoid as a very considerable danger to this simplicity which is so valuable and so central to your spiritual life. As you express it, it is certainly innocent enough, but I assure you that it is just the kind of thing that will muddle and dissolve your gift. For this point, in fact for all your spiritual life, I think you should first of all read carefully St. John of the Cross' *ascent of Mount Carmel*— which, by the way, is simply the first part of the volume which contains *[T]he Dark Night [of the Soul]*.

Do not bother with direct communication with souls—or communication through mediums however well minded. Enter into communion with *God*. All souls are in Him in so far as they are in His love. Having Him you have them. Keep the interior of your soul absolutely free for Him alone, and you will walk in peace: but the other way you will end up in confusion.

Another important principle is this: Do not concentrate so entirely on your gift of unitive prayer, contemplative prayer, as to neglect every other aspect of the spiritual life. There should always be a certain foundation of what amounts to external worship because you have a body and your body wants to be brought into this business too, in so far as it can. So there should be a liturgical element in your life. Since you are not a Catholic the only thing I can suggest is an occasional vocal prayer at set times. The spiritual life should have a kind of a material foundation, a framework of action in which our body is involved. Just how much this should enter into our lives depends on individuals, but I assure you also that if you were to throw away everything else and seek to reduce your interior life to nothing but this contemplative union with God, it would soon dissolve. That has been the effect of all the heresies that depreciated the body as though the flesh and all its acts were evil in themselves: they had for the time what seemed to be an exalted mysticism, but within a generation they were all murdering one another.

So use a vocal prayer—the Our Father, the Hail Mary—steadily at fixed times if you can, and if it is not awkward pray on your knees sometimes. It will do you good to overcome the embarrassment. In fact you ought to stop into Churches once in a while, and take holy water etc. and do what the people do. Hear Mass too and get to know what the liturgy is about—but don't think you have to do all this all at once. Just don't be afraid to follow any attraction in that line. All this will eventually help a lot to bind your experimental *sense* of God into your everyday life. But without such an element in your spirituality, faith will be relegated to the woods, and then your spiritual enemies—you have them too—will need only to amputate that one element in your life and you will be without anything to connect you with God. . . .

These are all suggestions at random. They might look as if they would swamp you, so I will cut through them all with just two notions: *simplicity* and *balance*—maintain your simple union by faith, and do not despise any of the ordinary traditional ways of prayer that incorporate the body in your spiritual life. Then, asking God for the things you need, you will go on integrating things more and more and you will find unity with a very solid foundation.

For you, detached as you are from the vital exterior Body in which this life flows, it will necessarily be difficult and haphazard to keep it all going as simply as a Catholic can with the Sacraments, spiritual direction and all the rest of our rich easy means of getting grace. But God is with you and He is guiding you and I am all happied up about getting a tangible answer to prayers for once! You pray for me too, and now I will get busy on that book.

In Corde Christi,
FR. M. LOUIS

13. TLS-2   Sept. 10th [1947]

DEAR LAUGHLIN

Thanks for the good newsy letter about all those people. I'll pray hard for Dylan Thomas because as far as I know there is not another living poet like him. . . .

Here is my idea of the book. *The Dark Night of the Soul* only, Spanish text of Burgos Edn facing Peers' translation, suppressing Peers' footnotes and adding notes and commentary of my own—at the back of the book?—plus a ten or twenty page preface about St. John and his doctrine. I would like to get busy on it next spring as it dovetails in nicely with some work I am just doing and what I will need most is the Spanish text. If you find it hard to line that up let me know and we will write to Europe. . . .

By all means go up and see the monks in Utah—

maybe take them a sack of potatoes if you feel like it. Last month they were not getting all the dinner they were entitled to because they didn't have enough things around to scrape up those two full bowls.

When you are full of work the way to pray is to remind yourself when you start and when you can during the bother of it that God's will is the life and value of everything and is woven into everything. The deficiencies in things come from what is opposed to Him in us. Therefore if you are working in union with Him a constant vital contact flows into you from Him through your very work itself. But if you are working against Him everything you do will blast your own energies and waste your own strength and leave you with your hands empty—or full of some kind of praise that is worthless and will eventually eat your heart out. Therefore the thing to do is to develop a keen interior sensitiveness to one's union or non-union with God's will. Ultimately this cannot be really successfully done without some kind of a sustained interior life, but if you will ask Him to sharpen up that sensitiveness within you He will do it. But you will have to be prepared to give up some things here and there.

I am very busy cataloguing the incunabula and medieval manuscripts in our vault. We may have to send many of them over to a monastery in Europe where they are establishing a sort of center of research, but Fr. Abbot is afraid this is dangerous and that the reds will come and burn the place down with all our manuscripts. . . .

In Xto.
FR. M. LOUIS, O.C.S.O.

/ · /

In Xto: "In Christ."

14. T L S - 1   Nov. 26th 1947

D E A R L A U G H L I N ,

Thanks for your letter. Glad you are settled in the mountains. I know how you feel. . . .

. . . Here is an idea I have that I think you will like. I am doing a book like Pascal's *Pensées,* just a collection of observations mostly about the interior life: but that sort of thing is very effective in its own way and I think it would make a nice little book, especially if it were nicely printed with a lot of space in the right places. The book is the kind that simply writes itself in a monastery—all I have to do is jot down the things that come into my head all day long. If you are interested I will send you all that has accumulated by, say, the beginning of February. After you have finished looking over that there will probably be a little more. It should run about the size of the poems. Will you be in the same place then?

Have you ever read the *Pensées?* But perhaps that might not suit your mountain mood. St. John of the Cross' *Living Flame of Love* would be better. Anyway, God bless you and give you all the graces of Christmas. Don't be afraid to use vocal prayer too and all the elementary means along with your recollection—and say a prayer for me.

> In Christo,
> F R . M . L O U I S

/ · /

Pascal's Pensées. The deeply religious French moralist, mathematician, scientist, and philosopher Blaise Pascal (1623–1662), whose *Pensées,* published posthumously in 1670, consists of notebook reflections and prose poem meditations on spirituality.

a collection of observations: This became *Seeds of Contemplation* (ND, 1949).

15. TLS-1   Feb. 8th 1948

DEAR LAUGHLIN

. . . I had been meaning to write but I have been too crowded. Proofs for several things came in all at the same time and I am also trying to finish a book about the Order. The devil is trying to mess up all that I do by getting me to do too much and involve me in such a network of projects that I will be neither able to work or pray.

Fr. Abbot was a little piqued that the *[Man in the] Divided Sea* was exhausted so soon but he will be glad to hear that they are printing a selection in England. Who is doing it, Burns [&] Oates? Please let us know so that we can order some as requests are coming in. Fr. Abbot has been ill. He is just back from the hospital today. . . .

I still don't have the Spanish text of St. John of the X.

About poems[,] I think I ought to try something new: and I feel guilty of not writing with sufficient discipline. And of trying to turn things out too fast. . . .

The book of *pensées* is growing. I think to call it *The Soil and Seeds of Contemplation* and maybe the book clubs might like it. But I won't send it to you until you come back from Europe.

The other books that have been bothering me are the life of a nun I wrote printed by a Catholic publisher in Milwaukee and the autobiography which is still tremendously long although it has been cut. I'll send you both as soon as I get them but if the life of the nun bores you don't worry.

One of the monasteries in America has bought a big dude ranch in the Pecos valley of New Mexico to turn it into a Trappist monastery. It sounds beautiful from the natural point of view except that it also sounds like the Atlantic City of the Southwest. Still, I guess they are isolated enough.

Apart from that all I can think of saying is that we cannot overestimate the value of contemplative prayer. It is more precious than any work or any activity. It is the highest activity of the intellect and will fused together and working on a plane that transcends our own nature in a deep and perfect love that is at the same time love and knowledge. The devil knows much more than we do how valuable it is and he does everything he can to keep us scattered and break up our recollection with useless activity. One of his strongest weapons is to fool people with false ideals and a false notion of their ability to save the world by their own ingenuity and energy. We lose immeasurably, sometimes, by pouring ourselves out in these things when we ought to remain contained and quiet and at peace before God. Nevertheless it remains a principle that the charity that is in us by contemplation does regularly need to overflow into good works for others. We do sometimes need to communicate our peace to others. But when this communication is willed by God it does not harm us, but feeds us and prepares us for deeper contemplation. So the thing is to develop much interior sensitivity to God's grace, so as to know His will, and always move with Him. . . .

> Pray for me.
> I{n Corde Xti}
> FR. M. LOUIS

/ · /

a book about the Order: Cistercian Contemplatives: A Guide to Trappist Life.
the life of a nun: Exile Ends in Glory: The Life of a Trappistine Nun, Mother M. Berchmans, O.C.S.O. (Bruce Publishing Co., 1948).

16. TLS-4   April 8th (I think.) 1948

DEAR LAUGHLIN:

. . . What I would like to do is get busy in a week or two typing out and reshaping what I have so far collected on the *Soil and Seeds of Contemplation*. I wanted to write a leaflet on contemplation and in fact did but the censor just made me a sign there is something he doesn't like about it. I hope he doesn't throw the whole thing out. I like to write leaflets. I'd like to write things to be given away to everybody for nothing.

When are you coming back, incidentally?

This is certainly a terrible world. Things seem to be cracking up very fast now. What impresses me about what I know of it is—on the one hand a small group of people with bright, defeated intelligences, gnawing themselves to pieces with an objectivity that is a final attempt to defeat nervousness: but its effect is terrifyingly *cold*. On the other hand masses of men being pushed around by crooks like cattle. But somewhere in the middle of all this is being formed a most terrific Christian elite. A very deep and serene and powerful sense of Catholic doctrine in its *wholeness* is coming back into the center of things. Books from France that have reached me are tremendously impressive.

My own stuff ought to be able to fit somewhere into all that: but it has to grow and I am beginning to realize how much it has to grow and get disciplined. Pray for me that it may do so. If my sanctification is tied up with being an artist—as I am more or less bound now to assume that it is—I have got to be a good artist to be a saint. But it brings with it a lot of perplexing problems. I am glad of them all because only Christ can get me through them. Which is what I want, because then the problems themselves will be the instruments and occasions for integrating me more fully in Him.

Christ is One Man. Those who live in Him are One in Him. They are one in His death, they rise with Him. That is why His resurrection is taking place in me *now.* The whole Church is rising with Him in the middle of all this black business, fighting its way slowly and with great strength and serenity out of the darkness. The thing to do is to be caught up in that resurrection, incorporated in the life of that whole Body and take one's place in that whole process. The term of it is infinite. And sometimes it seems very near. . . .

In Corde Christi,
FR. M. LOUIS, O.C.R.

/ · /

a leaflet on contemplation: Probably *Guide to Cistercian Life* (Abbey of Gethsemani, 1948), a pamphlet that includes a six-page section on "The Life of Prayer."

17. TLS-3   May 12th 1948

DEAR LAUGHLIN:

Thanks for the card from Ascona. I must have gone through there once in a train. And from the office they sent W[illiam] C[arlos] Williams and [William] Everson and the number of *[New] Direction[s in Prose and Poetry]*. Just looking at the books I liked the printing of them all especially the binding of *Paterson*. I haven't had time to read anything except a few lines of Everson which make me glad to be in a monastery. I had forgotten how disorganized things were outside—and how unhappy.

He is a fine poet and the book is beautiful and he has an eye and the stuff is balanced. But also he is a heretic—materially and through his not altogether blameworthy misfortune—in giving physical life an absolute value in itself. Sure, the pleasures connected with sex are good. God made them and they must be good, because they were supposed to be in the first place. But Everson like Lawrence and all the rest of them has that silly conviction that all that can be detached from the order of things and considered as something *sui juris* all by itself in a sort of vacuum into which morality cannot enter. The reason is, of course, that what passes for morality these days is, in reality, a bad joke and in most people it is a lesser value than the goods of a more or less animal order—which is how dumb we have come to be.

Nevertheless the true order exists which is this: all the good of the created order, all bodies, all the pleasures and activities of bodies and minds and souls have one purpose: the glory of God and the true joy of men and the two purposes cannot be separated. Or if they are, you get death instead of life.

Now among all the stuffy people for whom morality has become a false front for a lot of psychological unpleasantness, death has replaced life because physical goods have become warped and spoiled in the service of an idol—money, respectability, what not.

But that does not mean that the way to reestablish order is to liberate sex from all order and all morality. Just because some people have a false morality does not mean that the moral order does not exist.

And my proof of this is that Everson's poems are not the work of a completely happy man and one of the reasons for that is this fundamental disorder. Of course there must be plenty of other reasons.

There is only one way left to set things straight: to bring all these created things into relation to their true end and use them to glorify God. In doing that we will automatically get to be happy. And the way to glorify God by the use of things is to use them the way He wants them to be used. How is that? Well you don't have to take the word of Sunday school teachers. There are plenty of sensible people to tell us the answers—for instance St. Thomas Aquinas.

In other words just because the world is full of boy-scouts does not mean that everybody else has to give up all hope of making sense out of it.

At the same time I appreciate his problem and the thing that most struck me in the book was his statement of it somewhere where he talks about the tight lipped people who pray straining their heads at the rafters. To me that is a big problem too. In fact right now it is getting to be one of my biggest problems: that in a monastery there should be so many people that get no further than that, and for whom religion is still a complex of safe practices rather than a *life*.

But that will always be a difficulty. One of my solutions is that they are often not as dumb as they look. Behind the screen of mechanical gestures which they more or less have to use to keep their nerves quiet, there is a deep undercurrent (sometimes) of a life which even they are not capable of suspecting.

I like very much the idea of making the commentary on the poems a number of *[New] Direction[s]*. From the lineup I presume that would leave me until some time next year to get ready.

Here are some poems you might like to place somewhere in England—okay? Or if I catch you too late, perhaps they would come in handy over here.

Anyway God bless you and pray for me. I don't want to conceive myself in any way as having any kind of a mission in the world or the Church except to see God. That is plenty. But at the same time somebody who is capable of understanding them has got to worry about the people in the world who are wandering around in circles with tremendous talent and more tremendous sincerity and nobody to show them what to do about it. Sometimes I wish I were capable of it, but as I say it isn't my vocation, unless I can do it by prayer. Really this is a tremendously serious business. I hate to see a good world half rotten and full of the stuff that breeds wars and not be able to do anything about it.

{In Xto.}
fr. M. Louis

/ · /

Williams: ND published the bulk of American poet William Carlos Williams's (1883–1963) most significant work, including the *Complete Collected Poems* (1938) mentioned by TM. See Hugh Witemeyer, ed., *William Carlos Williams and James Laughlin: Selected Letters* (Norton, 1989).

Everson: An American poet and fine letterpress printer, William Everson (1912–) joined the Dominican Order and wrote under the name Brother Antoninus for eighteen years. Everson chronicled his disaffection from the religious life in *Man-Fate* (ND, 1974). JL sent TM Everson's *The Residual Years* (ND, 1948).

St. Thomas Aquinas: Italian Scholastic theologian and philosopher, St. Thomas Aquinas (1225–1274) entered the Dominican Order in 1243. His greatest work is the *Summa Theologica.* Known as Thomism, Aquinas's syntheses of philosophy and theology have become doctrinal cornerstones of the Roman Catholic Church.

the commentary on the poems: "Poetry and the Contemplative Life." See Letter #11.

18. TLS-2   June 28th 1948

DEAR LAUGHLIN:

First of all this is to say that I am about finishing the *Seeds of Contemplation* and want to know where to send the ms. Are you back from Europe?

Then thanks very much for the Vernon Watkins. That's what makes me think you are back, because I got two copies and I want to keep them both, one for one other monastery. I like him tremendously, and I am very happy that someone with so much energy is writing in the British Isles. He is alive and awake and has something of the innocence that a new age requires so that altogether he makes me very happy. For instance "the Broken Sea" is very fine. "The Sea Music" has a lot of Robt. Lowell in it, it seems to me. . . .

Did you ever get the copies of *Cist[ercian] Contemplatives?* . . .

I was thinking about that anthology and it seems to me that the only way I can possibly do it is to forget about any attempt at covering the whole field and taking just the poems that I know and like and can easily get hold of. How would it be to print one or two St. John of the X in Spanish and one or two others in Latin and a couple in Middle English and so on, and the bulk in English in which they were written? And include modern writers like [Robert] Lowell?

Anyway, it is a year already since you were down here and that should stimulate you to come here again and stay longer this time.

In Xto,
FR. M. LOUIS O.C.R.

/ · /

Vernon Watkins: Welsh poet and lifelong friend of Dylan Thomas, Vernon Phillips Watkins (1906–1967) is best known for his visionary poetry, the product of an intense midlife religious epiphany. JL sent TM Watkins's *Selected Poems* (ND, 1948).

Lowell: Robert Lowell (1917–1977), American poet, married the writer Jean Stafford in 1940, the year Lowell graduated from Harvard and converted to Catholicism. TM was particularly attracted to Lowell's first volume of poems, *Land of Unlikeness* (1944), and its depiction of the modern world as steeped in corruption, chaos, and spiritual bankruptcy.

19. TLS-2   July 9th 1948

DEAR LAUGHLIN:

I hope this will not have to chase you to Europe and
back. It is an answer to your beautiful Mont Blanc letter
about the angels and the rest of it. And a repeat invitation
to come on down here as soon as you can. Incidentally
the autobiography is out and I have asked them to send
you a copy and I sent you another letter about *Seeds of
Contemplation* being finished.

I don't think work is as important as any of us feel it
to be when the mood is upon us. Cultivate tranquility—
detachment—the purity of heart that does things simply
to please God. Think of yourself as swimming always *with*
the stream of His will and do not try to be fighting the
current with your own interests and ambitions and so on:
but rather hope for a life in which all your own interests
will veer around into the direction that coincides with
His aims for you, then things will move with a tremendous ease and swiftness. All this means cultivating His
presence by faith: keeping the eyes of your soul open
towards Him and His Being within you. To me, that is
my only source of comfort and happiness and without it
I think I would probably be hopeless about half the time.

One of the monks in Europe tells me about a first rate
French photographer who specializes in pictures of old
monasteries like Senanque but who is also a mountain-
eer—who has climbed something in the Himalayas. He
sounds like a fine fellow; I'd like to see the two of you
get together on some kind of a picture book.

In Corde Jesu,
FR. M. LOUIS O.C.R.

/ · /

the autobiography: SSM.
In Corde Jesu: "In the heart of Jesus."

20. TLS-1   Aug. 4th 1948

DEAR LAUGLIN:

Writing you this letter today is not nearly so gay as it would have been yesterday. Yesterday Father Abbot gave me your package of books on St. John of the X from Paris and your small book of poems from Milan and made me very happy. But last night he took a train to Georgia and they found him dead in the train before they got to Knoxville. I was glad that yesterday we had a long talk together about everything, anyway. And he was as cheerful as usual. Anyway, nobody gets very upset about anyone dying around here. I know he will be just as close to us as ever and will in some sense be able to help us out more. Besides, his troubles are over and his life of contemplation is really getting under way!

Still, he worked himself to death for his monasteries. Everybody saw this coming for a long time. He kept having strokes when he went on these journeys—had one in Utah last June. I was always afraid I would walk into his room and find him lying on the floor. So nobody was surprised. Say a little prayer for him—and I have no doubt he will do something for you in return.

The St. John of the X books will come in very useful for the preface to that *Dark Night [of the Soul]* job. Incidentally on the Spanish text of that I have finally written to a Carthusian monk I know in Burgos. Maybe he can get it for us. It looks like the job won't get under way until next year. I am very tied up now. The autobiography should be out any day and I have asked them to send you a copy. All that is holding it up now is the jacket.

The next few weeks will be turmoil here. The regular visitation is scheduled for next week. Then there will be the election of another abbot. This incidentally may mean a radical change in my own activities: they may find it necessary to take me away from the typewriter and put me on some other job: I don't mean abbot! But there is no telling what may come up. However I shall probably be able to wind up all the jobs I am supposed to be doing for you, at least in time. We shall see. If you really want them I think the next superior will be persuaded by anything you may say and your rights won't simply be thrown out the window. For my own part I am ready for anything—except perhaps that anthology, which still frightens me.

Was it you that sent a book in Italian on poetry and contemplation? If so, thanks for that too.

I don't suppose you would be free to get down here right away, and if not, don't come in September because the house will be full of priests trying to get some meditating done before another year of hard work. October would be a fine time. But I am very much looking forward to seeing you and really getting a chance to go over things. Anyway if you come in October you will be able to meet whoever is the new abbot.

Glad you are back. Did Naomi [Burton] send you *Seeds of Contemplation* yet?

In Corde Christi,
f r . M . L o u i s o . c . r .

/ · /

Father Abbot: Dom Frederic Dunne—see Letter #2. TM wrote about Dom Frederic's death in a poignant headnote, "Death of an Abbot," to Part Two of *SJ*.

your small book of poems from Milan: JL's *A Small Book of Poems* (ND, 1948).

the regular visitation: An official visit to the monastery conducted annually by the Father Immediate, the abbot of the Motherhouse of Gethsemani, Melleray, in western France.

21. TL-2   August 10, 1948

DEAR MERTON:

Thanks ever so much for sending me the corrections for the new edition of *A Man in the Divided Sea*. I will see that they are taken care of. We shall probably be producing it here by offset because the London deal fell through.

I was really considerably irritated with Hollis & Carter. After telling me for months on end that they were keen to do your book, they suddenly came out with the statement that they could not make up their minds which poems they wanted to choose, and didn't want to do anything right away. I don't see any reason why we should wait around several years for them to make up their mind. Accordingly, I gave strong fight talks about your work to [T. S.] Eliot at Faber & Faber and to Herbert Read at Routledge. They both promised that they would consider it seriously right soon, and possibly we will get an offer out of one or the other of them. They are both excellent houses, better, I think in fact, than Hollis and Carter. . . .

Miss Burton sent over the manuscript of *Seeds of Contemplation,* and what I have read of it I like terribly much. I shall be telephoning her shortly to proceed with making up a contract. I know that you want to work the thing over again, and possibly there are some spots where it could be somewhat polished. But I think it is full of marvelous meat and I must say that parts of it gave me a terrific lift and a good deal of new understanding and insight. I think it is a book which can do a great deal of good and I will try to give it a format which will make it so attractive that it will be helped on its way. . . .

I hope that I can get down to see you before too long but things here are in a terrible state of confusion, owing to my having been away for such a long time. I think I had probably better make a dent on the accumulated work before waltzing off on another trip. But I do very much want to come. Are there any particular times when it would not fit in with your schedule down there to have me?

Another idea I had was that I might ask Bob Fitzgerald to come along down with me. Did you ever know him? He is a poet and a terribly good one. He has also done those marvelous translations from the Greek with Dudley Fitts. He is a recent convert to Catholicism, and I think that he would get a great deal out of the trip and that you and he might be likely to strike up a long and lasting friendship which would mean a great deal to both of you. Bob is a very old friend of mine, in fact one of my best friends, but lately I never seem to get the chance to see him any more, what with the confusion and turmoil of this awful New York City life, so that it would be great to get off with him for a few days. But let me know if you don't approve of the idea.

Best wishes, as always
[UNSIGNED CARBON]

/ · /

Eliot: T. S. Eliot (1888–1965), the American-born and Harvard-educated poet who took British citizenship in 1927. Eliot was book editor at the London-based publisher Faber & Faber after serving as poetry editor at the literary journal *Criterion.* Neither Faber & Faber nor Routledge would publish TM's *A Man in the Divided Sea.* Only a trimmed-down version appeared in England: Robert Speaight, ed., *Selected Poems* (Hollis & Carter, 1950).

Herbert Read: (1893–1968), British poet, editor, literary and art critic. In 1951, ND published Read's *Phases of English Poetry* and, with Faber & Faber, *Collected Poems.*

Bob Fitzgerald: After graduating from Harvard, Robert Fitzgerald (1910–1985) wrote for *Time,* and in 1965, became professor of creative writing at Harvard. In addition to writing poetry, he was awarded a Bollingen Prize for a translation of the *Iliad* (1974). ND published Fitzgerald's collected poems, *In the Rose of Time,* in 1956.

Dudley Fitts: (1903–1968), JL's English teacher at Choate and translator of Aristophanes' plays, including *Lysistrada* (1954). With Robert Fitzgerald, Fitts translated plays by Sophocles and Euripides. JL recalled in a *Paris Review* inter-view (1983) that the inspirational Fitts "was my first introduction to modern poetry."

22. TLS-1   Sept. 27 1948

DEAR LAUGHLIN:

I was glad to get your letter and to know that things are going along on the book *[Seeds of Contemplation]*. My suggestions were only suggestions and evidently the printer knows his business better than I do. The format is perfectly ok with me. As to the decorations: it seems to me that they are a little stilted. The doctrine on con-templation that I hold on to for dear life is a pretty naked one and does not call for these things, rather the contrary. The book demands great simplicity. I see what he was doing: he had in mind medieval books and the decora-tions do give the book a high–medieval flavor. But that is not what the text needs. I would like to see something more bare and austere. . . .

In Corde Christi,
FR. M. LOUIS

23. TLS-2   November 18, 1948

DEAR MERTON:

You may remember that we were discussing the possi-bility of using a little design on the cover of *Seeds of Con-templation,* which would show grain, or wheat, or something like that. The girl who does our art work has turned out the enclosed sketch, and I thought I would send it down to you to see how you like it. Do you think we are headed in the right direction on this? . . . You said yourself that you used to do some drawing, and if you feel like it, maybe you would care to have a crack at this design. . . .

I went down to see [T. S.] Eliot in Princeton the other day, and we talked quite a bit about you. He is most interested in your work, but he thinks it is very uneven, and he wishes you would strive more toward form. That is probably an old refrain for you, and I won't rub it in. He asked whether it would be possible to see more of your early poems from which he might want to make further selections. Are there any others around with Mark [Van Doren] or with Bob Lax anywhere? I am having some carbons made of the ones that you gave me, and I will show him some of those that I think he would like. . . .

I have had several nice letters back from those Catholic poets, whose names you gave me. I had written to them, suggesting that they send in one or two poems which might be suitable for the Catholic anthology, and they have done so. I will assemble all this material before I bother you with it.

I hope that everything is going as well as ever down there. I am still feeling the good effects of my visit, which gave me an enormous lift.

> With best wishes,
> JAMES LAUGHLIN

24. TLS-2   November 22, 1948

DEAR JAY:

. . . I agree about not having enough form, but I can't figure out how I am going to acquire any: but thanks for *the Pisan Cantos.* Books help, and I think this is the best

of Pound I have ever read. . . . I'll type out some poems
I have that are old and unpublished, and I think Lax's
sister has some. I'll write. I'll ask Lax to make some suggestions about the anthology—but please don't ask me
about it until it is all lined up and ready for the
preface. . . .

In the refectory we are reading a book about the Byz-
antine-Slavonic rite—that is the "Greeks" who were here
with you. It is a good book, called *Windows Westward* by
Gulovich. It explains a lot of things about their liturgy. I
wish I knew when [Evelyn] Waugh was coming. A series
of mysterious phone calls from *Time* made arrangements
for him to get back and forth from here to the airport
but since then nothing has been heard. It will be fine
seeing him. . . .

Right now they have just elected Fr. Maurice abbot in
Utah and the pictures of the monastery look marvelous.

There goes the bell.

All the best,
In Corde Christi,
FR . M . LOUIS

/ · /

the best of Pound: The American poet Ezra Pound (1885–1972). Despite
espousing unsavory political views during World War II, Pound's poetry,
especially the *Cantos*, had a powerful influence on modern poetry. See *Ezra
Pound and James Laughlin: Selected Letters*, ed. David M. Gordon (Norton,
1994).

Waugh: English novelist, critic, and man of letters, Evelyn Waugh (1903–
1966) edited the English edition of TM's *SSM* under the title *Elected Silence*
(Hollis & Carter, 1949). Waugh arrived at Gethsemani the following week.
TM's letters to Waugh are collected in *Courage*, pp. 3–19.

25. TLS-1   December 18th 1948

DEAR JAY,

Here are the page proofs [of *Seeds of Contemplation*], with the censor's corrections made. I made every correction they suggested or desired. . . .

You said it would be possible to make a few extra prints of the picture of Our Lady for me to use as an ordination card. Could I have about four hundred of them if it is not too much trouble?

The Abbot General had another idea about those books for Rome. He suggested I send him copies of all I have written, for him to present them to the Vatican Library, where they will be seen and read. What gets sent to the Pope is just put on a shelf and forgotten. However I think it would be a good idea to send the Holy Father *Seeds* and *the Seven Storey Mt,* which there is a faint chance he might look at. I don't think he would have a lot of time for the poems. In that case, we would only bind these two, and send the others as they are to the General, for the Vatican. How does this plan strike you? In any case, it would be quite all right to get the job done at the New York place you mention, and charge it against the royalty account. Bob Giroux says he is hunting up a first edition of the *Mountain* and will pass it on to you.

Have you got the Eric Gill thing for the cover?

I have not had time to get around to any corrections on *Figures [for an Apocalypse]*. What is the deadline?

By way of a Christmas present, here is a little book on contemplation—the one Sister Madeleva printed. God bless you, and give you peace and joy this Christmas and always. Do all you can to get the spiritual graces of the Feast: I mean, ask for them, and penetrate into the meaning of what it is all about. Why don't you get to a Mass somewhere? Anyway, pray for me, and I'll be praying for you and all your family. Holy Christmas to you.

F R . M . L O U I S

/ · /

Giroux: TM's classmate and friend at Columbia University in the mid-thirties, Robert Giroux (1914–), became TM's editor at Harcourt, Brace where Giroux recommended the phenomenally successful *SSM* for publication. Later vice-president and editor-in-chief at Farrar, Straus & Giroux, Giroux serves as Trustee of the Thomas Merton Legacy Trust.

Eric Gill: The special edition of *SSM* that JL had bound for the Vatican Library was embossed with one of Eric Gill's original typefaces. Printer, typecutter, sculptor, and essayist (1882–1940), Gill's craftsmanship in service to religious commitment and social equality naturally appealed to TM.

a little book on contemplation: TM sent JL *Cistercian Contemplatives: A Guide to Trappist Life.*

26. TLS-1 Christmas Eve [1948]

D E A R J A Y

Here are one or two ancient poems I dug up. Not much good except "Dirge for Miami" and "Circe." Let me know if you are using any. May be some others somewhere. These are the only copies I have, so please be careful with them.

I shall pray for you especially tonight at Midnight Mass, which is very beautiful here. May God give you peace, and pour out into your whole family the graces that are given to families at this season. Ask Him to develop in you a spirit of supernatural discretion, and to help you separate what is worthless from what is valuable, and to keep you attending to what can really nourish your soul and give you spiritual health. I need that too— to keep myself from being swamped. Even in monasteries, no matter how much people try, there is always more chaff than wheat: whole mountains of it, in fact. Sometimes I think the more active we get the more chaff we produce.

Anyway, God bless you.

In Corde Jesu,
FR. M. LOUIS

27. TLS-2   December 29, 1948

DEAR TOM:

Thank you ever so much for several letters, for returning the proofs, and for the Christmas gift of the fine little red book, with your thoughts on contemplation, which has already been most helpful to me. I thought of you often on Christmas day, and wished that the circumstances were such that I could get into a closer relation with the things which you were thinking. We had a very nice Christmas, with lots of snow on the ground and a bright sunlight, but I'm afraid everyone was much too much preoccupied with the way their children received, and then promptly broke up their toys, than with things of deeper spiritual importance. How right you are about most of life being taken up with non-essential motions. I would say that about 95% of mine was. I wish I could do something about it, but it is hard to know where to start in to simplify things, and get down to bedrock. . . .

The reports that I get from Bob [Giroux] about the sale of *Seven Storey Mountain* certainly are wonderful. I don't see how such a large readership can fail to bring a lot of new souls to God, and you can be thankful that He has given you the opportunity and the power to do so much good in a wicked world.

I do wish that you could find the time to make the changes in *Figures [for an Apocalypse]* just as soon as possible. Why don't you try to do them this very week? We keep getting requests for the book every day, and I hate to let them back up too long, as a certain number of customers will lose interest, I suppose, if the thing doesn't get into their hands fairly soon. Do try to go over it right away, and let me have it right back, so that we can get ahead. . . .

Thanks ever so much for sending along the batch of older poems. I haven't had a chance yet to study them carefully, but they are on my desk up at Norfolk, and I will have a look at them next weekend. I note that these are your only copies, so I will have copies made of any that I send out to the magazines. We have begun to hear back from the bunch that I sent out a few weeks ago. I was very surprised that *The New Yorker* refused the one about the reader. I'm surprised at this. It strikes me as being one of your nicest things. Well, they always are peculiar. I'll send it somewhere else. On the other hand, *Poetry* accepted one of the group that I sent to them. I will keep sending these out, until we get them all placed.

Well, I must run along now to a conference of the salesmen, so that is all for now.

Very best wishes, as ever,
JAMES LAUGHLIN

28. TLS-2

Klosters
Easter Day [1949]

DEAR MERTON—

Today is Easter Day and I am thinking of you particularly because your letter came last night and your words of belief are very much in my heart and thoughts.

It is a glorious, heavenly day, with the sun streaming down from a clear sky. The mountains are still covered with snow, but here in the valley the fields are starting to green, and the crocuses are coming up through the grass. After lunch I shall walk down the valley through the little peasant hamlets to absorb the sun, and the sense of living, and the sense of joy because Christ is risen again.

This has been a trying and confusing winter—many problems, many blind allies [sic], many battles (I cannot yet seem to get rid of that tendency to fight back when someone harms me), and now we go into a confusing summer, and really the only thing there is to think about, that is not an affront to the intelligence, is what God can do for us, because surely Man has made such of a mess of it now that he can't extricate himself alone. . . .

The papers these days are just too horrible to read. Every day in Palestine there is a bombing from one side or the other. And a scientist reveals that our government has perfected an atomic cloud, which can move on the wind and annihilate everything it touches. Is this the anger of God?

I'm glad that you like your new book. Copies have reached me here, too, and I like it very much. The printing is not entirely first rate—it is a little grey and careless—but the general look and feel of the book is not bad. And the poems are full of beautiful lines and figures. I think the book will have a good reception and a considerable success. Rexroth wrote enthusiastically about it. He probably wrote to you, too. . . .

I shall surely be going to London, and so if you will send me the names of any books you would like me to look for there I'll be glad to. It is always fun to poke around in those shops in London and Oxford where you really feel that books are books and not just pieces of merchandise.

I shall also be seeing [Robert] Speaight and the others there in London and will try to get them to put their edition of your poems right into production without further delay.

I hope you can say a prayer too for dear Bill Williams. He is very ill, and there is no one we can afford less to lose. There is a man, not religious at all, but whose every action has the generosity of the naturally good. I'll ask the office to send you his new book—the second part of *Paterson*. It's a strange thing, but wonderful in parts.

As ever,
JL

I'll ask them to send you Everson and Watkins too. They are both good poets, in totally different ways—Watkins very polished, Everson very rough and direct. Everson was a CO in the War. Watkins is a schoolteacher in a little town in Wales.

/ · /

your new book: The Tears of the Blind Lions (ND, 1949).

Speaight: British author, editor, and actor, Robert W. Speaight wrote biographies of Eric Gill (1965) and Teilhard de Chardin (1967). Speaight edited and wrote a foreword to an English edition of TM's *Selected Poems* (Hollis & Carter, 1950) and recorded selections of TM's poetry at the Library of Congress in 1951.

29. TLS-2   [Spring 1949]

DEAR JAY

Thanks for your letter from Klosters. Today you should be back in N.Y. This is to repeat all I said about *Seeds* looking fine. I wish they would hurry up with that limited edition, or all the people to whom I want to send it will have read the book before the present gets to them.

This is also to ask if you will get the copies of *Seeds*

and 7 *SM* bound for the Holy Father as soon as you possibly can as I'd like to get them to him quick.

Also, I've thought it might be nice to get some of the fellows down here at the end of May or beginning of June when I am to be ordained priest and sing my first Mass. It will be a nice occasion and I'd like very much to have you come along with Mark [Van Doren] and Bob Giroux and one or two other friends. The date we are trying to arrange at the moment is May 26th but the Archbishop may get sick or change his mind. Anyway, I do hope you can make it. I'll let you know in plenty of time what the exact day will be. . . .

I was ordained deacon the other day and thought it would be a good idea if I quit writing poetry as though for good. I mean, drop it for several years anyway, and keep it dropped unless I get something right on a silver platter. The idea alone is enough to increase my interior liberty, and really the recent stuff, although it may be okay, is not on a level that demands that I continue to write.

In those circumstances you might get out a *Complete Poems*, from which I could drop half a dozen of the existing ones, and to which we could add the new ones I gave you—or the ones that are worth it, and perhaps one or two unpublished early ones. What do you think? Or is it considered bad manners for a person to get out *Complete Poems* at the age of thirty five, and then go into a shell? Maybe it would look dumb. In that case we could get out a *Selected* anyway.

I am expecting proofs on the new history from Harcourt. A sample page looks beautiful. They are using Cochin for the titles and Janson for the body. Cochin is superb.

Really I am happy about *Seeds*. That is the kind of stuff I ought to be writing. It has its faults, no doubt, but I can see my way more clear in that direction. The journal idea you spoke of would work out nicely too. Anything to get across some solid ideas about the interior life with enough "creative" about it to communicate something of the atmosphere out here, or something of the twelfth century tempo. I am still so swamped with mail that it is hard to keep a book rolling.

Honestly, activity gets in my hair. The things that go on in the depths of the soul are so much more important and fruitful! But anyway, the communication of all that is part of it, too. God bless you. Happy Easter.

In Christo,
FR. M. LOUIS

/ · /

proofs on the new history: TM's history of the Cistercian Order, *The Waters of Siloe* (Harcourt, Brace, 1949).

30. TLS-2   April 6, 1949

DEAR TOM:

Thanks ever so much for your letter that came in the other day. It was exciting news about your first Mass, and I am deeply touched that you should want me to come down and be there when you sing it. I'd love to do this if it works out all right for you, so please keep me posted about the dates. . . .

I'm sorry about the delays with the limited edition of *Seeds*. . . . Do we have here a list of people to whom you want to have them sent? If you sent it here, let me know and I'll hunt it up because it must be around somewhere.

The orders for the book continue to pour in every day, and we are all very excited about it. The second printing will unquestionably have been exhausted before the end of this week, and fortunately the third printing will be reaching us the first of next. With a printer who prints very carefully, and really takes pains on his make-ready, it is quite a job to keep up with the demand. The alternative would be to plate the book and run it in one of the big shops here in New York, but I think that would be bad because the books just wouldn't look the same. . . .

I was able to secure a set of sheets of the limited edition and these have gone off to the binder, together with the first edition copy of *The Seven Storey Mountain,* to be bound up in the special binding for the Holy Father. . . .

I don't exactly know what to think or say about your idea of giving up writing poetry. Most poets with your gift just wouldn't be able to stop if they wanted to, but of course, you in your regime there, have developed a kind of control over yourself which is like that of some of those yogis. Maybe you would be strong enough to keep your poetry submerged. Whether that would be desirable is something I'm just not competent to judge. You remember that when we talked about this before in connection with what you said on the problem in your essay, I said that it seemed to me that you were working out God's will in writing good poems, which also embodied a Christian message.

It would be quite feasible to put out a book of poems which would gather together your best work to date, but I certainly would stand against affixing the tag "complete" to them, because it really just seems to me impossible that you won't write poems later on. A faculty like that is just part of your being, and I don't see how any amount of will power can cut it off. . . .

We can talk about all these problems when I see you. I'm glad that you like the idea of the Journal. Let's hope that we can work out something along that line too. And then there's always the commentary on St. John of the

Cross when you find the time. There's no rush about these things and you don't want to burn yourself stale. . . .

With best wishes, as always,
J A M E S   L A U G H L I N

31. TLS-1   May 2nd 1949

D E A R   J A Y

Thanks for your card from Aspen. This is just to confirm the date. Ordination will be May 26th and I will say a low Mass on the 27th and sing my first solemn Mass on the 28th. So I hope all of you who come can plan on those three days. I am told Clare Boothe Luce wants to be there too and Father Abbot said okay. I have never met her before but she has been very friendly and has done us many favors. I had not invited any women on my own account because it is so hard to find anywhere for them to stay. Otherwise all the others will be old friends. Mark [Van Doren] says he will try to get there.

Bob Giroux has just sent me proofs of a beautiful cover they have designed for *Waters of Siloe.*

Apart from that I am entirely hemmed in by nuns. The news of the ordination has got around and they are sending me presents and holy pictures until I want to go and hide.

You asked me once about *the Catholic Worker* and they are certainly okay although perhaps some of the things some of them may write may sound a little funny at times. But they are definitely on the level.

With all best wishes,
In the Risen Christ,
F R .   M .   L O U I S

/ · /

Clare Boothe Luce: Dramatist, U.S. representative from Connecticut (1943–47), U.S. ambassador to Italy (1953–56), Clare Boothe Luce (1903–1987) was married to Henry Robinson Luce (1898–1967), publisher of *Time.* TM corresponded with Boothe Luce sporadically from 1948 to shortly before his death in 1968. She did not attend TM's ordination, but she gave him a typewriter that he used for writing *SJ.*

the Catholic Worker: A newspaper started in 1933 by two Catholic lay persons, Dorothy Day (1897–1980) and Peter Maurin (1877–1949). Under the influence of Day, *The Catholic Worker* dwelt on social justice issues from a Catholic perspective with particular stress on the importance of social witness, i.e., "works." "If there were no *Catholic Worker* and such forms of witness," TM wrote Day years later, in 1965, "I would never have joined the Catholic Church" (*Ground,* p. 151).

32. TLS-2   Aug 13th 1949

DEAR JAY,

About *the [Tears of the] Blind Lions*—I'd like to see the script before it goes to the printer. . . .

Do you think the title would be better as *The Blind Lions?* I mention that because now three of my titles have "of" in the middle of them. . . .

Many many thanks for the beautiful book on *Silos.* Those books make me feel happy and give me good ideas. Did you know this one was inscribed to Ezra Pound? What did he do, throw it out the window? Anyway it is a beautiful book. Pictures fine; text not up to the pictures, but the whole idea is swell.

I am writing the journal all the time. But I am getting scared of publishing it. Can you send me some good journals? Particularly some more or less religious ones— something by Kierkegaard. The fact that I am having qualms about this is a good sign. Good books are born in travail, and I am afraid if this one were published it would arouse a lot of comment and I might get hit over the head. That is why it ought to grow and mature slowly, and in fact that is what I am trying to do, now, with everything I write. Anyway, say a prayer that it will turn out the way Our Lady wants it to turn out. She arranges things very well. She has certainly been handling *the Seven Storey Mountain* nicely. Have you seen [Evelyn] Waugh's English edition? It is very fine. I owe him much. . . .

Father Abbot has been letting me go off by myself into the woods and it helps nicely with prayer. The abbey is very noisy with machinery these days. We have bought a huge new diesel tractor that roars like a mechanized army. I keep getting very nice letters from Jacques Maritain and from some other people he started me writing to in Europe. Wonderful calm priests with a very deep and simple view of things, and yet very living. They are really at the center of things, all right.

On the other hand I saw the twenty fifth anniversary number of the *Saturday review of Literature* and skipped through it and the impression I got was that half the writers in this country were cannibals. Really, Jay, I hope you can extricate yourself from that tangle—even though your natural integrity does preserve you to a remarkable degree. It's too bad, though, that you can't concentrate everything in the mountains where the air is clean. Interior silence is a thing to cultivate and it means relaxing and dropping projects for the time being in order to receive whatever comes from the depths of you, and keep organized. It is hard to do in a city.

Well, anyway . . .

In Corde Christi,
T O M
F R . M . L O U I S

/ · /

the journal: SJ.

Kierkegaard: Søren Kierkegaard (1813–1855), Danish philosopher, religious writer, and critic of modernity.

Waugh's English edition: See Letter #24.

Jacques Maritain: A French philosopher and social critic (1882–1973), whose book *Art and Scholasticism* (1920) had a major influence on TM's conversion to Catholicism. TM's letters to Maritain have been collected in *Courage.*

33. TL-2   August 26, 1949

DEAR TOM,

Your very good letter of August 13 reached me just as I was leaving for Nantucket. We have come up here for two weeks in order that the children may have a crack at the beach and the sea bathing. The place is far from what it used to be in the old days before they allowed automobiles on the island, but it's still very attractive architecturally, and if you drive out on to the back dunes in the distant beaches, you can get away from the maddening throng.

. . . I personally think that *The Tears of the Blind Lions* is a stronger title than just *The Blind Lions* by themselves. It is a very catching and colorful title which should stick in people's minds. . . .

What you write about the journal sounds extremely interesting, and I am keen to have a look at some of it. When I get back to town I'll look up some Kierkegaard for you and I will also try to locate a copy of that beautiful journal which Rilke wrote. No doubt other good journals will occur to me later on, and I'll send them along as I think of them. Would you care to have a look at some Albert Schweitzer? He is being very widely read in this country now, thanks somewhat to the big publicity he had this summer when he came over to the Goethe Festival, but due more probably, I think, to the fact that you just can't keep a good man down even in such a wicked world as this, and he certainly is a good man, if ever there was one. He has written a great deal but I imagine that *Out of My Life and Thought* or *On the Edge of the Prime Evil Forest* would be the volumes which would help you the most in what you are now doing.

Did you ever read a strange book called *Hadrian VII* by a wild character named Corvo? I am in the middle of it now and am quite fascinated. It's the story of a fanatical Catholic purist who imagines that he gets elected Pope and then what he does as Pope in the way of reforms and so forth. That is a very bare description. Actually, the color and atmosphere are absolutely knee deep and I have been learning all kinds of things about the inner workings of the church which I never knew before.

Well the bell is ringing on the dictaphone so that will be all for now.

With best wishes as always,
[Unsigned Carbon]

/ · /

Rilke: Rainer Maria Rilke (1875–1926), German poet, born in Prague. Rilke infused his poetry with a mystical depth and stylistic rigor that greatly appealed to TM. JL refers either to Rilke's *Die Aufzeichnungen des Malte Laurids Brigge* (*The Notebooks of Malte Laurids Brigge,* 1910)—a fictional diary of a young Dane in Paris, full of the same spiritual anxiety evident in TM's *SSM*—or to *Journal of My Other Self* (1930).

Albert Schweitzer: (1875–1965), Alsatian philosopher, ethicist, theologian, musician, and medical missionary, who was awarded the 1952 Nobel Peace Prize.

Corvo: One of many pseudonyms used by the English writer, novelist, and eccentric, Baron Frederick William Rolfe (1860–1913).

34. TLS-2   September 15, 1949

DEAR TOM:

Thanks eversomuch for your letter and for sending back the poems for *the Tears of the Blind Lions.* These have gone right off to the printer already and we hope to have

proofs for you and for the censor in a very short time. I
was very much intrigued by the poem written in French,
and also to notice that you have included the one written
for Dylan Thomas. I think this is going to end up as a
pretty powerful little collection.

That would be great if Father Abbot would let you
have a little hutch out in the woods. I see that you are
driving toward the Carthusian ideal.

Enclosed are two pieces of good news from England,
first that Robert Speaight will be willing to record the
poems next year when he comes to Harvard, and then
that Hollis and Carter finally want to make a selection of
the poems for publication in England. Please return both
of these letters to me as I haven't yet answered them with
any comments that you want to make. We will have
plenty of time to think which poems Speaight ought to
record.

. . . I have . . . been mulling over your query about
some famous journals by good writers which you might
like to see down there. I have thought particularly of
those by Dostoevski, Hopkins, Rilke, Kierkegaard, and
André Gide. Will you let me know which ones of those
you would like to have and I'll get ahold of them and
send them down to you there.

Now I want to speak a little bit about your manuscript
of *the journal of My Escape from the Nazis.* I read this over
the other day and enjoyed it very much. It is full of very
beautiful passages, and I like the overall idea and theme of
the book. I honestly feel however, that it needs a certain
amount of tightening up before it could or should be
published. I have tried to imagine what my reaction
would be if this manuscript came in to me from an
unknown young writer. I know that I would be very
enthusiastic, but I think I would insist that a good deal of
polishing and tightening be done. The passages of the
constructed language are interesting but naturally they
suffer by comparison with [James] Joyce. I realize that

you are not trying at all to do anything so ambitious as he attempted, but nevertheless anyone who has read Joyce cannot fail to set one against the other. I think that if I were trying it I would cut down the length of the passages in the invented language and try to make them smoother and richer, if you see what I mean.

Then we come to the question of whether you have the time at your disposal to do the work of revision, and whether such a job would be your own best use of your time. There is a clear and unmistakable human message in the book, with religious and pacifist overtones, but there is also an element of frivolity, which is definitely pleasant to me, but I am not exactly sure how some of your superiors might feel about it in the orders.

Mulling over all the pros and cons of this question I believe that I would give you this as my best advice. Devote a limited amount of time to polishing the novel and then let us publish it in a limited edition, which would not be distributed to critics but would be available to your friends and special fans. There could be an introduction, either by yourself or one of your friends, which would state very clearly that this was an early work written before you entered the monastery, and published now at the request of your friends.

But the above is only a tentative suggestion. Surely you will want to re-read the script yourself, and take advice with other people who have a disinterested regard for you and your career. I like the book myself. I like its spirit of adventure and experiment and I like its freshness. But I wouldn't want to push you [into] anything which wouldn't be for the best. Shall I send the script down to you there now? . . .

With best wishes as always,
JAMES LAUGHLIN

/ · /

the Carthusian ideal: The Carthusians are an eremitical monastic order. Unlike
the communitarian Cistercians, Carthusian monks live in isolation as hermits.
During the 1940s, their life—considerably more severe than that of Cistercians—was marked by isolation, silence, frequent fasts, and a limited diet.
After entering Gethsemani, TM began to experience a desire to transfer to
the Carthusians, as his journals bear out; it was not until 1951, however, that
the Carthusians established a foundation in the United States near Manches-
ter, Vermont.

Dostoevski: Feodor Mikhailovich Dostoyevski (1821–1881), Russian novelist.
JL probably had in mind the *Notes from Underground* (1864), a forceful portrait
of insanity written while Dostoyevski's first wife was dying from consump-
tion, her screams often filling the apartment while he wrote.

André Gide: (1869–1951), French novelist, essayist, critic, and playwright.
Gide won the Nobel Prize for Literature in 1947. JL no doubt mentions
his name along with that of Dostoyevski because ND had just issued Gide's
Dostoevsky (1949).

Joyce: James Joyce (1882–1941), Irish novelist, a genius with language experimentation and linguistic gamesmanship in novels like *Ulysses* (1922) and *Fin-
negans Wake* (1939). JL had good reason to believe that TM's "macaronic"
prose style would not compare favorably with Joyce. ND published Joyce's
Stephen Hero (1944), the first version of *A Portrait of the Artist as a Young Man,*
and a play, *Exiles,* in 1945.

35. TLS-1   Nov. 19th 1949

DEAR JAY:

[The] Tears [of the Blind Lions] have arrived, splendidly
done. Thanks again for a beautiful job. I like this as well
as anything you have done. I especially like the cover.
The type is fine. I am more pleased with this than with
any book of poems of mine since *Thirty Poems.* On the
whole I think it is more consistently worth while than
either *Figures [for an Apocalypse]* or *A Man [in the Divided
Sea],* though it is still not anything like what I would
really want.

Thanks for the Rilke. I am still entranced with Kafka's
diaries. They are swell. I also like the [Kenneth] Patchen
book very much. How is he getting along?

I am now busy teaching Scripture and mystical theology. It is very good for me and will result in many new perspectives and will ground me in much new material. It has been one of my faults that I have never really entered as deeply into the Bible as a monk ought to. Nobody does, nowadays. Nobody has been doing that since the middle ages. It is tremendously important for the contemplative life. People think the term "word of God" is a metaphor for human words about God. No. *Sermo Dei est vivus et efficax* and as John of the Cross says, God is the substance of His mysteries—God is the reality we arrive at in revelation, not human truths about God, but God Himself. Faith brings us into direct, but obscure contact with His essence as it really is in itself. I have found a marvelous Greek Father—St. Gregory of Nyssa. He would do wonderfully for one of your rare editions, the Verona man. Don't know just what book of his. They are all of reasonable length. I don't know enough Greek to handle him in the original but read him in Latin. The French are doing some good translations of these Fathers now.

Very busy but not writing: reading and praying mostly, and getting down notes for these courses. I am also giving an "orientation" course for the novices to try and get them around to a manner of thinking that will make them forget the funny sheets and appreciate the liturgy more. I must say they are very well disposed and the Holy Ghost is doing a much more effective job already than any course could do. But because of that, a course also helps much. Can you please send some more *Tears* as we are sending these all around. All the best.

in Corde Christi,
T o m

{p.s. Please don't give another plug to *Exile Ends in Glory,* because I am afraid it is too bad: but thanks anyway!}

/ · /

Kafka's diaries: The Diaries of Franz Kafka, 1910–1923, collected and translated by Kafka's friend Max Brod, had just been published. TM later wrote to JL (10 December 1949) that Kafka was a solitary "in a lost sort of way that has something of a greater integrity about it, in a certain sense, than my own safe solitude."

Patchen: Kenneth Patchen (1911–1972), American poet, painter, and pioneer of "Poetry-Jazz." Patchen and his wife Miriam lived in Norfolk for over a year (1938–39) and ran the ND office there. Although TM queried JL about Patchen's erotic and tormented work *The Journal of Albion Moonlight* (ND, 1941), JL never thought of sending it. The book TM refers to is probably *Selected Poems;* ND issued a third printing in 1949.

Sermo Dei est vivus et efficax: The literal translation is "God's language is living and powerful."

St. Gregory of Nyssa: (A.D. 335–394), Cappadocian philosopher and mystic. St. Gregory of Nyssa's writings range from doctrinal works and exegetical writings to ascetical treatises.

the Verona man: Giovanni Mardersteig, a German scholar and fine printer whose Italian press, Officida Bodoni, produced several special editions under the ND imprint.

36. TLS-2   Jan 7th 1950

DEAR JAY:

Weeks behind with everything. It is so long since I have had a chance to write, and so many things have come in from you, one way or another, that I can't remember all there is to deal with. . . .

Thanks for entering me in the Pulitzer. Somehow I find it hard to think of myself as winning *that.* But no harm will be done, I suppose. I am glad *Tears [of the Blind Lions]* goes well but when I think about my poetry I am rather dissatisfied about it all as a whole except some of the very first poems and some of those in *Tears.* A lot of it seems to me inadequate because it is somehow insincere. Not that I didn't mean what I said when I wrote it, but that I did not know what I meant, or ought to mean. . . .

I have been running about in the woods quite a bit. It has been raining a lot, but I especially like the woods in the rain. When I get out there I am delivered from the feeling that it is important for me to be anything, and thus I am free to be more happy about the one thing that matters, which is not a thing but God. I am appalled by the structures we build between ourselves and Him—half the time in His honor.

I keep liking the Rilke and Kafka you sent and anything more like that would help. Bob Lax wrote a swell poem about Our Lady which ought to go in any anthology under the sun but especially the one you are planning. But I can't find it right now. If you see him, ask him for it.

You know the old horse barn we had here? Well one of the brothers got a huge diesel tractor we have here and tied a rope to the thing and drove away and the building came down. Very spectacular and frightening. Now it is all sorted out and piled up in piles of lumber and it turns out that when it is out of the way one has a nice view of some hills.

God bless you, anyway, and give you a happy and a holy New Year filled with His peace. May He bless you from His depths and bring you into them.

> In Corde Christi
> T O M
> FR. M. LOUIS, O.C.R.

37. TL-3   February 8, 1950

DEAR TOM,

Thanks a lot for your good letter of January 7th. Please forgive me for not answering sooner, but I have been in a mad rush of work trying to get everything fixed up in the office so that I could get off for my annual winter vacation in the mountains. . . . It certainly will be great to get into the snowy mountains. I am just sick to death of the city. . . .

Business continues to go along pretty well, at least with your books. We get good orders for *Seeds* almost every day, and the *Tears* is also fairly active.

Naomi [Burton] and Bob [Giroux] both seem to be very much upset over a problem that has arisen in connection with the Journal you are writing. It seems that Naomi had you sign a contract with Harcourt Brace promising them your next book, because she thought that the Journal wouldn't be ready for a number of years, and she knew you had promised that to me. Now she tells me that you have decided that you want to bring the Journal out right away, and of course Harcourt Brace are clamoring for it on their option. It is rather a mixup, because I had wanted very much to do the Journal. Don't you think that it might be a sensible idea to let the Journal crystallize for a little while when you have finished it, and meanwhile go ahead with a book about the Saint for Harcourt Brace, which they want? Then you could go back over the Journal afterward and let me have that in due time. I honestly feel that with a book of that kind, its quality would improve by letting it season a little. Some kinds of books can be written in a white heat of inspiration and others need to lie fallow and grow with revision. Of course, it's impossible for me to make any kind of judgment, not having seen any excerpts from the Journal, but I should think it would be the type of thing which would profit from this sort of treatment.

If you decide that you wanted the Journal to come out right away I have made the suggestion to Naomi and Bob that we might have a joint publication. But Bob doesn't seem very keen about this. I suppose that he gets a pretty fat commission out of your books from Harcourt Brace, and I can certainly sympathize with that angle, as the cost of living is frightful these days. My situation, as you know, is a little different, but I would like to have you know that the profits which we make from your books here at New Directions are all turned back into the business and used to publish the books of young unknowns who need help to get started. I never take any salary or any profits out of the business myself. I have always thought of the thing as a kind of trusteeship, and having occasional successes, like your books, make it possible to do so much more than I would be able to do on my own for writers who do not fit into the commercial patterns and do not find it easy to be published by the big houses. However, I am getting off the track, and I know that there is nothing to worry about because you will surely find a solution which will please all concerned. . . .

Well, I guess that's about all for tonight. When I get out to Utah I'll drive up and see the Brothers at Huntsville and see how they are getting on. It ought to be very beautiful for them this winter, as there is a lot of snow in that part of the world.

A new printing of *Seeds* is just coming from the bindery this week. I think this makes the eighth. Goodness only knows what the total is by now. I'll have to figure it all out very soon now, as in March it is time to send Naomi a check. It will be a good big fat one for sure.

With best wishes, as ever,
[UNSIGNED CARBON]

/ · /

the Journal you are writing: SJ.

a book about the Saint: What Are These Wounds? The Life of a Cistercian Mystic Saint Lutgarde of Aywieres (Bruce Publishing Co., 1950). Passed over by Robert Giroux at Harcourt, Brace, Merton ranked the book years later as the worst he had ever written.

38. TLS-1   Feb 25th 1950

DEAR JAY

... I was typing a bit on the Journal but now I have
dropped it, on Naomi's instructions, to wait and see what
comes up. Material gathers slowly for the two books on
saints that Bob wants. I hope this Journal business will
not end by getting everybody sore. That is the last thing
in the world I want. I am still writing the Journal of
course, but not typing it out for printing. Anyway there is
no reason why the Journal should not extend into several
volumes if I live long enough.

Bob promised me Eliot's *Cocktail Party* and I am eager
to see it. The Novice Master would not let *Season in Hell*
through to his novice who wanted it so I've got it. Rimbaud writes about hell like someone earmarked for
heaven and I like the book.

It is Lent. I would be glad if I were less busy. . . . God
bless you.

> In Corde Christi,
> T O M
> F R . M . L O U I S

/ · /

Rimbaud: Arthur Rimbaud (1854–1891), French poet. At the request of one
of the Gethsemani novices, JL sent a copy of Delmore Schwartz's translation
of Rimbaud's *A Season in Hell* (ND, 1939). "The impression that I always get
out of it," JL wrote TM on 22 December 1949, "is that life in the world is a
perfect hell, which isn't much news to anybody. Rimbaud certainly had his
share of the world's suffering."

39. TLS-2   May 1st 1950

DEAR JAY

. . . I have been so busy down here that I feel just as rushed as a New York publicity man. It can't go on, and I am slacking down—as much as I can.

I agree thoroughly with all you said about the Journal and about your own set up there at ND. However the whole thing has been settled unexpectedly in a way that resolves all conflicts neatly. Father Abbot has decided that it would be too risky for the house[,] for himself and for me to let the book be published now. A lot of people, who would be a minority but who would be able to make things tough for Gethsemani if they wanted to, would simply not understand the publication of the intimate papers of a cloistered monk during his own lifetime. It would be like the effect of Edward VIII marrying Wally [sic] Simpson—if you can remember that far back. It is the only worldly event that I can remember that fits in here. It would be the end of the world for some conventional Catholics.

For my own part I see Fr. Abbott's point and agree with it. Although it doesn't mean much to me one way or another whether I am in the public eye or not—I mean it does not make me feel especially important or anything like that—my own personal preference is for complete obscurity and solitude. It would be an immense pleasure and relief to me if I simply did not exist for the world at large. Of course I just can't disappear like that now—I have a sort of responsibility and mean to fulfill it. But the fact that my own personal life and ideas won't be splashed all over everything is an immense relief to me. And even though I don't care one way or the other theoretically, the effect of being a public personage is really a strain on me, whether I like it or not.

Meanwhile I have a few other ideas to go ahead with

slowly. There is a small thing I am finishing which, Naomi agrees, will be just the thing for you. It is about the Psalms and contemplation and I like it fairly well. It is the sort of stuff I ought to be doing—at least partly.

Are you coming down again this summer? I would very much like to see you again and talk over everything. My plans for this summer are to work slowly and thoughtfully on minor projects. I am building up material for the bigger things as I go but I need to go slow and not wear myself out too much at this stage. . . .

Is Ezra Pound locked up? Poor guy. I like him a lot and am praying for him. . . . I am very interested in anything good from the Chinese—Mencius for instance. A Yogi chap in India is writing here a lot. He is old and blind and his Yoga has worn a little thin on him. Doesn't have the same grip on supernatural things anymore. He is a sad, patient old man, knows a lot of Sanskrit and is sending me books. I pray for him a lot too.

The more I think about solitude and silence and contemplation the more I am sick of being a writer and a teacher and all the rest. Writing can be made to fit in with solitude and that is what I am going to work on from now on. It will change things and change them for the better. You will see. I am in complete revolt against any way of working that reminds me even faintly of a city. Pray for me, and of course I keep praying for you. And come on down and we'll have time to chat. Bob Giroux will be down sometime this month, I think. All the best.

Yours in Corde Christi,
TOM
FR. M. LOUIS

/ · /

Edward VIII marrying Wally Simpson: Edward VIII (1894–1972), duke of Windsor and king of Great Britain, abdicated the throne in 1936 after marrying American Wallis (Wallie) Simpson (1896–1986).

a small thing . . . about the Psalms and contemplation: Bread in the Wilderness (ND, 1953).

Ezra Pound locked up: Pound returned to the United States in 1945 as a prisoner under indictment for pro-Fascist radio broadcasts from Rome during World War II. Judged insane at a pretrial hearing, Pound was incarcerated in St. Elizabeth's Hospital for the criminally insane, Washington, D.C., for thirteen years. JL visited him frequently. JL wrote TM (7 May 1950): "Yes, they still have Ezra locked up in the federal boobyhatch in Washington. . . . It's a shame that he's there. . . . But it's amazing how he triumphs over his surroundings. Never a complaint and he keeps on plugging away at his translations of Chinese and Greek, which he still does perfectly beautifully."

Mencius: (372–289 B.C.) Considered the second great Confucian philosopher and sage.

40. TLS-1   May 20th 1950

DEAR JAY

Thanks for the letter and the books. I sure like the way [Kenneth] Rexroth's is printed by your Verona friend. . . . Fr. Abbot and Naomi both think nothing more of mine should be printed this year. The fact that the Journal is not to be printed is a huge relief and I am daily more and more glad about it.

I looked into the Valéry and found some stuff that interests me very much. . . . Somebody sent me the *Bhagavad-Gita* and I am very interested in it. I think the trouble with Hinduism is not in the great original texts but in all the interpretations of those texts in later centuries—hence their screwy metaphysics etc. But the spiritual wisdom of the *Gita* is tremendous—and fits in very well with Christianity in its practical statements about detachment etc.

Do come down. You can read any bits of the Journal that you can decipher. Most of it is not typed.

I should think the book about Psalms and contemplation would do for next Lent—when would you have to have it, though? It is shorter than *Seeds*—much shorter at present but I mean to add something to it.

Right now my biggest job is the teaching. I sometimes type up the classes into articles, but they are not too wonderful. Teaching simply knocks me out, down here. Yet it is good to be able to communicate something to other people, and there is, too, something of that marvelous relationship you speak of with your children. Not nearly so much, of course, but something of that family bond that is so good—and builds things up inside you by making you give yourself to other people. Still, everything inside me simply clamors for silence and sometimes the sound of my own voice and the sense of my illusion of being something or somebody that matters fills me with a physical repugnance that almost makes me ill. In fact it *does* make me ill. It is one of the reasons why I couldn't write a poem if I wanted to. And I don't want to.

God bless you. All you write about the kids is fine. I pray for them too. I wish I could think of some books to give them. The Aesop sounds great.

In Corde Christi
T O M
FR. M. L O U I S

/ · /

Rexroth's is printed: The Signature of All Things (ND, 1950).

Valéry: Paul Valéry (1897–1945), French poet and philosopher. TM refers to Valéry's *Selected Writings* (ND, 1950).

Bhagavad-Gita: Part of the Indian epic *Mahabharata,* a classic Hindu Sanskrit text that records the dialogue between Krishna and Arjuna. See TM, "The Significance of the *Bhagavad-Gita,*" Appendix IX of *AJ.*

the teaching: TM had been giving lectures to the Novices at Gethsemani for some time. In June 1951, he was named Master of Scholastics, in charge of those in the Novitiate who would be preparing for ordination and solemn vows.

all you write about the kids: "My own kids," JL wrote on 7 May 1950, "are getting more and more wonderful. I play baseball every day with the boy down in the sheep pasture, and evenings after supper I am trying to teach the little girl some words in Greek." JL picked up in Milan a dual Greek / Latin translation of *Aesop's Fables* that he used for the Greek lessons.

41. TLS-1   June 26th 1950

DEAR JAY:

About the *[New Directions]* annual *[13]*. For you it is an aesthetic problem, for me a moral one. But I will handle it now only as a question of monastery diplomacy. *If* the material is such that it would get a write-up like the one last year in *Time*—attention drawn to fact that subject matter of some of the stories was homosexuality—it would be better for me to be out of it. People who would not read the annual would read the review and would not like or understand the situation. If on the other hand the material is simply outspoken in the sense that it would not get by the legion of decency in the movies and would be merely shocking in the way that the average good Catholic would expect a shocking annual to be shocking, they would understand my presence in it without necessarily approving. That is a rather shadowy norm. I think perhaps you ought to ask Naomi what she thinks. I'd definitely like the poem to go in, but not if it would cause a lot of comment and discussion in circles that do not understand or sympathize with your aims. At the same time, too, there is the possibility that my presence in the book would mean it would be sold to convents and girls academies. Well, you know the effect, if they run across someone like Henry Miller who does not write for the convent public exactly.

That's all for the moment. Naomi can settle the question adequately, I think. Later in the year I'll get busy and finish up that little thing about Psalms and Contemplation. I hear *Seeds* is creating a stir in Holland (where it is not yet translated)[;] there has been an argument back and forth about it between the Jesuits and the Carthusians. . . .

Here it begins to be hot.

> All the best, as ever. God bless you.
> In Corde Christi
> TOM
> FR. M. LOUIS

/ · /

an aesthetic problem: JL proposed to include TM's poem "Sports Without Blood—A Letter to Dylan Thomas" in the next ND annual anthology. "It is a most interesting poem," JL wrote (21 June 1950), "but I remember that at one time you thought that some question might be raised in the Order about your publishing in so wild a volume as the New Directions annual. It is quite true that we do print a good deal of rather outspoken material there. However, it is all artistically serious, and that outspokenness is part of the art." See Letters #42 and #43 below.

Henry Miller: The American writer and expatriate (1891–1980), whose early works (e.g., *Tropic of Cancer,* 1934) were punctuated by frank treatments of his sexual exploits. Starting in 1939, ND published several of Miller's most important books, including *The Wisdom of the Heart* (1941), *The Colossus of Maroussi* (1941), *The Air-Conditioned Nightmare* (1945), and *Big Sur and the Oranges of Hieronymus Bosch* (1957). In spite of Miller's celebration of the sensuous, TM was drawn to his writing. When TM sent Miller a photo in the early 1960s, Miller was taken by TM's resemblance to himself. "You too have the look of an ex-convict," Miller wrote, "of one who has been through hell and I think bear the traces of it." TM's letters to Miller are collected in *Courage.*

42. TLS-2   Aug. 19 1950

DEAR JAY:

The reason why I have not written, as you can guess, is that I have been trying to get organized with Naomi by mail. Now we are all set.

Of course the Psalm book *(Bread in the Wilderness)* is yours if you want it. I always meant that to be understood and Naomi thinks that Bob [Giroux] understood it that way too. . . . Naomi however balks at immediate publication. I mean to discuss that point further with her, however. You can see that the whole thing was a mix-up anyway, arising out of the use of the term "my next book" which is always coming up in my relations with Harcourt Brace! . . .

At the moment I am busy with the "next book" for Harcourt Brace. That will help gloss over the situation all right, I believe. I hope to be able to deliver it to them by the end of the year, and that will help matters toward speeding the publication of *Bread*. But first of all I want you to see it. It is theological all right and perhaps difficult for some but it is more the kind of thing I want to be doing—yet not completely.

I have been reading your Valéry and like it tremendously. Also Patchen's book—sorry, I mean Rexroth's.

There is one thing, though. You bring up, often, as a selling point with me, the idea that I can help you publish young writers. But, Jay, that involves a problem. I might as well write about it now as later.

You are in no sense preoccupied with the moral implications of what you publish: and neither am I—until you somehow make me partly responsible! If the appearance of a book with a "dangerous" theme depends on *my* help then, as a priest, I am in a tight spot. Because as a priest I cannot simply abstract the artistic value of a book from the moral effect it will very likely have upon people who are not as level headed as you are.

Let us take the question of a novel with a homosexual theme. You are capable of looking at the subject matter as it were clinically. So am I. But now, suppose some fool kid in college gets hold of it, and realizes that the theme is a very common one, and somehow becomes habituated to the idea as if it were just as common as going to the movies. It is something that would perhaps not normally interest him, but he reads a lot about it and then gets into it out of curiosity. . . [.] Behind all this is the book which was published because *I* helped make the money to float it! Where does that leave me?

Of course, this is rather theoretical. I have stated an imaginary case, which would be hard to verify in practice. Nevertheless, the fact that books with a possibly harmful character are coming out, so to speak, with my cooperation is not one that I can accept lightly. You know of course that I have absolutely no intention of telling you what or what not to publish, or of interfering with your business in any way: but I do wish I could somehow feel that I were not involved in it to the extent that you sometimes like to tell me that I am. But if I am involved, and if, as you say, you want to cut down a little—what I have said might help you make up your mind where to do some cutting.

Well, that is a difficult topic. But I think I have stated my problem more or less clearly. Do think about it a little, and try and see it from my point of view—and let me out in any way you can. It is not just a private question because some busybody might take it into his head to connect up some success of mine with other titles on your list and remark on the connection in print, to our disadvantage!

The best thing for both of us would be for you to come down here again, and I hope you will. Meanwhile I must get busy and write to Naomi. God bless you—

> As ever,
> Sincerely in Christ,
> T O M
> F R . M . L O U I S O.C.R.

/ · /

the "next book" for Harcourt Brace: The Ascent to Truth (1951).

43. TL-4   September 12, 1950

DEAR TOM:

Many thanks for your good letter of August 19th. . . .

Naturally I am terribly pleased to have you confirm that we will be doing your book about the Psalms at such time as Naomi thinks best. I felt all along that you would not want to let me down about this, but I also feared that difficult pressure might be being put upon Bob up there where he works. Bob has always struck me as a sensitive and understanding soul, but I know there are some very tough men above him in the firm. . . .

The point which you raise about your involvement in my responsibility for the moral tone of our books, is one that I want very much to discuss with you the next time I get down there . . . and if I should fail to make it right away, I might as well say now how I feel about this question.

First of all, I would never want to cause you or the Order any embarrassment, but even deeper than that, I would never want myself to publish anything which would lead anybody into sin. For years I have been carrying on the classic argument with my mother as to why we publish books about what she calls "the unpleasant side of life." It is the same sort of argument that one has with people who don't understand modern art. It is so difficult to make them see that there can be formal qualities of order, which achieve a kind of beauty, in things which are not in themselves pleasing and beautiful. Similarly, I try to explain to my mother, that when a writer writes well and with perception and truth about bad people, the result can still be a work of art, which can have beauty as art, and can even exercise moral persuasion in the right direction, in spite of the subject matter, though that is not a requisite of good art.

These are things which I don't need to explain to you

on that level, because you know and understand them just as well as I do myself. What you and I should talk about is how to help me draw a practical line. It is easy to deal with obvious cases; smut, or pornography, or books which incite to violence or perversion, can be easily rejected and detected. The borderline cases are the difficult ones. As you point out in your letter, one has to beware of the good artist who makes vice attractive, or seems to make it acceptable.

I have tried very hard to steer clear of these pitfalls, and I hope I have not failed too badly. On several occasions I have rejected very promising works, because it seems to me that they did make wrong doing attractive and persuasive. The hardest case to decide which faces me at the present time is that of Jean Genet in France. You have probably heard something about him. He is clearly a genius of the first order, and just as clearly a terribly twisted personality, who is all mixed up in homosexuality and the glorification of crime. Strangely enough, he is also profoundly religious in a sort of fanatical, in reverse way. I am under great pressure to translate and publish him here, because he obviously is the most exciting and important person writing in France today. On the other hand, I have held back to date, except for some short and harmless excerpts in the anthology, simply because I could not reconcile myself to the way he celebrates the life of sin and evil. He certainly doesn't make it attractive, but he writes so brilliantly that he makes it fascinating. There is the danger.

My present best judgment is that I should not publish him, for this reason. I would like to talk to you more about it when I get down to see you. I feel, as you know, a responsibility to help the unconventional writer, who cannot find a regular commercial publisher. But I definitely do not want to contribute in any way to any kind of moral delinquency.

This is just a very brief summing up of my feelings

about this difficult problem, but I did at least want you to
know that I have been giving it serious consideration,
and that it troubles me, from both points of view. We can
talk about it more when I get down there, and I know
that you will be able to help me to steer a straight course
through these treacherous waters. . . .

Thanks again for your very reassuring letter, and
please, for your part, feel assured that I will use the help
which your publishing with us gives us for worthy ends
consistent with your own ideals.

As ever,
[UNSIGNED CARBON]

/ · /

Jean Genet: (1910–1986), French novelist, poet, and playwright. Genet came
out of the closet in the early 1940s.

44. TLS-2   Oct. 3 1950

DEAR JAY

. . . The doctors say I got colitis and have to eat funny
foods. Means no more of the nice brown bread here and
some other things, but on the other hand the little Irish
brother in the kitchen stuffs me with eggs and other lux-
uries unseen for nine years. Am also getting out to do
field work four or five times a week and this is just precisely what I most need. It is fine. Won't slow down the
writing too much either because it clears up my dumb-
head and helps ideas. Also it is always most intelligent to
live the way monks are supposed to live—i.e. by farming
and not to get too theoretical about it the way I have
done.

[Robert] Lax wrote a book about a circus maybe you

ought to see. Now I don't know what he is about to do. Told me something about going to Rome barefoot. Someone has mimeographed the notes of the talks I had been giving to the novices here and I'll send you a copy for fun (I hope!)[.]

Wish you would come down some time and rest and discuss things. . . . Got a nice letter from Rexroth, maybe I told you. There goes the whistle. I pray for you and the children and N[ew] Directions—and I liked a lot your letter about the problem of moral tone. I know we see things very much alike and it is just a question of exchanging a few more ideas. God bless you.

As ever
In Corde Christi,
TOM
FR. M. LOUIS

/ · /

a book about a circus: A poetry collection Lax worked on from 1949 to 1951, entitled *The Circus of the Sun*. Published in *33 Poems* (ND, 1988).

45. TLS-1

St. Joseph Infirmary
735 Eastern Parkway
Louisville Ky
November 13, 1950

DEAR JAY:

Being in the hospital I have come by this typewriter and dare to write letters. Here too is a poem which I wrote in the hospital and since I write so few I am sending it to you. Maybe you would have an idea about some magazine to give it to. I do not know whether or not it is a good poem. It seems to be rather like some of the more early ones.

Naomi tells me that she has given you the material for *Bread*. I am glad. I really want to get it in proof not only to send it to Fr. [Jean] Danielou but also to have a theologian go over it. Do you mind if I make some additions (small) while it is in galleys? There is still some work to be done on it. But I cannot conveniently handle that until I get galleys as I do not have a complete copy put together around the monastery anywhere and the ms. I sent Naomi is rather a mess like all my mss.

The doctors are keeping me here another ten days or so. I had an operation on my nose last week. They cut some bone to help me breathe. It is healing fine. But I also had a bad chest X-ray and they are giving me rest and penicillin. And they have not yet cleared up the other business—colitis. They want to work on that too. I sound like a wreck but I really feel pretty good. I have no objection to being fixed up, but I would like to get back to the monastery. . . .

The drawings for *Bread* are not finished but it would be a bit of pressure if I had to do up the unfinished sketches. There are about six that are I think presentable. Would you like to take one or two of them and leave it at that? Anyway I am anxious to hear what you think about the whole job.

> As ever, all the best. God bless you.
> In Corde Christi,
> TOM
> FR. M. LOUIS

/ · /

a poem which I wrote in the hospital: "Early Mass" first appeared in *Commonweal*, 56 (18 April 1952). Collected in *The Strange Islands* (ND, 1957).

Danielou: Cardinal Jean Danielou (1905–1974), a distinguished Jesuit theologian and professor of primitive Christianity at the Institut Catholique in Paris. TM was influenced by Danielou's work on St. Gregory of Nyssa.

46. **TLS - 1**   St. Joseph's Inf.
                                           Louisville
                                           November 22, 1950

DEAR JAY

Here is the completed ms. of *Bread in the Wilderness.* I only have to add some material in a couple of footnotes. It is all ready to set up. Because of the precarious state of the ms. material (so many bits and pieces, so many additions and rewritings that have not been put together in the various carbons) I am anxious to see it set up as soon as possible and hope [Alvin] Lustig can get busy on it. . . .

The hospital has not been so bad. I have not had to stay in bed much and have been able to get out in a nice quiet sort of field with a couple of willow trees in it. There I say the office or just walk around keeping away from people. The nose business went off all right. As for the chest I have no TB, but I have had to watch myself for the last 5 or 6 years and have to go on doing so. Yes, I have to take things slower. It means less writing, but there is no hurry about turning out a lot of books, especially since these two are coming out together more or less. I can take my time with the next one. It is silly for me to rush into overproduction anyway. That is not the way I write best.

Being here has done me good in more ways than one. I find that I am pretty much unconcerned about where I am or what I am doing. It is all the same, because the one thing that really matters is union with God. And the world—which is manifested somewhat harmlessly by Louisville—is certainly not interesting enough to be much of a distraction. Louisville is fortunately a silly, colorless town—not like New York which I remember as being actively unpleasant in so many ways. Maybe New York would worry me and make me feel bad still, but I can't bring myself to feel any resentment about anything in Kentucky. In fact, as soon as I am out of town I find that I am very fond of everything. It looks as though I have finally grown some roots.

Well, God bless you. Have a good Thanksgiving.

As ever,
In Christ,
T o m
f r . M . L o u i s

/ · /

Lustig: Alvin Lustig, ND's primary book designer.

47. TLS-1   April 6th 1951

D E A R J A Y

It was good to get your letter from the Canadian Alps. The thought of a hut that one reaches only by plane made me green with envy. It is something I shall take with me to the wagon shed. I shall think it over, looking at the hills. Concerted efforts of all my publishers might persuade the abbot general that I need to have access to such a hut once in six months in order to be a glory to the Order. But when I got there I would see that the plane never came back. . . .

We are having a lot of fun here. One of the Brother novices has turned out to be a genius in designing liturgical vestments and has turned out one or two that are clearly better and more original than anything that has hit this country yet. Now I am just going to get busy and try to design a vestment for one of the monks who is getting ready to be ordained. I hope it turns out as I have never done anything of the kind before. . . .

Well, this is the end of the piece of paper. God bless you always.

As ever,
TOM
FR. M. LOUIS

48. TLS-1   July 7th 1951

DEAR JAY

. . . Tonight I am on as night watchman and maybe I will have some fun sitting up in the Church tower looking at the stars when everyone is asleep and the place is really *silent!*

God bless you always.

As ever—
TOM
FR. M. LOUIS

49. TL-2   July 9, 1951

DEAR TOM

. . . I'm glad that you and Father Abbot will back me up with Naomi. I must say I was very much upset by the tone she adopted at our last meeting. To me, the matter is plain as black and white, and I had expected that she would be grateful to me for being willing to bow out on a fair compromise. Instead of which she seemed to be trying to put me in the wrong, which she didn't succeed in doing, as I simply declined to argue with her.

In the end she tried to put me off with some vague promises, but I don't think that is a proper solution at all.

I feel that this ghost ought to be laid to rest at once, don't you? By that, I mean that you and I should decide what we want to work out, and then get both Naomi and Bob to approve it definitely so that there need be no more misunderstandings. . . .

So let us hope that Naomi and Bob will be able to see the beauty of the idea too, so that everybody will be happy and pleased all around.

With best wishes, as ever,
[Unsigned Carbon]

/ · /

the matter: In January 1951, Robert Giroux proposed to TM's literary agent, Naomi Burton Stone, that "henceforth Harcourt, Brace act as exclusive American publisher of Thomas Merton. . . . Sound business judgment . . . suggests such an arrangement." The proposal immediately jeopardized ND's plans to publish TM's next book, *Bread in the Wilderness.* "By exclusivity," Giroux argued, "we mean . . . all his work in whatever form, non-fiction, fiction or poetry." TM addressed the matter in a letter to his agent, 27 January 1951. "The only new note I am introducing into this" proposal, he said, "is that of charity. Look, Naomi, to put the thing on a concrete and human plane. Jay is a good guy. He likes to come down here. It does him good to come down here. He has a soul and a destiny to work out for himself which is more important than books. There is a certain amount of good for him and for the people he most reaches, in our tie-up. He may not be a very orderly business man. I sympathize with him intensely on that score, because I am even worse. I do not see that it would be necessarily any hardship for Harcourt Brace to let Jay get first chance at a few insignificant pamphlets of poems. . . . If I promise to behave myself and let you call the plays, I do not see why the whole thing should not be very simple—with Jay getting the little scraps of stuff that he is perfectly willing to cook up into something and Bob getting the real books. If, on the other hand, we just simply close Jay out completely and refuse him the poems which, after all, he started printing, and if we do so on the grounds of practical expediency he will get the idea that Father Abbot and I are in this thing for the fame and fortune angle of it and that we don't care anything for his indigent poets etc etc.

"Off the record," TM continued in the same letter, "as far as I am concerned, the thing I like best about New Directions is that they did absolutely nothing to make me 'rich and famous.' . . . [A]t least he can't afford to plaster me all over the papers. I realize that it is business. But it seems to me that I am going to get some of those [Harcourt, Brace] ads and that publicity [over *SSM*] fried out of me in purgatory, unless I do something about it now. May God help me, and have mercy on me."

50. TLS-1   Oct 29 1951

DEAR JAY

Thanks for your letter and cards from various parts. . . .

I would like very much to get the book *(Bread)* under way. I do not know what Naomi has in mind, but I shall write to her suggesting next spring. In any event, I wonder if you could please go ahead and start getting it set up for two reasons: first of all because the ms. is the only complete copy and it is in a bad mess anyway. If anything happened to it I doubt if I could get the book together again as it is. Secondly this bird in France has been waiting for over a year to get a piece for his magazine and I would like to send him something.

If the book is not for spring, at least it ought to come out in the summer and it is not too soon to start production.

I don't know if you got a copy of *the Ascent [to Truth]* but I am sending you one. I think it is supposed to be doing all right, but am not sure.

Things are swell here—I got a job in the woods after all. Nothing I love better. At the moment I am ranging all over the place marking trees to be felled, also transplanting small maples etc etc.

Well, here comes business—

God bless you always,
TOM
FR. M. LOUIS

51. TLS-1   Dec. 21 1951

DEAR JAY—

. . . Here is another poem you can try on someone, maybe together with "Early Mass" which I guess you still have. I am not too enthusiastic about *Saturday Review,* frankly but give one of the poems to them if you like. What about the *Hudson Review* maybe—one of their editors is a Catholic and a friend of Dan Walsh and from a copy I saw a few years ago they seem to be pretty good. Or maybe something in England?

This Christmas poem was written because the Carmelite nuns, according to their custom, drew a subject out of a hat for themselves and one also for me. They compose poems every Christmas and sing them (often very badly) at the crib on Christmas eve. They sent me my subject which is "Little Jesus comes to us through the Immaculate Heart of Mary." So there we are. I sent them the poem but I don't know if anyone is going to sing it at their crib.

In any case, may God bless you and all your family and I wish I had some time to draw a few birds or something for the children. But I have my hands full with twenty four children of my own. Anyway, a holy and happy Christmas to all of you.

> As ever, in Corde Christi,
> T O M
> F R . M . L O U I S

/ · /

Dan Walsh: TM's professor of scholastic philosophy at Columbia University, and later his friend. Ordained into the priesthood in 1967, Walsh lived at Gethsemani during the 1960s and taught at the abbey and Bellarmine College, in Louisville. TM first heard of the Trappist monastery in Kentucky from Walsh.

the Christmas poem: "The Annunciation," collected in *The Strange Islands* (ND, 1957). The poem first appeared in *Commonweal,* 57 (26 December 1952) under the title "Christmas, 1951."

52. TLS-2   Norfolk
                                               January 2, 1952

DEAR TOM—

It was good to get your Christmas letter. Many thanks, and best to you for the coming year.

Victor Weybright is delighted with "Sports Without Blood" and is very grateful to you for letting him have it. Their check will be along to you in due course. His new magazine promises well.

This new poem of yours is very lovely, I think—and I'm very glad that you are writing verse again—but I wonder whether you have perhaps left out a "were" or something in the fourth line of the fifth stanza. The rhythm strikes me as suddenly prosey there in contrast with the flowing cadences of the rest. Please cast an eye on this, will you, and then shoot it back to me and I'll send it out for you. *Hudson [Review]* would be a good idea. They do a very fine job.

The proofs of *Bread* aren't back yet from the printer ([Eric] Gill's old firm) in England, but should be along soon and I'll pop them right down to you. Are you going into a huddle for Lent this year, or will you be communicado?

There still has been no word from Naomi on when we can release this book, but I am cultivating patience, which is probably good for me, and trying to be a good boy. Was supposed to have lunch with Bob just before Christmas but he took sick at the last moment. I guess he isn't too strong.

I hope you will be saying some special prayers for a man named Grenville Clark up in New Hampshire. He has written a little book called *A Plan for Peace* which seems to me the best hope for the world that I have seen. It is a plan for revising the United Nations Charter in such a way that it might take effective steps for disarmament. Clark is perfecting the plan now, and then there is to be a big drive to get people interested in it so that there will be an extra-political movement toward getting it adopted. I think everyone, almost, feels now that the politicians are quite incapable of straightening things out and that there will have to be a worldwide spiritual re-awakening.

The last few weeks I have been working very hard on a job for the Ford Foundation, which is the pilot issue of an international cultural magazine I suggested to them, which will try to export American highbrow culture to Europe. I don't know whether anything will come of the idea, but at least it is worth trying. I hope it is all right with you that I included one of your poems—"Christmas Card"—in this pilot issue. The pilot issue is not for sale, but is just to show around and work out typographical problems, but they gave me a little budget for permission, and I am sending $10 to each poet represented. . . .

I will be writing you a real letter soon, but just wanted to get off these business points right away. Life, as ever, is much too full of occupation.

Best wishes for 1952,
J.

/ · /

Victor Weybright: (1903–1978), Author and editor-in-chief of New American Library of World Literature, publisher of Mentor and Signet paperback books. TM's "Sports Without Blood—A Letter to Dylan Thomas" appeared in the New American Library's "First Mentor Selection" series, *New World Writing* (1952).

Grenville Clark: (1882–1967), Internationalist, civil rights activist, co-founder of United World Federalists (1947), and consultant to the U.S. War Department. Grenville Clark's *A Plan for Peace* (1950) advocated world law and the international union of all democratic countries as the basis of durable disarmament agreements and as hedges against the outbreak of nuclear war.

a job for the Ford Foundation: See Letter #55.

"Christmas Card": Appeared in *Perspectives USA* (January 1952); first published in *Figures for an Apocalypse* (ND, 1948).

53. TLS-2   Jan. 15 1952

DEAR JAY,

Just sent off Weybright's agreement. I like the idea of his *New World Writing* and am glad to be in it. Here is the corrected edition of the Christmas poem. . . .

About Naomi's release for *Bread in the Wilderness.* They all write that *the Ascent to Truth* is having an unusual sale, largely because of the fact that it has the Catholic field almost to itself. Hence they request that *Bread* be not rushed into the field. I see their point of view—I don't know what kind of delay they envisage—probably indefinite, depending on how long the sales keep up. They have sold 45,000 and just issued a 2nd edition of 10,000. Jay, this will not hurt you at all, because if you hold off a little, *Bread* will then have the same advantage and will have at least "my" market to itself and in return for this concession on your part I think Naomi ought reasonably and justly to leave you the field with *Bread* for a good space, so that you will have a chance to do something with it. The Journal will probably be along next, but no one wants to hurry with that, so it will leave you quite in the clear. I think this is the only decision I can come to for my part, at the moment. . . .

I shall be praying for Grenville Clark. At first sight one might think that an isolated individual with a certain backing might end up by accomplishing almost nothing, but I am inclined to feel that in the end the mess will probably be wiped up just in such a peculiar way—by a man cropping up in New Hampshire and telling everybody what to do. The more such a one will be like St. Francis the better chance he will have of succeeding quickly. In any case, somebody is going to walk out of somewhere unexpected talking like St. John the Baptist. On the other hand, it is surprising the number of kids who come here convinced that antichrist has appeared in Chicago or even, what is worse, half afraid that they might be him. The ones who cannot be disabused of this conviction are sent away, I am delighted to say. So far none in my scholasticate. My scholastics are all very simple and very holy and radiate an atmosphere of tranquility so thick that it is like a blanket: I mean the kind of blanket that is warm and protective in the winter. It is good to have that sort of thing all around you. It keeps me warm in the woods, when no one is around anyway. I am still trying to figure out how we are going to plant ten thousand loblolly pine seedlings in March and April with all the monks busy with jobs they cannot drop. Maybe I'll have to plant them all myself, and if I do I won't be unhappy. . . .

Now I have a million Christmas letters to answer. I won't be able to do it, but I have to try. God bless you always.

In Corde Christi,
T o m
f r . M . L o u i s

54. TLS-2

June 5, 1952

d e a r J a y

Bob MacGregor said I could reach you through American Express in Geneva. We have cleaned up the first batch of proofs for *Bread*—did some necessary rewriting. I will be happy when the thing is finally in print: of all the patched up jobs it is the most patched I have ever done and I don't know if I am going to be happy about anything except the layouts and the pictures. . . .

Everything has been busy here. The kids are my big job now—and teaching Scripture. It is nice though.

Planted trees this winter, now planting beans. Trying to
think up a plan for landscaping part of the place so that
we can have a nice quiet spot to go and pray in. I still
wish I had a hut in the woods. Can't you dig up some
millionaire who wants to endow a hermitage for a few
contemplatives, in some land where potatoes grow easy
and where the corn comes up without too much fighting
with the weeds?

God bless you. Hope all goes well with *Perspectives.* I
liked the first issue.

As ever, in Christ,
Том
fr. M. Louis

/ · /

Bob MacGregor: JL hired Robert MacGregor (1911–1974) as editor and gen-
eral manager after taking on work for the Ford Foundation (see Letter #55).
Founder of Theater Arts Books, MacGregor stayed on at ND and became
JL's valuable right hand. See also Letter #68.

Perspectives: See the next letter.

55. TL-3   August 19, 1952

dear Tom,

I feel terribly badly that I have let so much time go by
this summer without writing you. I think of you and the
Brothers down there very often, and have meant to write
a dozen times, but the new job at the Ford Foundation is
keeping me very over-worked, and on weekends I just
seem to go into a sprawl of rest. . . .

I had lunch with Bob Giroux the other day and was
glad to have his report that all was well down in Kentucky.

Bob showed me a copy of the letter which Father

Abbot had written to Naomi about plans for your books, and it seems to me to be all in order. I am very happy that Father Abbot continues to recognize the commitment to New Directions. . . .

I also hope, of course, that you are going to start writing poetry again soon, and that we will be able to do those books for you. I just can't really believe that you have given up writing poetry, and I hope it won't be too long before you feel that you have enough good ones together for another book.

On the question of the release date for *Bread in the Wilderness;* in regard to that for *The Sign of Jonas,* I am sure we can work this out all right with Bob. There will certainly be no conflict. As you have correctly pointed out, we will benefit greatly from the big promotion which they are going to put on for the Journal, and we will simply try to time our release date to profit from it the most. Since our book will be expensive, and is very suitable for gifts, I hope we will be able to have it ready for Christmas, but we will probably wait and put on our big circulorization drive at Lent. That will give us two good whacks at it, and we ought to do awfully well.

I don't think you ever answered my question about whether you could serve on the advisory board for the new magazine *[Perspectives USA].* As I told you, I want to be very sure that Catholic writing in America is properly represented in our effort, and I think you could give us good leads from time to time. I don't believe your presence on the board would commit you to anything which would not fit in with your obligations down there. It would simply be a matter of sending me a postcard now and then if you ran into something in your reading which you thought would be suitable for us to reprint.

Work on the new magazine is coming along pretty well, and I think we will have copies of the first issue next month. The Italian translators have given us quite a headache—they keep losing their scripts—but the French, German and London editions are shaping up well, and should be pretty powerful.

I am planning to get off for Europe on September 15th to do some work there, and then will be going on to India for a month in October. The Foundation is interested in the possibility of doing some Western books in cheap editions in translation in the native languages there, and they want me to look over the scene and recommend a program. Here again you could help me, if you would, with suggestions of books which you feel would be of interest to the Indians. I wonder whether your English publishers have done much with *Seven Storey Mountain* down there.

I do wish I could get down to see you before going off, but it is going to be a hard pull to get all the work done in New York that needs to be done. So I guess I'll have to put it off until my return. . . .

> With very best wishes, as ever,
> [Unsigned Carbon]

ps: Would you like me to get for you this new book that is announced about the Carthusians, or would that just be stirring up an old wound? Bob's news about your little hut in the woods is fine.

/ · /

the new job at the Ford Foundation: In 1952 JL became president of Intercultural Publications, Inc., funded by the Ford Foundation. Under its sponsorship, JL edited and published a quarterly journal, *Perspectives USA,* in American, British, French, German, and Italian language editions. Intercultural Publications also sponsored supplements to the *Atlantic Monthly* profiling the contemporary arts and letters of foreign countries for American readers.

56. TLS-2   Sept 28 1952

DEAR J.,

I am astonished to see that it is already a month since I got your letter. . . .

It was good to hear that everything went off well between you and Bob [Giroux] about the time element in the production of these . . . books. I know the way we have it now will be for the advantage of everybody. Frankly, I think I am wasting my time writing books like *the Ascent to Truth*. There are plenty of other people who can do that a lot better than I can. As for *Bread,* it looks to me like a botched piece of work, now that I see it all in one piece. But no one will expect it to be pretentious or perfect. Your job of presentation will make up for most of its defects—I hope. Your staff has been very patient and cooperative and I am grateful to them. After all, I made things rather difficult with all those changes I suddenly had to introduce this summer.

About being on the masthead of *Perspectives*—it seems better that I should not be. The reason is that Father Abbot has got me refusing all such offers—rightly—otherwise I would be on all sorts of magazines etc etc. But that means that I cannot accept the ones I would really like to be on. The idea is to say no to all alike. The only exceptions are things like a big Franciscan committee in Italy for the 7th centenary of St. Clare, at Assisi. That is not a publication. So I am sorry not to be able to help out. I had to say no to Ed Rice too, for his picture magazine.

Are you back in the US—? Come down and see us. Except in the middle of November and the first week in October everything is clear. Yes, Father Abbot let me have a hut in the woods but I don't live there or anything like that. I wish I did. I really need something like that. God bless you, and hope to see you soon.

In Corde Christi,
T o m
fr. M. L o u i s

/ · /

Ed Rice: Among TM's closest friends at Columbia University, Edward Rice (1918–) was TM's godfather. Rice edited the Catholic "picture magazine" *Jubilee* for fourteen years. He was also TM's first biographer (*The Man in the Sycamore Tree: The Good Times and Hard Life of Thomas Merton* [Doubleday, 1970]).

57. TL-2

Paris
August 13th [1953]

DEAR TOM—

I'm sorry not to have written for so long. I was three months out in India and had a great time. Such marvelous people, so naturally gentle. I think we have the Foundation's book program there pretty well set up to roll now.

This is a crazy typewriter with half the letters in the wrong places, so I will brief (be) today, but promise to send a proper account soon. . . .

Have you written any poetry lately? I hope so. Quite apart from the New Direction interest (we should have your things in a gathered form when we have cleaned up the back stock on the separate volumes)[,] I would like to run a good solid poem of yours in *Perspectives* before we wind it up next year. It will stop as a magazine with Number 16, but we may find European publishers who will keep occasional book form anthologies under their own steam without the Ford subsidy.

Except perhaps for occasional consulting jobs, I shall be leaving the Foundation next fall, and getting back full time to New Directions. This pleases me very much. The experience with the Foundation has been most educational, and I think we have done a lot of good contact work abroad with our publications, but New Directions, though on a smaller scale, is more personal and vital. I think we can say of *Perspectives* "mission accomplished." When we started it contemporary American culture was a post-war question mark in many parts of the world. This is no longer true. The channels are open again and books and magazines are getting through to most places.

Well, I must rush off now to catch a plane to Sweden to join my Mother. Will be back in New York soon and write you again from there. . . .

As ever
[UNSIGNED]

---

58. TLS-1   Sept. 25, 1953

DEAR J.

Many thanks for the various editions of *Perspectives* which are coming in. I think it is a very nice job and have looked into a lot of it with interest. I like the poems very much, feel I have been out of contact with much that is good: especially by its simplicity. [Yvor] Winters and Co. are very clean cut and I liked the [Stanley] Kunitz piece. For the rest I would make the following statements about what I have seen: best article: E. B. White. Best reviewing—Seldes. Best miscellaneous item: selections from periodicals. Best face: Learned Hand. Best name: Learned Hand. I haven't read the rest, but I plan to read Learned Hand. It seems he knows English.

[Robert] MacGregor wrote me a hairraising letter

about what nearly happened to all the stuff that was being summoned from the 4 winds for the ultimate composition of *Bread in the Wilderness.* He said he had dictated a letter to me, about its loss, into a dead dictaphone. But it turned up. . . .

I have written a long poem about the Tower of Babel and a short one about the cowbarn burning down here this summer, and there are one or two others and on the whole I think I had better write something different. I am tired of hearing myself talk like that article on St. John of the X.

Did you know we grew a lot of tobacco here this summer? I felt at last that I was of some use, providing some guy with a few smokes anyway. Tobacco is fun. You have to hang it up in a barn, and my scholastics were swinging around in the rafters like monkeys doing this. I never saw them so happy. But now we come to the season of the forest fires.

I have about five minutes in which to write five more letters. God bless you, and let me hear from you—and come down when you can.

As ever,
Yrs in Christ
T O M
FR. M. L O U I S

/ · /

Winters and Co.: Yvor [Arthur] Winters (1900–1968), critic and poet, began a distinguished teaching career at Stanford in 1928 where he edited *The Gyroscope,* a literary magazine. Published in 1952, Winter's *Collected Poems* spoke to TM's desire to achieve restraint, simplicity, and sharp moral judgment in his own poetry. ND published Winter's *Maule's Curse* in 1938. JL included Winter's poem "To the Holy Spirit" in *Perspectives USA,* 4 (1953), along with a cluster of poems by Richard Wilbur, Richard Eberhart, J. V. Cunningham, and others—the "Co." TM refers to.

Kunitz: Harvard-educated editor, translator, and poet, Stanley J. Kunitz (1905–) won the Pulitzer Prize for his *Selected Poems* (1958), which included selections from *Passport to War* (1940). TM singles out Kunitz's poem "Benediction."

best article: E. B. White: "Here is New York," a prose "observation" by Elwyn Brooks White (1899–1985), a contributing editor of *The New Yorker* who also wrote columns for *Harper's.*

Seldes: Gilbert Seldes (1893–1970) contributed a commentary on "Recent Trends in Motion Pictures and Television" to *Perspectives USA,* 4, Seldes, managing editor of *The Dial* during the twenties, directed television programming for the Columbia Broadcasting System from 1937 to 1945.

Learned Hand: (1872–1961) The distinguished American jurist Learned Hand wrote hundreds of landmark decisions. His speeches, including the piece TM notes—"Democracy: Its Presumptions and Realities"—were collected in *The Spirit of Liberty* (1952).

Tower of Babel and . . . the cowbarn: "Tower of Babel: A Morality" first appeared in *Jubilee* (October 1955) and, along with "Elegy for the Monastery Barn," was included in *The Strange Islands* (ND, 1957).

that article on St. John of the X: The article JL generously selected for *Perspectives USA,* 4 "St. John of the Cross," excerpted from TM's *The Ascent to Truth* (1951).

59. TLS-2   Dec 21, 1953

DEAR JAY,

   After all the crises and difficulties the new book went through, it was wonderful to see *Bread in the Wilderness* turn out as it did. I agree with you that [Alvin] Lustig did a marvelous job. The text looks a hundred times better in such surroundings. (When I saw it in proof I was a bit discouraged by it.) Father Abbot is delighted with the book. Everybody who has seen it is very impressed. I am sending copies around—even to Beatrice Lillie who was down here. I had a little talk with her. Her former script writer is one of my scholastics and she came to see him. She asked if there was anything I wanted and I mentioned the record of Honegger['s] *Jeanne d'Arc [au bucher].* She sent not only that but a deluge of other marvelous things which I play to the kids on occasion. But I think that

Jeanne d'Arc is a marvelous thing. One of the few really religious works of its kind that has been seen in our time. And it makes me sick to think how few supposedly religious people know anything of it—or would appreciate it, perhaps. That is another reason why I am glad of *Bread in the Wilderness* and the way it looks. At least it proves that all religious books do not have to be horrible, or stupid looking, or just vulgar and dull. . . .

We are going through the grey, cold days that come just before Christmas, which seem empty but are really very wonderful. You miss their emptiness there, where you have stores all over the place. Here there are no shop windows, only the bare trees, and a marvelous silence, and the rain. And fasting. Today is the Feast of St. Thomas, and the archbishop was here for ordinations. It seems strange that it is almost five years since I was ordained. It is also getting to be rather a long time since you were last down here.

I have a little sort of a hut out in the woods. It has a stove. Squirrels live in the wall of the thing, and get excited by the warmth and try to eat their way through the insulation board to get in on the heating. Such are the small problems of solitude. I read there and work a little and pray and the squirrels gurgle in the wall. The more I think about solitude the more I know it is essential. But still I only get it in morsels. We are fools to work so hard. It is an illusion. We kid ourselves that we are doing something. That is what I say. As soon as I say it a new, unavoidable assignment lands on my neck. But the thing is to do what is unavoidable without adding to it uselessly out of the stores of our own futility. . . .

They tell me Dylan Thomas is dead. God have mercy on his soul. He was a good poet. And a mixed up guy.

God bless you, Jay. Happy Christmas. Don't work too hard. Come down when you can. If there is anything good in the way of poetry coming out, I'd like to see it.

Naomi thinks that if I write poems again it will solve the Harcourt-Brace-New-Directions impasse.

As ever, with all the best,

Devotedly in Christ
TOM
FR. M. LOUIS

/ · /

Beatrice Lillie: (1894–1989), Canadian-born singer, actress, comedienne who appeared in popular Broadway and London revues.

Honegger: Arthur Honegger (1892–1955), the Paris modernist, composed *Joan of Arc at the Stake* in 1938.

Dylan Thomas is dead: See the next letter.

impasse: See Letter #49.

60. TL-2 January 7, 1954

DEAR TOM,

Thank you so much for your good letter of December 21. Needless to say, I am very happy that you like the appearance of *Bread*. I think it is a very beautiful book, one of the best we have done, and does justice to the contents. Bob [MacGregor] tells me that it has gotten off to a very fine start, and that we may have to consider reprinting, as soon as we see what the re-orders are like from the stores. Apparently the Thomas More Book Club took a larger quantity than we had anticipated.

I don't think I have ever heard of Honegger's *Jeanne d'Arc,* but I shall get a hold of the record, and thanks for the tip. It sounds fine. Do you know Copland's *Appalachian Spring?* That seems to me a piece of modern music that will probably survive, though of course it isn't religious specifically. . . .

Your little hut out in the woods sounds terrific. Now you get those squirrels organized so that they will bring you your meals and then you can really have the kind of Carthusian life that you have been waiting for.

The death of poor old Dylan Thomas was one ghastly mess. I don't like to write about it, but will tell you the whole sordid tale when I see you sometime. Surely there was a miracle that anyone who was so hopelessly messed up in his living could have turned out such beautiful poems. That was some kind of Grace all right, for there could be no other explanation.

You ask about other poetry that has been coming out that might be good. Frankly, I haven't seen much that interests me. The one I like the best is Ted Roethke. Have you had his books? If not, let me know and I'll have some sent down to you. Then I know that T. S. Eliot thinks very highly of Dick Wilbur, but to me he has always seemed a little ornate. I have been rereading Wallace Stevens lately because we want to represent him in the magazine, and surely that is about the most elegant language that anyone is turning out, and I'm often at a loss to know exactly what he is trying to say. There are scattered poems of other young people that I have liked, but none of them seem to me to add up to anything very big.

It would certainly be wonderful if you started writing poems again. You know how I feel about that—and quite apart from the interest of New Directions—so I don't need to go into it again. I just keep hoping that you will get back in the groove.

. . . I expect to be working around Western Europe for about six weeks, and then head on through Turkey and Israel to India and Japan. Did you see the job that we did on India? I'll ask them to send you another one from here, in case you didn't get it. Well, I am going to tackle a similar one for Japan, and look forward eagerly to

seeing what I hear is a most marvelous culture and wonderful people.

With best wishes, as ever,
[U N S I G N E D   C A R B O N]

/ · /

Copland: Aaron Copland (1900–1990), The American composer, whose bal-
let *Appalachian Spring* (1944) embodies the clarity, serenity, and sense of balance that established him as a popular modern figure in music.

the death of poor old Dylan Thomas: Dylan Thomas died in 1953 in St. Vincent's
Hospital, New York City, of acute alcohol poisoning compounded by a mor-
phine injection. Thomas's wife Caitlin smashed a crucifix and a statue of the
Virgin over his deathbed. After attacking various people at the hospital, she
was hauled off in a straitjacket to a private clinic on Long Island.

Ted Roethke: Theodore Roethke (1908–1963), Michigan-born poet who
began a long teaching career at the University of Washington in 1947. JL sent
TM Roethke's visionary *Praise to the End!* (1951) and the Pulitzer Prize-
winning *The Waking* (1953).

Dick Wilbur: Harvard-educated poet, Richard Wilbur (1921–) started teaching at Wesleyan in 1955. JL published six of Wilbur's poems in the *ND Annual
10* (1947), the year Wilbur published his first book, *The Beautiful Changes.*

Wallace Stevens: (1879–1955), American poet and insurance company execu-
tive Wallace Stevens wrote his most significant poetry after he was fifty. JL
included five Stevens poems in the first ND annual (1937). For *Perspectives
USA,* 3 (Spring 1953), JL selected Stevens's "To an Old Philosopher in
Rome," and for *Perspectives USA,* 8 (Summer 1954), "The Auroras of
Autumn."

61. TLS-3   Norfolk
July 3, 1954

D E A R   T O M

Thank you so much . . . for your kind wishes for Ann
and myself. She has read a number of your things, and
liked them, and is eager to meet you, if that is possible

some day. The new guest house at the Monastery sounds encouraging and perhaps we can get down next fall. Right now we are all tied up getting ready for a trip to Germany this summer, where we will collect material for a "Perspective of Germany" anthology for *The Atlantic Monthly.*

The three new poems which you sent along are extremely interesting. This is sort of a new vein for you and I like it. They will be a real addition for the book, and meanwhile I have sent them along to Naomi, giving her a couple of suggestions for placing them, in addition to yours. . . .

I am so pleased that you like the various books of poems that we sent down. I know how busy you are, but if you can spare a moment, do send some postcards to the various authors, because each, in his particular way, is in a position greatly to appreciate a word of praise.

Tennessee [Williams], for example, is terribly shy and apologetic about his poetry. He just doesn't seem able to realize how good it is, and thinks because he doesn't write in the fashionable vein of the day, that he isn't as good as the others, when actually, I think, he is much better. He isn't ashamed to put his feelings, whatever they may be, right into the work, and the result, I feel, is at times a terrific intensity. He has gone abroad for the summer, but a card would reach him % American Express in Rome.

Ezra, as you know, is at St. Elizabeth Hospital in Washington. I had a couple of visits with him recently and it is amazing how he keeps his spirits up in those depressing surroundings. He keeps hoping, of course, that he will be let out some day, and a number of us are working toward this end all the time, though there isn't much to show for it yet. But the editorial in *Life* was terribly encouraging, and I do hope that you won't fail to let Mrs. [Clare Boothe] Luce know that it was appreciated. Perhaps if Eisenhower gets himself re-elected that may be a favorable moment to beg his indulgence for genius. The way the matter stands now, there are apparently certain elements in the Department of Justice who would be glad enough to drop the indictment and get the matter off their records, but none of them is high up enough, or has guts enough, to take the risk of the criticism which might follow from certain quarters.

Poor Kenneth Rexroth is in really terrible shape. It seems that his wife wants to leave him and take the two little children, to whom he is utterly devoted, along with her. He is really broken-hearted and talking about suicide and such things. I know that a word from you that you like the Japanese translations would cheer him up. I can sympathize with his wife, because I know how moody and difficult he is, but he really seems prepared to turn over a new leaf, and take a regular job, which might remove some of the tension. The situation has been that she had a job as a secretary at the college there, and Kenneth devoted himself to his work. But he was very good about doing all the housework, cooking, and taking care of the children. I have never known a more devoted or attentive father. He has a basket on the front of his bicycle so that he can take them out for rides in the park there in San Francisco.

On top of this, more sad news, in this letter just received from Harry Duncan, from The Cummington Press, saying that his partner and colleague Paul Williams has been killed in a motor accident. Harry asks in his letter that you say a special prayer for Paul, and I know you will want to do so. I didn't know him very well, but he was a fine and sensitive person, and the work that the two of them did there at The Press was quite unique in this country. Now Harry feels that he won't be able to go ahead with the special edition of "The Tower of Babel." Naturally, this isn't entirely emotion on his part, though that would be reason enough, because it takes two people to run a hand press effectively.

How do you feel about our going on with this special project with another hand printer somewhere? I had initiated the idea out of a great desire to do something for Harry and Paul, who needed the work, but I still always like the idea of beautiful editions. I've suggested to Naomi that perhaps I might take the script with me to Germany this summer and find out who is doing the best work there now. Does this idea appeal to you? Or have you heard of other hand printers whose work you like?

The news from the Patchens in Palo Alto is fairly cheerful. He [Kenneth] had his spinal disk operation a few weeks ago, and the doctors seemed pleased with what they accomplished in there, and now he will be in a cast for several months. His wife's health also, is a constant worry, but apparently she is not too bad at the moment.

I am so pleased that you liked our "Perspective of Indonesia," and I'll ask them to send copies again of "Perspective of Greece" and "Perspective of Brazil." I didn't feel that our Brazil issue was quite as good as some of the others, but there were some absolutely marvelous poetry in the Greek one. I am deep now in the editorial revision work on "Perspective of the Arab World." This is one of the most interesting cultures we have approached. I have been simply amazed to discover how close Islam is, in theory at least, to our own Christian Protestantism. We haven't been able to turn up much modern Arabic poetry that is very good, but some of the stories are extremely interesting. This will be coming out in the fall. . . .

Your job with the novices sounds fascinating. And it's particularly interesting that you are doing a little analysis on some of them. Frankly, that whole area is one that I just don't know much about. Somehow I have shied away from it, and there seems to be so many different schools with conflicting principles and theories. Why don't you invite Merrill Moore to come down there and pay you a visit? He's the poet, you know, who writes all the sonnets, but has a very successful analytical practice in Boston. He might be able to give you a lot of interesting practical leads, and I am sure it would fascinate him to meet you and find out what is going on in the Monastery.

My children are with me now, between boarding school and their camps, and both of them are developing into most interesting personalities. My little girl writes like a dream and is also a terrific worker. This morning she cleaned the attic, shined 12 pairs of shoes and ski boots, and then dug dandelions out of the lawn until lunch time. The boy is not so determined—he likes to ruminate about space travels and such matters but he is very companionable and intelligent.

With best wishes,

As ever,

J. LAUGHLIN

/ · /

Ann: Ann Clark Resor, JL's second wife. See Letter #65.

three new poems: These included "The Stranger" (placed by Naomi Burton Stone in *Sign* [March 1956]) and "Sincerity" (*Poetry* [December 1956]). Both poems were published in *The Strange Islands* (ND, 1957).

Tennessee: Tennessee (Thomas Lanier) Williams (1911–1983), American writer and dramatist. After publishing Williams's verse drama "Dos Ranchos or, The Purification" in *ND Annual 8* (1944), ND became Williams's principal publisher. His major works include *The Glass Menagerie* (1944), *A Streetcar Named Desire* (1947), and *Cat on a Hot Tin Roof* (1955).

Harry Duncan: Duncan and Paul Wrightman Williams operated the Cummington Press of Cummington, Massachusetts. JL hired Duncan and Williams to print several fine limited letterpress editions for ND.

Your job with the Novices: TM became Novice Master at Gethsemani in 1955—see Letter #66. On occasion, he and the novices experimented with Rorschach blots. TM dabbled in psychoanalysis and wrote an essay, "Neurotic Personality in the Monastic Life," which Br. Patrick Hart edited for *The Merton Annual 4* (New York: AMS Press, 1991), pp. 7–19.

Merrill Moore: The Boston poet and psychiatrist Merrill Moore (1903–1957) published several volumes of sonnets, including *Clinical Sonnets* (Twayne, 1949). JL published Moore's *Sonnets from New Directions* in 1938, which first appeared serialized in *New Directions in Prose and Poetry,* 1/2 (1937–38).

62. TLS-2   Feb. 16, 1955

DEAR J.,

It was good to hear from you again and to get the Japanese *Perspectives.* You must have had a fine time there. I am getting more and more interested in Japan, especially since getting a letter and some books from a very alert missionary there, Fr. Van Straelen in Tokyo. He has written some good things about the awful mistakes made by missionaries who try to impose a second rate European or American culture and "art" on the Japanese and how important it is to let the Japanese Christians express themselves in art and architecture in their own way, and arrive at something genuine and spontaneous.

The Japanese *Perspectives* please me very much. I especially liked the wonderful Samurai story about the ten gold pieces, and read it out to the students as a lesson in virtue—I might also have said in civilization. How barbarous we are in this country. Aren't the Japanese aware of how much *we* have to learn from them?

By the way I notice you are sending out lists of books about Japan. Could you put me down for one? And have you ever run across any books by D. [T.] Suzuki (I think that is how you spell him) on Zen Buddhism? I am anxious to track some of them down and have them, but I can't locate the titles right now.

I have had a busy year. You will probably see a new book out with the Harcourt imprint pretty soon. I'll get Bob [Giroux] to send you one. I didn't know anything about the deal he has been getting there. Glad you told me, I'll keep it in mind. I talked to him on the phone a couple of weeks ago—that was the closest I had been to New York for a long time, and I walked back from the gatehouse feeling as if I had been parading down Madison Avenue.

I like the Japanese poems in *Perspectives.* Have you any

in a volume? I thought I remember Rexroth editing one such. The main reason why I write little is that I have little to read—I mean in the way of poetry, because I continue to write too much prose.

However, I think I have another small volume of poetry shaping up. I will send you the stuff when I have it all together and all censored, and you can see it all at once.

I do not know what to suggest for your *Perspectives*—I have read little of anything except *Animal Farm* and some stories of J. F. Powers. Have you run anything by him? I do think before you close down you ought to run a poem or two of Fr. Daniel Berrigan S.J. Did you ever get to see any of his stuff? I do not know where he publishes, but you can reach him through, or rather at Weston College, Weston, Mass. How is [Robert] Lowell doing?

Talking of poetry, I hear they are bringing out commemorative numbers of various magazines on Dylan Thomas—I'd love to see some of them. I very much enjoyed the Christmas piece of his that you sent down. I think he was a terrific mind. What a poet. I cannot get over his death, but something like that has to happen to someone so gifted in a sad mess like ours. What place is there for real talent in this kind of a world?

Everything here is as usual, except that with enormous bulldozers we have dug many lakes and now at last they are all full of water. More than full. Last summer was dry, and so was the one before. In fact a lot of trees died in the forest. Talking about the forest, it seems the state is going to put a fire tower on top of one of our hills. The foresters are coming over tomorrow to see me about it, and it looks as though I may get a chance to sit out there and think a bit during the forest fire season. I certainly hope so. In fact I imagine that will help everything considerably. It ought finally to materialize in that little book of sentences I once promised you. Really the kind of writing I think is most natural and fitting for me is something gnomic like that, that can be thought out in the silence of the woods. Any other kind of thing distresses me to write—except I was happy writing a longish poem which you will see, called "Elias[—Variations on a Theme]."

Well I have a bunch of letters to get out of here before Lent starts, so I will stop. But I will only remind you that it is an awful long time since you have been down here. I hope the children will grow up happily and wisely and well. They must be getting big—a few years are enough for that, and it is astonishing how fast three or four years go by. Is it that long since you were last here? I think it must be, pretty nearly. Come on down again when you can. You will find the place quite changed, with a lot of new buildings. . . .

God bless you, Jay. It was good to hear from you again. As I say, don't wait too long before coming down.

As ever
Devotedly in Christ
T O M
FR. M LOUIS

/ · /

the wonderful Samurai story: "An Unbalanced Account on New Year's Eve" by Saikaku Ibara appeared in *Perspectives of Japan,* an *Atlantic Monthly* supplement, 1954.

D. Suzuki: Daisetz T. Suzuki (1870–1966), the Japanese-born Zen Buddhist practitioner and scholar whose writings are central to the ecumenical dialogue between Eastern and Western religions. Starting in 1959, TM and Suzuki began an extensive correspondence. Their letters are collected in *Ground* and Robert Daggy, ed., *Encounter: Thomas Merton and D. T. Suzuki* (Larkspur Press, 1988). TM and Suzuki's collaborations include *Zen and the Birds of Appetite* (ND, 1968), which contains TM's moving tribute to Suzuki.

a new book out: *No Man Is an Island* (1955).

the deal he has been getting: Robert Giroux was in the process of leaving Harcourt, Brace & Company. By June 1955, he was an editor at Farrar, Straus & Cudahy.

Rexroth editing one such: *One Hundred Poems from the Japanese* (ND, 1956).

Animal Farm: Popular novel by the British Socialist writer George Orwell [Eric Arthur Blair] (1903–1950), first published in 1954.

J. F. Powers: John Farl Powers (1917–), American novelist who wrote about Midwest Catholic clergy in novels like *Morte d'Urban,* which won a National Book Award in 1962. In an essay first published in *Worship* (November 1962), TM wrote that the novel epitomized Powers's "usual style: sustained and withering irony." According to TM, Powers "trenchantly satirized . . . the kind of superficiality in thought, in life, and in worship" the contemporary Catholic Church was slipping into. JL published Powers's poem "Are These Our Children?" in *ND Annual 17.*

Fr. Daniel Berrigan: Daniel J. Berrigan (1921–), Jesuit priest, poet, and peace activist. TM's letters to Berrigan, begun in 1961, are collected in *Ground.* They attest to a close friendship and the two men's shared commitment to peace and social justice issues.

the Christmas poem: ND published Dylan Thomas's *Conversation About Christmas* in 1954.

63. TLS-2   Aug. 16, 1955

DEAR JAY:

Writing a letter to you these days is like writing to some Jules Verne character in an airship. I wonder where you are and the whole earth opens before me. Wide horizons—India, Burma, Uganda, Finland. Maybe that last one is a dull country, and if it is you are not in it. But, by the way, I got a very nice copy of the Swedish translation of *Seeds of Contemplation*. It is the only one that comes up to the beauty of the American edition. When you come back here to visit us, which I hope you will do some day again, you can see it. And that reminds me that it is a very long time since you were last here.

The main reason why I am writing to you is that I am cleaning out my files, and have been rereading the momentous correspondence between us through the time when *Bread in the Wilderness* was in production—all the accidents that could have happened, and nearly did, or did. I was thinking that instead of throwing everything away, I ought to send them to the librarian at the University of Kentucky who likes to have that sort of thing, in a collection he is making. I am writing to ask if you would object. There is nothing especially private in any of the letters. Let me know. . . .

You told me *Perspectives* is closing down. I thought the numbers I saw were very good. Sometimes it occurs to me to suggest a story or an article by someone, but I never get around to doing it. I suppose it is already too late to suggest you use something from Randall Jarrell's book *Pictures from an Institution,* which I liked very much. And I also suppose you have already used something by J. F. Powers. Or would that be bad publicity for the Church in the U.S.? I suppose it would be. But he is accurate as he can be.

Right now I am busy with the State Foresters who are putting up a fire tower on one of our "knobs" (which is what they call the hills around here). I am very happy about the whole thing because it is likely that I may have a chance to sit up there and be a stylite from time to time. Although all the things I like best are hotly opposed by people whose opposition alas makes quite a lot of difference. But I have Father Abbot with me on this anyway. I haven't been writing much, or rather I have but it has stopped for a time more or less long. There are a lot (four or five) of things lying around to be printed bit by bit and it is agreed with Naomi that you get your share but don't get after her too fast because she told me to keep everything quiet. Act like you just guessed, and please don't push her so as to get her upset. When I say it is "agreed" with her, I mean I have agreed to let her do it her way.

Well, I wish I had some news. Here it rains rivers. And we sweat bad. And we think this is how it must be in the tropics, everything wet unless you sit around in your skin. Speaking of India, this isn't news because he was here a year ago, but a little Indian Archbishop was here and he wanted to see me and they sent me to eat supper with

him and I scandalized him by eating. Bob Lax, where is
he? He is worse than you, because you travel I suppose
in trains, planes, and stay in hotels. But he travels under
hedges and the last I heard from him he sent me a postcard signed with a false name and false whiskers from the
poorhouse in Turin. Him, I envy. Not the poorhouse in
Turin, however.

If you ever go to France, (if you ever! You are always
in France) you ought to stop and see the out of the way
and hidden Benedictine monks which they have tucked
away in a corner of Burgundy called La Pierre qui Vire
(Yonne). They put out some nice books and do some
good painting and sculpture and are very nice and intelligent people, with whom I am agonizingly going through
the process of getting out a book with a lot of pictures of
the monastic life with a text by me. Beautiful book, terrible headaches, more accidents than *Bread in the Wilderness*
and so many complications I am surprised we have not
all ended up in Devils Island. Each one turns around and
finds the other one has just made a contract for the whole
thing to be printed on leather by a firm in Moscow or
something. Then we forgive one another by letter and
begin all over again with our monastic drolleries.

The rain stops, country, houses and trees crawl back
again out of the water and act fresh, and this is the end of
the letter. But come and see us. God bless you in all that
you do, and wherever you go. And your children.

> As ever—Yrs in Christ
> T o m
> fr . M L o u i s

ps. Oh, Dom Mauritius, the abbot out in Utah: well, he
died, good soul. He had cancer for about a year, was on
his way here to visit and the cancer jumped up and bit
him on a street corner in St. Louis and he had to go to
the hospital with it and kept it ever since.

/ · /

Randall Jarrell: (1914–1965), Tennessee-born poet and literary critic who graduated from Vanderbilt in 1935. His only novel, *Pictures from Our Institution* (1954), satirized faculty at a progressive liberal arts college for women. JL wrote TM on 19 September 1955 that "Jarrell's stuff is a little too tricky for us, though we used his essay on Whitman once ["Some Lines from Whitman," *Perspectives USA,* 2 (1939)], but we definitely ought to have a Powers story before we wind up." JL had, in fact, already published J. F. Powers's story "Death of a Favorite" in *Perspectives USA,* 15 (1953).

stylite: From the Orthodox Christian tradition, a stylite is a recluse who sits atop a "style," or column.

a book with a lot of pictures of the monastic life: Silence in Heaven (1956).

64. TLS-1   May 7th 1956

D E A R J A Y —

For a long time I have been meaning to write about several things. For one, I at last sent off the *Dhammappada* (or however you spell it) and the Tamil *Kural.* I was especially interested in the former, and I guess it must be a pretty important Buddhist text. A lot of the material is thoroughly familiar—detachment, purity of heart and so forth. I was glad to have the chance to look through it, and I kept a few notes. I have finally found the Zen books I was looking for in the Library of Congress and am borrowing them from there. Zen is fierce, but terrifically practical. I think after all I am innately Chinese (Zen is really Chinese—combination of Taoism and Buddhism, reduced to its practical essence, all doctrines thrown out, naked contact with reality).

Then I meant to send you some poems by an interesting kid who was here in the novitiate for a while. But I seem to have misplaced them. I think he has real talent—too much for here. We sent him away to get orientated, and he is now batting around the mid-west. He is getting psychoanalyzed in Kansas, for one thing. (I couldn't undertake to psych him, which was what he really needed.) But I think he has the makings of a very good writer and his brief experience in the monastery seems to have been valuable to him. I am sending just one of his poems, written recently, not as interesting as the others, but it will give you an idea. He could easily get together a group of manuscripts for you. Are you going back to Young American Poets again?

I sent Naomi a couple more poems, in fact three or four more. Where did I leave off with the stuff you have? Do you have the "Landscape" and the "Spring Storm?" And after that "Birdcage Walk" and "A Letter to Graham Greene" (about *The Quiet American,* which I surprisingly got to read. I was impressed with the central moral point, somewhat unconvinced by the ending. All the business about the little Annamese lady is perhaps not strictly monastic reading, but I guess I am now beyond all norms).

Anyway if you have these new poems, I wonder if you can do something with them for some magazine (exception made perhaps for the "Letter to Greene"). Naomi I know sent them out to things like the *Ladies Home Journal* (perhaps not the new ones) but I am sure she never got to the people who would really be interested like maybe *Sewanee Review* or some little reviews, or what have you. I keep thinking of the *Hudson* as the best.

How's with Ezra [Pound]? Last chance I had to write to Clare Luce it was a big project a Doctor friend of mine had about getting medicine to the Viet Nams, and I didn't wedge in anything about Ezra. How's his case? Would it help if I said anything to anyone?

Any good new books, especially poetry, over there with you?

And don't forget to come down.

God bless you—as ever—

Devotedly in Christ,
M E R T O N

/ · /

Dhammappada . . . and the Tamil Kural: After returning from India, JL wrote TM (19 September 1955), ". . . while out there, I was nosing about a bit in translations of the various Indian classics and ran into some interesting things, such as the Buddhist Dhammapada, which no doubt you know . . . and the Tamil Kural, which has some of the beautiful poetic quality of the Song of Songs." Later on (14 December 1955), JL admitted that "the principles of Zen are pretty far beyond my comprehension, but I have been getting a lot out of the more orthodox 'Dhammapada.' I have lent my extra copy of the little Bombay edition to a friend, but will get it back and send it air mail to you soon. I'll also lend you my copy of the *Kural* and can get you one to keep if you like it." The sixth-century *Kural,* by Tiruvalluvar, is a collection of hundreds of moral epigrams. Arranged into 26 chapters, the writings of Dhammapada, a Theravada Buddhist dogmatic theorist, consist of 426 verses on the basics of Buddhist teaching.

an interesting kid: Dan Quinn. See the next letter.

Young American Poets: In the forties, ND issued a three-volume series called *Five Young American Poets* collecting the early work of Randall Jarrell, John Berryman, Karl Shapiro, Paul Goodman, Jean Garrigue, John Frederick Nims, and Eve Merriam.

"A Letter to Graham Greene": Although TM wanted to include "The Sting of Conscience: (A Letter to Graham Greene)" in *The Strange Islands* (1957), his agent, after an unusually heated exchange of several letters with TM, urged him to drop the poem. It has never been published, although it is excerpted in Patrick F. O'Connell, "Sunken Islands: Two and One-Fifth Unpublished Merton Poems," *The Merton Seasonal,* 12, no. 2 (Spring 1987), pp. 6–7. TM admitted that the poem was "neurotic," but he still felt it was a good poem, unlike anything he had written before, and he only reluctantly acquiesced to his agent's advice. The poem was inspired by Graham Greene's stinging indictment of smug inaction amid social injustice in his novel *The Quiet American.*

> You have written, Greene, in your last book
> The reasons why I so hate milk.
> You have diagnosed the war in my own gut
> Against the innocence, yes, against the dead mother
> Who became, some twenty years ago,
> My famous refuge.

> This one place that claims to know peace,
> This is the very den
> Where most damage is planned and done.
> Oh, there are quiet ones among us
> And I live with the quietest of all.
> Here we are, victims, making all the trouble
> Loving the pity and the ignorance

With which the light stands firm
On our most righteous candlestick.

And now your book has come
To plague the hapless conscience of the just
While war boils in my own hard-praying heart.
Not out of charity,
Rather out of idleness do we refuse to hate.
O, if I were less desperately meek
And could win back some malice, once again
And tell the people what I mean
I would perhaps hate them less
For having so loved me.

I know: the decision is fatally made.
I shall never return. I cannot reach again
Those dear bad shores, to which prolific life
Is not altogether alien.
I cannot see again
The world of lively, prodigal sin!

Yet look, Greene! See Christ there,
Not in this innocent building,
But there, there, walking up and down,
Walking in the smoke and not in our fresh air,
But there, there, right in the middle
Of the God-hating sinners!
But here I stand, with my glass in my hand
And drink the pasteurized beatitudes
And fight the damned Ohio in my blood!

Tell me, at last, Greene, if you can
Tell me what can come of this?
Will I yet be redeemed, and will I
Break silence after all with such a cry
As I have always been afraid of?
Will I so scandalize these innocents
As to be thrown clean out of the wide-eyed dairies
And land in heaven with a millstone around my neck?

65. TLS-4   May 24, 1956

DEAR TOM:

. . . It was good to hear from you again and I'm glad
that they are letting you read all that wonderful Buddhist
stuff. I wish I had your philosophical training with which
to approach it.

I agree with you that it is a good idea to place some of
the new poems in magazines before they appear in the
new book. However, to avoid duplication, since I know
that Naomi has been sending some out, I shall suggest
that Bob MacGregor check over the list with her first,
and also let her know to which magazines he decides to
send what. . . .

As you will doubtless have heard from Naomi, we
seem to be delaying the publication date on the new
book of poems to oblige Roger Straus. It is now scheduled for the beginning of Lent in 1957. I hope this means
that you will keep on writing new poems all summer
which you can send us, since we won't have to go to the
printer until late summer or early fall. The more the better, I say. I like the recent ones very much indeed.

Naomi may also have written you about the possibility
that we might want to do about 200 copies of a special
edition of the little play by itself hand-printed by the two
lads up at the Cummington Press who do such gorgeous
work. There are various problems to work out on this,
and I think that Naomi is writing to Father Abbot about
them, but I hope it works out, because I think we should
all do what we can these days to support the dying art of
fine hand printing. I think I have written you before
about those boys at Cummington Press, who lead a very
monastic life and endure all sorts of physical hardship in
order to have the independence to keep up their work on
the hand press in a little farmhouse up in New England.
They really have guts as well as great taste and skill.

Thank you for sending me the poems by Dan Quinn, whose story is interesting. I can't really tell from this one specimen whether I like him or not, there seems to be a certain vagueness, if you know what I mean. But I have written him . . . and hope he will send me along a group to look at, and that he will be someone with whom we can do something interesting.

One of the things which distresses me is that I haven't been able to locate any new young poets who really excite me very much. We are getting out some five books of poetry this year, but all of them are by old hands— Tennessee Williams, Rexroth, Patchen, Pound, and yourself.

I'll ask that copies of these be sent you as they come along, and trust that some will filter through, and that you will find things to like.

The new Pound *Cantos* are ready now and should reach you in the next week or so. They seem to be getting more and more fragmented, but there are still some beautiful spots.

Ezra's situation appears about the same. I was down to see him in Washington this spring, and found him as delightful as ever, and full of plots and plans. A great many articles about him and his imprisonment are appearing now in European magazines and newspapers, and he feels certain that their weight is bound eventually to be felt in Washington. Mrs. Luce hopes that something will be done about him after the election. After receiving communications and deputations from a great many different Italian writers and groups, she has responded rather nobly by planting a fine editorial in *Life* on behalf of Ezra. It did not plug openly for his release, but said that his case should certainly be reexamined in the light, perhaps, of what history is going to think about the whole affair. If you write to her I suggest you express appreciation of what she has done so far and urge her to continue. I see where Drew Pearson is plugging her in his column to replace Dulles as Secretary of State. But I gather her health is poor and that she is in a nursing home in New York. Everyone connected with the situation is hoping that if Eisenhower gets reelected he will feel able to do something about a pardon. Actually, from the legal point of view, one shouldn't speak of a pardon, because there has never been a conviction. But rather, of simply persuading the Justice Department to drop the indictment and forget about it. The feeling is that he is afraid to do anything about it now for fear of further antagonizing the Jewish vote, but that if he gets reelected, he might feel safe in doing it at once, thinking it would be forgotten before the next election. Which is how the world gets run, I suppose.

Poor Patchen is in bad shape again. He is just going into the hospital at Stanford any day now for another complicated operation on his back. What is equally serious is that his wife, Miriam, who has been supporting him by working in a department store, has come down with multiple sclerosis, or something like that, and is no longer able to help, and is sick most of the time herself. Their plight is pretty desperate, and I don't know how they are making out. Or rather, I suspect that they are on some kind of relief, except for a few contributions from friends now and then. Hope you can get the boys to pray for them especially, and, if you hear of any people who want to help out a poet, this is certainly a case. The address is 852 Bryant Street in Palo Alto, California.

Poor old Rexroth is also having a tough time. It seems that his wife, the third one, has now run off with some other poet, leaving him with the two small girls to take care of. Did you see, by the way, the very beautiful Japanese poems which he translated for us at Christmas? I'll ask that another copy be sent along to you, and hope it will get through.

The big news in my own life is that I have just gotten married again, to a very ideal and sweet person, whom I will hope to bring down one of these days for your inspection, if that is possible. We are off on a bit of a honeymoon now—I am dictating this from the beach—and expect to be working in Germany this summer, getting together a "Perspective of Germany" for the *Atlantic*.

I'll ask them at Intercultural to send you the "Perspective of Indonesia" which we have just gotten out. Now I am working on the Arabs, who are the trickiest of all.

As I think I wrote you, *Perspectives USA* will be folding up in July of this year, but we still have the Arab and German collections for the *Atlantic* to finish up, before Intercultural tapers off. It has been a fascinating experience, and I think we have really accomplished a lot in terms of intercultural exchange, but, for myself personally, I'll be glad to get back to New Directions.

Well, I guess that is all for now, and I hope this finds you in the usual serenity of soul. It pleases me very much that you are writing poems again, and I hope this will continue. . . .

As ever,

J .

/ · /

the new book: The Strange Islands (1957).

Roger Straus: Publisher of Farrar, Straus & Cudahy, who insisted that TM's *The Silent Life* be released before ND's publication of *The Strange Islands* (1957), TM's first book of poems since *The Tears of the Blind Lions* (ND, 1949).

the little play: The Tower of Babel (1957), printed in an edition of 250 copies for ND by a German printer, Richard von Sichowsky, with woodcuts by Gerhard Marks.

Drew Pearson: (1897–1969) Popular American newspaperman whose syndicated (and muckraking) column, "The Washington Merry-Go-Round," often featured exposés of Washington officials and federal government scandals.

Dulles: John Foster Dulles (1888–1959), American lawyer and diplomat, was appointed Secretary of State by Dwight Eisenhower in 1953. Considered the most powerful Secretary of State in U.S. history, Dulles held the post until his death.

66. TLS-2   June 16, 1956

DEAR J.,

First of all, congratulations on your marriage. By all means bring her down when you come. I would love to meet her—and maybe you were not here when the new ladies' guest house was open. It has been in use for a couple of years now. The only trouble is that they sleep all over the place on couches, there are usually so many relatives visiting. But you could stay in Bardstown, if it comes to that.

Thanks for all the new books. Tennessee Williams has done exactly the thing I want to do—gone over all his poems and thrown out what he didn't like and changed a lot and finally produced a volume of what he really wanted to hold on to. I would very much like to do the same—some time. After the selected poetry and prose.

Here are three more poems. They are a bit prosy and Horatian or something. But still. I suppose a new approach is not out of place. I like all your suggestions for magazines to which we might send material. *The London Magazine* sounds okay, and I bet Naomi didn't try *The Nation*. Of course the more pious ones would not do for most magazines, I suppose. And a lot of those have already been printed, maybe twice over, by things like *Commonweal* and so on.

How do you like *Birdcage Walk* as title for the whole volume? It is getting to be my preferred title—I sent some suggestions to Naomi some time ago.

To return to the things you sent—I like the Tennessee Williams poems tremendously. I particularly like Ezra's "Canto 90," which is a monastic theme transposed no doubt into a different key, but basically monastic. Anyway it is beautiful. I think it is one of the best things he has ever done. The Plays I have not yet read. Lax sent me *Waiting for Godot* which is very funny and I don't see why people are running up and down asking themselves what is its message. But of course they always do, so in this case also they must. I like the look of the Chinese ideograms on Pound's pages. When I go to Louisville, which I sometimes do, I read Pound's letters in the Public Library, and browse around looking for Chinese paintings, also recently I found some No plays. How marvelous they are. Maybe someday I ought to do something like that, but I can't think about writing much or anything at the moment. (That is of course a very good situation out of which might come something worth while, instead of so much stuff I wrote before.)

I like very much the idea of getting the play *[The Tower of Babel]* done by the Cummington fellows, and wish I could think of something more for them. I haven't been in contact with the stuff written on behalf of Ezra P. I'll encourage Clare Luce when I write to her. If I ever get around to it. I wish I could do something for Patchen. I'll keep my eyes open, and see what turns up. I read some of his stuff in the Louisville Public Library the other day too. Yes, I got the Japanese poems of Rexroth and they are wonderful. Maybe sometime I [will] write Rexroth about Zen. The Indonesian *Perspective* (the only one I have received since Japan,) is beautiful too. I wish I could have seen the Greek one. . . .

Most of the time now I think about psychoanalysis, since it is important for my job. I am trying to learn how to give the Rorschach test. Such fun. But it all takes a lot of time. You knew, didn't you, that I am now Master of the Novices?

Now I have to stop. God bless you, and your wife, and the kids too.

Thanks for everything. Hope you'll come down this

way soon. Mark [Van Doren] is going to be doing something at the U of Louisville and I hope to see him soon.

> All the best—
> in Christo Domino,
> MERTON

/ · /

Waiting for Godot: Absurdist two-act "tragicomedy" by Samuel Beckett
(1906–1989), first published in 1954.

No plays: Japanese musical dance-dramas dating to the fourteenth century,
No plays are highly ritualized performances reflecting an essentially Buddhist
view of existence.

67. TLS-2   Aug 30, 1957

DEAR J.,

How—and where—are you?

There are lots of things to write to you about, if only
I can remember them. For one thing, perhaps you may
be interested in this ms. which is just a rough draft of a
"play" I am thinking about. It may have possibilities, or
at any rate I am interested in it myself. Perhaps you will
look it over and return it when you have finished with it.

How are the *Strange Islands* going?

I feel better about *the Strange Islands* than about any
other verse I have written since *Thirty Poems.*

It is an awfully long time since I have written to you
or heard from you. Have I told you that for the last couple of years I have been Master of Novices? That means
I occupy myself with those who have just entered, and
try to get them lined up for a lifetime in the monastery.
It is interesting work. They are mostly good kids—all
kinds, not necessarily kids. Some are priests, some are

old, some are young, some come from Latin America, and we have got one coming in a day or two who ran out of Hungary last fall.

One of our novices is a Nicaraguan poet, Ernesto Cardenal. I don't know if you have seen any of his work. He was recently in the *Revista Mexicana de Literatura,* and he did a good anthology of Nicaraguan poetry. He has up his sleeve a very interesting crazy poet of Nicaragua called Alfonso Cortes, whom I like a lot.

He tells me Dudley Fitts did an anthology of Latin American Verse for you. Can I bum a copy? Especially I'd like to see some of [Pablo] Neruda's stuff—English or Spanish. You know, I have been reading Pound, and he is a terrific poet. I mean some of his early stuff—I knew it all before but I had never really read it. I had to get in here and be here a few years to appreciate it. And then going on to the *Rock[-]Drill* Cantos, I find them fascinating, packed with stuff. I haven't been able to track down most of it, but the general gist of the thing is very impressive. He really is talking.

While I am bumming books then: could I ask you for [Pound's] *Great Digest of Confucius,* and *Guide to Kulchur.* The Nicaraguan brought with him most of Pound's verse, *Deo Gratias.* And if you run across any good South American novelists—let me have something of theirs too, English or Spanish.

I think an awful lot about South America these days, and want to read everything I can lay hands on, especially about the Bolivar countries up in the top left hand corner—Venezuela, Colombia, Ecuador. We are getting a lot of men from down there and may someday make a foundation. The idea of starting something in the Andes I find most exciting and it has got me very interested indeed.

Mark Van Doren has written his autobiography: that ought to be quite interesting. I saw him for a moment when he was down here last year talking at the University of Louisville.

[Robert] Lax was here last fall too and may come down again. I still think you ought to bring out a book of his poems and stuff. It would be very good.

Working in the woods as usual. This time we have a real job. We are putting up a power line up to the fire tower. Digging holes for telephone poles, cutting down trees etc. I never saw so many yellow jackets as we have in our woods, and mad too. Everyone has been bitten quite a few times. They seem to have nests in or under every tree.

I haven't been writing much, but that is good. If I am batting my brains out on one of those stuffy prose jobs, I am too beat for anything else. When I am not "writing" I have time to think a little more and poems are more likely to come to the surface. There is altogether too much "writing." However I did have to "write" a monastic job this summer, and I will send you a copy when it is printed. We are doing it ourselves. I suppose since we last wrote you have been twice around the world. You said "Perspectives" was all finished. Anything else?

Oh by the way: how about that limited edition of *the Tower of Babel* with the woodcuts and all the rest? I never saw or heard anything more about it. Last I heard, you wanted me to sign the first pages, but nothing ever happened—though perhaps Father Abbot may have decided it was not a good idea: and that perhaps was wise. Was the book ever printed? Could I see a copy?

How's Rexroth coming along? I think of him. I like all his Chinese poems very much. I think of all your poets—Patchen, Pound, Tennessee Williams, all of them. Did I tell you how much I liked the [Robert] Fitzgerald book? That I think is really good.

When are you ever going to stop by here again? You

haven't been around here in ages. Come by and rest your bones for a couple of days.

> God bless you—
> Sincerely in Christ—
> T O M

P.S. Just got a letter from Bob MacGregor with news of you and of the sheets for the limited edition. Fine! I'll send everything to [Richard] Von Sichowsky as soon as I can.

Have you published any new French poets? Like these Martinique guys? I like this Aime Cesaire.

/ · /

a "play" I am thinking about: Most likely "Atlas and the Fatman," which first appeared in TM's *The Behavior of Titans* (ND, 1961).

Ernesto Cardenal: Cardenal (1925–) entered Gethsemani in 1957 and left for health reasons in 1959. Poet, priest, revolutionary, and minister of culture for the Sandinista government in Nicaragua, Cardenal's short tenure at Gethsemani fueled TM's passion for Latin American culture and literature. TM greatly admired Cardenal's talent for "getting poetry out of the confusion and pathos of the modern world, without being bitter about it," and remarked on one occasion that Cardenal "will be one of the most significant spiritual voices in the two Americas." For his part, Cardenal always looked to TM as a teacher and spiritual mentor; "it was an incredible privilege," Cardenal recalled, "to be instructed by this great master of mysticism who for so many years had been my mentor through his books." TM's letters to Cardenal are collected in *Courage.*

Alfonso Cortes: (1893–1969), Nicaraguan poet who went insane in the house of Ruben Dario, Nicaragua's most famous poet. Although he translated some of Cortes's most lucid metaphysical poems (*Emblems of a Season of Fury* [ND, 1963]), TM remained ambivalent over Cortes's confused genius. "It cannot be said without qualification," TM demurred, "that Cortes' verse is that of a madman."

Neruda: Pablo Neruda (1904–1973), Chilean poet, diplomat, and winner of the Nobel Prize for Literature in 1971. After joining the Communist Party in 1939, Neruda served as Chilean ambassador to France under Socialist President Salvadore Allende. Translated by Angel Flores, Neruda's poetry appeared in *ND Annual 8* in 1944. In 1972, ND published Neruda's *The Captain's Verses;* in 1973, *Residence on Earth* (both translated by Donald D. Walsh).

a monastic job: Basic Principles of Monastic Spirituality (Abbey of Gethsemani, 1957).

the Fitzgerald book: In the Rose of Time (ND, 1956).

Aimé Césaire: (1913–), Surrealist Martinique poet and dramatist whose major work has been translated by Clayton Eshleman and Annette Smith, including *Collected Poetry* (University of California Press, 1983) and *Lyric and Dramatic Poetry, 1946–1982* (University Press of Virginia, 1990).

68. TLS-3   Norfolk
                                               November 8, 1957

DEAR TOM:

What a wretch I am to have let so much time go by without answering your wonderful letter. Believe me, I think of you often down there, and have meant a dozen times to write, but the past weeks seem to have been more hectic than usual. . . . I'm not quite out of the woods yet, but it should be a little better soon.

Thank you so much for signing the sheets for the German book *[The Tower of Babel]* and sending them back. The binder reports that the mail did not treat them too kindly on the return journey, but he thinks he will be able to fix them up by dampening them and pressing them. . . .

Now to get back to your letter, which was such a joy, particularly because you sound so wonderfully happy down there. Out here in the unreal world, which gets unrealer every day, we have the whirling Sputniks, and the last one with a poor little dog trapped in it. It looks as if the Russkis are really serious about getting hold of the Middle Eastern oil, and I see nothing but trouble ahead. I don't see why one of our peerless leaders wasn't smart enough to give them half of it spontaneously, but I guess I am just not a practical fellow.

I am intrigued with your little play in the vein of Gertrude Stein. As I think I told you, I knew her fairly well, spending some time down at her place in the French countryside one summer. In fact, I tried to write a book about her, but got bogged down and never finished it. Because what you came up against in the end, I found, was automatic dictation, and somehow, with all allowances for genius, that just ain't art, at least in the mass.

What you are doing in this play seems to me more rewarding, because you set limits to the free association and give it some shaping and control. Do by all means go on with this when the spirit moves you, and I'll be eager to see how it turns out. I'm sorry to have kept it so long and hope that my doing so has not dulled the inspiration.

Strange Islands has been doing very nicely, and is somewhere around 2000 copies now, which is excellent. We are all very pleased with it and happy about it, and feel sure it will continue to do well for a long time.

That is very interesting that you have a young Nicaraguan poet down there in your midst. How is his English? I ask because I think it would be fine if we could have a little group of translations from Nicaraguan poetry in the next number of New Directions anthology, which is to be an international one. And the crazy one sounds good, too. Will you pass the word to Cardenal that I am interested, and perhaps he will send me something?

Yes, [Dudley] Fitts did a very fine anthology of Latin American poetry for us, and I'll ask Bob [MacGregor] to send a copy down to you.

I wish that I could also send you a copy of the book we did of Neruda's stuff, but, unfortunately, it is totally out of print. But I think there is a Spanish book store in New York and I'll call them up and see what they have of his.

I am delighted that you have found your way back to Ezra again. He really is incomparable, in his wacky way. I'll see that his books are sent along, too.

I'm ashamed to say that I don't know too much about

Latin American novelists—I know there are some good ones, but I just haven't had time to get any reading done in that field. What I shall do here is to telephone over to Herbert Weinstock at Knopf's, who is a specialist in that area, and see what he can recommend that is in print. I do know about a fascinating Argentine short story writer, named Borges, whom I think I can get for you from Indiana Press.

I'm afraid that we haven't done any of the new French poets. Here again, I just haven't managed to keep up with them, as there are so many of them who seem promising. But I have gotten interested in that fascinating German, Gottfried Benn, who died last summer. He was sort of the equivalent of Pound in German—opened up German verse and brought all the modern insights into it—and we are getting up a selection of his prose and poetry that ought to be along in about a year.

Burma was just terrific. I liked it so much better than India, and, without getting very deep into it, took a great shine to Buddhism. Of course, there are some things you can criticize about it there, such as the fact that they spend their money on gilding the spires of pagodas rather than building hospitals, but they really have faith, and it seems to make them very happy. A number of my good friends out there, and I made a lot of them, are members of meditation groups, and get a lot out of it. But it seems to be rather different from the kind of meditation that you do down there, as the object seems to be to empty the mind of all thought. If I understand them correctly, they don't try to think about the Buddha, or what he stood for, but just to eliminate every form of self or sensation.

Did Bob [MacGregor] write you that he has a namesake? That is our little Robert, who was born on May 6 and is now a thumping creature 27 inches long. He is named for Bob Hutchins, too, and for Bob Fitzgerald.

With three such Bobs to model himself on he really ought to turn into something!

Well, I have rambled on too long, but it is always a pleasure to sit down and talk with you, as it were.

Oh yes, Rexroth: he came up and spent a few days with us at the ranch in Wyoming, my wife's father's ranch, that is, when we were there in August. He is in better form than I have seen him for many years, and really coming into his own, as he gets more and more recognition for his poetry, his radio station broadcasts, his translations, and his very sprightly essays which appear almost every week in *the Nation*. He had one of his little girls with him, Mary, age 7, and we all went off together on a pack trip in the mountains on horses. Kenneth is the world's most fascinating talker and he kept us in stitches the whole time.

Best to you all down there,
J.

/ · /

Gertrude Stein: (1874–1946), Expatriate American writer whose Paris salon became a hub of literary and artistic activity in the 1930s. Stein moved to France in 1902, where she lived until her death. What JL refers to as "automatic dictation" Stein explained as her philosophy of composition: the business of art, she thought, was to capture "the complete actual present," uninterrupted by temporal categories and divisions. JL visited Stein and her partner Alice B. Toklas in August 1934; he wrote press releases for Stein's American tour the following year. In 1936, Arrow Editions, published by Florence Codman in New York, announced plans to publish JL's *Understanding Gertrude Stein,* but the project was dropped.

anthology of Latin American poetry: Anthology of Contemporary Latin-American Poetry (ND, 1942).

the book . . . of Neruda's stuff: Residence on Earth, and Other Poems (ND, 1946).

named Borges: A Buenos Aires-born writer best known for his short stories, Jorge Luis Borges (1899–1986) was recognized by an international literary circle. After teaching Anglo-Saxon literature at the University of Buenos Aires, Borges was demoted by the anti-intellectual Perón regime to chicken inspector in 1946. After Perón's fall, Borges became director of Argentina's National Library.

Gottfried Benn: (1886–1956), Novelist, essayist, dramatist, poet, and M.D., Benn was an influential German writer little known in America. His thirty-seven books include selected writings published by ND in 1960, *Primal Vision.* Benn's poetry also appeared in *Contemporary German Poetry: An Anthology* (ND, 1962), ed. and trans. Gertrude Clorius Schwebell.

Bob Hutchins: Robert M. Hutchins (1899–1977), youthful president of the University of Chicago, leader of midcentury American liberalism, democratic idealist, and founder of the Center for the Study of Democratic Institutions, Hutchins's influential writings include *Education for Freedom* (1943), *The University of Utopia* (1953), and *The Learning Society* (1968). TM and JL's mutual close friend W. H. Ferry served as vice president of Hutchins's Fund for the Republic—best known for defending Hollywood screenwriters during Joseph McCarthy's HUAC hearings—and later as an officer in the Center for the Study of Democratic Institutions. See Letter #90.

69. TLS-1 March 6, 1958

DEAR BOB [MACGREGOR]:

For a long time I have owed you and J. letters. This will have to pay you both.

What I have been thinking about first of all is [Adolfo] Bioy [Casares]'s novel—*Plan de Evasion.* It is a good, curious book, certainly the sort of thing I think you ought to publish. Story of a Frenchman who is sent on a job to Devil's Island, as a kind of assistant to the governor of the Penal Colony. Finds the place in the grip of mysterious experiments conducted by the governor with the help of some of the prisoners. Experiments in penology—the governor, by operating on the prisoners' brains and putting them in a weird group of cells with mirror-walls, introduces them into a strange imaginary world in which they are "happy" and don't really know they are in prison. Those who live in these mirror cells remain in some strange kind of contact with each other, psychically or what have you, and in the end they are murdered more or less by the thoughts of one of their number. It is a weird and amusing book—French rather than South

American. I am glad to have seen it. I am sending the book back, now.

Also I am returning the article on Neruda which is otherwise interesting. Bioy seems to me to be somewhat up a blind alley. Neruda too in his own way: but Neruda remains in contact with the roots of his country and with the real South America, and I can see tremendous possibilities in his best stuff. I would very much like to have the collected works, published by Losada of Buenos Aires, of which this is a review. Could you somehow, by hook or by crook, get it for me? A review copy or something? Someday I really want to write an article about Neruda, perhaps even to do some translations of him—as if I would ever get the time.

I am in contact with one of the best sculptors in Ecuador, Jaime Andrade, in the hope of getting him to do a statue for us. He is very interested in the project—I only fear he may turn out to be beyond our means. There are interesting artists down there, including one who would be able to do some fabulously wonderful decorations for a book. Maybe we can rope him in on a project some time.

. . . I will keep reading lots of things and someday something will come out of it, I am sure. You would be amazed to realize how rich Spanish America and Brazil can be in *everything.* We look very shabby in comparison, culturally. Take for instance fantastic mystery plays (in the old sense of the word) in a combination of Spanish and some Indian dialects like nauhuatl. . . .

Thanks again for the books and for the Neruda article. Keep sending things, I am more and more interested. . . . Some monks might think this sort of thing a dissipation: to me it is a real part of the contemplative life. Without something that has to do with real people and their aspirations, the contemplative life becomes, alas, purely abstract and platonic. And then, what good is it? One has to see God in the dynamism of man's development, as well as in all His other mysteries. Thanks for the news about *the Tower of Babel*. I was wondering what had become of it.

All the best, as usual!

Yrs in Christ

FR. M. LOUIS

/ · /

Bioy: RMM wrote TM on 18 November 1957 about "an Argentine writer named Adolfo Bioy Casares, published by Sur in Buenos Aires and now translated into French and being published by Gallimard, although his first and perhaps most interesting novel, *Plan de Evasion,* was published by a minor publisher in Buenos Aires named Emece. He first was brought to our attention by Paul Bowles, and now I occasionally hear about him from friends in Paris, London and other places. He has not been translated into English. . . . Do you read Spanish? I can send you this novel, either in Spanish or French. He is an extraordinarily original writer, and I think that you would get him as I do."

the article on Neruda: In February 1958, RMM sent TM an "article from the *Times Literary Supplement* about Neruda . . . [that] argue[s] a sensible approach towards some of the problems Neruda's politics and other matters present."

Jaime Andrade: See Letter #72. Andrade's sculpture arrived at Gethsemani in April 1959.

the news about the Tower of Babel: Although TM's "morality play" *The Tower of Babel* bears a 1957 publication date, it wasn't released until mid-1958 due to numerous printing errors.

70. TLS-1   October 16, 1958

DEAR J.

Thanks for your letter, and for the Pasternak *Selected Writings* which came in today. I was not trying to rush you, I would have been content to wait for the new one. However I am glad to have this. I hope to write a study of Pasternak, and this will help out. Thanks also for forwarding the letter Pasternak wrote to me. It was exciting to get it and his few words confirmed my conviction of the deep understanding that exists between us, or rather the identity of certain basic ideas and attitudes in both of us. I had written to him about this and he replied in kind. His *Zhivago* was a tremendous piece of work, not of course perfect in every respect, but all the better for it. Pantheon sent the ad. I am glad to have been able to speak out for him.

Your idea about the "Letter to an Innocent Bystander" seems to me to be a very good one. It is now censored so everything is ok. It would of course be essential to check with Naomi [Burton] but I am sure she would not mind your sending it to Ted Weeks [at *The Atlantic*]. It seems to me to be a very good idea.

I have written to Cuadra asking him to hurry up and send some of his illustrations. As far as I know they will be copies of Indian ceramic designs, and though quite good might not warrant a special finely printed book. I should be inclined to go for the [New Directions] World Poets idea and I hinted as much to him when I wrote. He is editor of a paper down there and has rather a tough time with the local Dictator. In the meantime I am glad you will go ahead with some of his material in the anthology. As I said you can have the two poems of mine, but can you wait until I let you know about the censors? The "Letter" is censored but the poems not yet.

Mark Van Doren sent his autobiography and I have been enjoying it: it is full of good things and all about everybody I used to know, so it is a lot of fun to read.

Don't forget that you are supposed to be thinking of coming down here, now!

Oh yes, *Babel* arrived. It is splendid and lavish and we are all very happy with it. The printing and the woodcuts are superb. . . .

I would very much like to see the Octavio Paz book you refer to in your earlier letter. [Ernesto] Cardenal (Frater Lawrence) knows him and thinks highly of him. I have just been reading some Cesar Vallejo, who is terrific. I have not read any of Paz. I threaten to translate some Jorge de Lima from the Portuguese for you, when I get a chance. But I like to keep time free for writing of my own. I have done over completely that Atlas thing and it is shaping up into something better I believe. Or I hope. Larry Ferlinghetti's stuff sounds interesting. I now have permission to read anything so there are no problems about the nature of the material. I don't know the whole [William] Everson story (we had a friend of his here for a while) nor have I seen his late poems. On the whole I think a monastery is not ordinarily a place to write good verse in. Too much triviality is dictated by the walls.

Am always interested in everything that is alive, and anything that strikes you as something I ought to know about, please send. All the best of everything.

Faithfully in Christ,
T o m

/ · /

Pasternak: TM developed a very deep attachment to the Russian poet and novelist Boris Pasternak (1890–1960). He wrote a moving, insightful monograph on Pasternak—"The Pasternak Affair" in *Disputed Questions* (1960)—which includes a detailed rendering of the events surrounding Pasternak's refusal of the Nobel Prize for Literature in 1958. In publishing *Dr. Zhivago,* Pantheon circulated an advertisement decrying the censorship of Pasternak's novel in Russia and his expulsion from the Soviet Writers' Union. The ad included a quote from TM taken from a letter he wrote to Aleksei Surkov, head of the Soviet Writers' Union, hailing *Dr. Zhivago,* "which burst upon us full of turbulent and irrepressible life, giving us a deeply moving image of the heroic sufferings of the Russian nation and its struggles, sacrifices, and achievements." TM and Pasternak's brief correspondence was published by the University of Kentucky's King Library Press (1973): *Boris Pasternak–Thomas Merton: Six Letters, 1958–1960.* TM's letters to Pasternak are included in *Courage.*

Ted Weeks: Poetry editor at *The Atlantic.*

Cuadra: Pablo Antonio Cuadra (1912–), Nicaraguan poet, intellectual, journalist (cousin of Ernesto Cardenal), who became editor of Managua's largest daily newspaper, *La Prensa,* and its literary supplement, *La Prensa Literaria,* in 1954 during the repressive Samoza regime. Later at odds with Sandinista ideology, Cuadra went into exile after the 1979 revolution. TM translated Cuadra's *The Jaguar and the Moon* (Unicorn Press, 1974), a collection of poems inspired by pre-Columbian Chorotega pottery that earned Cuadra the Ruben Dario Prize, Nicaragua's highest literary honor. The "Letter to Pablo Antonio Cuadra Concerning Giants" (in *Emblems of a Season of Fury*)—a screed on superpower arrogance—is without question TM's most powerful political statement. TM began corresponding with Cuadra in 1958 (see *Courage*).

World Poets: World Poets Series, a short-lived series of 64 page pamphlets selling at one dollar begun by JL in the late fifties. Poets in the series included Octavio Paz, Alain Bosquet, and Chairil Anwar. JL published fifteen TM translations of Cuadra's poems in *ND Annual 17*.

the two poems of mine: "A Practical Program for Monks" and the often-anthologized "An Elegy for Five Old Ladies."

Octavio Paz: (1914–), Mexican poet, critic, and essayist whose poetry resonates with images of Mexico's Indian past and landscape. Paz was awarded the 1990 Nobel Prize in Literature. JL mentions in an earlier letter the *Anthology of Mexican Poetry* (Indiana University Press, 1958) edited by Paz. ND published *The Collected Poems of Octavio Paz, 1957–1987,* edited and translated by Eliot Weinberger, in 1987.

Cesar Vallejo: (1893–1938). In a brief essay introducing his translations of the Peruvian poet Cesar Vallejo's poems in *Emblems of a Season of Fury,* TM wrote: "Certainly one of the greatest Latin American poets of the present century . . . Vallejo is a poet of . . . deep compassion and . . . inextinguishable humanity." Vallejo went to Madrid during the Spanish Civil War, then returned to the high Andes of Peru, "torn apart," TM commented, "by the inexorable forces that were plunging the world into disaster."

Jorge de Lima: (1893–1953). Brazilian poet who wrote in Portuguese. Just a week earlier TM had written to Boris Pasternak about his "particular fondness for a great Negro poet of Brazil, Jorge de Lima."

that Atlas thing: "Atlas and the Fatman," first published in 1961 in ND's *The Behavior of Titans.*

Ferlinghetti: Lawrence Ferlinghetti (1920–), Beat poet and publisher of City Lights in San Francisco, which issued celebrated books by counterculture writers Jack Kerouac, Gary Snyder, and Allen Ginsberg, among others. Ferlinghetti published TM's deadpan indictment of Auschwitz atrocities, "Chants to Be Used in Processions Around a Site with Furnaces," in the *Journal for the Protection of All Beings* (see Letter #90). Before leaving for Asia in 1968, TM spent the night at the City Lights Bookstore (see Letters #200 and #201). TM's letters to Ferlinghetti are collected in *Courage.*

the whole Everson story: JL did not want to publish the new book Everson had just sent ND. "Just couldn't convince myself that it was very good poetry," JL wrote TM on 23 August 1958. "No real incandescence that I could feel. Devotional, the right ideas, but, for me, anyway, not much charge. I wonder about the girl [Everson fell in love with]. No doubt he has found satisfaction, if not peace—the poems show an awful lot of torment—but what about her? I'd like to know what has happened to her." See Letter #17. JL's query is answered by Lee Bartlett in chap. 8, "The Rose of Solitude," of *William Everson: The Life of Brother Antoninus* (ND, 1988).

71. TLS-1   January 17, 1959

DEAR J.,

The "Perspective of Italy" has arrived together with
your copy of your letter to P. A. Cuadra. I am sure he
will be happy with it. And in spite of your misgivings the
"Perspective" looks very good to me. I have only read
one or two poems and looked at the pictures so far but
though the poems are not super special I like them, and
the art certainly strikes me as being vital and spontaneous
after the awful junk that was put out under Mussolini—
the last stuff I saw from there.

I am still working on the other poems of Cuadra that
belong in the book, by the way. There is not [a] terrible
rush, I understand—I can turn on the heat if necessary,
and finish it in a few days. But at present I am only giving
it one afternoon a week, the rest of the time I am busy
with a lot of other things, including learning Russian.
Someday perhaps I will be able to translate some Russian
verse for you. I wish I could handle Pasternak—but not
yet. I am still at the stage where Ivan Ivanovitch works
without rest all day in the factory. And other such
things—"At our club we have a real fine radio."

Have you any simple Russian reading you could ship
down to me? I'll be in a position to read simple prose in
a week or two, I think.

Naomi tells me she sent back the "Letter to the Innocent Bystander" not having unloaded it on *the Atlantic*. I
myself had sent it to [Stephen] Spender at *Encounter* and
got a letter back saying it was "too generalized" for him.
. . . If you still have any magazine leads and want to use
them ok, or if you want to just use it in the Annual ok. I
am not planning to try anything more with it myself.

It is however being printed in the magazine *Sur* of
Buenos Aires. But you are the only one doing anything
with it in America so the field is yours. I gave Naomi a

long article on the Pasternak affair too and don't know what is becoming of it—she says it is at *Harper's*.

To Bob MacGregor I sent an emended text of the essay on "Poetry and Contemplation" for the selected verse. And a list of poems. And the promise to work over a couple of new ones yet. . . .

Spender says he is coming to this country. If you see him and can encourage him to stop off in this backwater on his way somewhere, I hope you will do so. Always of course let me know first so I can arrange permission for a visit. And this reminds me again that you are overdue and always welcome. Happy New Year—all the best of everything.

Faithfully in Christ,

T o m

/ · /

poems of Cuadra that belong in the book: Emblems of a Season of Fury includes ten TM translations of poems by Pablo Antonio Cuadra.

Spender: Stephen Spender (1909–), British essayist, poet, and literary editor of *Encounter,* edited by Irving Kristol and published by the Congress for Cultural Freedom. "Letter to an Innocent Bystander" never appeared in an American or English periodical. It was collected in TM's *The Behavior of Titans* (ND, 1961).

a long article on . . . Pasternak: "The Pasternak Affair in Perspective" was published in *Thought,* 34 (Winter, 1959–60).

72. TLS-1   Feb. 12, 1959

D E A R J . ,

It was good to get your letter of Jan. 26th, and I can imagine how hard it must be to get out from under the mountain of letters you must get from everywhere. Thanks too for offering us the Apel book on *Gregorian Chant*. It would be a very worthy addition to the novitiate library, as of course the kids are always up to their ears in chant and struggling with the technical side of it. So if you send it we will all be happy about it.

Really I think [Giuseppi] Ungaretti is terrific. His intensity is overwhelming—and the honesty with which he refuses to hammer anything but the nail. Most poets knock down the wall of the house. He is from now on one of my favorite poets.

Octavio Paz you sent, I guess quite a while ago, and this I liked too. Our man Cardenal one of the novices is a friend of his and he was glad to see it too. I like Octavio Paz and the Mexican poets in general.

You ought to see the fine statue of the Virgin and Child that is being done for us by a man in Ecuador [Jaime Andrade]. Somewhat Indian and astute and a good working out of a special idea of mine. Hope you will see it someday here.

I have done a little volume of translations of some sayings of the Desert Fathers. They might be very popular in their way, having as they do a kind of Zen flavor about them. It might even be interesting to get someone like Suzuki to write a little word of preface—but in any case I am passing the thing on to Naomi and she will probably pass it to you. In the meantime a very limited hand printing is to be done down here by Victor Hammer (62 copies). I think you will be interested, though.

I have written a brief introduction which, in a further edition, could be expanded to about twice the length in a little study of the background.

. . . Do you know Victoria Ocampo. . . ? She is quite a person. This is a short rush letter—tomorrow we go on retreat for a week. I expect to be busy in the woods.

With all the best—God bless you

Faithfully in Christ,
Tom

/ · /

Apel: Willi Apel, author of *Gregorian Chant* (Indiana University Press, 1958).

Giuseppi Ungaretti: (1888–1970), Italian poet. ND published Ungaretti's *Life of a Man,* translated by Allen Mandelbaum, in 1958. JL included Ungaretti's "The Promised Land" in *ND Annual 10.* Ungaretti was one of the voices TM took along with him when he moved to his hermitage in 1966.

sayings of the Desert Fathers: TM's translations of the sayings of the fourth-century Desert Fathers were published in two editions: *What Ought I To Do?,* a fine letterpress book printed and designed by Victor Hammer (Stamperia del Santuccio, 1959), and an expanded trade edition, *The Wisdom of the Desert* (ND, 1961). Although D. T. Suzuki agreed to write an introduction, neither edition included one. See Letters #77 and #78.

Victor Hammer: (1882–1967), Vienna-born artist, type designer and cutter, printer, and Lexington, Kentucky, resident who became, along with his wife Carolyn, close friends with TM, often traveling to Gethsemani for afternoon picnics. See David Cooper, "Victor Hammer and Thomas Merton: A Friendship *Ad Maiorem Dei Gloriam,*" in *The Kentucky Review* (Summer 1987).

Victoria Ocampo: Born to a wealthy Argentine family, Victoria Ocampo (1891–1979) earned an international reputation as a writer, feminist lecturer, and editor of the much-respected literary magazine *Sur,* which published work by, among others, TM, Henry Miller, Albert Camus, Evelyn Waugh, and Simone Weil.

73. TLS-2

Sarasota, Fla
February 20, 1959

DEAR TOM

Many thanks for your fine letter of the 12th, which reached me down here in Florida, where I am visiting for a few days with my venerable Aunt, well on toward 90, a lady of unbounded vigor and great antique charm. I think I told you about her once. She is the one who is a follower of "Unity," holding that God is thought, and in all of us, if we will but listen. This is compounded with her contacts with an angel named "Lester" who communicates via a lady who does automatic writing in Pleasantville, New York. I see these communications from time to time. They are full of exhortation to high thought and benevolent action, which my Aunt puts into practice with much generosity, but not very precise in detail. "Lester" spends his time trying to help people in this life who are in difficulties, and the dear lady has been assured that a similar role awaits her when she is happily liberated from the limitations of this plane. Since she has done little but help people for the past seventy years, and is very good at it, she looks to the future with great cheer, and, insofar as my temper of doubt permits, I share in her happiness.

I am so pleased that you like Ungaretti, and have asked my pal [Filippo] Donini at the Italian Cultural Institute to see if he can't get you the complete poems in Italian. It would be fine if you could translate a few of them. . . . How would you feel about letting us use your praise of Ungaretti in some ads? I know it would help a lot, and we are rather in the dumps about this book so far, because there have been no reviews yet, and no notice taken. It is always hard to push a foreign poet here, unless he gets some flashy publicity from his private life, but, in this case, I am not prepared to take it without a struggle.

I'm very much interested in what you write about the Desert Fathers translations. I hope so much that Naomi will want us to do that, and I've dropped her a line to that effect. These texts should lend themselves to a beautiful treatment. I'm glad that Hammer is doing them first. I admire him greatly. Saw some of his recent things at a show of fine printing in the NY Public [Library], and they were lovely. . . . The other crashing thing in that show was the missal that Bill Everson had printed on his hand press. Did he send you one? Absolutely stunning!

That's fine that you approve the "Letter to the Innocent Bystander" for ND. I propose to wind up the selection for the next number as soon as I get North. . . .

Yes, I share your enthusiasm for Victoria Ocampo—a great person. I met her once when she came to New York, very quiet behind the constant dark glasses, but giving off a lot of microwaves. I never quite followed her rage for T. E. Lawrence, but she has done a great work down there, with fearless persistence, and really carried their culture on her back during the bad years. She and the Princess Caetani in Rome have the same wonderful determination to see that good things get printed, and that poets are paid well for their work, while keeping themselves in the background. . . .

I want so much to get down to see you this year. I thought of stopping off on the way North from this trip, but I gather this is the time of year when you are in seclusion. But perhaps along about May or June we can work it out at a time that would be convenient for you.

As ever,

J.

/ · /

Donini: Filippo Donini, whom JL remembers as a poet and director of the London-based Italian Cultural Institute.

the missal that Bill Everson . . . printed: Novum Psalterium Pii XII (Los Angeles), an edition financed by Countess Estelle Doheny in 1955.

T. E. Lawrence: Thomas Edward Lawrence (1888–1935), British writer, soldier, and archeologist, famous as Lawrence of Arabia.

Princess Caetani: Princess Marguerite Caetani, a wealthy American married to an Italian prince and editor of the international literary review *Botteghe Oscure.*

74. TLS-1 April 18, 1959

DEAR J.

I want to rush this off to you, so it may be a little incoherent. But the main thing is . . . Naomi Burton saying that Bob Giroux had regretfully turned down *[The Wisdom of the Desert: Sayings from] the Desert Fathers* which means they are clear for you. I am very happy because I think this is clearly the right decision and I think we are going to have a tremendously interesting time with it. I am very happy about this book for various reasons, and the chief of them is that I have contacted Suzuki in Japan and he is most probably writing a preface, for his letter sounded very receptive and friendly, and he liked very much the few samples that I sent him. I think this is all going to be very worth while, and meanwhile I send you a larger edition of the text. The text sent to Bob [Giroux] is nothing but the short text that is being set on his hand press by Victor Hammer. For the definitive edition everything is somewhat enlarged, and I may add even more. In fact it is certain that I am going to go over the introduction again and add perhaps two or three pages of clarifications, because I am not yet satisfied that it makes my meaning at all clear. I am sure it does not. But what you have here will give you a good idea of the book, and of course I think Suzuki's preface will be excellent. I have tried to stimulate him to open up and take all the space he wants. I sincerely hope he does so.

It seems to me that this material will also lend itself to some very fine typography.

[Giovanni] Mardersteg's idea of making an Oratorio of *the Tower of B* is of course very close to my own, in fact the original project was something I went into with Hindemith. He was down here, and we started from some conversations, and this was the result. However it was too long and involved and not enough the kind of thing he is interested in the moment (he likes to bring in the public to sing choruses etc.). I think it would be fine if some young composer wanted to try it, and if you know of one who might be interested, by all means suggest it. . . . It is all a bit vague, though, because I feel that in its present form it would scare a composer, there is too much of it. If someone could work up an interest in parts of it, and regard other parts as meant to be spoken rather than sung, and remember finally that I would want to shorten it in places—then I think there would be a possibility of doing something with it. . . .

I got the Ungaretti and it is very fine. About translation—I'll think about it, I don't know if I am up to such excellence. . . . More later. Come down.

God bless you
T O M

/ · /

Mardersteg: Giovanni Mardersteig, Verona book designer who JL called "the greatest printer in the world." Mardersteig urged JL to find a composer who could set TM's *Tower of Babel* to music, "for it reminds me," Mardersteig wrote to JL (1 April 1959) "in many ways of an oratorio. I can imagine that music might be a better way of bringing out the inner meaning of the text. . . ."

Hindemith: A central figure among the composers who came into prominence in Germany after World War I, Paul Hindemith (1895–1963) left Germany when Hitler came to power and spent two decades in the United States, where he taught at Yale University and at the summer school in Tanglewood, Massachusetts. His works include a choral setting of Walt Whitman's elegy to Lincoln, *When Lilacs Last in the Dooryard Bloom'd* (1946).

75. TM ALS-2

St. Anthony Hospital
St. Anthony Place
Louisville, Kentucky
Oct. 19, 1959

D E A R J.

I am here in the hospital for some minor repairs—will be going back to the monastery in a few days.

Suzuki has just wired that he is mailing his manuscript [for *The Wisdom of the Desert*] on the 20th so we will have to wait just a little. I am glad he is finally coming through with it. There is not that much rush anyway. How is Mardersteig coming with the plans?

This gives me a chance to bring you up to date on the things I was talking to you about when you were down here. Application has been made to Rome for permission for me to go to Mexico. The Cuernavaca solution seems to be the most feasible & I have heard that chances are quite good. I haven't the faintest idea whether or not Rome has yet contacted Father Abbot, or what is happening.

Ernesto Cardenal, the poet, has gone down there. I told him if there were some hitch to contact you—but I don't think it is likely that he will.

I am not very definite as to what's likely to happen, or when, except I have hopes that by the end of the year or early in 1960 I may be in Mexico. The project is to eventually start a hermitage back in the mountains in a place that can only be reached on horseback. Sounds great. I hope it works out.

If between now and the end of November you are likely to be coming this way, perhaps you could write to Cardenal & ask him to give you all the available dope as to how things are going with my plan, & what has developed so far. He is at the monastery there and can tell you all the news. Then you could relay it to me on the way through if it should happen to be anything important. The final decision ought, I suppose, to come direct from Rome but I don't know—it may be sent to them down there. . . .

Don't bother to go out of your way for this, but if you *do* happen to be out this way it might be a good idea.

I'll write more about business from the monastery.

All the best

Cordially in Xt.
TOM

/ · /

permission . . . to go to Mexico: Dom Gregorio Lemercier, visiting Gethsemani from the Benedictine monastery at Cuernavaca, tried to persuade TM to join the monastery in Mexico. TM petitioned the Congregation for Religious in Rome to do so. Permission was denied in December 1959.

76. TLS-1   December 14, 1959

DEAR J.,

Your letter and Bob [MacGregor]'s together with one copy of the *Selected Poems* reached me today. The book is very attractive and I am quite happy with it. The cover came out very well. The only thing I regret is that I should have left out one or two poems from *Figures for an Apocalypse* and inserted some more from *the [Tears of the] Blind Lions.* I hope the book does well. I have just been looking over the illustrations done by Armando Morales for the Spanish edition. They are tremendous but extremely abstract, still I think it would be a wonderful idea to bring out a limited English edition of poems with his work to illustrate it. I leave it until I have the Spanish book to send to you, and we can talk about it further then.

About *The Wisdom of the Desert.* . . . [S]ince the book has shaped up the way it has, growing organically so to speak, and since the Suzuki material, which is so good, would have no *raison d'être* detached from the sayings of the Fathers, I still think that we ought to keep the lot together, even though it may be untidy and disconcerting. The point is that Zen is a great drawing card now, and it is a good thing to tie up the Zen viewpoint with the Desert Fathers' attitude, and that is why I set about it all in the first place. The kind of people who like Desert Fathers might perhaps take an interest in the Suzuki bit, and vice versa. And a few will find the whole tie up intriguing, as I do. The book will be what it started out to be—something quite unusual.

About *Problems and Pardons,* I shall definitely tell Perry Knowlton that I think it ought to go to you. The understanding has always been that ND would handle these out of the way things. He might have to show it to Bob [Giroux] first. But in the long run I think the way would be clear. It was Naomi that was the obstacle to your handling "Atlas [and the Fatman]" for magazines—she was so sensitive about her rights. Now I don't see any special point in trying it on any Catholic magazines except perhaps *Renascence. Jubilee* of course, but I have given them plenty stuff. I would rather see you try the more likely literary magazines. It has been to *Evergreen [Review],* no it hasn't, either. "The Public Confession" went to them and *New Yorker.* Bob Lax may be doing something with *that.* But "Atlas" and the other things have not been anywhere as far as I know. New American Library as a last resort would probably take it. But I'd like to see it go somewhere good. Bob [MacGregor] suggests waiting a little on this small book, of course. We can talk about it when you come down and of course I am eager to see you and go over all these things.

I'll dry up now for the moment—best wishes to all of you for Christmas. God bless you all. As ever

Faithfully in Christ,
TOM

/ · /

Armando Morales: Mexican engraver who illustrated TM's *Poemas,* translated by Ernesto Cardenal and published in Mexico by Imprenta Universitara, 1961.

Problems and Pardons: Early working title for *The Behavior of Titans.* See Letter #80.

Perry Knowlton: TM's new agent at the Curtis Brown agency. Naomi Burton Stone left Curtis Brown in November 1959 to become an editor at Doubleday.

"The Public Confession": "A Signed Confession of Crimes Against the State" eventually appeared in the inaugural number of the *Carleton Miscellany* (Fall 1960).

77. TLS-1   Jan 29, 1960

DEAR J.,

We are in an emergency. There are going to have to be drastic changes in our plan for *the Wisdom of the Desert.* The Abbot General has finally come through with his decision based on the decision of the censors, as usual very late. And as usual (or as often usual) very bad. He absolutely excludes Suzuki from the book, and my reply to Suzuki almost necessarily goes from it too. I do not think there is any special way of getting around this or coming to an arrangement with him, and so the first point is, definitely, that I think we had better publish the *Wisdom* merely as part one, that is my essay on the Fathers and the Sayings. This brings us back to the suggestion Bob [MacGregor] made, and since it has a lot to be said for it, I think it is perfectly satisfactory, at least up to a point.

Hence—this part being duly approved and without anything to hold it up—we can go ahead immediately without further delay to get *the Wisdom of the Desert* under way in this form. It has the advantage of being uncomplicated and pure. I am not worried about that, especially since the Suzuki article takes such a different tone, and puts the second part in a whole new atmosphere.

However I do want to make use of the Suzuki article and my own too.

Nobody can stop anyone from printing Suzuki, naturally. No obstacle there. The General hints that under certain conditions and with renewed censorship my own reply can be published. He was thinking of possible publication of my reply in the *Wisdom* itself. But that is absurd.

I am wondering if this would be a possible solution: to print part two of the *Wisdom,* meaning Suzuki's article and my reply and the other two short pieces, in ND annual. The objection of the General was that in me and Suzuki appearing together, it might lead Catholic readers to dabble in Buddhism which would be very perilous. He hasn't seen Suzuki's article himself, and doesn't realize how little it might make anyone a Buddhist. I do not know whether he would object to me and Suzuki appearing together in the annual, and this I will ask him. It would seem a little extreme to put it that rigidly. But meanwhile, how does that look to you? . . . Catholic writers all the time appear in magazines in dialogues with nonCatholic thinkers and the Annual would correspond to that sort of situation. As I understand it, his objection was to my inviting Suzuki to appear in "my" book, all officially Catholic.

Let me know what you think of this, and any other problems which may arise at your end. . . .

> Best wishes, as ever—and God bless
> you.
> Tom

78. TLS-2

Norfolk
February 10, 1960

DEAR TOM,

Just back from some very pleasant skiing up in snowy Vermont with my daughter and some friends, and find your letter of January 29th.

You really are much more philosophical about disappointments than I am. I feel quite badly that we cannot use the Suzuki material in *the Wisdom of the Desert*. I had become much attached to the idea, and probably just for the reason that troubles the Order. It seems to me that it is a good thing for members of one religion to learn about others, in order to develop sympathy and understanding. As you know from our conversations, I felt that the book would bring many Zen followers to a more open mind about Catholicism, and never worried about Catholics being led away from the fold.

However, it will still be a wonderful book just with the text and your introduction, so let us concentrate our thinking on that.

But certainly we should try to get the Merton–Suzuki interchange published somewhere and at a time that will fit in with publication of the book. For this reason, I am hesitant about scheduling it for the New Directions anthology, because I don't just know what the release date of that is going to be. Wouldn't it be a good idea to try to place the interchange in one of the weeklies, say perhaps the *Saturday Review,* to come out at the same time as the book? We have plenty of time to work on this, and should be able to line it up well if we start right away. So please let me know how you feel about this. And what steps are necessary to get the censorship approval for the magazine appearance? . . .

I talked with Perry Knowlton on the phone this morning and he said that we could send *Problems and Pardons* to the printer as soon as we get confirmation back from the Abbot that the contract is all right. . . .

I like the little poem, "Love Winter [When the Plant Says Nothing]," a lot. It is very crisp and clean, yet the images are rich and float out into space, so to speak. . . .

I hope you will say a few prayers for poor old Kenneth Patchen. He is in terrible shape again, and has to have another operation on his back, and is in real despair, having just been turned down for a Ford Foundation grant.

As ever,

J.

/ · /

The Merton-Suzuki interchange: First published in its entirely in *ND Annual 17* (1961) as "Wisdom in Emptiness: A Dialogue between Daisetz T. Suzuki and Thomas Merton." Later included in TM's *Zen and the Birds of Appetite* (ND, 1968).

79. TLS-2   April 20, 1960

DEAR J.,

Finally the [Joseph] Delteil book *[François d'Assise]* starts back to you. I can see where Henry Miller would like it, and I like it too in the same way. Looking further into it I think it is rather not for Naomi. Doubleday wouldn't want a book that the conformist types will be angry at. If anybody publishes it, you should. The only trouble is that it won't send the Catholics and it probably won't send the beats. . . .

The [Jacques] Barzun book I enjoy very much and find salutary. It has a lot of good things in it, and it is time someone deflated so many of the poses that otherwise intelligent people think they have to take. Thanks very much for it. We do have an obligation to be serious and honest and to work with the minds God has given us, rather than repeat clichés—even the most refined and sophisticated of them!

. . . I'd like someone like [Lawrence] Ferlinghetti to come down. The other people you mention sound very fine. Why don't you some time plan to come down with one or two like Jack Mills and Arthur Cohen, informally, for a visit, and I think it would be very profitable. At least it would make sense. I have several groups of protestant seminary professors coming, but I don't want to get holed in to that sort of specialty. What would be ideal would be ten or twelve groups a year, small ones: writers, beats, protestants, buddhists, intellectuals, who knows, even politicians. But the less professional and formal I get about it, the better. I think [Robert] Lax would bring [Jack] Kerouac and has already spoken of it. Do let's think more of this. . . .

Did I yet thank you for the Aeschylus books[?] I am very glad of them, and will probably write abit about Prometheus in the preface [to *Behavior of the Titans*]. It needs explaining. Incidentally I don't have a question mark on this new typewriter. I picked the keys myself to get some French accents in case I should some day order a ton of *pâté de foie gras,* or *boeuf rôti* or even a dozen bottles of *kümmel.* Really it is for letters to foreign brass, of course. But in picking everything either I didn't allow for the question mark that was pushed out by one of those accents, or else the guy in the typewriter place didn't note down what I said about not necessarily wanting an exclamation mark! Well that is what I've got!!!!!

Finally, and most inexplicable, is an accented ù. For Roumanian names or Sicilian underworld slang. Think what the next book might be!

Féioèst zazù çerdönt à gêtù!! Galà pù çonq!

That reminds me, don't forget *Zazie dans le métro.* . . .

Well, for the moment this will have to do. Thanks for everything, and God bless you. With best wishes,

Cordially in Christ,
T O M

/ · /

The Delteil *book:* Henry Miller sent Delteil's book on St. Francis to TM in July 1962, two years after JL's copy arrived. TM later wrote to Miller (7

August 1962): "The Delteil book is frankly remarkable. It has an unusual zest and life. He works in big energetic blocs of symbol." See *Courage,* pp. 275ff.

The Barzun book: Either *God's Country and Mine: A Declaration of Love Spiced with a Few Harsh Words* (Little, Brown, 1954) or *The House of Intellect* (Harper, 1959). JL wrote TM (4 April 1960): "Jacques is a very old friend of mine, and I'm devoted to him, but sometimes I think his writing is just a little too glib. But there is some very good stuff in that . . . book, all right."

Jack Mills: JL mentions John F. Mills in a letter to TM (4 April 1960) as "someone to think of sometime. [He] works now in the Print Room of the Museum of Modern Art. Not at all famous yet—he is quite young—but a rather wonderful person, who tries to relate the tendencies in art to other humanistic areas. He is not at all one of the faddists who are promoting the new splatter painting. He has written a book on Ruskin, that isn't published yet, and spent a lot of time in India visiting temples there, and also studying Romanesque churches in Europe." Mills died in India in the mid-1960s.

Arthur Cohen: Head editor at Henry Holt. A "person you might enjoy," JL wrote (4 April 1960), "who has been working with Bob Hutchins on the religion panel of Bob's Center for the Study of Democratic Institutions, which is now out in Santa Barbara. Arthur was educated to be a rabbi, but then came over into publishing, and has done a marvelous job with his Meridian Books."

Kerouac: Jack Kerouac (1922–1969), Massachusetts-born writer whose energetic novels chronicle the Beat movement, especially *On the Road* (1957), *The Dharma Bums* (1958), and *Desolation Angels* (1965).

the Aeschylus books: On 19 February 1960, TM asked JL to send "the Chicago translations of the Tragedies of Aeschylus," referring to the Greek tragedian whose short plays were performed from 499 B.C. until his death in 456. Later in the year, on 5 December, TM repeated the request for "the Loeb Classical Library edition of Aeschylus, in Greek and English. . . . I want to do some more on his Prometheus, maybe a full dress essay on it, or on him altogether. He is a wonderful tragedian, and a key to so much in western culture." TM's "Prometheus: A Meditation," first published in 1958, later appeared in *RU,* pp. 79–88.

80. TLS-1   May 31, 1960

DEAR J.

A problem has arisen. Bob Giroux thinks that *Problems and Pardons* as a title comes too close to *Disputed Questions* which is the title of the book he now has in galleys, and which will probably be out at the end of summer. He has been asking that *P and P* be put off indefinitely, which of course I do not agree to. Instead, I am going to propose to him a new title for *P and P,* and so I want to propose it to you also. I hope it is not too late to do this. The title I have in mind is better, and I think that perhaps Bob is right in making the point about the two titles, though I am not overpowered by the resemblance personally.

It seems to me that since both Atlas and Prometheus are titans, we can profitably use a title with Titans in it. Hence I propose

The Behavior of Titans
How Titans Behave.

I like the second title better, and I think it is far superior to *P and P.* Though I did like that. Yet it doesn't really convey anything. This does. I realize of course that by now you may have printed up a catalogue with the other title in it. This may be a snag, and perhaps you can work that out with Bob Giroux. But in any case, for what it is worth, I make the proposal of the above change in the title. I hope that can be a simple way of working out the difficulty. (Another possibility: *How Titans Ought to Behave.*)

I just learned of the death of poor old Pasternak. He is a great loss to the world. I suppose he didn't finish any of the things he was working on. I must write to Helen Wolff and find out. He has had a remarkable life, a very significant one. It was amazing that he survived to be seventy. I cannot help thinking that within a few years Russia is going to regard him as one of her very great writers, and *Zhivago* will be widely read there. It is certainly one of the few books worth reading that have come out of Soviet Russia. I do not, as he did, repudiate his earlier work. To my mind *Safe Conduct* is still very remarkable and there are some passages in it which are superb. I must reread his earlier stories too. I hope Pasternak will be a vital link between Russia's past and her future. They need one.

I have been reading the ND book on Brecht's theater. It is very interesting. Have you printed any of Brecht's plays! If you have, I would love to read them. I like his tough style and I think it would do me good. . . . Now I must get this into the mail.

All the best as ever

> Most cordially in Christ
> T O M

Victor [Hammer] did a superb job on *the Solitary Life* and you will be seeing it shortly.

/ · /

Helen Wolff: Publisher at Pantheon Books (and later at Harcourt, Brace), which brought out Pasternak's *Dr. Zhivago* in America.

Safe Conduct: Autobiographical novel by Pasternak published by ND in 1958.

Brecht: Bertolt Brecht (1898–1956), the Expressionist German playwright and poet. Brecht's theatrical techniques emphasized estrangement and alienation and became his significant contributions to modern theater.

The Solitary Life: Issued by Victor Hammer's Stamperia del Santuccio, 1960, in a limited edition of sixty numbered copies.

81. TM TLS-1   June 20, 1960

DEAR J.

Here is the full Suzuki text [for "Wisdom in Emptiness"]. I have had the preface retyped with a lot of necessary changes and I have rewritten my own epilogue. I think the footnotes ought to be right with the text throughout. I wonder if it would not be possible to do quite a few separate offprints that could be stapled together and these I could send around to those souls who would be shocked at some of the other material in the Annual [17]. . . .

I am really glad that this has been salvaged and that we can get along with it.

Glad you and Bob [MacGregor] like Herakleitos [the Obscure]. I think it will really add to *the Behavior of Titans,* though it is not poetic. . . .

These fragments of H[erakleitos] I have amended to suit myself and considerably changed in many places, and furthermore I have strung them together in my own way to make a "poem" out of them. . . . One more thing about the Suzuki dialogue. I think that in order to draw attention to the original Desert Father texts, the sayings alluded to ought to be printed in footnotes with references to the book. This applies especially to the one about the hermit whose disciples caused a robber to be thrown in jail and who told them to go break into the jail and let him out.

In rereading this [exchange] I like it very much and I think Suzuki's essay is really superb. I wish mine were equal to it. He is a great man and a great contemplative (although I don't maintain that this term has an awful lot of meaning).

Hey you ought to see what is happening down here, with my retreat scheme. Some people in Louisville got interested and have designed a very simple and pleasant hermitage type of place, all glass practically, for a place with shade and a lovely view, quiet and out of the way, and now we are going to try the Ford foundation to see if they will subsidize it. I'll explain what I am trying to do and I will mention you among the people who are interested and likely to participate in the gatherings. This might turn into something very nice indeed. Later we might get someone to pay the fare for intellectuals who can't make it and I think that in itself is very important.

One man who was here recently is a very interesting Bishop from Ceylon (native) a tremendously deep character, whose Christianity, on an oriental basis, is really tremendous. Those fellows have something.

Well, I'll try to get this into the mail. God bless all of you.

> Very cordially in Christ
> T O M

/ · /

my retreat scheme: On 18 March 1960, TM wrote to JL about a plan that had "been working on me for some time, of very informally discussing basic things with small groups of intellectuals, writers, etc. Not in order to accomplish some very specific end, but just in order to open up communications between the contemplative life as I live it and the intellectual life or what have you. It is not really something to be dignified by the name of a project, it is not an enterprise, it is not a plan, it is not a campaign, it does not endeavor to sell anybody anything. It is just an ordinary human activity which offers itself as possibly much more fruitful than one might think. The way to approach it would be rather as a kind of visit down here than as a grandiose sort of a project. . . . [W]hy not you, Lax, Kerouac, and a few other assorted people picked by the two of you, make an expedition down here and we could solve the problems of the world for two or three days, perhaps on the edge of some quiet lake. . . ."

82. TLS-1   Nov. 28, 1960

DEAR J.,

. . . Now that I am not working through Curtis Brown I presume that you will take care of foreign editions of the books of mine done by ND. In that case, I want it to be clear that for Spanish rights I have been tied up for all forthcoming books with Editorial Sudamericana . . . Buenos Aires. They will probably get [Ernesto] Cardenal to do *Behavior of Titans.* They will want a copy as soon as it is ready, or even proofs. And for French rights I want my good translator, Marie Tadie . . . Paris to both act as agent and translator. I think this will be easy and ok.

The only reason why I mention this is that in confidence I am getting some funny impressions, indirectly, from certain actions of Bob Giroux at F[arrar,] S[traus] and C[udahy]. He will not play along with this situation at all though he knows my promises and obligations. He doesn't answer questions and he is busy finagling around with other people: I don't what he is doing, but I think he simply wants to dispose of the books according to his own ideas. He even spoke of very kindly taking care of the foreign rights for books published by you. He seemed quite willing to do this. Well, if the question arises, I want you to know that I am not willing, and that I am beginning to see you were right in having doubts about my leaving Curtis Brown. They are no great wonders but at least they save a lot of trouble in one way. Perhaps I may yet have to go back to them.

Do please let me know soon when I would have to deliver the new revised version of *Seeds of Contemplation.* I want to really get at it. It could be a rather notable revision job and we could even call it NEW *Seeds of Contemplation,* though of course the substance of the old book would remain. . . .

Best wishes always—

Cordially in Christ
Tom

Victor [Hammer] has finished a Broadside from Mencius. You will see it I presume, he said he would send some around. . . .

/ · /

not working through Curtis Brown: TM's literary agent, Naomi Burton, had just moved on to Doubleday.

a Broadside: Broadside II: Meng Tzu, Ox Mountain Parable (Stamperia del San-tuccio, 1960). Introduction by TM.

Dec. 17, 1960

DEAR J.,

Well, it is pretty bold of you to let authors write their own blurbs. I did however slightly revise the copy [for *Behavior of Titans*] you sent and passed it on to Bob [Mac-Gregor]. He can appraise it sanely. . . .

Would you make a note for someone to send copies of *Behavior of Titans* when it appears to . . . Dr. Abraham Heschel . . . and half a dozen to Laurens van der Post, to whom it is dedicated. I will send him one of my own copies signed. . . .

I looked at the Japanese "perspectives" and like very much the print ["Symbols of the Tea Ceremony"] by [Sabro] Hasegawa. And I would indeed like to have it. It would add greatly to the simplest and most hidden room of the little house. I have not seen anything of the Aeschylus arriving yet but am very grateful to you for sending it. Of course my commentary on Prometheus is a little confusing. It is certainly not a critique of the Prometheus of Aeschylus (rather of his Zeus). I tried to say that in a little note which will only leave the reader confused, I am afraid. But I am glad your daughter likes Prometheus. I mean the one of Aeschylus. I am all for him. Does she read Sophocles? Like *Antigone?* Wow. I am really going to have to write a little something on the Greek Tragedians. There is a tremendous amount of spirit material there, very real and very powerful.

Bob [MacGregor] sent me your *Wild Anemone [& Other Poems],* which I reproach you for never having told me about. It is a very fine little book. I like your Propertian and Catullan trends, though they are in some sense refreshingly innocent. Or at least very healthy, put it that way. But there are many fine and subtle variations of mood that one enjoys very much in the book.

I unearthed this ad for a book on Zen, and as I am still

very interested in that, and if you have not heard anything saying it is a stupid collection, I wonder if you could get hold of it in some convenient and not too expensive way? You could charge it to royalties if there is any monetary difficulty.

Finally here are two new poems. These are all censored and everything and I rather like them, though they are nothing special. If you think they would find a place somewhere (I am all ready to disagree that they should be sent to *Atlantic*) by all means try them out. Or if you think they are not interesting . . . they could go to *the Commonweal*.

I have to close now and get to choir. A young guy from Lexington is coming over with a table he made, a copy of one Victor [Hammer] made, in V's house.

Very best and most cordial Christmas wishes, blessings, joy, peace, grace to you and the kids and to your wife and to the whole houshold (middle English spelling all of a sudden).

Cordially in Christ,
T O M

/ · /

Heschel: Abraham Joshua Heschel (1907–1972), Warsaw-born Jewish theologian and writer (*The Prophets* [1936], *Man's Search for God* [1954], *God in Search of Man* [1955]). Heschel fled Poland after the Nazi invasion of 1938 and moved to the United States, where he enjoyed a long and distinguished teaching career at the Jewish Theological Seminary in New York. He visited TM at Gethsemani in 1964 for fruitful discussions about the Vatican Declaration on Jewish-Christian relations.

Laurens van der Post: (1906–1996) Distinguished English-South African writer, soldier, explorer, and close friend of the Swiss analytical psychologist Carl Jung. Among his best known books are *Journey to the Interior* (1964), *The Lost World of Kalahari* (1958), and *The Heart of the Hunter* (1961).

Wild Anemone: A pocket-sized edition of twenty-eight short poems by JL (ND, 1957).

84. TLS-2   Norfolk
                                     December 26, 1960

DEAR TOM,

Thanks so much for you fine letter of December 17th, enclosing the two good poems—"Advice to a Young Prophet" and "A Dream at Arles [on the Night of the Mistral]." I particularly like the "Young Prophet" which has a lot of dash, and gets at something important in the social pattern as we now see it. What would you think of our trying them out on Stephen Spender at *Encounter* in London? Have you sent him anything in recent years? I am pretty disgusted with [Ted] Weeks at *The Atlantic*. He returned that poem of yours he had been holding for so long, with one of those picky little comments about how such-and-such a group of lines didn't seem to be quite right. I don't know whether to laugh or cry about Ted's taste in poetry. Ninety percent of the time he prints such anodyne drivel that when something comes along that has a little punch in it, or some verbal color, he pretends to find fault with something in the structure. He is always very polite about you, and asked to see something more, but I'm getting a bit tired of this procedure of his.

I'm dictating this from up in the country, where we had a beautiful "white Christmas," as the saying goes, about ten inches of snow, which is a lot here for this time of year, and good skiing in the forest roads until there was a bit of rain which put a crust on it, so I'm not fully up-to-date on how things are progressing down at the office, but I think there ought to be a proof of the jacket of *Titans* in a day or so, and I'll ask Rhoda to try to snag one for you. I hope you'll like the way it came out. I think our new girl—Gilda—did a very fine job of interpreting my pretty rough sketch. And I do want to say again how grateful I was for the fine jacket copy you provided. . . .

I am so pleased that the Hasegawa print may find a home in your new little house in the woods. I'll shoot it along down as soon as I can find a way to pack it so that it won't get bent.

The two little volumes of the Loeb Aeschylus ought certainly to have arrived by now. . . . I do hope you will write more about the Greek tragedians.

Thank you so much for those kind words about my poems in the little book *[The Wild Anemone & Other Poems]*. I certainly hadn't meant to hide them from you, but, personal as they are, I have come to have a rather detached feeling about these random communications from another orbit. I enjoy them when they turn up, but don't really work at them.

I've ordered the anthology of Zen for you—the one for which you sent the clipping. . . .

Well, I hope that 1961 will be a great year for you, and certainly it should with the wonderful new little house in the woods coming along so well, which I hope to see come spring.

As ever,
J L

/ · /

Weeks: Edward Weeks, an old friend of JL's, editor at the *Atlantic Monthly.*
Rhoda: Rhoda Rissin, JL's assistant at ND.
Gilda: Gilda Kuhlman, ND art director.

85. TLS-1 Jan 4, 1961

DEAR J.,

I got your good letter of Dec. 26th and am glad you liked the poems. I certainly don't think there is any point in sending anything more to Weeks. Spender, yes I did send him one of the other ones, the winter one, when the plant says nothing. I still don't think that has appeared anywhere. Maybe you know of some better bet in England. Why not lump together all the ones you have excepting only the one *Sat[urday] Review* took, and send them to someone good like that?

Yes the Loeb Asechylus is here and I am very happy with it. I so much to want get down to Greek again myself. Have also an awful urge to study Sanskrit and then Persian. . . [.] Yah, it is probably crazy. I will never have the time. But I do have an interesting contact in Pakistan, a Moslem scholar with a lot of interesting information about Sufis, and he says he prays for me in his morning prayer.

Yes the little house is in full swing. All it needs is a bit of paint on the outside, for the rest I am in there as often as I can be and I can't tell you how wonderful it is. Utterly quiet and bright and with a wonderful view of the valley. Nice pine trees all around. It is perfect. The more time I can get to be there the better. I do hope you will get down to see it in the spring. I don't yet have the Hasegawa [print], should it have arrived by this time? I can ask about it. Bob [MacGregor] said he was sending a Japanese mat but I haven't heard anything about it yet. People in Japan were going to send a Sengai calendar and I never saw hide nor hair of it, but maybe it was not sent. You know Sengai? Zen man, artist.

I wonder if I sent you yet an offprint of the thing I did on Creativity. It is now on the way, at any rate, I am sending one. . . .

Do you think this year would be a good time to let Harcourt Brace start on a *Merton Reader* they wanted to do? It seems logical, if they include what will have been done up to the end of 1961 or so.

By the way I am going great guns on the revision of *Seeds.* Have got about half way through having made at least thirty pages of additions. I enjoy doing it and I think it is worth while. Certainly it will be a whole new book, built of course on the old one.

All blessings for the New Year.

Got a nice letter from Pablo Antonio Cuadra who says he is starting a literary magazine and wants to use a lot of my stuff in it.

As ever, Cordially in Christ
T O M

/ · /

the winter one: "Love Winter When the Plant Says Nothing" first appeared in the *Catholic Worker,* 26 (June 1960) and was included in *Emblems of a Season of Fury* (ND, 1963).

an interesting contact in Pakistan: Abdul Aziz. TM's letters to Aziz are collected in *Ground.*

the thing I did on Creativity: "Theology of Creativity," in *LE.*

Cuadra . . . wants to use a lot of my stuff: See Letter #92.

86. TLS-2

March 3, 1961

DEAR J.

First of all the Hasegawa print certainly did arrive and I am overjoyed with it. We have given it a nice cedar frame. . . . It is a wonderful addition to the hermitage which is now bright and pleasant with white paint on the outside walls. You must come and see it. . . . June is the only month that looks like being crowded so far. May is always the best of months.

Victor [Hammer] by the way is coming over tomorrow. He will give a little talk to some of the monks on the kind of attitude they should have to art and work.

Thank you so much for having Claude Fredericks send his admirable little sermon on Eckhart. It is beautifully done and I enjoyed it very much, particularly since it is one that Suzuki was referring to. I am going to write to Fredericks as soon as I can. I have a great desire to get him to print something for us here. I don't know just what, but I am sure something will come along. A broadside or something. Did you get the thing on the atomic bomb I did for Bob Lax? There is to be more of it. That is the best I can do about this non-violence bit. The marchers move and concern me. The worst thing about being in a deeply committed position, such as I am in here, is that one's freedom of action as a individual even in the best of things is reduced to dependence on an institution. I would like very much to say or do something. The book of Gandhi selections will be another opportunity, of course.

The trouble is that there is nothing very clear or unequivocal that a man can do these days, about peace. Everything, every action, every utterance, can be twisted or exploited by some group. Silence to my mind takes shape more and more as a valid witness. But it has to be a certain kind of silence. This is something I have to think about.

The Wisdom of the Desert sans jacket blew in today and I am really happy with it. The end sheets are very pretty and the whole design is pure and great. The Desert Fathers would, I think, heartily approve. It is in their spirit. It is one of the books I am most pleased with. The censor is all right and everything is fine. I wrote to [Cardinal] Spellman about the slip up on *Titans* and have heard nothing. It is after all possible that Bob [Mac-

Gregor] got it through the censors and someone forgot to put the imprimatur in the book.

I quite understand how concerned you must have been, and probably still are, about Bill Williams' plays. I hope everything comes out fine. Did I tell you how much I enjoyed reading his essay on Daniel Boone up in the hermitage? It was very appropriate there, and very moving. Deeply symbolic. Especially with Boones living in the hills all around me and Andy Boone's buzz saw going like mad a quarter of a mile away; (he is my next door neighbor). . . .

> All best wishes always, and
> blessings . . .
> T O M

/ · /

Claude Fredericks: Playwright and handpress printer from Pawlet, Vermont.

Eckhart: Meister Eckhart, born at Hochheim in Thuringia (1260), Dominican friar, preacher, mystic, and a major figure in the history of Christian mysticism.

the thing on the atomic bomb: Published originally in *PAX* (1961), *Original Child Bomb: Points for Meditation to Be Scratched on the Walls of a Cave* came out in an elegant limited edition with drawings by Emil Antonucci and in a trade edition (ND, 1961); it was later reprinted by Unicorn Press (1983).

the book of Gandhi selections: Gandhi on Non-Violence: Selected Texts from Mohandas K. Gandhi's "Non-Violence in Peace and War," edited and with an introduction by TM (ND, 1965).

Bill Williams' plays: JL wrote TM (9 February 1961) and apologized for "having fallen behind in our correspondence" because he had "the proofs of Bill Williams' plays to go over—he isn't able to do them himself, still very ill. . . ."

essay on Daniel Boone: Williams's "The Discovery of Kentucky: Daniel Boone" from *In the American Grain* (ND, 1956).

87. TLS-1   April 5, 1961

DEAR J.

. . . I think that everything possible ought to be done
to get across the idea that *New Seeds [of Contemplation]* is
a whole new book, though it has all the material of the
old one in it. This does not exclude using the same format and a cover that recalls the old one, particularly the
very first one, if we can.

The little paperback anthology celebrating your [ND]
anniversary sounds good. Twenty fifth! I got in pretty
near the ground floor, didn't I? It makes me feel good to
realize that I have been with you all the way since the
first little man and the funny horse appeared on your letterheads. In fact long before Mark [Van Doren] sent you
my poems I had sent you some from St. Bonaventure in
1940 or 41. I don't know if "Candlemas Procession" is
one of the stronger poems. It is a religious one, though.
And which "Song" is it? I wrote so many things called
just "Song." However I don't see any reason for me to
stick my nose into the choosing. Hayden Carruth has his
reasons and I will respect them all right. So go right
ahead, unless you yourself think there is some better
poem to substitute for "Candlemas."

I got a very nice letter and a long poem from Jack Mills
and will be answering him when I crawl out from under
the big pile of mail. I do look forward to seeing you both
some time soon. May would certainly be the best month.
I leave your poor Aunt in God's hands and to His mercy:
He knows best what He intends in her regard. Anyway,
we will plan on a visit sometime, when you can make
it. . . .

I would very much like to try the Atom Bomb piece
with Claude Fredericks. I guess I will send him a copy.
[Robert] Lax has suddenly gone off to France and wants
to print it "when he gets back." As you say it is a terrible

and central issue. This country is getting sicker all the time. I have begun to hear about these John Birch people. In fact I think I am already on their list. Well, you have already published a confession and I have only to sign it. Somebody was sending me complaints and reproaches because I came out in support of the Dean of the Vanderbilt Theol[ogical] Seminary when he resigned on account of the expulsion of a negro student. The country is scared and stupefied. They can't do anything to stop the real Reds, so they compensate by plaguing poor college professors and getting them thrown out of their jobs. Because this *looks* like "results." Thus they delude themselves and try to delude others. Meanwhile the really dangerous people have a nice smoke screen behind which to maneuver. . . .

I have been taking things easily, relatively speaking. You will be glad to hear that things are getting under way on a project of selections from Chuang Tzu about which I spoke to Bob [MacGregor]. I have got in touch with a wonderful Chinese Catholic scholar, John Wu, a marvelous person, and he is going to translate the passages I select, while I will do an essay on Chuang. I think this will be most rewarding and am delighted with the work so far, though for my part it has been only reading and note making. . . .

All the best always. Victor [Hammer] is fine. I hope to see him again soon.

> Cordially, as ever, in Christ
> T O M

{I'll try to drop Doc Williams a line—sometime.}

/ · /

The little paperback anthology: *A New Directions Reader,* edited by Hayden Carruth and JL (ND, 1964). The "Song" Carruth selected for the anniversary anthology was TM's "Song from Crossportion's Pastoral."

your poor Aunt: JL's aunt was seriously ill. She died later in the year.

a confession: "A Signed Confession of Crimes Against the State," in *The Behavior of Titans* (ND, 1961).

selections from Chuang Tzu: The Way of Chuang Tzu (ND, 1965), with "Interpretations" by TM. Chuang Tzu was a fourth–third-century B.C. Chinese poet and philosopher whose writings embody the philosophy of the legendary Lao Tzu, founder of Taoism.

John Wu: Scholar, diplomat, and member of the National Legislature of the Republic of China, Wu was born in 1899 in Ningpo, China, and served as a research professor of Asian Studies at Seton Hall University. TM's letters to Wu are included in *Ground.*

88. TLS-1   July 1, 1961

DEAR J.

Good to hear from you. Lax wrote in the same mail and said Antonucci had designed something already for *Original Child [Bomb].* I told him to get in touch with you. I think what we ought to do is go ahead with the Lax[/]Antonucci project as they are moving with it. You can figure out with him how it is to work. Originally you remember I gave the thing to Lax for his little broadside magazine and I suppose this is what is happening. I would like to let Ferlinghetti have it of course, but since Lax has been promised it and has it and is going ahead first, then that seems to settle the matter.

In any case one principle I have to work on at the moment is to remain dissociated from any and every group whatever, including Catholic ones if possible. Just to appear on my own in odd places and when occasion demands, especially when it is a question of statements like this, of which I shall probably have to make several. They should be made in the air, so to speak, without any connection with anybody else's statements. Hence I cannot get into any protest group. Much as I sympathize and much as I would enjoy doing so.

I liked Ferlinghetti's long Cuba poem and other material in that connection. Say hello to Bro Antoninus [William Everson], and while you are there you ought to look up Czeslaw Milosz who might do a very interesting collection of Polish poets for you, or something of the kind. He is in the dept of Slavic languages at Berkeley and Bill [Everson] knows his address as I told him to visit him.

Pretty busy with people coming in a lot, maybe too many people now. That is an angle I am going to have to watch because if I get swamped in that way I won't have time to write any more. So it sort of defeats itself. . . .

Sorry for poor old Patchen. I'll at least pray for him. And everybody.

All the best. In haste,

Always cordially in Christ
T O M

/ · /

Czeslaw Milosz: TM felt that the Nobel laureate Czeslaw Milosz (1911–) was "one of the most important Polish poets and writers of the twentieth century." After seeking political asylum from his native Poland in France, 1951, Milosz moved to the United States in 1960. TM read Milosz's *The Captive Mind* in 1958 and considered it "the most intelligent and stimulating book it has been my good fortune to read in a very long time." Of the hundreds of writers TM corresponded with, the letters of Milosz and TM stand out as especially insightful and penetrating. TM letters to Milosz are collected in *Courage.*

89. T L S - 1   July 22, 1961

D E A R J . ,

It is good to get your roundabout letters from the coast, and it sounds great out there. Especially about the Rexroth autobiography which ought to be his best book and certainly the one that will make the biggest splash. As you say, it might mean a lot of libel suits. . . . [sic]

I look forward to seeing it. I'll ask Naomi about it at Doubleday.

Here is a poem about Auschwitz which I am also sending to Ferlinghetti. This he can have for his magazine if he wants it. Only it will probably have to go under an assumed name if he wants it now, because if I try to get it past the censors it will take a couple of months more and then may not get past, though I don't know. It may seem silly to have to fuss around with such a lot of trivialities and I hate to do it, but remember if I don't cooperate with them they have the power to shut me up completely and I prefer to retain some power of expression in case I might need it some time. I wrote to him about the assumed name and all the rest.

Meanwhile you must have received from Lax the wonderful plan and layouts and design [for *Original Child Bomb*] by Antonucci and I hope you liked them. I hope you want to go along with the idea of a little book. Presumably you have got in contact with Lax about this, and I am eager to hear how the idea is developing.

It is getting hot here now, after all. Today we are going on eastern standard time, from central, which seems a little screwy to me. But all the people around here are involved in it and we think we have to go along with them. I suppose in a way we do. But we used to stay off daylight saving time, and had an hour's difference then. Well, it is all in the head I guess. Not mine, though. I can't cope with such wonders. . . .

All the best of everything, as ever, and God bless you. Hope you can drop by at the end of August. . . .

Cordially in Christ
Tom

/ · /

the Rexroth autobiography: "I have been reading [a typescript of] Rexroth's autobiography," JL wrote TM (14 July 1961), "which really is extraordinary.

The only trouble is that nobody will ever believe that he hasn't made it all up, because he has done so many strange things in one lifetime, and has met so many really weird and wonderful people." Doubleday would publish Rexroth's memoirs under the ironic title *An Autobiographical Novel* in 1966.

a poem about Auschwitz: "Chant to Be Used in Processions Around a Site with Furnaces," which Ferlinghetti published in the inaugural number of the *Journal for the Protection of All Beings* (1961). See Letter #91.

90. TLS-3   Salinas, California
                                                        August 11, 1961

DEAR TOM

Please forgive my delay in replying to your good letter of July 27th. I have been moving about a bit out here— and am still in California—and I have fallen behind with the correspondence.

Most recently I have been down seeing [Robert] Hutchins and [W. H.] Ferry at Santa Barbara. We talked a great deal about you and I showed them that wonderful poem ["Chant to Be Used. . . "] you wrote about the German extermination camps, and they were deeply moved by it. I hope I did not do wrong in letting them make copies of it. They are most eager to see the "Bomb-piece" but, unfortunately, I didn't have a copy of it with me. As you may know, Hutchins has transferred the Fund for the Republic into the Center for the Study of Democratic Institutions, and they have a kind of "think tank" in an old estate at Santa Barbara, with great minds like Scott Buchanan and others grouped there to think about the major issues of the day. They have been getting out a wonderful series of pamphlets, sort of study papers based on their deliberations, and are doing a great job, I feel, trying to figure out what needs to be done with our "institutions" to make them serviceable in the present, modern complicated times we live in. It occurs to me that you might like to see some of these papers they have been getting out, and, if you would let me know, I will ask that they be sent to you. One of the men there is a priest, but I didn't get to meet him, and failed to write down his name. As a matter of fact, I think they have several Catholic thinkers on their advisory boards, one of whom, I believe, is Father Courtney Murray. Do you know him or his works?

As I was there and got the feel of all this high thinking that is going on, I thought that you ought to be there too, helping them with it, but, of course, that is out of the question. The next best thing would be if Hutchins or Ferry could come to see you. Hutchins does not travel too much these days, Ferry does, and I believe he is very eager to come down there, if you could get him an invitation. As far as international politics go, he is the most advanced of the group, being an advocate of unilateral disarmament. He has published a number of articles on this topic, and has given speeches around which have raised up quite a ruckus. The group is very much divided on this crucial issue, as a number of them still seem to believe in "preparedness." They do not seem to hold to the view, as Ferry and I do, that if everybody prepares just as hard as they can prepare something is bound to go boom by accident.

Your thoughts about what we should do about the *Bomb* book were fine, and I agree with them, and have written the necessary letters to New York, and hope that everything will move along smoothly with Antonucci. This, then, could be a very handsome book, using his lay-outs, perhaps a couple of hundred copies, or a few more, which you would sign the sheets of, and we would sell them at a good price. This would be necessary to afford the kind of job that Antonucci wants on his design. I think that is wonderfully generous of you that you would want Antonucci to have all the royalties, and I hope this will spur him on to the work. Though, I shouldn't say that—I'm sure he would do it for love and nothing, he being such a wonderful person. I hope it will be time enough for us to work out the contract for all this when I get back to New York early in September. But I am still hoping to get down to see you first, on my way back east. This would probably be toward the last days of August. . . . At the moment, I am hung up in a small town in California, with trouble with the transmission of my car, and great difficulty in getting the repair work done as the mechanics quite naturally feel that they have first responsibility to take care of the farm vehicles that are broken down, which are needed for the harvests which are now coming in. The town is loaded with Mexican agricultural workers, and their lot does not appear to me to be a very happy one, though I judge it is some better out here than with the ones which work the East Coast from Florida up north. At least here, there appears to be a real effort on the part of the local authorities to provide decent housing for them.

While I was in Santa Barbara, I met a most fascinating young Spaniard, Miguel Moreno, who is doing some very appealing religious paintings. He is one of those Catholics who no longer goes to church but has great faith, which is apparent in his paintings. His wife works for Hutchins at the Center, and they have given him an old barn on the place to paint. I am hoping to be able to buy from him one of his little altar triptyches, and then to get it photographed, and if you like it, you can have it for down there. . . . What he is doing is kind of a new twist on folk painting, and most appealing, to me at least. On the other hand, it might not "go down" with some of your colleagues, because he distorts the figures, and things like that. But certainly, he is a deeply religious man and we had some wonderful talks about Spanish literature, which he knows very thoroughly. His father was an old-line Spanish socialist, and he himself fought in the civil war in the Loyalist Army and then fled out of Spain and has been living here.

I was glad to hear about the "Hagia Sophia" that Victor [Hammer] is doing. I hope we can see Victor when I come down.

Well, I must trot off to see if anything is being done about my car, which I rather doubt. I suppose if I stomped and hollered things would move faster, but I can't really believe that whether I get to San Francisco a few days sooner really matters that much.

As ever,
J L

/ · /

Ferry: William H. "Ping" Ferry (1910–1995), born in Detroit and educated at Dartmouth College, Ferry and TM hit it off from the start of their friendship in 1961 when Ferry began to correspond with TM, visit him regularly at Gethsemani, and shape his political consciousness. Ferry collected TM's letters to him in *Letters from Tom* (Fort Hill Press, 1984). See also *Ground.*

Scott Buchanan: (1895–1968), Philosopher, author of *Poetry and Mathematics* (1929), Dean of St. John's College, Annapolis, and a key figure in the extraordinary group Hutchins assembled in Montecito, California.

Father Courtney Murray: Rev. John Courtney Murray (1904–1967), Catholic theologian and professor at Woodstock College, a Jesuit institution. Murray's statements on foreign policy issued by the Center for the Study of Democratic Institutions (where Murray served as a Fellow)—e.g., *Foreign Policy and the Free Society*—had an influence on the Kennedys and Henry Luce, publisher of *Time.*

91. TLS-2   Aug. 18, 1961

DEAR J.

Thanks for your good letter. By now, as you know, a series of accidents has led to the publication of the

Auschwitz poem both in the *Catholic Worker* and Ferlin-ghetti's *Journal [for the Protection of All Beings]*. And it is still not censored. Since I am in the clear I have no sor-rows about it, though I may get into some trouble.

What you wrote about your visit to Hutchins, Ferry etc. is very interesting. I should very much like to see their pamphlets, and if you give me the address I shall write asking Ferry or any of them to drop in here. You will have to give me the full name, the address, and all.

Personally I am more and more concerned about the question of peace and war. I am appalled by the way everyone simply sits around and acts as though everything were normal. It seems to me that I have an enormous responsibility myself, since I am read by a lot of people, and yet I don't know what to begin to say and then I am as though bound and gagged by the censors, who though not maliciously reactionary are just obtuse and slow. This feeling of frustration is terrible. Yet what can one say? If I go around shouting "abolish war" it will be meaningless. Yet at least some one has to say that. I am in no position to plan a book about it. There is no purpose to a silly book of editorial-like platitudes. Some more poems like Ausch-witz, maybe. But the thing is to be *heard*. And everything is perfectly soundproof and thought proof. We are all doped right up to the eyes. And words have become use-less, no matter how true they may be. But when it comes to action, then I am more helpless than anyone: except within my own very limited sphere of prayer, with which I have no quarrel at all. That is perhaps the last great power that can do anything: and the less said about it the better. Not only prayer but holiness, which I don't have. We are all wound up in lies and illusions and as soon as we begin to think or talk the machinery of falsity operates automat-ically. The worst of all is not to know this, and apparently a lot of people don't.

I sent a sermon on "the Good Samaritan" to Claude

Fredericks. I don't mention this as a move to save the world, but just as evidence that I have given CF something to print. . . .

What Miguel Moreno paints doesn't have to go down with the other monks, I can always put it somewhere where it isn't their business. He sounds good and I am eager to see a picture of his work. There must be quite a lot of people like that around, without too many people knowing of them.

I don't want Ferlinghetti to be paying me anything for that poem. If at all, he can send some books. In any case I will send him a list of books which he can charge to the royalty account. . . .

All blessings and good wishes to everyone out there.

Cordially in Christ
TOM

92. TLS-2   Sept 19, 1961

DEAR J.,

First of all the book of Denise Levertov just arrived. I think her book from Jonathan Williams was the best I got in that whole lot and this one is one of the best you have published. This is poetry that really means something to me, not just poetry I like with my head, poetry that I intellectually approve, that I can say "is good." She is one of the few poets into whose experience I can enter fully and with complete agreement and total acceptance. I think there are really very few poets I can read like this today, so I think it is worth stating, and I want her to know my gratitude and appreciation. I think the Toltec poem about the artist is a tremendous beginning and completely wise. I will tell everybody [what] I respect about this book. She sees things as they are, in their spiritual nature, not with what Blake called single vision. But what is not seen in the seen.

I am enclosing a thing I am just sending to Caudra. It is a kind of tirade, maybe too bitter. It could go in the *Last Words of Everybody,* along with the bomb piece maybe and Auschwitz and other things I will write soon perhaps. I wonder if this is just a silly and bitter thing, or if it has value. When things are as serious as they are now it is perhaps better not just to sound off for the sake of protesting or making one's voice heard. Let me know what you think.

It could go of course to Ferlinghetti except hold on, because Fr. Abbot read much of the first issue of the *Journal [for the Protection of All Beings]* and said it was dirty and I couldn't be going on publishing in something like that. They can have the bomb piece as they already got it. . . .

I am very sorry about the people at Farrar Straus, and the trouble you must go to. However you are in business and you have to consider what the Hindus teach about *Artha.* There are hard headed actions that have to be done without compunction. You simply have to stand for your rights and do so effectively. No point in going at it with doubts. Certainly you will feel distaste but do not be divided, to your own distress.

The Hammers were over again Saturday and told of your visit. We had a good time except it was shortened by the new time change here. Here I am asking for books again. There is another Tuttle book on Zen *[First Zen Reader]* which looks v. good. . . .

I could really use it if it can be got without trouble, and if it is expensive just charge to the royalty account. I guess we can afford it all right. I don't want to put you to a lot of expense and trouble.

Best wishes as always, and God bless you,

In Christ
TOM

{Here is a poem too, not very good, might conceivably go in *Last Words of Everybody.*}

/ · /

Denise Levertov: (1923–). TM refers to Levertov's *Overland to the Islands* (Jargon, 1958). ND published thirteen Levertov titles. She was born in Ilford, Essex, and lived in London briefly after World War II before moving to the United States in 1948.

Jonathan Williams: (1929–), Student of Charles Olson's at Black Mountain College in the early 1950s. Poet and book designer, Williams was executive director of the Jargon Society (Highlands, NC) and editor of Jargon Books, devoted to publishing fine editions of non-commercial books by poets like Louis Zukofsky, Denise Levertov, and Robert Duncan, among others.

a thing I am just sending to Caudra: "A Letter to Pablo Antonio Caudra Concerning Giants," translated into Spanish by Jose Coronel Urtecho, first appeared in *El Pez y La Serpiente* (1962). A condemnation of the Cold War, the "Letter" is TM's most incisive piece of political commentary.

Last Words of Everybody: TM would eventually split this material into two books. He edited the prose passages together into *Conjectures of a Guilty Bystander* (1966); the poems became *Emblems of a Season of Fury.*

the trouble you must go to: A conflict over publishing rights involving another author. "A friend of ours is trying to push me around," JL wrote on 12 September 1961, "or rather, I prefer to think, his associates are using him to do so. . . ."

93. TLS-1   Oct 24, 1961

DEAR J.

This letter is overdue and there are a thousand things to say. Shooting all over the target I'll begin with Ferry who wrote yesterday and said he would like to come, and I will expect him. He sent some rather good things including a very fine speech by Lewis Mumford. Sounds very sympathetic and eager to work on ideas, even though this is a pretty rough time for ideas. Things have gone pretty far. But there is no use giving up our basic task, because nothing else makes sense anyway. I refuse to join the readers of *Life* and *Time* running around making loud and incoherent noises.

The monies arrived and I am grateful, certainly it was agreed that I would pay for the offprint [of the D. T. Suzuki exchange in *New Directions 17*] out of those same monies, to wit royalties thereof in the first part and in the second party of the part as mentioned hereinafter in the clause. So everyone is happy, and I am glad to have the offprints.

Also many thanks for the books which have come, not only from Ungar but also from Tuttle. All fine. And Henry Miller's too, which I have read mostly with a great deal of interest and sympathy, especially the essay on bread which is one of the best. He wrote Bob [Mac-Gregor] that he liked the Suzuki exchange and this was encouraging. [Miller's] "Murder the Murderer" is in many ways like something I wrote at the time, on a much smaller scale, in *the Secular Journal* (did you ever get that by the way?) It will be in the *[Thomas Merton] Reader.* Editor of the *Reader* is down here now and we are working on the final details. We are *finalizing* the *Reader,* I mean. Got to use the right language.

Man is now typing a little book I got for you[:] *Clement of Alexandria,* introduction and translations about twenty five pages, selections from his *Protreptikos,* most interesting both to philosophers, religion people, Zens, and Classical scholars. I think you will like this. I think of it as a small format, discreet little book, perhaps a little bigger than your poems usually are, I mean your own bks. of poems, but small and unassuming like that. It could be very attractive. The ms. will be along in a few days.

I also want to put everything aside and work on the *Gandhi [on Non-Violence]* now and in November. Probably won't have time until next week, but once I get at it I ought to have it done in short order, meaning of course *finalized.*

As to *Last Words[,]* well there has been some work on that too, but assuming Divine Providence has given us a little time before *everything* is finalized. . . . [sic]

. . . I am sending you a recent piece ["The Machine Gun in the Fallout Shelter"] of topical import, very seasonal for the autumn fallout season. Don't do anything with, just peruse and we'll see later if I can get it censored. If you have any ideas however by all means let me know. Yes, "the Letter [to Pablo Antonio Cuadra] on [sic] Giants" is certainly patchy and too vehement to be perfectly straight and clear at the end. There is a lot that can be done about it, and I am waiting to hear from Cuadra. . . .

Again thanks for the monies, the books, and everything else. God bless you.

As ever, in Christ
T O M

/ · /

Lewis Mumford: An American intellectual and critic whose books—*Technics and Civilization* (1934), *The City in History* (1961), and *The Myth of the Machine* (1967, 1970), among many others—are highly regarded works of cultural criticism and intellectual history. Although he never received degrees, Mumford (1895–1990) attended Columbia University and New York University. He contributed an essay, "The Morals of Extermination," to a book edited by TM on the threat of nuclear war, an idea TM hatches in the next letter.

the essay on bread: Henry Miller's "The Staff of Life" in *Remember to Remember* (ND, 1961).

Reader: A Thomas Merton Reader, edited by Thomas P. McDonnell (Harcourt, 1962).

Clement of Alexandria: Clement of Alexandria: Selections from the Protreptikos. An essay and translation by TM (ND, 1962).

94. TLS-1   Oct. 30, 1961

DEAR J.

An idea has occurred to me for a ND paperback for next spring, on Peace. It could be a kind of anthology of good straight articles on peace and on the struggle against war at the present time. I could contribute besides the little mimeograph I sent you the other day, another article on peace ["Peace: A Religious Responsibility"] which is being typed up now, and the *Catholic Worker* article, "The Root of War," which is a chapter of *New Seeds* with a special beginning added to situate it in the present crisis.

We might add the pamphlet they [The Center for the Study of Democratic Institutions] did at Santa Barbara, "Community of Fear." Ferry also sent a fine talk ["The Morals of Extermination"] by Mumford. I could get something from Erich Fromm, think I have an offprint around. And seven or eight other current pieces, maybe Tillich and Niebuhr have something, and Ferlinghetti's outfit. It would be a hasty job but it is emergency pamphleteering and it would have to be done as fast as possible. Do you agree? I think you will. I will be glad to hear from you and your ideas about this.

Just got in touch with a small outfit called the Fellowship of Reconciliation, practically nothing, but good. They want to do "The Root of War" as a pamphlet of their own. They need permission of ND for this as it is in *New Seeds.* I told them to write pronto to the NY office. And that they would get permission without difficulty.

The man [Thomas P. McDonnell] was down here editing the *Merton Reader.* I think it will be a satisfactory job. We are of course using a lot of ND material and permissions will be asked for in due course. It is satisfying to try to gather in one book all one's most urgent ideas and statements, as well as some more placid material to back it up and give perspective. Maybe this is the self love of the middle aged author, but I haven't time to go picking on my soul for it, God will take care of any deordination there may be. The lesson of this time is first of all to leave absolutely everything to Him, while attending to your own job whatever it may be. I am a contemplative and a writer, and consequently my job is to speak as one and write as one in the present situation in which there is a massive denial of all the values of the spirit that man has ever possessed including a denial of Christ, implicitly, even by some of the most solid and respectable "Christians." We all have the hammers and nails in our hands and are ready to go to it with the utmost gusto, while in our hearts compassionating with some image of a Jesus Who is a million miles away from the scene. . . . [sic] This is the crucifixion. . . . What a horror. No wonder people are unable to see it.

Do let me know right away about the paperback idea. . . .

These days I seem to have gone around some kind of a corner and run into a clear straight stretch, like in Nevada. So vrroom.

All the best, and all blessings,

Cordially in Christ
Tom

/ · /

Erich Fromm: A Berlin-trained psychoanalyst and social philosopher, Erich Fromm (1900–1980) left Nazi Germany in 1934 for the United States, where he taught at several universities before taking a permanent post as professor of psychoanalysis at the National University of Mexico, Cuernavaca. Among his many books, Fromm's *Escape from Freedom* (1941) and especially *The Sane Society* (1955) shaped TM's social conscience. TM wrote to Fromm in 1954 after reading his *Psychoanalysis and Religion* (1950); despite their differences over religion, they carried on a rich, mutually rewarding correspondence until TM's death. See *Ground.*

Tillich: Paul Tillich (1886–1965)—Prussian-born author, philosopher, theologian—who taught philosophy and theology at Prussian and German universities until his leadership in the Religious Socialist movement brought him into conflict with National Socialism. He emigrated to the United States in 1933 and enjoyed a distinguished teaching career at the Union Theological Seminary, Harvard University, and the University of Chicago Divinity School.

Neibuhr: Reinhold Niebuhr (1892–1971), influential American minister, liberal, theologian, writer, professor of theology and philosophy of religion at Union Theological Seminary, and founder of Americans for Democratic Action and Fellowship of Socialist Christians. Niebuhr's efforts to integrate Christian ethics with a pragmatic political philosophy (e.g., *Moral Man and Immoral Society: A Study in Ethics and Politics* [1932]) had much greater influence among secular politicians than Catholic figures like TM.

Fellowship of Reconciliation: An affiliate of the Catholic Peace Fellowship, a social justice activist organization whose leader, James Forest, became a close friend of TM's in 1961. The FOR printed a monthly magazine, *Fellowship*, that published several of TM's anti-war essays and poems. TM considered *Fellowship* "a very good little publication and the FOR . . . impresses me as a living and efficacious movement. . . ." (*Ground*, p. 259).

95. TLS-2

Norfolk
November 3, 1961

DEAR TOM,

. . . I'm most enthusiastic about your idea of a little paperback anthology of pieces on peace. Do let's by all means try to get it up, and as quickly as possible, and I would like to urge you to bring Ferry into the picture, as I think he would be invaluable in adding some range, through his contacts. He must certainly be in touch with a considerable number of brilliant people who are thinking along these lines whom neither you nor I know about it.

This idea fits into something that had been in my mind about a year and a half ago. I wanted to do then such a little anthology whose focus would be in terms of satire against what I call the "Pentagonian" mentality. I gave it up because I just wasn't able to lay my hand on enough really first-rate material. Now, of course, things have gotten past the point where one can laugh at them. This collection, I feel, should be a direct appeal to reason and Christian morality. . . .

Another good person to ask for advice, though not to be a collaborator exactly, would be Carey McWilliams at *The Nation*. They have published some really remarkable pieces along these lines. . . .

I'm glad to hear that the Fellowship of Reconciliation people—I have heard of them vaguely myself, but am not just sure what their line is—want to do your "The Roots of War" out of *New Seeds* as a pamphlet. I assume that you want them to have this permission for free, which is certainly all right with us, in such a good cause. But perhaps Rhoda [Rissin] can work it out with them so that they will give a good plug to the *New Seeds* somewhere in the pamphlet.

I was glad to hear that the *Merton Reader* was coming along so well, and that you are satisfied with the editing job that has been done on it. Here again, I see no problem about the permission. . . .

Going back to the peace anthology—have you any ideas yet on a good title for it? The conference with the Lippincott salesmen will be coming along about Thanksgiving time, and I know they will be excited about this, and it would be good to be able to tag it with a definite title. They start their road trips just after Christmas, so we would want to have even more information for them then.

As ever,
J L

96. TLS-1   Nov 25, 1961

DEAR J.

Have not yet received the dictated letter you spoke of
with copy of letter from Ferry. Has it gone astray somewhere? However I did just get letter from Ferry with a
fine article by Gerald Piel, publisher of the *Scientific American,* which is a gem for the book. This we must get.
{Ferry says he is sending you a copy.}

Furthermore I have run across an excellent small book
of articles on *Nuclear Weapons and the Christian Conscience*
by English Catholics. It is edited by one Walter Stein, and
the contributors are young English Catholic intellectuals,
mostly university professors, who think straight and write
well. It is much better than some of the good but loose,
informal and meandering material by some of the older
English Catholics. I want very much to use this whole
book, 6 articles. I have already written to the publisher
[The Merlin Press] tentatively, it came out this summer,
but I don't want it to be snapped up by someone else. . . .

It is really very good. With this and the material we
already thought of, supposing we can get it and Ferry
approves of it, I think we almost have enough for a book.
Just one more guy I want to try is Gordon Zahn, at Loy-
ola U in Chicago. He is very fine. . . .

This is certainly enough for a good solid book. Ed Rice
sent me one that has been brought out just now, *God and
the H Bomb,* with Tillich and [Bishop Fulton J.] Sheen and
all the big wheels in it, religious like. It is quite fair, I have
not gone all through it. But I think with our stuff we are
much more solid and tight and hit a great deal harder.

In a word, I think as soon as we get this stuff together
and look at it in a bunch we will be ready to roll. And I
will get busy on the preface when I see it all together.
Will have to get the preface in the works way ahead of
time because of the censors.

Ferry gave no sign of objecting to the [Machine Gun in the Fallout] Shelter piece, on the contrary liked it a lot. Probably Giants, but I am not considering that for the bk. though it is being grabbed all over Latin America and translated into German.

Last Words is coming along good. Will consist of three parts. The first two come from notebooks I am typing up, are called "Songs of Innocence," "Songs of Experience." Third part would be "Endings and Elegies," and I think could include "Original Child," Auschwitz, poems like . . . "Hemingway" and "Thurber" [elegies] and others of that type and maybe a finale not yet written.

All the best, in Christ
TOM

/ · /

Gordon Zahn: Sociologist and pacifist, Gordon Zahn's biography of Franz Jagerstaetter, an Austrian conscientious objector who refused to fight in World War II and was beheaded after a military trial in 1943, moved TM so much that he mentioned it repeatedly throughout his growing correspondence to peace activists during the early 1960s. Zahn studied at the Catholic University of America and Harvard University. In 1980, he edited *The Nonviolent Alternative,* a revised edition of *Thomas Merton on Peace,* a collection of TM's writings on the principles of peace, non-violence, and Christian conscience, since updated by William Shannon, ed., Thomas Merton, *Passion for Peace: The Social Essays* (Crossroad, 1995).

Last Words: See Letter #92.

97. TLS-2   Dec 1, 1961

DEAR J.,

Carey McWilliams [at *The Nation*] wrote suggesting I do an article for him. I thought I would try a review article on that little book I told you about, *Nuclear Weapons and Christian Conscience* but I am waiting to hear what he has to say about it. This will have to be censored of course.

"The Letter to Cuadra on [sic] Giants" has on the other hand got through the censors (in England) and is therefore cleared. I think this really would go good in *the Nation,* though not their usual kind of thing. I would very much like to see it there. . . .

Thanks for the quote from Henry Miller. Well, that is a testimonial. I am really warmed by it. To me that is an indication that I am perhaps after all a Christian. I believe that this element of inner recognition that cuts right through apparent external barriers and divisions is of crucial importance today. It is in this kind of recognition that Christ is present in the world, and not just in the erection and definition of barriers that say where He is and where He isn't. *There are no such barriers.* Those who imagine them too literally are in illusion. Not that the Church isn't visible, but there is that little man in Boston who says that only the ones who are members and Catlicks are really saved: and he is excommunicated for saying it. . . .

. . . All the best always, and of course warm regards to Henry M.

Yrs in Christ

T o m

/ · /

the quote from Henry Miller: JL (27 November 1961): "In a recent letter from Henry Miller to Bob [MacGregor], Henry speaks very warmly of you, as he always does, as follows: 'Was happy to get the new annual with Merton's fragment on the Desert Fathers. Do give him warm greetings from me whenever you write him. I feel closer to him, his way of thinking, than any American writer I know of. . . .' "

98. TLS-1   Dec. 15, 1961

DEAR J.

I have two new ideas about the paperback, which I think should now be called *The Morals of Extermination,* using the title of the other Mumford article which is very fine.

First: It would be wonderful to get some of Ben Shahn's "Lucky Dragon" pictures and run them in the middle of the book somewhere, perhaps with a note by him. They are on exhibit at some gallery in New York and it ought to be easy to get reproductions and permission to use them. I think this would really make something great out of the book; as you know Ben Shahn paints pictures about the Japanese fishing boat that got loaded with fallout from the Bikini test and he has statements written all over the pictures. I think this would be tremendous, and would make the difference between a good book and a really remarkable one.

Another idea, would be to get a certain memorandum of Senator [William] Fulbright to the Senate this last summer, from the *Congressional Record,* something about the Generals getting their fingers into everything in sight and out of sight. It is apparently a very forceful statement. . . . This too I think ought to get in to the book. Can you hunt it up some way?

I asked Mark Van Doren for a piece on the subject when he was here and he said he might do it. I hope he does. . . .

The Norman Cousins articles are really fine. I hate to do so much on fallout shelters but these three editorials are really powerful and we ought to use them, maybe quite edited and somewhat shortened. What do you think about this?

Ferry came up with a couple of names I told you about, like Sir Watson something who invented radar but

I would hate to ask an important personage to write something special, and then find it was not quite what we wanted. I have not written to him yet, I am waiting to hear how you feel about it.

The first copy of *New Seeds* got to me the other day and I like it very much. I wrote to Gilda [Kuhlman] telling her how much I liked her cover.

Only problem I have now is that the book I have been typing up is not turning out at all to be *Last Words of Everybody*[.] [T]hat will have to come in a month or two, I got clean out of that mood, and this is simply a collection of quite direct notes on the whole business and it is called *The Guilty Bystander.* I will keep at this and it ought to be finished and on the way to you soon.

All the best wishes. This really is [a] Christmas card now, I guess. Merry Christmas, and stay out of all shelters. . . .

> All the best, yours cordially in Christ
> T O M

/ · /

The Morals of Extermination: ND published the book under the title *Breakthrough to Peace: Twelve Views on the Threat of Thermonuclear Extermination,* edited and with an introduction by TM, who also wrote the "Notes on Contributors." The book included essays by TM, Lewis Mumford, Tom Stonier, Norman Cousins, Erich Fromm and Michael Maccoby, Howard Gruber, Gordon Zahn, Walter Stein, Herbert Butterfield, Allan Forbes, Jr., Joost A. M. Meerloo, and Jerome Frank.

Ben Shahn: (1898–1969), Russian-born American artist and political satirist.

Norman Cousins: (1912–1990), Author and American editor of the *Saturday Review.* TM combined Cousins's editorials into a single essay and included it in the "Bomb book" *(Breakthrough to Peace)* under the title "Shelters, Survival and Common Sense."

The Guilty Bystander: Conjectures of a Guilty Bystander (1966).

99. TLS-2   Dec 31, 1961

DEAR J.

Thanks for your last letter. I will be eagerly expecting you on the 15th, and we will go over all the material together. I still don't have the piece from Fromm, or one promised by Dr. Rollo May. Nor have I heard at all from two people I wrote to, Etienne Gilson and a Protestant theologian, Norman Gottwald. They will be too late if they come through at all. What are we going to do about some of [C.] Wright Mills' *Causes of World War III?* Are you the one that had Martin Corbin send me some copies of *Liberation?* There is some good stuff in these issues I have here. We can take care of all that when you come.

Now about the big question of censors. It is a big question, so I had better try to make it clear.

First of all I have apparently shocked both you and Ferry and given you the idea that I am indulging in some kind of monkey business. Not at all. We have some very strict censorship laws, and I have hitherto been very conscientious about keeping to them. But I have absolutely no intention of keeping laws that we don't have. A subject after all retains his rights, as long as his Superior leaves him the liberty which is his. If the Superior wants me to refrain from something, he is in a very good position to make me refrain. It is understood that if I do something of which he might personally disapprove, if he has not forbidden me to do it, and continues to let me do it, then he cannot complain if I do it. But I do not even have any indication that in this case the Order would be completely unwilling to have me do what I am doing. On the contrary, it is well known and tolerated that mimeographed material be circulated without censorship. This is the common practice and most would agree that to interfere with this would certainly be abusive—except in a case where something definitely out of line was getting circulated, and then the powers that be can always take plenty effective measures against it, in that particular case.

Besides that, there are a lot of other things that are not normally censored at all. Most magazine articles, actually, are never censored. But in our Order the rules happen to be stricter. Yet even our censorship statute provides that material that is to be printed in a publication with very limited circulation does not need to be censored at all.

What I envisaged was the purely private circulation of some mimeographed copies of the material I mentioned, and this certainly conflicts with no known regulation of the censors and with no established practice. On the contrary, I have a perfect right to do it, unless forbidden by the Abbot here, which is not likely.

Finally what I am up against is not the formal matter of "faith and morals" and the possibility of doctrinal error, but rather the very sweeping and I think arbitrary powers the local censors of the Order have to completely veto an article just because they don't like the subject matter or the way it sounds. In the question of peace, we have in the Order a lot of well meaning but completely uninformed men, whose ideas may be narrow and even infantile, and who would be horrified at a lot of the things I have said already. They do not realize the situation, and they are apt to block any effective statement about peace. However, they can only block it getting into print, and I will certainly exercise whatever rights I have a) to get the material recensored by somebody else more intelligent, if possible, and b) to circulate the material privately. It would be nonsense for me to do otherwise. However I would make an exception in a case where the Abbot General personally declared that he did not wish the material to be circulated in any form. Or, of course, if the local Abbot did so. As for private circulation, that is none of the censor's business. All he can do is say whether or not there is a possible objection to its appearing in print, strictly speaking *published*. Circulation of a couple of hundred mimeographed copies is not publication.

Be sure that I have not closed up the hermitage. It is very nice up there. We have a bit of snow, but no one knows how much snow to expect. It might turn out to be quite warm, like the day when Victor [Hammer] came down a couple of years ago.

Oh yes, back to the censors. The most important thing is this: it is very risky for me to simply shoulder publicly the editorship of the paperback. If my name appears as the "editor" then it is likely that the whole thing will have to pass the censors. That is to say they will want to see it and will want to judge whether or not they think I ought to be editor of it. Obviously they can't stop you printing it but they can stop me from being "editor" and they might well do so. As for the preface, I can get that censored separately and there will be enough trouble right there, probably. I am ready for them to get very nasty about the whole peace business, though they might not. But as I say their lack of comprehension is sometimes monumental, and it is something one has to put up with, as far as getting into print is concerned.

Well, I have to stop now. Let me know exactly when you are coming. I hope all the material will be available by then.

All the best for the New Year . . . [sic] that in itself would make a subject for a pretty letter. It is curious to face a New Year with the expectation that there might be nothing left standing at the end of it.

Cordially as ever, in Christ
T O M

/ · /

Rollo May: Psychologist and popular author, born in 1909, whose influential works include *Man's Search for Himself* (1953) and *Love and Will* (1969).

Wright Mills: Charles Wright Mills (1916–), an American sociologist and educator (Columbia University) whose most significant work addressed labor issues—*New Men of Power: America's Labor Leaders* (1948)—and analyses of America's middle class, including *White Collar* (1951).

some kind of monkey business: One of the ways TM sidestepped censorship difficulties was to circulate his writing widely in mimeograph form. He proposed to W. H. Ferry that *Peace in the Post-Christian Era*—a monograph-length work that set out TM's views on Catholic Just War Theory—be privately circulated through the Center for the Study of Democratic Institutions' mailing list. JL wrote (27 December 1961): "Your idea of working on circulation through Ferry's organization is interesting, but would that really be 'cricket'? I am never very clear in my head about these matters. With my background, I would be inclined to look on a situation like that as a kind of game, sort of like the taxpayer's relationship with Uncle Sam every March, where you don't do anything 'dishonest' but try your darndest to find all the loopholes."

100. TLS-1   March 4, 1962

DEAR J.

I am glad you got the [Herbert] Butterfield article straightened out and that we can use it. The censor has approved the preface to the paperback but there is still some ambiguity about whether they want to see the whole book. There has been a misunderstanding at headquarters and I think it will soon be straightened out. But in any case I hope you are moving along with the book. I have incidentally lost my copy of the Fromm article before finishing it, but it must be around somewhere.

Original Child Bomb got here all right, the first copy that is. I think it is very handsome and I hope it goes well. Hope to have a few more copies when they are available, and will send them out. Would you like to send a review copy, among other places, to the *Catholic Worker.* Also Fellowship [of Reconciliation]. . . . Many thanks. . . .

Here is a new poem about the space flight, and I hope you will like. You can ask Rhoda [Rissin] to handle it and send it around if convenient. I forget if she is doing something with the "Song for the Death of Averroes," can you check on that? I think you took it along with the idea that she would send it around, but I am not sure.

Victor and Carolyn [Hammer] were over the other day and we had a nice time. He brought me a fine flossy Italian book with a lot of pictures, a book of ancient myths etc, which a friend of his did. He wants me to help get a translation published. Would you be interested? I feel there is too much in the way of pictures for you and that this would be a book for Doubleday or someone like that.

Macmillan offered me a ten thousand dollar advance for a book on peace, after the recent *Commonweal* article. It seems to me that if they suggest a book like that I can do it for them without that affecting my option with Farrar Straus. However FSC is being a bit messy about the *Reader* as far as I can understand. I do not have all the dope. What do you think about my doing a book on peace for Macmillan at this juncture? Just the articles really, and it would include the one we are using in the paperback and perhaps also a revision of that chapter in *New Seeds.* Any ideas?

I am sorry to hear Bob [MacGregor] has not yet fully recovered, but I hope he is better now. Tell him I will write but I am absolutely behind the eight ball with letters now, as there have been visitors and retreats and I am not caught up.

Have they started nuclear testing again in this country yet? I hope not, but I suppose it is inevitable.

All the best, in haste,

Cordially in Christ
Tom

/ · /

Butterfield: Sir Herbert Butterfield, Professor of History and Vice-Chancellor of Cambridge University, England. TM selected Butterfield's "Human Nature and the Dominion of Fear," excerpted from *International Conflict in the Twentieth Century* (1960), for *Breakthrough to Peace.*

a new poem: "Why Some Look Up to Planets and Heroes" first appeared in *America,* 108 (30 March 1963). See also *CP,* pp. 305–307.

the recent Commonweal Article: "Nuclear War and Christian Responsibility," *Commonweal,* 75 (9 February 1962). See also Shannon, ed., *Passion for Peace,* pp. 37–47.

101. TLS-1   March 16, 1962

D E A R J.:

Thanks for the lineup on the *Human Way Out.* I am glad we can get moving on it and that everything is now settled except the last irritating delay from the Abbot General. And there is still just a vague possibility that he *might* want the whole book to be censored, which is impossible. . . .

The *Clement [of Alexandria]* just got in this morning, I don't know how it got held up so long, maybe Fr. Abbot wanted to read it or something. But anyway I will look over the suggestions and shoot it back to you.

About the space flight poem: yes, the sun rose and set on the guy six times each time he went round. Three rounds, eighteen sunsets or sunrises or both, but I am pretty sure about that. So I am sending it right back, and you can go ahead with it, also "[Song for the Death of] Averroes" which I am glad Rhoda [Rissin] is pushing.

Hope the opinion makers get in there behind *Original Child [Bomb].*

A friend in Washington sent me the *Catholic Standard* of that city, and it has in it a hot and hostile editorial about my article in *the Commonweal* which is the basis for the article to be in the anthology. It is not signed but is evidently by the auxiliary bishop of Washington. This is bad. It means there is going to be a lot of determined opposition to the stuff I have written and it may mean that if I don't watch my step they will clamp down. What this means is that I have got to be a lot more smart and qualified about theological statements that they cannot pull apart even according to their own standards. This is going to be difficult. This opinion of this bishop is the official Washington-Pentagon line all the way down. We have got to test, we have got to have plenty of bombs, etc. And of course lots of quotes to prove this is authoritative.

This may make it very difficult for the book Macmillan wants ever to get out at all. We'll see. But this was to be expected.

Of course if you run into any other comments, especially adverse ones, let me know. I presume there will be a lot of them. . . .

All the best,
Cordially yours in Christ,
T O M

/ · /

Human Way Out: Another early variant title for *Breakthrough to Peace.*

102. TLS-2   Norfolk
                                               March 28, 1962

DEAR TOM,

. . . I am very sorry to hear about the attack on your *Commonweal* pieces in the *Catholic Standard* of Washington. But I know you will stick by what your conscience tells you is right. I certainly hope that this kind of pressure will not prevent you, or Macmillan, from going ahead with the big peace book with them, which can do so much good in this crisis.

There was a terribly frightening hour on television Sunday night. It was a very well put-together documentary done by NBC News Service, and the subject was the growing arms industry and its effect on our social and political life. It was an expert job of filmscript cutting. It would jump from terrifying pictures of the earth opening up, to the sound of a gong that sounded like doomsday, to allow the Titan missiles to get ready to fire off, and then switch to interviews with workers who had been thrown out of work near Baltimore by the closing of one of the Martin Company plants there, when a certain aircraft was abandoned in the Pentagon planning in favor of a better missile. There were actual politicians explaining, very candidly, how they got votes from arms plant workers in their campaigns by advocating increased armament spending. It showed the Mayors of cities waging campaigns to influence Congress to keep up the arms budget, and things of that kind. It all really made me feel pretty hopeless, but how can one blame these people, who think of their jobs and stomachs, when the rest of us really do so little to fight the evil? . . .

I have a nice compliment to relay to you about your poetry from somebody whose opinion I value. Hayden Carruth, for his own pleasure, has been reading your poems and he tells me that you have the quality of natural rhythm in your idiom which Pound and Eliot had in their young best days. What would you think of our asking Hayden to do an introduction for your next book of poems? It always galls me that the critics do not pay enough attention to your poetry. Perhaps a good strong blast from Hayden—and he writes very well indeed— would set some of them to rights about your importance as a poet, which I think has been neglected lately.

Did I tell you that I ran into Mark Van Doren at the National Book Award fiesta and that he spoke very warmly of his visit with you? That affair turned out an awful mess, at least for us, as they gave the prize to what is, in my opinion, an extremely inferior book, done by a young man named Duggan. I got some inside scuttlebutt later—not from Mark, but from a man on the *Tribune*— who said that after the first voting, our candidate, Denise Levertov, was ahead 2 to 1, which I think would have been the votes of Mark and Leonie Adams, but that the third judge, who was William Jay Smith, could not be brought around, so that in the end they gave the prize to a "compromise" candidate. Well, he sure was. All of these prize deals are pretty unsatisfactory. [Lewis] Mumford, who got the prize for the best non-fiction book, his big work about the history of cities, gave a magnificent talk, and got in some nice plugs about the regression of civilization to cave-dwelling.

As ever,

J.

/ · /

Hayden Carruth: An American poet and editor who worked with JL on the staff of *Perspectives.*

Duggan: Alan Dugan (1923–), whose first volume of poetry—*Poems* (1961), issued by the Yale Series of Younger Poets—won the National Book Award and a Pulitzer Prize.

Leonie Adams: Leonie Fuller Adams, New York poet who taught English at New York University, Bennington College, and Columbia University.

William Jay Smith: American-born poet, writer, and translator, who served in the Vermont House of Representatives and began teaching at Hollins College in 1965. Married to poet Barbara Howes.

103. TLS-2   April 28 1962

DEAR J.,

   . . . Now here is the big problem of the day. After all the trouble I have had with censors, the Abbot General finally clamped down and I have been practically ordered to write nothing more about war. The only question that remains concerns the little book on peace I have just finished, and I am asking him if it is ok to try to get that one through. But after that it is nix on the war. Reason given: this is not fitting for a monk, a monk should not concern himself with worldly affairs, this preoccupation with war and peace will "falsify the message of monasticism," a message of detachment and contemplation. In other words they are concerned with the image of monasticism they wish to present to the world, an image built on conventional and party line standards. The judgment seems to me to be rather foolish and uncomprehending, and to sensitive people it will tend to be a confirmation of their suspicions about the obtuseness and artificiality of the monastic ideal in some quarters. It reflects in reality a complete misunderstanding of the deep meaning of the contemplative life and the prophetic character of the monastic vocation, and this I regard as a very serious deficiency indeed. This one runs up against at every turn. A rigid and confused concept of contemplation that in reality has nothing to do with God, and is a more or less contrived psychological state, maintained by negation and setting oneself over against something else which is classified as less good and which is studiously rejected. This is a misconception altogether, and it leads nowhere. It accounts for the fact that there is so little real contemplation in some monasteries. For the rest I am not preoccupied with this question. I have no desire to carry on a running campaign against every phase of the arms race. I have said enough for people to know exactly where I stand, and that is sufficient, monk or no monk. I don't feel somehow that the monastic order will suffer by this. I note also that there are many other things which monks do which in fact bring the monastic state into disrepute but these are not questioned or reproved at all: they make money.

However this has several consequences of importance to us. The command of the Abbot General (it is not yet a completely formal command, but this is his wish, though it is actually formulated rather by his secretary who is in charge of these things) is that I write only things which are "fitting" in a monk. That means of course things which *they* consider fitting. Knowing their minds, that lets Gandhi out. Surely they would not imagine it fitting for a monk to know about Gandhi, still less to defend his ideas. I can send you the ms. [of *Gandhi on Non-Violence*], and maybe someone else would like to do a brief preface to it? Or do you want to drop it? I could just get it mimeographed and send it around.

As I say there is no law against mimeographing things, and I do not think they would specially object to this. However they might well object to the *Cold War Letters.* I am sending you a copy, but this must be kept under wraps. They would not categorically forbid my sending this around, but if there was too much discussion of the ms. and it got back to them there might be repercussions. I will therefore have to be very careful who I send it to. . . .

I don't know if I have written since Ferry was here but the visit was fine. We got some great pictures of an old distillery, the red one down at Dant Station. You will like them. I'd love to do a photo essay on it but of course perish the thought. A monk writing about a distillery, what a scandal. The funny part about that one is that the distillery at Dant Station has actually more of the qualities of early Cistercian architecture than the monastery has. This one would not be expected to say with any degree of acceptance.

Well, I have to get this in a bag and give a conference. God bless you, and best wishes always.

Cordially in Christ,
Tom

/ · /
the little book on peace: Peace in the Post-Christian Era.
Cold War Letters: The mimeographed collection of forty-nine letters on the themes of war and peace that TM wrote to a wide variety of correspondents between October 1961 and March 1962. TM assembled a second edition of sixty-two additional letters that included items dated through October 1962. Collected in *Witness,* pp. 17–69.

104. TLS-2   May 1, 1962

DEAR J.,

Thanks for all the letters, clippings and so on. I hope we have finally got squared away on all the material for the Peace book. . . . About a subtitle, how do you like: "Essays against Extermination" or better "An Extermination of Conscience." That is about as good as I can do at the moment.

Here is one very important point though. Please do not under any circumstances put me down in print anywhere explicitly as editor of this collection. This is likely to cause an awful lot of trouble for me and might even prevent the publication of my own peace book, which is right now hanging over the abyss like the guy in the Zen story, clinging to a branch with his teeth while a bystander asks him "what is the meaning of Zen?"

All that I have received permission for was to print the preface together with the book without having the book go through the censors. There is no official favor or blessing upon my editorship simply because I have not drawn this fact to their attention one way or the other. If it were to come out that I were editor, they would raise over again the whole question of approval of the entire book, which needs not be raised now as my editorship is not public. So for heavens' sakes don't print my name on there as editor. If you want to print "Preface by T. Merton" all right, that is true and nobody has objected to that. If anyone wants to figure out from that who the editor is, all right, no objections to that either. But there would be very much trouble if I just appeared as "editor" simply, without further permission. I know this is all very tiresome, but I am having a difficult time with these people, and their Byzantine formalities.

In case I did not tell you, the last article on war finally came back with thumbs down from the censors and a recommendation that I submit nothing further for censorship on this subject. The Abbot General seems to back this decision up though he has not formally said so, he has certainly indicated that was his idea. Hence I have had to ask him special permission just to send my new book to the censor at all, and that is no guarantee it will even begin to get past the censor after that. This is extremely stupid and frustrating but there is nothing I can do about it and if now there is further indication of what he feels to be a spirit of insubordination then everything will stop, period. And this General of ours is very quick to interpret things as insubordination, I can tell you.

Besides, people at the *Catholic Worker* have let me down badly, publishing things without my consent and without corrections the censors had asked for, etc. So at the moment all my writing at least about war and peace is in a very precarious spot.

As to the ad [for *Original Child Bomb*], I can't get over my feelings of doubt about it, because the book is so short and tiny, and that can never be clear in an ad. When a man sees it in a bookstore and picks it up and then buys it, all right. That is my feeling. Also it is not a worldshaking statement, it is just a statement. A very unpretentious statement, and its whole value comes from its unpretentiousness. As soon as it gets apparently blown up into something the whole picture is changed. I don't know how you can go about advertising it effectively without making it look like something special, which it isn't: unless of course you say, "This book, itself the size of an atom, this peanut among all books, will knock you off your can o reader, just wait, only 8 pp. but what a wallop, etc. etc." or even better "If you can find this book with your microscope you will be wowed by it."

But anyway, go ahead. I cannot be of much help here. . . .

Now I have to stop and get down to a bunch of other letters. Sorry this one is full of negations. Better next time.

All the best always, in Christ,
T O M

/ · /

the Peace book: Breakthrough to Peace.

the last article on war: "The Machine Gun in the Fallout Shelter," published as "The Shelter Ethic" in Shannon, ed., *Passion for Peace,* pp. 20–26. Convinced that the bomb shelter craze was a clear expression of the moral chaos and spiritual malaise which nourish the roots of war, TM continued to write about the fallout shelter until this article eventually led, in early 1963, to a complete, but short-lived, ban on all his writing dealing with political matters.

105. ALS-1   May 3, 1962

D E A R J.

I ran across this quote from Einstein again and want to get it to you before I forget. I think we should put it in the front matter of *Breakthrough for [sic] Peace.*

It reads:

"The splitting of the atom has changed everything save our modes of thinking and thus we drift toward unparalleled catastrophe."

That suggests a subtitle: "Modes of Thinking in Nuclear Crisis." Or is that too pretentious?

The quote can give suggestive leads in the blurb.

Best, as ever, in Xt,
TOM

---

106. TLS-1   May 10, 1962

DEAR J.

. . . Sorry *Original Child* got in with Peter Rabbit in the stores. You never know how you will be understood. I think we have tried to make too much of this book. It is not for everybody. But I do hope nevertheless that it will reach those for whom it *is.*

I got in touch with Leo Szilard, who seems to me to have the best and sanest idea for peace. Practical anyway, consists in getting everybody like us together and getting us represented by a peace lobby in Washington. Szilard is about the most impressive authority in that field anyway. I am reading the curious book by [Edward] Teller who also seems obsessed with the moral angle, but in a strange ambiguous self justifying way because he also wants to use that old bomb, man. He just wants to use it second, so he isn't guilty.

Unconsciously there is great danger these cookies will get around to war not by honest outright war but by goading somebody else into starting it. . . .

Ferry just sent some transparencies of Miguel M[oreno]'s work which I like very much and he says he sent a triptych to the abbot but the abbot is away.

All the best always,

In Christ,
TOM

Henry Miller wrote. I am very glad to hear from him and will write. He is sending that [Joseph] Delteil book, he says. I will look at it again and probably reading it at leisure will see more in it than before, though at a glance it seemed quite good.

/ · /

got in with Peter Rabbit: JL wrote to TM on 11 May 1962: "It's absolutely amazing to think that the reviewers and columnists may have thought *[Original Child Bomb]* was a juvenile, but perhaps 'Child' in the title, and the shape of it, made them think so."

Leo Szilard: The Budapest-born physicist and biologist Leo Szilard (1898–1964), convinced that Germany might be first to develop nuclear bombs, helped persuade President Roosevelt to launch the Manhattan Project. However, Szilard opposed the use of atomic bombs on Japan at the end of World War II, and he subsequently became a prominent and active proponent of arms control. His popular satire about war and peace, *Voice of the Dolphins,* was published in 1961.

Teller: The Hungarian physicist Edward Teller (1908–) studied under Niels Bohr and Enrico Fermi. Teller was principal scientist for the Manhattan Project. He later returned to Los Alamos in 1952, where his work contributed significantly to the explosion of the first H-bomb on the Marshall Islands in November 1952. Unlike fellow Hungarian Szilard, Teller remained a strong advocate of U.S. nuclear superiority during the Cold War, and in 1963 he testified against the nuclear test ban treaty.

107. TLS-1   May 30, 1962

DEAR J.,

. . . Well, I finished my book on nuclear war *[Peace in the Post-Christian Era],* the one I was going to give Macmillan and for which they have offered a ten thousand dollar advance. But the Abbot General vetoed it. Some American Abbot of the order wrote to him complaining that I was writing about nuclear war for the *Catholic Worker* and that a friend of his in the intelligence service had assured him that the *CW* was "communist controlled." Some intelligence service. Anyway there is nothing for me to do but accept the decision, and that means that *Conjectures of a Guilty Bystander* is out of the question also. I have been instructed to stop writing on controversial and secular subjects. I hope this will not affect any of the poems in the new book. . . .

I think the decision of the General also lets me out as far as the *Gandhi* preface is concerned. It is lucky that we are able to get through by the skin of our teeth with that peace anthology. . . .

The Peace Book *[Breakthrough to Peace]* will be mimeographed shortly, the typing of the stencils was all done when the General's letter came. I am sending a few copies around to friends, and you and the gang will all have copies, anyway. Perhaps I will do the same with *Conjectures.* They will just have to be handled discreetly, to make sure no one grabs a bit of one of them and publishes it. . . .

> All best wishes, cordially as ever, in
> Christ,
> T O M

---

108. T L S - 1   July 30, 1962

D E A R J .

I just got through writing to Bob [MacGregor] and I typed out a list of things that would be in the paperback built on *Behavior of Titans* plus. I have a good title, and the title seems to be one that would also cover the poems, so really since the last few minutes I have been considering the possibility that you might put the poems in the same book.

The title: *Emblems from [sic] a Season of Fury,* with a line from Shakespeare on the title page or somewhere: "His sicatrice [sic][,] an emblem of warre[,] here on his sinister cheeke" (*All's Well,* II, 1.) That ought to cover some of the poems that are like wounds.

In a word then we would have a nice sized paper back with some twenty five poems and then also the appended list of poetic prose pieces, including *Behavior of Titans* (minus perhaps "Herakleitos" which would be out of place I think). I like the idea, and hope you will. . . . When we think that there will be the "strange" poems like "Chant for the Furnaces," "Averroes," "The Space Man," "Lee Ying," "Moslem's Angel of Death," the Elegies for Hemingway and Thurber etc., I think it builds up to an interesting volume and we could go ahead on it for spring of 1963, no?

As soon as you let me know I will get busy with the censors for the poems that have not yet been done (about four new ones you have not seen).

Note that I am including *Original Child Bomb,* it really ought to be in. For that we might have to wait until Fall. I never thought *Original Child* would sell, to tell you the truth, but the salesmen thought it would. I was thinking more in terms of the limited edition. However, all is well. Ferry sent me a copy of a fine letter in which David Riesman spoke highly of it. . . .

So far no Henry Miller paperbacks have gotten in: did you send them? Should I go ask? All the mail has been held up, there is a bottleneck in the front office somewhere. I am reading that St. Francis book of [Joseph] Delteil seriously and it has a lot. It has plenty of life and imagination and it wallops hard. I think it really ought to be published and if you want to do it, by all means go ahead, though I think it would be more for one of the outfits like Doubleday. Why do I think that? Maybe I am totally unreasonable. It is a good hard hitting book, and you would like it. No pansy St. Francis in this. I think

Ferlinghetti would like it. I think Bill Williams would like it. I think all decent clean living American hundred percent beatniks like you and me would like it. I think the squares and the cardinals might not like it but who cares? It is a religious book that calls horsedung by its popular name, which is one of the things it has in common with St. Francis.

Sorry about Williams: I wish there was something I could do. I have so many hundreds of letters to write that if I wrote him it would be a stupified hasty note that would only puzzle him.

> All the best, cordially always in Christ,
> To m

/ · /

David Riesman: (1909–) Lawyer, professor of social sciences at Harvard University, and author of acclaimed *The Lonely Crowd* (1951), David Riesman is deeply committed to studying trends in American society, values, character, and especially higher education. His praise of TM's *Original Child Bomb* was no minor endorsement.

sorry about Williams: On 20 July 1962, JL was sad to report to TM that "Poor old Bill is really having a very tough time. . . . He hasn't come back very well from his last stroke. . . . All terribly sad, but that beautiful radiant smile still breaks through now and then."

109. APCS   [August 16, 1962]

DEAR J.

Yes I have the H Miller books, they got here with a brief delay. The *Wisdom of the Heart* is extraordinarily good & I'm discussing it with a priest[/]poet here who is a fine guy and thinks like [Eric] Gutkind (it is Dan Berrigan, the Jesuit—know his work?)[.]

Ok about waiting with *Emblems [of a Season of Fury]*.

Most of it is censored, but some poems need processing. Terrible news about *Breakthrough* but maybe the delay is salutary.

All the best
T O M

/ · /

Gutkind: (1877–1965), German-born theologian and philosopher whose principal work—collected in *The Body of God: First Steps Toward an Anti-Theology* (1969)—attempted a radical reinterpretation of traditional Judaism in light of Marxism. Gutkind fled Nazi Germany, settled in New York City, and lectured for many years at the New School and Yeshiva University.

terrible news: "Something pretty awful has happened," JL reported to TM on 9 August 1962, "a cruel blow of fate. . . . We received a few advance sewn, but unbound, copies of *Breakthrough* only to discover, to our horror, on examining them, that something in the folding machine slipped and some of the pages 'bounce' very badly. This means that facing pages do not line up, some are slightly askew, and, on some pages, the top or the bottom comes unpleasantly close to the trim line."

110. TLS-1   Nov 2, 1962

D E A R J.

It is ages since I have written and I don't know what I have not said that I ought to have said. I think the *Clement* is most handsome and am very pleased with it. [Giovanni] Mardersteig is always great.

Original Child Bomb has been stopped in France. The Abbot General is being beastly about the whole thing all down the line, with serene authoritarian righteousness. He is another DeGaulle and more so. I think that if anyone wants foreign rights anywhere for *Breakthrough* there is going to be a problem with permissions. I have to get a new permission, for each new language, *before translation,* for my peace articles. I doubt if many of them will ever be translated at that rate. . . .

You are right, the Cuba business was rough for a while. I don't like to say glibly that it came out "all right" except that it might have come out a great deal worse. I am not one for going about scoring up Cold War victories which may well be laying eggs for more chickens to come home to roost. We sure got them chickens coming in all the windows. I haven't heard anything much since Sunday, anyway. Maybe something worse has started up. How are the Chinese in India? And in China for that matter?

Macmillan has got a book of mine about prayer coming out next fall, and maybe since that is the case we ought to put off *Emblems* until early 1964, by which time I will have more poems and perhaps other things that can go in it. But let's keep thinking about it.

I am working on some very interesting people in the 12th century, the School of Chartres. Very little known as yet but fascinating material. The [Gloss on the Sin of] Ixion poem is partly the result of a jolt from them . . . [sic] and contemporary history.

Let's hear from you. I am glad you liked the *[Thomas Merton] Reader.* Hope it will get around, I have rather put my heart into it, and it says a whole lot of things I want to say clearly and in one place. I hope it gets reviewed.

> With all the best, as ever,
> Cordially in Christ,
> T O M

/ · /

the Cuba business: On 22 October 1962, President Kennedy ordered a naval blockade of Cuba after Soviet missile sites were discovered on the island. The subsequent nuclear brinkmanship between the Soviets and Americans was averted on 29 October when Nikita Khrushchev agreed to dismantle the sites in exchange for Kennedy's promise not to invade Cuba—a reference to the failed Bay of Pigs invasion of April 1961 conducted by U.S.-trained anti-Castro activists.

a book of mine about prayer: TM refers to the never-published *Prayer as Worship and Experience.* See Letter #121.

111. TL-2

Alta
November 26, 1962

DEAR TOM,

This is dictated from out in Utah, where I have stopped off to see our new ski lift—which is really a dandy—but I'll be back in New York Monday or Tuesday.

Have you seen this very fine review of *Breakthrough* by Sidney Harris of the *Chicago Daily News?* It is our first big piece of luck in the larger press, because Harris' column is syndicated by Field Enterprises and reaches, I believe, nearly a hundred small papers. Of course, some of them may not have run it.

I had a good three days in San Francisco and saw all the gang there, and they all send you their best. Ferlinghetti is much occupied in writing little plays, and they are pretty good. They are of the new "non-realistic" variety, but he manages to get across a lot of message. His City Lights bookshop is still going strong—it's the center for everything advanced in literature in that area—and he is also keeping up with his publishing activities, doing some very fine small pamphlets, etc.

Rexroth is in great form, he has become very much of a big wheel around San Francisco, thanks to his twice a week columns in the *Examiner* in which he writes about everything. I was a bit miffed with him because he hadn't done a story on *Breakthrough,* but he seems to be moving into a rather "conservative" phase in his thinking, a strange change in character for one who was so "far out" as a young man. But he is still a great deal of fun, and one of the best "confabulators" that I ever ran onto.

Poor old Kenneth Patchen is still in pretty bad shape. His ulcer is better, but his back is still bad, and I am afraid that the doctors have pretty much given up hope of finding out what is really wrong with him and curing it. He spends most of his time lying down, though he did get up and get dressed the day I was there to see him. He still writes a bit, but mostly is devoting himself to his painting, which is pretty good. We will be doing a little book of his "picture poems" of which you may have seen some in *Liberation* this spring.

Unfortunately, I didn't have time to get over to Oakland to see Brother Antoninus [William Everson].

Ferlinghetti has also been extremely active in the peace work in San Francisco. He was chief organizer of quite a sizable peace parade on Armistice Day. They got the peace people fitted out with placards and then they marched down the side of the street right along with the Army and Navy! But apparently it was a pretty grueling experience, as the comments on them from the crowd were rather horrible, and a lot of old ladies actually spat at them. Some world, isn't it?

I am rather coming to the conclusion that the sitdowns and the peace marchers don't do too much good, because the public just identifies them with local Communists and beatniks. I hope there can be more of the kind of thing that [H. Stuart] Hughes did in Massachusetts, actually moving into political action with the voters. I hear that Hughes got about fifty thousand votes in Massachusetts, which would have been between 3 and 4% of the votes cast. I heard that there was a man out in Iowa, a farmer named Herbert Hoover, of all things, who ran on a peace ticket for Congress and did much better, getting nearly 15% of the vote. Dworkis, the man in New York who was running on a peace ticket, didn't have much of a chance because he was running against the young Republican Sir Galahad, Lindsay, who is such a fine fellow, that he is practically unbeatable. I had sent *Breakthrough* to Lindsay, but didn't get any specific response, just a thank you note. I'm afraid that Lindsay plays ball with Gov. Rockefeller on the shelter business.

As ever,
[Unsigned Carbon]

/ · /

Hughes: Henry Stuart Hughes, Harvard history professor, ran as an independent in the Massachusetts senatorial campaign, 1962, on a peace program of American initiatives to end the arms race while advocating a liberal domestic program.

Lindsay: John V. Lindsay, congressman from New York and former mayor of New York City, 1965–73.

112. TLS-1   Dec. 4, 1962

DEAR J.

Victor and Carolyn [Hammer] were over yesterday and we had a fine visit, sitting up by the lake. We even built a little fire on the shale, and this was enough to take the chill out of the air. Very pleasant indeed. Their trip to Italy was not all roses and they kept speaking of crowds everywhere. I haven't much desire to see Italy again, I can tell you.

The magazine *Ramparts* is located at 1178 Chestnut Street, Menlo Park, Calif. I sent them "Hagia Sophia" and they are delighted to have it. I want to encourage them as much as I can as they really want to do a good job. They have had Bro Antoninus of course, and a lot of other stuff, but there is not an unlimited amount of good Catholic material, and of course they are not limited to the club, that's true. Anyway like I say I gave them "Hagia Sophia.". . .

Great about *Breakthrough* getting a good review. The ads have been fine. About the book with Macmillan, I didn't work it out with Farrar Straus at all. First I have let them know that we are no longer friends and I have indicated I am thinking of quitting them. However I have several times mentioned the "next book" question, should it be a collection of essays which they have? Never get a reply on this. The heck with them, I think I am entitled to just go ahead with Macmillan, for this one book. Maybe after that, for the big books, I could go back to Naomi at Doubleday. I still wonder if it would not be smarter to have a good *agent*. Or even just to go back to Curtis Brown, though they are so torpid and easily confused. Any ideas not so much about agents as about the general plight?

> . . . Cordially as ever, in Christ,
> T O M

---

113. T L S - 2   Jan 11, 1963

D E A R J .

First of all, I am sorry for not responding more quickly about the books on peace. I suppose I wait to read them and comment, and by the time I have read them I forget I owe you an answer. But I liked *Kill and Overkill* very much, if like is the right word. I thought it was very intelligent and informative in the right kind of way. I have recommended it to people in connection with the [Vatican II] Council, where the issue may eventually come up for some kind of discussion. My own Peace ms. *[Peace in the Post-Christian Era]* may be taken up by somebody on one of the [Council] commissions. I hope it will, but this is to be treated with discretion. *Breakthrough* is also in a dossier of my stuff that has been got together by responsible persons for discussion in this connection.

. . . Yes, I read the James Baldwin article [about race relations in *The New Yorker*], which I thought was terrific, except that toward the end it just went on and on. The thing that struck me most forcibly was the confirmation given by the ads all along the side of the columns. They were even more eloquent than he was, in showing what the trouble was. I do think there is much wrong, and deeply wrong, with the whole society of man but ours in particular. I am reading the Rachel Carson book, *Silent Spring*. That too is powerful. Have you seen it? You certainly should. It is about the destruction and pollution of wildlife and natural resources through the use of insecticides which have been promoted commercially beyond all reason. Another aspect of the same basic trouble.

Let us by all means go ahead with the poems for Fall 1963. . . . I have done some new translations, this time from Raissa Maritain, Jacques Maritain's wife, who was a most remarkable person. Her poems are very individual and reflect a deep and simple spirituality that is most impressive. Probably won't be wildly popular with some people, but I think they have, as the blurbs say, "lasting significance.". . .

To return to the peace books, I have also received *Preventing World War III* but have not got into it yet. But I am very grateful. A long time ago I got E[t]zioni, but have not read that yet either. But don't think I don't appreciate these things: I just get at them very slowly as I have great masses of reading to do on so many other subjects. . . .

It is getting late so I must stop. Personally I have no worries about *Breakthrough*. I think the response has been very satisfactory, all things considered. Did you see the review in a thing called *Manas*? Ping Ferry sent it along and I will pass it on if you have not seen it.

All the best always, in Christ,
T O M

/ · /

Kill and Overkill: Kill and Overkill: The Strategy of Annihilation (1962), by Ralph Eugene Lapp.

the James Baldwin article: "Letter from a Region in My Mind," *The New Yorker* (17 November 1962). JL wrote TM on 18 December 1962: "Speaking of the 'white man's religion,' have you read that extraordinary piece that James Baldwin recently had in 'The New Yorker' about the black-white situation? It's pretty terrifying." Baldwin's *New Yorker* Letter slightly predated his bestseller *The Fire Next Time* (1963), a powerful essay on racial tension that predicted outbursts of black anger which would wrack American cities in the decade ahead. Baldwin (1924–1987)—novelist, essayist, lecturer—remains a passionate voice on race relations in America.

Rachel Carson: (1907–1964). TM wrote Rachel Carson a long letter the following day, 12 January 1963, to compliment her "on the fine, exact, and persuasive book you have written . . . it is perhaps much more timely even than you or I realize. . . ." (*Witness,* p. 70).

Raissa Maritain: TM wrote a biographical essay on Raissa Maritain (*LE,* pp. 307–308). His translations of her poetry from the French are included in *CP,* pp. 962–969.

Preventing World War III: Preventing World War III, Some Proposals (1962), by Quincy Wright.

Ezioni: Amitai Etzioni, *The Hard Way to Peace: A New Strategy* (1962).

Manas: "Wisdom and the Bomb," a review of *Breakthrough to Peace* in *Manas,* 25 (26 December 1962).

114. TLS-1   Feb 8, 1963

DEAR J.,

About the title [for the next poetry book]: I'd still like to use that "Emblems" one. I like the word emblems in this connection, and do you still have the Shakespeare quote?

Here are the possibilities:

Emblems of War
Emblems of a Season of Fury
Emblems and Elegies

Just plain *Season of Fury* does not fit because it makes the whole book sound much angrier than it is. "War" in the title might scare people. . . .

For the translations: I would like to add a few more of [Ernesto] Cardenal: and I really think his little notes on Gethsemani which you quite understandably did not take as a book in itself, might go in here. What do you think? Especially if I write a little note on Cardenal and explain how he was a novice. I think that puts the whole little collection in an entirely different light. . . .

Just thought of another title:

Emblems of a New Season. I like that *best*. Cheery. Will exhilarate the reader and make him think he is getting a book full of sunshine. Maybe too peppy, hah? How you like *Emblems of a Wicked Season?* This gets fanciful, I stop. . . .

That's all for the moment. Best of everything. . . .

Ever in Christ,

Tom

/ · /

notes on Gethsemani: Ernesto Cardenal, "Selections from 'Gethsemani, Ky,' " translated by TM and included in *CP*, pp. 849–855.

115. TLS-2   March 28, 1963

DEAR J.,

Many thanks for the Norman Thomas book *[Ask at the Unicorn]*. I will read it with pleasure and tell you what I think. It just got here. Funny about the name. You had me wondering for a while if old Norman T. had suddenly taken to turning out Upton Sinclair stuff in his old age.

I am glad the book *Emblems* is lining up nicely. October is a fine date. Clear, because Macmillan is publishing in February. I think also that I am getting gradually straightened out with Farrar Straus but I don't know what I will finally do. Probably the thing that makes the most sense is to get Naomi back into the picture somehow. I think she can keep all the threads uncrossed, and if necessary I will go to Doubleday, though I am not too hot on them as a publisher. Maybe she can just be agent, exceptionally.

Give me a few days to think about words of eulogy for myself in the blurb. I don't know that this is exactly the best thing for me to do, but if it will help I will try to describe the book accurately. Did you see the fuss *America* made with the spaceman poem? I suppose they want to be controversial or something.

There is a possibility of a Yogi coming around here in May. Any more about Raja Rao coming down? I haven't seen his book *[Serpent and Rope]*. I will have to inquire about it from Fr. Abbot. I think you said it was sent, didn't you? That is strange. But they get a little arbitrary sometimes about books. Or else things just get lost. I am sorry about this, but you know how it is.

As for the cover, your ideas about the photo of a tormented bit of metal sound fine to me. I am sure there are all sorts of interesting things you could dig up. I would like to see anything you think worth while. I certainly have nothing here.

Too bad about Bill Williams. I will keep him in my prayers and masses. May God be good to him, and there is no reason why not.

It is spring and Lent. I am empty. But it is nice and the birds sing. Do you think you might come down with Raja Rao? Let us keep it in mind, because I will have to plan a bit. Maybe June, now. Though that is a hot time all right, but I suppose he won't mind. I have to make sure too many visits don't get jammed up together because that throws everything out of whack.

I dug up a fuller text for the inscription at the beginning of *Emblems:* see if you like it. . . . It reads:

"You shall find one Captain Spurio with his cicatrice, an emblem of war, here on his sinister cheek. It was this very sword entrenched it."

All's Well, II. i. 44.

Well, here we go with another page and nothing to say on it. I wrote a long article on Zen which I will send along when I have made a few corrections.

Did you ever hear of a fellow called John Howard Griffin? Very interesting, and much concerned with integration and Martin Luther King etc. He was here.

All the best, always. Happy Easter.

Yrs in Christ,
Tom

/ · /

old Norman T.: TM recalls Norman Mattoon Thomas (1884–1968), editor of *The Nation* in 1921–22, who, like the novelist Upton Sinclair, ran unsuccessful but popular Socialist candidacies for public office—Thomas in New York, Sinclair in California. Not to be confused with the novelist Norman Thomas, whose novel, *Ask at the Unicorn,* had just been issued by ND.

the fuss America made: The 30 March 1963 number of *America* included a full-page layout of TM's poem "Why Some Look Up to Planets and Heroes" (p. 433), accompanied by TM's short commentary. The editors announced the poem prominently on the magazine's cover.

Raja Rao: Indian novelist, author of *Kanthapura* (ND, 1963). Pantheon published *The Serpent and the Rope* (1960).

Too bad about Bill Williams: JL wrote TM on 19 March 1963: "I hope you can say a few prayers for dear old Bill Williams who went to heaven, or so I assume, two weeks ago. They didn't have any religion at the funeral at all, but just read from his poems and had a eulogy, which sort of upset me. He was a dear and wonderful man, and it was best that he should go, because he had been utterly miserable in recent years, being unable to write, and completely frustrated. I really will miss him."

John Howard Griffin: This first visit by John Howard Griffin (1920–1980) was followed by many others after Griffin and TM became good friends. In addition to strong commitments to racial justice—Griffin wrote *Black Like Me* (1961), a book that moved the racial conscience of America—both men shared a dedication to photography; Griffin edited TM's photographs in *A Hidden Wholeness: The Visual World of Thomas Merton* (1970). Chosen by the

Thomas Merton Legacy Trust as TM's official biographer, Griffin completed only one part, which was published after Griffin's death as *Follow the Ecstasy: Thomas Merton, the Hermitage Years 1965–1968* (1983).

116. TLS-1   April 21, 1963

DEAR J.

Where are you? You can't be skiing now. It is as hot as summer here, and we certainly have had no rain. Are you likely to be coming down with Raja Rao? I am expecting Victor [Hammer] over the first Saturday in May. Later, June 5th, Victor is representing me at the Commencement of the University of Ky where, of all things, he will receive in my name the honorary LL D. Home town boy makes good. I think I get an orange and red gown, with the Lord knows what sort of hat, and am planning to wear the lot in choir.

I forgot if a man called John Howard Griffin sent you a "portrait" he took of me. He took some fabulous pictures up at the cottage, and I want you to have one. Let me know if he did not, I may have forgotten to tell him.

And now to continue further the narcissism of this letter, here is the blurb [for *Emblems of a Season of Fury*]. I forgot all about it, but remembered today for some reason. I guess I drank coffee for a change, and that stimulates the brain, or at least it seems to for me. So here is the stuff, and I know you will be able to make all sorts of better things out of it, pruning the indecencies. That phrase in the 4th line is not "chronic understatement" but *ironic* understatement. Just in case you can't read my corrections.

Everything is going quietly along, and I have decided that the best thing for me to do about business is to try to persuade Naomi Burton to be my agent again, no matter what. I think she probably will. This may get me off the hook with Farrar Straus, who are still maintaining a mysterious silence. I am not writing much except short articles. I want to stay with things like poems, and some translations. Shortly I will send you a few things. I dug up some interesting texts on peace in the seventeenth century (spiritual) writer [François de Salignac de la Mothe] Fénelon. They are very powerful. They might make a nice little collection like the Clement one. You will see.

The Pope's encyclical on peace is very heartening, especially when it is very carefully read and all the implications of the early, seemingly theoretical parts are digested. What he is really doing is laying down solid principles for Catholic conscientious objection to nuclear war. I hope people will grasp this in time.

Friend of mine [Justus George Lawler] has started a new magazine, *Continuum*[,] which he thinks of as a kind of Catholic *Dissent*. It is quite good. I am sending you a copy. You might want to help him out with an ad once in a while. He gave a great push to *Breakthrough,* as you will see. . . .

All the best, always,
Yours in Christ,
T O M

/ · /

Fénelon: TM's "Introduction: Reflections on the Character and Genius of Fénelon" appeared in *Fénelon: Letters of Love and Counsel* (1964), translated by John McEwen.

encyclical: Pope John XXIII's encyclical *Pacem in Terris* was released on 1 April 1963. "*Pacem in Terris* is a magnificent document," TM wrote in "In Acceptance of the Pax Medal" (*The Nonviolent Alternative*, p. 258); "it was written in order to prevent nuclear war, and indeed to rule out all further consideration of war as a reasonable and just means of settling international disputes. As a consequence *Pacem in Terris* is a reminder to the conscience of every reasonable human being on the face of the earth that each one of us has a strict obligation to work for world peace, for the peaceful arbitration of all disputes, and for the peaceful settlement of the social, international, interra-

cial, religious, economic and political problems in which we may be directly
or indirectly involved."

117. TLS-1   April 26, 1963

DEAR J.,

. . . did I mention June as a good time for coming
down? Up until about the 15th it will be a bad time, as
Fr. Abbot has given me permission to make a little retreat
up at the hermitage and I certainly want to take advantage of this, as it will be invaluable, and of course it is just
what I need. . . .

But I do hope to see you some time.

By the way did you know that H. Stuart Hughes had
awarded me a peace prize. Some New England Group, a
medal or something. I am glad he thought of me, and am
glad to accept it, except that I can't go. The editor of the
reader, Tom McDonnell[,] is in Boston and we are asking
him to pick up the medal for me, otherwise I would have
suggested you, and maybe he may not be able to. If not,
would you be able to run up to Boston for a day? I don't
know when. I would hate to bother you with this,
though, as I know you are plenty busy. But you would
be a logical choice, and it would be at Harvard and so
on. Probably McDonnell will field it anyhow.

Glad you got good skiing in Utah. We are still short of
rain here. But the country has been splendid.

> Best wishes always, and most
> cordially in Christ,
> TOM

/ · /

a peace prize: The Pax Medal.

118. TLS-1   May 11, 1963

DEAR J.,

Boy, were you ever right in that intuition about the tormented metal [photograph]. This is magnificent. Wham, what a cover [for *Emblems of a Season of Fury*]! Go to it, man. This is great.

I am so happy about Bill Williams getting the Pulitzer, even after he isn't around to enjoy it. It is important for the work, anyway. I have recently been looking through the *Pictures [from Brueghel]* and there is very fine stuff in it.

It looks as though I am finally going to leave Farrar Straus and get over with Naomi at Doubleday. Not that I like Doubleday, but Naomi is a good one to keep things going in the right direction. I write too many square books anyway, got to stop. I'd rather write more New Directions books.

This is just a quick note, to get the emblem back to you.

                                      In Christ,
                                      T O M

/ · /

the tormented metal: A detail from a photograph of *Manes Flayed No. 2,* a huge metal sculpture by the New York sculptor Elio Martinelli.

Bill Williams getting the Pulitzer: William Carlos Williams was awarded posthumously a Pulitzer Prize for *Pictures from Brueghel and Other Poems* (ND, 1962).

119. TL-1   June 12, 1963

DEAR TOM,

Many thanks for the copies of the two new poems, both of which are fine, especially the one about Birmingham ["And the Children of Birmingham"]. You suggest *Partisan Review* for that one, but they are so slow coming out, wouldn't it be better to try somewhere else first, and perhaps something with a big circulation, since this is so topical? It might be too "good" for them, but what about something like the magazine of the *Sunday Times?* Or, failing that, *Saturday Review,* which does come out very quickly.

I'm so pleased that you liked the Martinelli "tormented metal" sculpture for the cover of *Emblems.* He has given his permission, and I think it is going to look very fine indeed.

That sounds like a good idea to get tied up with Naomi again. I always liked her, and found her very understanding and efficient in business matters. But I'm especially glad to hear you say that you will want to be doing some more of our kind of books, too.

You must have been very sad, as we all were, that that dear wonderful old Pope had to have such a painful going. He really was a great man, I think. I hope they will vote for one half as good, who will keep the Council going, and keep up with good work for peace and reconciliation with the Iron Curtain countries.

Kennedy's speech yesterday seemed very hopeful. It really looks as though he means to try to do something about the situation. But it will be rough going with all those idiots around Washington who want to "hard line."

Ned asked me again the other day whether you had any bits of paper that give the factual details about your honorary degree and peace prize up in Boston. He would like to add this stuff to the biography that he keeps current in the promotion files. People keep writing in for biographies of authors, and he does a good job of keeping them up to date.

As ever,
[UNSIGNED CARBON]

/ · /
Ned: Edwin Erbe, ND assistant editor.

120. T L S - 1   June 14, 1963

D E A R J .

   Thanks for your letter: you are probably right about
not sending the Birmingham poem to the *P[artisan]
R[eview]*. On the other hand the *Times Magazine* would
be a bit fast at the moment, as the poem is not yet censored. Would you want to try some other big magazine
that is not so fast as all that? Then maybe the *Saturday
Review,* and by that time it will be, I hope, censored. If
you see *Liberation* this month, it appears I have a letter in
it about the race deal, which sounds bad. Keep sending
me things about it if you see anything worth while.
   Do you think the "Birmingham" poem should be in
Emblems? I really do, myself. I hesitated to suggest it as
everything may now be set up. But if it is not set up, I
would like to exchange "Birmingham" for one of the
"Macarius" Poems, about the same length. It really ought
to be in this book. I am sorry to keep inserting things at
the last minute. What do you think?
   I will see Victor tomorrow, I hope, and will learn more
about the big jamboree [at the University of Kentucky
commencement]. I really don't quite know much about
this LL.D. business. I guess I get a hood of some sort.
What I do then, I can't imagine. Maybe if I sleep in it I
can shut out some of the noises. There is regularly a cat-
fight under my window every night and last night some
infernal machine got going and sleep was impossible.
   However they sent me a copy of the citation, which
makes me out to be quite the lad. I am sending that, if it
is any help, only for heaven's sake I think it shouldn't get
into advertising, not that way. Ned can tone it down or

use the material some other way. I think it would be ok in a *file*. I am sending it because it is all the info I have.

As to the peace medal, I am getting that by proxy (Allen Forbes) some time in August at a dinner somewhere. I wouldn't mind going to the dinner. I still don't know much about this either, but he can find out from H. Stuart Hughes, though I don't think it is very important.

I am finally getting down to reading that great big book of Mumford's, *the City in History,* and it is great. I haven't read the Kennedy speech yet, will do so after dinner. It sounds like it would be safe after dinner.

Read a life of old Henry Miller, which was interesting. I really like him.

> Best wishes always,
> Cordially in Christ,
> T O M

/ · /

a letter . . . about the race deal: "Cuba Project: Letter to the Editor," *Liberation,* 3 (April 1963).

One of the "Marcarius" Poems: All three poems ended up in *Emblems of a Season of Fury:* "Marcarius and the Pony," "Marcarius the Younger," and "And the Children of Birmingham."

121. TLS-1   July 19, 1963

DEAR J.,

Word has come from the censor that the "Birmingham" poem is clear, so you can go right ahead with it with anyone who wants it. . . .

Tom Burns says he might help with *Emblems* in England. I gather Hollis and Carter is no more, and that Burns Oates do not publish verse. I would like to see

Emblems done by a decent outfit there. How about the Harvill Press?

Farrar Straus is still talking of suing Macmillan. I tried to get the *[Prayer as Worship and Experience]* ms. back from Macmillan and sent them their advance back, but no soap. I see no point publishing a book on prayer if everyone is dragging it through the courts. I can't get much sign of action out of [Robert] Giroux, he won't answer questions or tell me what's next. I am supposed to do some more books for them, on contract, but don't get any cooperation. I am really fed up with them and want to get out. I suppose they realize this by now and want to do everything they can just to block me and hold everything back, simply by being inert. As long as it is not quite definite that I have fulfilled my contract, they can prevent me from publishing anywhere else. I mean full length prose.

I don't know when you plan to come down with Raja Rao, but August is going to be bad. I have a Jewish mystic and an Anglican priest and then an interesting guy from India, a Benedictine who has an ashram there. (Rao might like to meet him, but we'll want to be talking a lot. I could send him along to you in NY.) Perhaps the best thing would be to plan something early in September, but after the first week the guest house is full of clerics on retreat.

Your new list looks fine. I'll be after you for some of the titles when I can find it and check which ones. Especially any new Henry Millers.

> All the best always, in Christ,
> T O M

/ · /

Tom Burns: Publisher at Hollis & Carter in London.

122. TLS-1   Sept 5, 1963

DEAR J.,

   . . . I saw the Xavier Rynne book: who hasn't? I think
it is pretty good, but I think the tone of conspiracy and
fantastic revelations is a little overdone. In the long run I
think it is a good job, but I think too that it is so obstrep-
erously anti-conservative that, in the end, the bishops will
be much more kind to the conservatives to compensate.
That is the way those things work out. I am sure everyone will be much more considerate of the Ottavianis in
the next session, and they may make a few gains as a
result. Only thing is that this is not, thank God, just a
party convention. There is more to it than that.

   Yes, saw *Catholic Digest* piece. Not worried about cats,
man. Or spilled beans. It is a little jolly and trumped up,
and some of the beans that got spilled were not really
there in the first place. However, it is nice, and it has
got all the nuns congratulating themselves that I am still
here. . . .

   Glad you want to send out *Emblems* for one of the
prizes. Hope we make it this time, though I can't imagine
the Pulitzers going out for us. How about some of them
clubs? Maybe there is a left wing prize around someplace,
too.

   I hope to see Victor soon. Have been overvisited this
summer, and am looking forward to a little respite in
September when the guesthouse is reserved for local
clergy. However, it is too bad you didn't get down with
Raja Rao. Maybe next year. Ferry thinks to come in
October.

All the best always,
Yours in Christ,
TOM

/ · /

the Xavier Rynne book: Letters from Vatican City (1963), Rynne's popular jour-nalistic account of the 1962 Second Vatican Council.

the Ottavianis: Reference to the conservative Cardinal Alfredo Ottaviani (1890–1979).

Catholic Digest piece: TM refers to Gerald Groves, "My Fourteen Years with Thomas Merton," in *Catholic Digest,* 27 (August 1963).

123. TLS-2   New York City
                                              October 11, 1963

DEAR TOM,

I have now managed to get caught up with those new things that you were good enough to send me in mimeo-graphed form, sometime ago, the ones that the Post Office lost for nearly a month, and I find them very interesting indeed. Lots of imagination, good images in the language, and very pungent on the salient points at issue. I hope you will find time to keep experimenting and exploring with these types of "new directions." When you go over them later, there are certain passages where you may want to tighten up a bit—the range of imagery becomes at times almost so profuse as to cloud the line of meaning—but they are essentially very good indeed. I wonder if we should not think about these for the next number of the New Directions annual, which I hope finally to get going on later this fall. I have been so busy with major editorial projects the last year I haven't managed to do much in shaping up the next annual, and I really should.

The "Devout Meditation in Memory of Adolph [sic] Eichmann" is right on the button, in its different way, too. As you pointed out, it is the "supposedly sane" peo-ple who make most of the trouble in world politics. They can appear to be perfectly normal in all exterior behavior, but, evidently, they are driven by some sort of terrible compulsion inside that leads to the kind of madness the world is now plagued with. I think that, too, would be fine for the next annual, if you like the idea. . . .

As ever,

J.

/ · /

those new things . . . you were good enough to send: "The Early Legend: Six Fragments of Work in Progress" led off the next *New Directions in Prose and Poetry,* 18 (ND, 1964): 1–9; TM later revised it and, under the title "The Early Legend: Notes for a Cosmic Meditation," included it in *RU,* pp. 125–138. The mimeograph items also included an early version of "Atlas Watches Every Evening," which JL printed in *ND* 18, pp. 10–15. It too later appeared under a slightly different title—"Martin's Predicament, or Atlas Watches Every Evening"—in *RU,* pp. 111–121.

Eichmann: Adolf Eichmann (1906–1962), a German Nazi who oversaw the execution of Jews from 1942 to 1945. Apprehended by Israeli security forces in Argentina in 1960, Eichmann was brought to trial in an Israeli court (1961) and sentenced to death for crimes against humanity. "One of the most disturbing facts that came out in the Eichmann trial," TM wrote in the "Devout Meditation," "was that a psychiatrist examined him and pronounced him *perfectly sane.* I do not doubt it at all, and that is precisely why I find it disturbing" (*RU,* p. 45).

124. TLS-1   Oct. 15, 1963

DEAR J.

. . . I am glad you like the two pieces, ["]Early Legend [(Six Fragments of a Work in Progress)"] and ["Martin's Predicament, or] Atlas Watches [Every Evening"]. I would be glad to have one of them in the *Annual,* or indeed both, but I was rather planning to try "Atlas" on *El Corno Emplumado,* which is bi-lingual, in Mexico. Would that make any difference to publication in the *Annual?* It would be *before* the *Annual.*

You are right about the need for revision, and I will be going over them both.

Ping Ferry was on his way down but I have just heard he had to go back and help out a niece who is trying to kill herself. I hope I won't miss him, but that he will be able to get here later maybe. I am sorry for him, to have something like that on his mind on top of everything else. He seems very fond of her too. From the way he talks, the next time anybody leaves her alone she is really going to do the job too. Maybe they'll just have to lock her up for keeps.

. . . As for the Eichmann bit, I can't quite remember if it was picked up somewhere else. I have no record of it, but if it was not, and you still want it, it will be yours.

Nice fall weather here. My back is ok, relatively. It is not a problem of exercise with me, I am always getting that. The vertebrae and one disc are injured and to some extent deteriorated, but I think I am getting them back in shape with heat, traction, rest and what not.

Any good new Spanish poets? I mean to translate a few Cuban Catholics who are having a rough time—if I can ever get to them. Maybe some for the *Annual*.

All the best always,
TOM

125. TLS-1   Nov 26, 1963

DEAR J.

Here is a copy of a letter to a Brazilian publisher [Father Wemhoff] who is interested in my part of *Breakthrough*. The project is all right with me, if he can get past all the other watchdogs. But the Abbot General died recently, so maybe things will ease up. I hope so.

Rhoda [Rissin] sent me a copy of *Emblems* and it looks fine. Sorry I cut so much when there were some pages left at the end. But it doesn't matter, maybe the stuff that went needed to go. I hope to get the other copies soon as I gave that one away. Glad *Poetry* took "Seneca."

I haven't heard from you for a long time. We have not come to any final decision about the two longish pieces I sent you, "Atlas Watches" and "Early Legend." You said something tentative about wanting them in the *Annual*. If this is definite, you can have them, otherwise I was thinking of trying the "Atlas" one in Mexico. Though it is so much part of the same project that was in *Behavior of Titans* that I suppose it logically goes in a ND publication. Whichever way you like is all right with me.

Isn't this business about the President awful? Everybody seems to be upset and shattered by it. Naturally we heard all about it and the shooting of Oswald and all the rest. The whole thing is very strange indeed isn't it? What is the intelligent comment on it? I hope to heaven things will calm down and that some good will come out of it all. The speech he was going to read at Dallas when he was shot down, is being read in the refectory. Strange thing: he lists all the increase in our weapons, missiles, bombs, polaris submarines etc. etc., and after doing so says that this would put a stop to any sinister plans of aggressors and . . . *assassins.* With all those missiles and submarines, all it took to do him in was a rifle and two bullets—one extra for the Governor of Texas. I think probably this angle of it is one of the things that has unconsciously unnerved so many people. But then too he was young and vigorous, energetic, lively, etc. It is this sudden stopping of *life* that shocks everyone. And in such a figure. So symbolic. I am very sorry for him and his family, but more sorry for the national dance of death, which is of course understandable, but it is such a symptom of our whole condition. Oof. What times to live in.

Finally, could you please do me a favor: someone has recommended an article by [Martin] Buber in the September 1963 *Commentary*. Do you think you could scare one up and have it sent to me, please? Charge any expense to the royalty account. Do you have a copy of Sartre's *Nausée* around in French? I know you did it in English. I am working on him a lot and find him smart. Since I was in the hospital I have been reading him right along. Sounds drab, superficially, but underneath is not so dumb or so negative either. Best wishes always, and God bless you.

Cordially in Xt.
Tom

/ · /

"Seneca": Appeared in *Poetry,* 103 (March 1964).

an article by Buber: Martin Buber (1878–1965), a Jewish philosopher, writer, and Hasidic theologian. Buber's writings include *The Prophetic Faith* (1949) and *Tales of the Hasidism* (1961). TM refers to Buber's article "Interpreting Hasidism" in *Commentary,* 36, no. 3 (September 1963), pp. 218–225.

Sartre's Nausée: Largely autobiographical novel by the French philosopher and writer Jean-Paul Sartre (1905–1980). *La Nausée (Nausea)* describes a growing awareness on the part of the character Roquentin of the purposelessness, absurdity, and gratuitousness of his own existence and the obscene overabundance of the world around him. From Sartre, Albert Camus, and others, TM encountered one of the core insights of modern existentialism: Human freedom is both limited by and made possible through responsible ethical action in the world.

126. TLS-1   Dec 7, 1963

DEAR J.,

The copy of *Nausée* reached me this morning. Many thanks. I will get it bound here, as it is rather beat up. Do you want it in your library, if so I will return it bound. Otherwise I will keep it here, but I would just as soon return it (bound) rather than accumulate more books. Thanks very much.

Thanks also for [William Carlos Williams's] *Patterson*. It is impressive to have the whole thing in one, and I can see that this is the only really proper way to read it. It is certainly a powerful poem. One of the great things of our time: by one of those people who are dying off on all sides. What is going on? Everyone seems to be departing. Taking off. Vanishing into better realms. One begins to wonder about this realm, then. What is being prepared for it?

The new Rexroth is very good too. I certainly like his poems. They are clear and alive. He has a classic touch. I suppose he gets it from his contact with the Chinese.

Thanks also for the big non-violence anthology. If they are going to have everybody in it, they might as well have me. I feel slighted. But I guess they have no notion that my stuff exists. One can't see everything.

I wrote to Bob [MacGregor] about a piece by Marco Pallis as a possibility for the [New Directions] anthology. He said send it along, but I have yet to find it. I know a man in Minnesota who has a copy, and if I can't find the one I had I will get him to send it along. Bob says the anthology is coming right along. If that is the case and you want "Atlas" etc., that is fine with me.

Here at Bellarmine College they are starting a sort of collection with a lot of odds and ends of mine, mostly mss. If there is anything you can do for them, they would be delighted. But I think you send stuff to Harvard, no?

The little Chuang Chu book you sent (Mentor) is unfortunately the same stuff I was working on. I will continue anyway. But slowly and without trying to get anywhere special, just because I like the guy, and there might still be room for my "versions."

. . . This is a hasty note. I have been extremely busy. Shoulder still hurts a bit, but not too steadily, and I can get a fair amount of work done on occasion.

All best wishes always.

Yours in Christ.
TOM

/ · /

the new Rexroth: Natural Numbers (ND, 1963).

Marco Pallis: Mountain climber, student of Tibetan art, author of *Peaks and Lamas* (1939), and TM correspondent (see *Ground,* pp. 463–477).

Bellarmine College: The Thomas Merton Collection was initiated at the Bellarmine College (Louisville, KY) Library in September, 1963, by a committee chaired by Father John T. Loftus. See "Thomas Merton Studies Center" by TM, John Howard Griffin, and Msgr. Alfred Horrigan (Unicorn Press, 1971). See also Letter #136.

127. TLS-1

Feb 13, 1964

DEAR J.

Just a short letter. Old back acting up, lousy raw weather, can't type much. Mainly I want to send back the Polish poets. Sorry to have kept them so long, they are great. I really hope you will do a small volume just of these. Really. Don't miss it. [Czeslaw] Milosz must have more by this time. It could go in your pleasant little series.

I am sending also "Message to Poets." It was read at the meeting of Latin American poets in Mexico and the last I heard it was read by old Henry Miller himself. I haven't any news about it however, so I don't know. Where should this be published? I think it should be in some medium sized magazine, not worth attempting *Atlantic* etc. If you have any ideas . . . [sic] I will have to send you a corrected text meanwhile. I will wait to hear from you.

All the best, in Christ,
TOM

J, while I am in the big envelope with cardboard backing, here are some abstract calligraphic drawings I have been doing lately. I think they are interesting enough to get [Emil] Antonucci perhaps to think up some sort of a little book, perhaps with wayout texts. What do you think of these?

/ · /

"*Message to Poets*": First appeared in *Americas,* 16 (April 1964); later included in *RU.* TM's "Message to Poets" was read by Miguel Grinberg at a gathering of Latin American poets in Mexico City, January 1964.

128. TLS-1   Feb. 27, 1964

DEAR J.

Just a quick note. I am getting a touch of 'flu and feel a little washed out. Thanks for everything: the copies of the letters to widow [Cesar] Vallejo etc. etc. Suggestions about Hans Kraus is much appreciated, but I think it is out of the question right now. Part of the monastic poverty idea is that the monk can't afford to take exceptional steps to guard his health and going to a specialist in NY seems a bit more than we ought to attempt. I can live with the thing as it is now. It slows me down a bit. But certainly I want to avoid an operation, and if it seemed that an operation was necessary, or claimed to be, we could look into the question. As I say, though, I think New York is just out and as far as I am concerned just being there would probably make me ill in some other way, though I am very grateful for the offer of a little room at 9 Bank. Used to have a girl friend on Bank, it would revive old memories. That is not what I am objecting to. Thanks again, anyway.

I have gone through this copy of the "Message to Poets" and found there were not as many corrections as I thought. I think that the *Saturday Review* would be the best. I don't cotton on to *the Reporter* for something like this. *Harpers,* maybe, if you think so. You can send it to

[John] Ciardi or to [Norman] Cousins direct. Cousins has been very friendly all along and says he wants to see everything I do etc. etc. So that might be a good approach.

Sorry to hear about widow [Aristodes] Stavrolakes and the hitch with the annual [ND 18], but I hope everything will work out all right. That section sounds interesting. I do not know his work. How is the new Henry Miller, by the way *([Stand Still Like the] Humming Bird)?* I think it was Henry who read the "Message" to the poets down there, I am not sure. Miguel Grinberg is supposed to be coming this way any time now.

As to the abstract drawings. I agree with you really. I liked Victor's book *[Concern for the Art of Civilized Man]* very much and of course I agree with him. Yet at the same time I think there is a place for this other kind of thing as long as it in no way pretends to be "art." Actually it is something totally different. But it seems to me that a book or collection of these things coming from me would be highly ambiguous and maybe we had better just forget it. I think a friend of mine has already showed some of this to Antonucci.

Best wishes always and I hope the Annual will be a smasher.

Yrs in Christ,
Tom

/ · /

Vallejo: TM's biographical essay on the Peruvian poet Cesar Vallejo appears in *Emblems of a Season of Fury,* along with TM's translations from the Spanish of Vallejo's poetry. See also *CP,* pp. 999–1002. See Letters #135 and #153 regarding Vallejo's widow.

Hans Kraus: JL wrote to TM on 24 February 1964: "I was mighty sorry to hear that the old back is giving you trouble again. I do wish we could get you up to Hans Kraus. He is the German doctor, a mountain climber himself, who fixes up all the skiers. We all swear by him. . . . Would Father Abbot let you come so far away?"

a little room at 9 Bank: JL's new apartment in New York City.

Ciardi: Poet and critic John Ciardi was poetry editor at the *Saturday Review* (1952–72) where Norman Cousins was editor-in-chief.

Stavrolakes: Greek writer, pupil of John Hawkes's, who killed himself in 1963. A civil suit brought by Stavrolakes's widow held up publication of the *ND Annual 18.*

Miguel Grinberg: The Brazilian writer, publisher, and poet Miguel Grinberg (born in 1937) edited a literary magazine, *Eco Contemporaneo,* and founded Acción Interamericana, an organization dedicated to promoting cultural exchange. TM's letters to Grinberg are collected in *Courage,* pp. 195–204.

129. TLS-1   March 20, 1964

DEAR J.

Many thanks for Miller's *Hummingbird* which reached me and which I have begun. As usual, I am completely in agreement. He is wise and persuasive and I think is one of the very few people who really makes any kind of sense. Thanks very much for the book. I will write to him when I get a chance.

I think I told you Miguel Grinberg was here. He seems a very good guy very open and genuinely promising in many ways. His magazine sounds and looks good and so do his other projects. By now you may have seen him in NY.

The other day I was going over the material for that Gandhi book *[Gandhi on Non-Violence]* and I would like to get the introduction done and get it in print, but I have been in trouble with the General (new one) about writing on non-monastic subjects (such as peace, love etc.) and I don't know how nonviolence would go down. But if things seem clear perhaps we might do this book finally.

Another thing I have been thinking about: doing some translations of the Negro poets of Africa and West Indies who write in French. Three I think of in particular: Jean Joseph Rabearivelo (of Madagascar), Leon Damas and

Aimé Césaire (of Martinique). Do you have any of their stuff in originals, or are you likely to run across them? Cesaire is especially good, and I think the others are from what little samples I have seen of them.

I read your little book of Chairwil Anwar and like it, also [Alain] Bosquet. Sunstone is the best, though. I like Octavio Paz very much indeed.

Victor and Carolyn may come over tomorrow if it does not rain or snow. Apart from that things are quiet.

> All best wishes for Easter,
> Yours in Christ,
> T o m

/ · /

Aimé Césaire: JL tracked down and sent to TM Césaire's *Les Armes Miracul-euses—The Miraculous Weapons* (Gallimard, 1961).

your little book: Part of ND's World Poets Series of 1963; poets in the series included Octavio Paz, Alain Bosquet, and Chairil Anwar.

130. T L S - 1   April 15, 1964

D E A R J . ,

Too bad about the "Message [to Poets]" and *Saturday Review.* I suppose it is logical though. Where else? Perhaps one of the University Magazines, though perhaps also one of the better Little Magazines. And there is always *the Commonweal* or *Jubilee.* Perhaps try Ed Rice at *Jubilee,* and save trouble. One thought also came to me: why not shoot a copy to John Beecher to make a little leaflet on his press? As long as it does not turn into anything that can in any sense be described as a book. I am as usual on thin ice with Farrar Straus and I wish I could finally get free of them. One more book and I think I am loose.

I wrote Bob [MacGregor] a couple of words about Stevie Smith. I love her, I am crazy about her, she is innocent and smashing like a Blake only new, and a lot of pathos under the deadpan sad funny stuff, a lot of true religion.

The *Gandhi* is coming along fine. I wrote seventeen pages yesterday and got a hemorrhage in my throat which had nothing to do with the writing or the subject, but just that there is something funny in my throat which bleeds. Doesn't amount to anything but it could turn into a nuisance I suppose. Meanwhile I hope to get the Gandhi stuff to you right soon and in fairly good shape. . . .

Cardenal and a fellow called [Jose] Coronel Urtecho (a good poet) are planning an anthology of my stuff in Spanish, and I am telling them to go ahead and use anything they want. They will be in touch with you soon, I suppose.

I have no books of Aimé Césaire so anything that may come along is fine. I suppose you are right in regarding him simply as a French poet. Titles of the others, I will send when I find them.

All best wishes always, in Christ,
T O M

{Did you read I. F. Stone on the missile racket? Wow!}

/ · /

John Beecher: Jon Beecher—printer, poet, Agrarian radical.

Stevie Smith: (1902–1971), English poet and novelist, recipient of the Queen's Medal for Poetry, 1969. ND published her *Selected Poems* in 1963.

I. F. Stone: Isidor F. Stone, writer, political commentator, and editor of the influential *I. F. Stone's Weekly.*

131. TLS-1   April 25th 1964

DEAR J.

The little Gandhi book was suddenly finished and seems to have turned out quite nicely. I am sending you the ms. herewith. The introduction will have to go to the censors and I will take care of that. Meanwhile you can be looking the book over. You will note that I have written introductory notes for each section of quotes. In these notes I take care of explaining terms like "ahimsa" and "satyagraha."

The only small gaps are references to pages from which citations were taken. I do not have the books here and cannot check, but I can get them and do so eventually. The very last one should be near the end of volume ii, in any case. I cut out one or two sections that seemed unclear and a couple of others that would give violent scandal in the west: the same is said more subtly in other selections anyway.

Don't worry about the throat. I haven't had any more bleeding and in checking with the doctor I found he agreed that there was nothing much to it. But I will be careful. Who knows, it may be some weird new thing. Lately I have tried to lay off most kinds of medicine (except bufferin which seems innocuous and is good for the back) because I have dimly heard about the awful racket that has been carried on by the drug companies. It seems to me that one of the basic things Gandhi is talking about is a kind of quiet liberation in which we become independent of these producers and simply do not use their products. I guess we are all far from that. The economy is so tightly interwoven with strands which are part of every life. The reason I mention the medicine is that you never know when some strange reaction is a side effect of a miracle drug. I heard of one miracle drug that cleared up arthritis temporarily but also produced softening of the bones and a flock of other things including psychosis. Nice, eh?

I sent John Beecher the "Message to Poets" and also "Answers on Art and Freedom." But today I discovered that the "Message" had been printed in part in the magazine of the Pan American Union, *Americas,* in English and Spanish. I forgot that I had said yes to the guy who asked about that, some time ago. But I don't think it will matter much, as this magazine does not get around in the U.S., as far as I know and is sort of a glorified trade journal anyway (though the editor now is quite good, and is a poet).

All the best, always, in Christ,
TOM

[P.S. deleted]

132. TLS-1   May 24, 1964

DEAR J.

First, many thanks for Aimé Césaire. I have the book now and I find it full of good things but of course I will keep in mind your warning that he may be much translated already and if I get down to anything I will take the proper steps and all. That "special" book on Vallejo I did manage to get from Cordoba through poets in Argentina, so I have that. It is fairly good, has a lot of material by people who knew him. His wife, incidentally, comes through it all as a rather unpopular figure and probably a harpy who made his existence miserable. That happens, I suppose. . . .

I have not yet dug up titles of other African poets and am in no hurry. I suppose it is best not to get too mixed up in too many things at a time. But there is one thing I really need, and I wonder if you could get it for me, charging the account as usual. That is an ATLAS, and I mean a really bang up one with plenty of details on European countries. I really don't need to know about every whistle stop in Nebraska but I do need to be able to find things in Germany, Ireland etc. etc. and in Africa and South America for that matter. Can you think which is the best? We have here in the library a big idiotic *Life* picture book that claims to be an Atlas, and some rather old ones.

Still no news from censors on *Gandhi*. They always take time, and I am hoping that they will not be troublesome though I am afraid this time the stuff had to go to the two tough ones, as the friendly ones have done too many things all at once and it begins to look fishy if the mean ones don't get in the game. Well, they have. I am still not cleared away with Farrar Straus, and Naomi, moving to Maine, does not have much to say about what goes on.

Archbishop [Thomas] Roberts, the only really pacifist Catholic bishop I know of, was here. A very sound guy, he seems to me. Knew Gandhi. Also the people from Hiroshima, or one group of them, were here and we had a nice little meeting in the hermitage, but it did not last long enough. I was happy to see them. I forgot your request about [donating] the slightly damaged *Original Child Bomb* books. John Heidbrink at the FOR [Fellowship of Reconciliation] would probably know a good thing to do with them. Incidentally the *[Thomas Merton] Reader* which Harcourt Brace put out is doing very badly too, which is a shame because I thought it was well done.

Anyway, all the best, and God bless you.

Ever yours in Christ,
TOM

/ · /

Roberts: Former English archbishop of Bombay, one of the liberal bishops at the Second Vatican Council, who resigned in favor of a native bishop.

the people from Hiroshima: Led by Hiromu Murishita, a member of the Hiroshima Peace Education Institute, a group of *Hibakusha*—survivors of the 6 August 1945 bombing of Hiroshima—toured the United States in 1964, and visited TM at Gethsemani.

John Heidbrink: Presbyterian minister and civil rights activist who joined the Fellowship of Reconciliation in 1960 and served the organization as Secretary for Church Relations. See *Ground,* pp. 401–430.

133. TLS-1   July 8th 1964

DEAR J.

Thanks for the good batch of new [ND] books. . . . The [George] Oppen and [Charles] Reznikoff books are both great as far as I can tell, and I know I am going to enjoy going into them deeply.

John Beecher wrote that he had not got down to printing the "Message to Poets" yet, but that he would some time, and if I wanted to send it to a magazine meanwhile . . . [sic] I think it would probably be a good idea to send it somewhere. Ping Ferry saw Beecher lately and said B. was in a kind of despair and the likelihood of his printing anything was about zero, at least at the moment. Do you still have a copy or shall I send you one?

I got a very good letter from Henry Miller. I had sent him a snapshot of me and Miguel Grinberg and he said I looked like an ex-convict and also like him (Miller) and also some like Genet. These are all compliments and I am pleased. I also look like Picasso, this I have been told by others, and I got a letter from a Cuban poet who said I looked Chinese. So far for what I look like.

Thanks for the info about [Fernando] Pessoa. I shall be very glad to get anything of his, including the French

translation you mention. I really mean to try to do something with his stuff one of these days, and think I will.
But I haven't forgotten Chuang Tzu either. About the
Atlas, maybe a good foreign one would be the best idea,
perhaps English or German. Or did I have that idea
before?

All the best, hope *Gandhi* is clicking.

Yrs in Christ
Tom

/ · /

Oppen: George Oppen (1908–1984), poet and leader of the Objectivists
whose spare verse was inspired by Ezra Pound's poetics. ND published
Oppen's *The Materials* (1962) and *This Is Which* (1965).

Reznikoff: (1894–1976), Part of the George Oppen circle—the Objectivist
School—Charles Reznikoff's *By the Waters of Manhattan* (1962), introduced
by C. P. Snow, was co-published by ND and the *San Francisco Review.*

Pessoa: In *LE* (p. 309), TM spoke fondly of the Portuguese poet Fernando
Pessoa (1888–1935) and his "Zen way of seeing."

134. TLS-1   Oct 2, 1964

DEAR J.

By all means go ahead with the new title *Gandhi on
Non Violence.* The only thing is that you might have to
check as it sounds awfully close to nine other Gandhi
titles. I don't know for sure that this exact title has been
used, but it is close. A subtitle could clarify.

As to the glossary of Indian words: I don't really think
I used enough of them, and the few I used I explained in
the little prefatory paragraphs to each section. I believe
there were not more than six technical Indian words. Not
enough for a regular glossary, it seems to me. However, I
don't mind if you want to put one in there.

No news from Victor lately. I will try to find out what is new. The last I heard he was going to get out of the hospital. Perhaps the recent silence means that things are not going well.

The poem ["And the Children of Birmingham"] in the *New York Review [of Books]* got there via Bob Giroux, it was his idea to send it there. I would not have thought of it. Ping Ferry had suggested *Commentary* and I sent it to Bob [Giroux] who knows Podhoretz. By the way Bob sent me their new Purdy novel. Very funny indeed.

What an awful thing about [Robert] Hutchins' house. I thought about them all when I heard of the [Santa Barbara] fires, thought most about the center [for the Study of Democratic Institutions]. One tends to assume that the people who get their houses burned in brush fires are all sort of share cropper types like around here. But I would not like a good big fire to get in around this hermitage either. Last year we fought a fire around an old guy's house and he just sat on the porch with another gaffer talking about the *real* fires they used to have in the old days. And flames thirty feet high climbing up in some young willows a hundred yards away, less than that. And a big gas tank right up against the wall of his old shack. Some experience.

By no means send any money to the Bellarmine thing. I don't see where they need to raise a lot of funds, though they are doing it, and I think they are pushing things too fast and too far. I don't think they rate as a really "worthy cause" though it is all right by me for them to collect papers and things. Still, I appreciate their kindness. But they make too much of everything.

Do let's look forward to a sort of visit early in the year if you can.

All the best, always,
T o m

/ · /

the new title: TM originally proposed the subtitle *A Primer of Non-Violence.*

Podhoretz: Norman Podhoretz (1930–), Brooklyn-born, Columbia-educated literary critic and conservative political commentator who became editor of the right-leaning *Commentary* in 1960.

Purdy: James Purdy (1923–), Ohio-born novelist, known for his comic and satirical fiction. TM refers to Purdy's novel *Cabot Wright Begins* (1964).

the Bellarmine thing: See Letter #126.

135. TLS-1   Nov. 21, 1964

DEAR J.

Thanks for your good letters, especially the one from Yucatán. I was delighted to hear you had run into Nicanor Parra. He is the Spanish American poet who interests me most at the moment and I have not been able to get hold of any of his stuff except a couple I have seen in magazines. I wonder if I wrote to you about him, but evidently not. Naturally I am most anxious to have all his books. I like your collaborated translation. I would be delighted to try a few myself, except it is always understood that much of this projected translation stuff ends up by being only a fond hope. Still, I would really like to do this. (Still have not touched Pessoa, same kind of anti-poet in a way). I would be delighted to be in contact with Parra, though next year in general I am cutting down on correspondence.

Actually, about widow Vallejo, I kept that letter of mine on ice and then decided not to send it at all. In the long run I think this is better with these deranged people. They get all steamed up and write in a fury, and then the letter goes away into the blue and they get excited about something else, so that when you come back at them you simply start it all over without good reason. And there is no placating them because they do not want to be reasonable, they want to make a scene. I feel very sorry for her, but I don't think that my writing to her is going to help much. And in this regard I have been having quite a bit of trouble with Marie Tadie in France. That is enough for me. . . .

Best wishes always, as ever,
T o m

/ · /

Parra: The Chilean physicist and poet Nicanor Parra visited TM with JL in May 1966. TM was greatly influenced by Parra's *Poems and Antipoems* (ND, 1953) and considered him "one of the best South American poets, a no-nonsense anti-poet with a deep sense of the futility and corruption of social life." TM's translations of Parra's poems are in *CP,* pp. 972–981.

that letter of mine: JL wrote TM on 1 October 1964: "Here is a terribly sad letter which has just come in from the Widow Vallejo. As you can see, she is in a very disturbed mental state. It is terribly sad." TM wrote JL (3 October 1964): "Here is some stuff from widow Vallejo. I enclose [a] copy of my letter to her. Do you know what one is supposed to do about such things, I mean irrational things like this?" Vallejo's widow often became unreasonably and unpredictably angry and confused over permissions requests governing her late husband's literary affairs. At one point she threatened to sue ND. See Letter #153.

Marie Tadie: TM's French translator.

136. TLS-2   Dec. 13, 1964

D E A R J .

Thanks a lot for your letter of the 8th. I am glad to hear that books of Nicanor Parra will soon be on the way. I got an interesting offprint . . . with selections from young Peruvian poets. Very much impressed. Maybe I will write to him. . . .

Here is an important thing I have been pondering and wanting to write you about. Next January I am fifty, and besides that I am in a real corner-turning mood. It is always the same corner but this time the way is open, since it looks almost certain that I will get permission to live a great deal of the time alone in the hermitage. And that is fine. I have been sleeping up there, spending all the time I can there, taking some of my meals there (the ones that don't call for much cooking). I find it agrees with me perfectly, is just what I always expected, wanted and hoped for. It seems to me that I am finally getting in to what I really came here for in the first place, twenty three years ago today, by the way, I entered the community.

This will bring with it certain adjustments. Naturally I hope to go on writing, and to write only the more creative and meditative sort of stuff, not turn out manuals of spirituality etc. Poems, meditations, and the freer kind of commentary, I hope. Journal too, and all that. The kind of stuff I really like, along with some scholarly studies for the monastic reviews too, on occasion. The Abbot is going to cut down on external contacts, I don't know how much, but of course I will remain in contact with you, Naomi, etc. And I hope perhaps to occasionally see people, exceptionally, like for instance Parra if he comes around. Cardenal is supposed to be coming to this country in 65 too.

At this point I think it makes sense to get my affairs in some sort of order, and what I would like to do would be to ask you and Naomi jointly to take over the responsibility of being my literary, artistic etc. executors. This would also involve someone at Bellarmine, to some extent . . . as in fact most of my mss. and so on are already there. There is really quite a lot of unpublished stuff around, and there are also lots of bits and pieces that have appeared all over the place at random and have never been collected. Someone would need to look after all that and get it collected some day. As long as I am alive and kicking, I would of course do my share. But I would want the thing to go into effect whenever I started living in the hermitage more or less continuously. Naturally, the monastery would get the royalties as usual.

If you could get down here some time next year, we might discuss this and make some sense out of it, as you understand these things and I don't. I have not mentioned it to Naomi, still less to the Bellarmine people. I think it is workable though. It is certainly Fr. Abbot's idea that my stuff should not stay in the monastic library but should be at Bellarmine, and no one here would know how to go about publishing it or disposing of it.

My idea would be to get the Bellarmine people, once they have catalogued the stuff, to let me have a list and I could give a complete checklist of unpublished work. Perhaps also it might be a good idea to let you have at least a partial collection of unpublished mss. on file there. Indeed, there would be no harm in publishing some of it in the ordinary course of things. For example I thought of one idea that we need not rush into: but how about a paperback consisting of *Behavior of Titans* plus a lot of other short bits like the three that were in *ND 18,* poetry and poetic prose? It could make a good little collection, I think.

Then there would be plenty of letters that could eventually be published too. I have at least two full length books for which, for one reason or another, have not been published. One because of the jam we got into between Farrar Straus, and Macmillan. Another because I am not satisfied with it. Maybe another somewhere. And there are stacks of Journal material, some of which by the way is going to be in the next *Sewanee Review.*

In the long run, you and Naomi could decide between you who would get what, proceeding on the principle that we have always followed: poetry and offbeat or exceptional small prose books to ND and the full length prose books to, in this case, Doubleday, or whoever Naomi is with, or decides to give it to.

Does this make sense? I do think it is important, at any rate, to get things straightened out at this point. There is a great deal of stuff around and I would not want it simply to kick around the monastery until it gets lost, and believe me things certainly do get lost fast in this place.

Ping Ferry saw the drawings and liked them. I am selling them by the way with the idea that any money they make will go toward a scholarship for a Negro girl at Catherine Spalding College. Do you think there would be any point sending them east to be exhibited somewhere around NY? Any ideas?

Please let me know what you think of all this.

> With my most bouncing Christmas wishes,
> T O M

/ · /

the three that were in *ND 18:* "Atlas Watches Every Evening," "A Devout Meditation in Memory of Adolf Eichmann," and "The Early Legend: Six Fragments of Work in Progress"—later collected in *RU.*

137. TLS-2   New York City
December 21, 1964

D E A R   T O M ,

Many thanks for your extremely interesting letter of December 13th. I am {fifty} now too, and I know how you feel. There are many days when I wish that I could just sit and read a book, or go chop in the woods, rather than busy myself with all the turmoil of the office and all its complicated business affairs. That is really great news that Father Abbot is going to let you live more and more in your little hermitage in the woods. But I hope you won't cut yourself off entirely from all contact with your old friends.

It makes me feel good that you have enough confidence in me to ask me to serve as one of your literary executors. I will certainly be glad to help out in any way that I can. I'm sure that Naomi will too, and she is a fine person to work with. But before you make up your mind, let me inject here a few thoughts on the negative side of my own participation.

Would it not be better to find someone twenty years younger than I? This would make for more continuity in the executorship. While I am lucky to be enjoying wonderful health, except for my dratted sinus, and expect to be around, or hope to, for some time, we are, after all, of about the same age, and so, I guess, is Naomi.

I am sure that publishers have served as literary executors for writers, but wouldn't Father Abbot or his successor, feel that there was a "conflict of interest" in having either Naomi or myself serve, since we are both in the publishing business, and might have a tendency, no matter how objective we try to be, to steer things our own way in our own interest? Wouldn't the Order prefer that one of its own people be the executor? That, of course, may well be something that you want to avoid, being fearful that they would suppress some of the more exciting stuff, thinking it too literary, or "far-out" and not sufficiently religious.

Bellarmine: I hope you have been careful to get up proper legal documents and specifications when you made the gift of manuscripts to them. Is the stuff simply on deposit with them, still your property, or that of the Abbey, or do they think that they now own it? If so, do they own only the "physicality," or do they also own publishing rights? This is a very important distinction which we run onto all the time. For example, when a library buys a paper or letters they usually get only the "physicality," and the publishing rights remain with the writer of the letter, the author or his heirs. It is important, I think, to get all this down in very clear black and white, so that there can be no later misunderstandings.

As I see it, the really ideal literary executor for you would be some able young Catholic lawyer, with literary taste, someone in his thirties. Can you think of any such person?

I hope you won't misunderstand my questions and suggestions. Nothing would give me greater personal satisfaction than to be able to do some work for you which might be of real help and value to you, now or in the future. But I just want to try to look at the problems as objectively as possible, and urge you to make sure that what you are planning will really achieve all the objectives that you want. Also, I wouldn't like to feel that I was moving into anything which might make Father Abbot unhappy. Have you talked out all these angles with him yet? Why not sound out Naomi, in a tentative way? I think she has a lot of good horse sense about things of this kind.

Yes, I think we ought to be thinking about a paperback collecting various of the literary pieces, both prose and poetry. Of course, there is still a fairly good stock of hardbound *Behavior of Titans* on hand, but it's hardly fair to deny the paperback audience, the students and such, forever, on account of that.

That's great that the drawings are going well, and a very nice idea that you are selling them for a scholarship for a Negro girl at Spalding College. Would you like me to ask around a little bit among the bookshops in New York to see if any one of them would like to have a little show, and perhaps to sell some of the drawings here? I suppose they would probably want a commission, but we could find out. I would think a bookshop would be better than an art gallery, or another possibility might be something like the Catholic Student Center at NYU on Washington Square, if they ever do that sort of thing.

The day after Christmas, I'm flying over to Switzerland to meet my son Paul for a bit of skiing. He gets a little vacation from his school in the Lebanon, and I think he needs some cheering up—it's a pretty austere life there, I gather—and some good food for a while. After that I'll drop down to see Ezra in Venice and other members of the Pound family, but should be back not much later than the middle of January. I hope I can get down there for a good visit with you in the early Spring. I hope you will have a fine Christmas down there, in the Abbey, or in the woods, as the case may be.

As ever,

J.

138. TLS-1   Jan 1. 1965

DEAR J.

Thanks for your good letter of the 21st which clears up a lot of points. I agree with the difficulties you raise concerning the executorship, and I had seen them to some extent. I still think you and Naomi are the most logical ones to get it in motion, and then perhaps the "young lawyer" type can be brought into the picture and survive us, like they say "hopefully."

Father Abbot agrees with me that you and Naomi are the two people who understand the business enough to handle it. As for the fact that you might want to publish some of the stuff yourselves: well, who else? You have a right to it. We both feel that the only essential thing as far as the monastery is concerned is to see that they get the royalties to which they are entitled. Fr. Abbot felt, as I do, that the question of submitting everything to strict order censorship would not arise if I were dead, the only point he raised was that if there were question of something that might hurt the reputation of the monastery or of someone in it, then perhaps a member of the community with some sense could be called upon to give an opinion. Otherwise all the initiatives would rest with you, because I don't think anyone around here understands the situation well enough.

As to Bellarmine, that is a very good point about "physicality" and "rights" and we can get that ironed out too.

The one thing I am concerned with is to make quite sure that if I kick off the material I leave around will be in the hands of people who will understand what it is all about and know what to do about it, and not simply lie around in the normal confusion of the monastery where everything gets lost if not immediately, then within a week. Or if it is not lost then worse still it gets into the hands of half cultivated morons with printing presses in Labrador or something like that. It is not that I think my stuff is all that important or that it deserves to survive, but that I still have enough self respect to want to see the results of a lot of work dealt with at least according to the norms of commons sense and ordinary equity.

I keep thinking about the paperback collection and will write more about it, or better talk with you when you come down. And yes, I think it would be fine if you could interest some bookstore in the drawings. They are now going to New Orleans, after that probably to St. Louis, maybe a few other places.

Hope you are having a fine trip. Best wishes and blessings,

Cordially in Christ,
T o m

---

139. T L S - 2   Feb. 3, 1965

D E A R J.,

First of all here are some prints of the drawings. They are not any good for reproduction nor do they represent the whole drawing in the sense that the whole sheet is not taken: there is much more white space. But they can give a fair idea. Good enough to interest a possible exhibitor. . . .

Naomi has agreed that the executorship is a good idea and is glad to get in on it, with, as you too said, the proviso that there will be a Catholic lawyer in it somewhere. That can certainly be worked out. Father Abbot's most recent contribution to the question is that I ought to "publish everything I can" before I kick off, and I have no objections to *that*. So I think it would be great if you and Naomi got together and discussed it.

I am interested in what you say about [your son] Paul. A friend [Abdul Aziz] (Moslem) is trying to urge me to learn Arabic, but I am wary of that, at least when there is no instructor in the picture. I know how much time one can waste trying to get Russian by oneself (I soon gave that one up after I had got as far as ["]Ivan working like the devil in his factory["]). I probably will not start Arabic. What you say about Ezra Pound['s severe depression] is not surprising. He must be affected by the deaths of Eliot, Edith Sitwell etc., even though they were perhaps not all close to him (Sitwell?).

It is not news to say we have had cold weather. It has been good for me to be sleeping in the hermitage in sub zero weather, though I hope I don't make a career out of it. Last night some water I had in a cup near my bed was frozen solid (only a little bit of water, not a full glass) and I must admit that even under a pile of blankets I ended by feeling the cold. I try to keep the fire going, but when I am not around the place gets plenty cold. I am still waiting for the Electric Cooperative guys to get the line up there so that I can have light and also a heater (small one) to supplement the wood fire. An outdoor jakes in sub-zero weather is also interesting (though nature takes care of it, I find, one is not pulverized with cold after all).

It is all right when one is in good health, but I would not like to try that regime with a bad cold.

Nicanor Parra's books came and they are splendid. He has a good tough and sensitive delivery, straight face anti-poet style, very eloquent and impressive, and dour. I must write to him. I really want to get down to translations of Pessoa and thought I would do a little book of Parra and Pessoa, call it say "Two Antipoets." But first I want to get Chuang Tzu done. I mean to.

There is a new magazine, the *Lugano Review,* which is going to print some of the drawings. Later I mean to send you some abstractish photographs I have taken. They might be interesting for covers of paperbacks. You will see. Or when you come down, for I hope you are coming down this spring.

All the best always,
Cordially in Christ,
T o m

/ · /

the drawings: TM put together a collection of his abstract calligraphic ink drawings which were exhibited in several U.S. cities. Fifteen drawings are reproduced in *RU,* along with TM's explanatory "Signatures: Notes on the Author's Drawings," pp. 179–182.

what you say about Paul: In early January JL accompanied his son Paul, on vacation from school in Lebanon, on a skiing trip to Switzerland. JL wrote TM (26 January 1965): "I am afraid he is finding that Arabic is a hopelessly difficult language, the kind of field where you could go on and on for a lifetime and never get really to master it."

Edith Sitwell: (1889–1964), British poet, critic, and novelist.

Nicanor Parra's books: Poemas y Antipoemas (1953) and *Versos de Salon* (1962). TM's translations of Parra's poetry appeared in *Poems and Antipoems* (ND, 1967). In 1972, ND published Parra's *Emergency Poems,* translated by Miller Williams.

Lugano Review: Very stylish literary review founded and edited by James Fitz-simmons, TM's Columbia University classmate.

140. TLS-1   Feb. 25, 1965

DEAR J.

Thanks for your letter, and thanks especially for the two [W. H.] Auden books which arrived yesterday. I am glad you thought of including [Auden's essay] ["T]he Dyer's Hand["]. I hope you are charging these to me, because I also want to ask for his *Collected Poems.* I find we have nothing of his in the library. I have been using him a bit in some classes on poetry to the novices and I think he is about the best one to get them familiar with the modern idioms. Used some Rexroth too.

Here is a copy of the letter I just wrote to Mons. Horrigan [at Bellarmine College]. I share your respect for him. He is a very good and capable person, broad minded and very straight. I am glad Naomi has an attorney up her sleeve. All can thus be sewed up right. As I say in my letters to Mons. H. I hope that the thing will not be nailed down so tight that no scholar can freely use the material in publishing some possible study. Just so that it is properly controlled and the Abbey is not cheated of anything that is reasonably to be expected from the publication.

I would gladly translate some Parra soon. I wonder just what I should do? Just anything, or should I avoid duplicating what may have already been done by the other guy? In a few days I hope to send some samples of Pessoa, perhaps for the Annual? I also thought that some of the letters Lax and I have exchanged ought to be typed up and they might be worthwhile for the annual also.

This mad skin trouble is back on the hands and I am typing with gloves. Saw the skin specialist yesterday and he is baffled by it, as to saying what it could come from. Obviously it is not poison ivy, there is snow on the ground. I am working on some sleuthing: maybe some plastic objects or some funny process, e.g. in some new offset choirbooks we have. I hope I can place it.

Since it is hard to type I will stop, more later.
Thanks again for the books. Let me know about Parra.

All the best, in Christ,
T o m

/ · /

Auden: Wystan Hugh Auden (1907–1973), British-born, Oxford-educated poet who became a U.S. citizen in 1946 and turned to his Anglo-Catholic roots in books like *For the Time Being* (1945) and the Pulitzer Prize–winning *The Age of Anxiety: A Baroque Eclogue* (1948). JL sent TM Auden's *The Dyer's Hand* (1962), a major collection of essays and lectures, and Monroe K. Spears's *Auden: A Collection of Critical Essays* (1964).

done by the other guy: Miller Williams. See note to Letter #139.

141. TLS-1   March 19, 1965

D E A R J .

Before I got your letter of the 8th I had already translated a few of Parra's "Versos de Salon" and since then
they have been typed up. Here is a copy for you to look
at. I am probably going to send them to the *Lugano
Review*. . . . Do not have the copy of the Letters between
me and Lax which I promised you, but will send them
soon. I think they will be lively enough for the annual.
You will see. Meanwhile about the [Parra] antipoems, I
will see if I get a chance to do a few of these between
now and the time you come down. I am still looking
forward to that.

However, in regard to coming down, much of April is
ruled out by Holy Week and Easter, but after Easter is all
right. Whenever convenient for you. Easter is April 18th
this year. So after that we will be in the best season of the
year anyway.

Thanks for the two [Homero] Aridjis books. I have

not read them yet, but they are attractive. I will drop you a note about them later. Thanks also for the Cortazar novel, which I think is excellent. I have heard a lot about him. This one sounds in the beginning like *Ship of Fools* but actually it turns out to be much better and with a special twist that is very intriguing. I think Cortazar is great, and will be doing things that will make everyone sit up and pay attention.

A priest who was with the marchers in Selma came through here on his way back to Chicago, last night. He was not on the big march which I understand does not take place until today. Had some very exciting things to say, and I think this is another big step, perhaps the biggest, in the whole civil rights thing so far. We will see. The most unfortunate and miserable people, the ones who need the most help, turn out to be the Southern whites. I hope that this gradually gets through to them. But with all this, we still may forget that the problem is only really beginning. There is far to go.

Meanwhile I am going to write to Parra, if not today, then soon. If you want a couple more copies of these translations, I will send them.

All the best always,
Cordially in Christ,
Tom

/ · /

two Aridjis books: On 8 March 1965, JL "sent down to you two little volumes of poetry by one of the good Mexican poets, Homero Aridjis, which a Mexican editor dropped at my office the other day." Aridjis's "Los Espacios Azules: Six Poems" appeared in *ND Annual 29.*

the Cortazar novel: Julio Cortazar's *The Winners* (1965).

Ship of Fools: The Katherine Anne Porter novel, first published in 1962.

the marchers in Selma: Led by Martin Luther King, Jr., 4,000 civil rights demonstrators marched from Selma, Alabama, to Montgomery to deliver voting rights petitions. Judging from the severe race riots in Watts, Los Angeles, the following August that claimed thirty-five lives, TM's assessment of the problem was right on the mark.

142. TLS-1   May 13, 1965

DEAR J.

I trust your judgment about not publishing the letters to Lax. So just keep one for the file and send another down here. I will let it be part of a collection and that will be that.

Carolyn wrote a note that Victor was very happy about the visit but had to go to the hospital again. I quickly got over the bug I had, because the doctor finally gave me an antibiotic that was effective in knocking it out, or at least I hope it has done so. Everything is fine now. The brother has not got the pictures out yet. I certainly agree that it was a historic visit, and a wonderful day in the country.

I made a collection of some Irish hermit poems for the novices, and it occurred to me that this would make a nice little anthology, if you are interested. They are mostly poems by Celtic hermits of the 6th–9th centuries, perhaps a few later ones, and they are charming. I could write an essay on them to go with it. No hurry of course about what list it would be on, but I am sending a copy along for you to look at. I am glad about being on the next [ND] list and have already got three or four more poems or pieces to go with it. I ought to have it all done in a month or so, preface and all. I hope so anyway.

Victor is probably ok, but just tired, and again each time he goes to the hospital he slides down a bit, poor man. But I am not worried, nor is Carolyn. Though of course with the heart anything could happen.

All the best always, in Christ,
TOM

/ · /

the pictures: The monastery sought JL's help in locating a printer to publish what TM described to JL (8 May 1965) as "a book of photographs we are putting out about the monastery."

a historic visit: JL visited TM the first week of May 1965. The Hammers
prepared a picnic lunch; it was the first time that TM, JL, and the Hammers
spent time together.

143. TLS-1   Aug. 10, 1965

DEAR J.

Many thanks for your letter from Wyoming. The Arab
manuscript sounds interesting, but as I am just in the
middle of moving out to the hermitage and getting all
my stuff cleared out of the novitiate, this is not the best
time for me to try reading it. I think I can consider that
kind of project again in a couple of months when I have
got settled down and have only very small piles of work
confronting me.

I was glad and surprised to get the *Chuang Tzu* proofs
so fast. But they do present a bit of a problem. I don't
know if I mentioned to you that Bob Giroux is bringing
out a book of mine *[Seasons of Celebration],* now scheduled for December. Actually, I was expecting it to be out
by now, and so I did not think there would be any conflict between it and *Chuang Tzu.* But for some reason it
was delayed, but I had proofs of it a couple of weeks
before *Chuang Tzu* parachuted in, and Naomi said she
would be writing to you about it.

Actually, I think that it would be to the interests of all
of us to put off *Chuang Tzu* until say Easter season or at
least somewhat early in 1966 (if you and Naomi work
out something better that's fine with me). With *Gandhi*
delayed, and the book at Farrar Straus and Giroux, that
would mean three books of mine in one publishing season and I think that would be a bad idea for all of us. I
am sure you will agree. I leave it to you and Naomi to
figure out what is best.

Chuang Tzu really looks good and I am happy that my

friend John Wu is really enthusiastic about the result. He is a very good judge in such matters. He has by the way written a very interesting book on Zen which I think you ought to see, it is just getting finished in ms.

As to the Irish poems, yes, I am sure you are right. The translation is really inadequate. I will think it over and see if I get some good ideas.

All the best always,
Cordially in Christ,
T O M

/ · /

moving out to the hermitage: TM "retired" as Novice Master in August 1965, and began living full time in a hermitage close to the abbey that the novices had built for him. He explains his reasons for moving into the hermitage in "A Life Free from Care," *Cistercian Studies,* 5 (1970); TM writes about a typical day at the hermitage in *Day of a Stranger* (Peregrine Smith, 1981).

144. TLS-1   Sept. 2, 1965

D E A R J.

About the Paperback consisting of *Behavior of Titans* and other material. I realized when you spoke of sending the list to Naomi that I no longer had the complete list myself. I must have sent the copy along to Bellarmine with all the other stuff when I cleared out the novice master's office before coming up to the woods. Still, I have a rough idea: I think I suggested the "Meditation" on Eichmann and other stuff that was in *ND 18.* What else? I am not too sure.

I am therefore enclosing more material that I think might possibly go in.

To Each his Darkness[: Notes] On [a Novel of] Julien Green

Flannery O'Connor[: A Prose Elegy] Message to Poets
[Answers on] Art and Freedom
Rain and the Rhinoceros

These I think ought to go in for sure, plus perhaps an article of which Naomi has a copy, ["]the time of the End is the Time of No Room.["]

I am also enclosing, just in case—no I am not either, I changed my mind.

I have what I think is a better title for the book:

Raids on the Unspeakable

Do you like that any better? I think it is an improvement. But now, will you do this: when you have editorially gone over all the proposed material and decided what you think ought to be in the book, will you please send it all to me so that I can go through it and make a few corrections, do some editing and so on? Then we can move.

While we are on the subject of this book, *Raids on the Unspeakable,* I might mention that Bob [Giroux] will also be planning another one, and this time I think we must make sure they do not clash. His will be *Mystics and Zen Masters.*

All the best. Hope you like the title.

Cordially in the Lord,
TOM

---

145. TLS-1   Sept. 12, 1965

DEAR J.:

I haven't heard a word from the *Lugano Review* people about [the poem] "Man the Master" so if you want it for the annual *19* and are in a hurry, I would say plan on using it. Let me know what you decide, and also, what else of mine are you using in this annual? I got a couple of good letters from Parra. Did I ever send you the correction he wanted made? Which reminds me that I don't think I have the copy of those corrections I made either. When I moved out of the novitiate I cleaned everything out (which explained the pictures I sent you) and these corrections may have gone also.

It is certainly going to be a joke if *Gandhi* appears now, while India jubilantly dashes off to war with Pakistan in the most material and self-congratulatory fashion. Surely the book ought to be ready by now. Are you sure that the printer isn't a John Bircher or something? Sounds like sabotage to me.

Looking forward to *Chuang Tzu,* that is one book I am happy about.

Guess that's all for the moment. Have finished out my contract with Farrar Straus and am busy moving over to Naomi and Doubleday with my next one, though FSG still have two in the works.

Best wishes always. Send a clipping once in a while so I can follow what these crazy people are doing in Asia: at least the worst or biggest or most relevant bits of news.

Cordially always in Christ,
T O M

/ · /

"*Man the Master*": Printed in *ND Annual 19* (1966). See also *CP,* pp. 637–640.

146. TLS-1   Sept. 27, 1965

D E A R J .

Many thanks for the list. There is no conflict between the Answers on Art and Freedom and the Art book to which Naomi refers, also Notes on Art and Freedom are the same as the "Answers" of which you have the text, so that problem is liquidated.

I would prefer not to pad out the book, but to keep it short. As I said, I am delighted with the idea of [my calligraphic] drawings in it. What about adding five or six of my recent poems, like Man the Master, Tune for Festive Dances [in the Nineteen Sixties,] the [Picture of a] Black Girl and [sic] White Doll and a couple of others like that. The section of poems could have the title of the book, "Raids on the Unspeakable"??? Or does the mere addition of another seven or eight pages just complicate matters and demand even more, plus padding etc. to round it out to the next size? Let me know what you think.

Have you a copy of a magazine called *Choice* and of another called *the Sixties* lying around? I have never seen some and they sound like something I ought to know about, from the poetry viewpoint.

I wonder if we should have Atlas Watches along with Atlas and Fat Man. There might be some confusion, this early flippant version being somewhat like the other. Maybe better to omit it? Or at any rate explain that it is an earlier attempt?

Naomi can certainly give you a copy of "Time of the End." I did not have it mimeographed but I will send copy as soon as it is printed in the magazine *Motive*.

Yes, I will probably write a preface if there is space, and will do when I get all the copy to go over.

Things are going fine. Chopping wood and getting ready for winter. The woods are great.

All best wishes always,
T o m

/ · /

the Art book: TM's never-published *Art and Worship*. See David Cooper, *Thomas Merton's Art of Denial* (University of Georgia Press, 1989), pp. 89–129.

Choice: Academic review published by the Association of College and Research Libraries.
Sixties: Poetry magazine edited and published by the poet Robert Bly.

147. TLS-1   Oct. 25, 1965

D E A R J.

Chuang Tzu not here yet, but it might be down at the monastery when I go down. Nice fall weather. I have been working steadily in the woods and my back feels it a little, but seems to hold up all right. I have the traction outfit up here on my bed so I can resort to that when needed.

What I wanted to write about mostly was: I am doing some notes on [Rainer Maria] Rilke, and would appreciate any books you have put out of his or about him. I don't know what the notes will turn into, but I think they will eventually be publishable.

Another thing I must have forgotten: what do you think of slipping Original Child Bomb into *Raids on the Inarticulate?* It would be good there, but you may have other reasons for not wanting this. . . .

That's all for the moment. All the best, as ever,

Cordially in Christ,
T O M

148. TLS-1   Nov. 6, 1965

D E A R J.

. . . I am working on *Raids* and find that I may have to do quite a bit of rewriting on some of the pieces so be patient with me.

Did I ever answer your question about letting *Behavior of Titans* fall into the void? Do whatever is best, it is ok with me. I always think in these [remaindering] cases though that we might be able to use a few of the sheets down here, to bind up this way or that, and use as gifts or something, rather than just throwing everything completely out. Is this practical? I asked it concerning *Tears of Blind Lions.*

Thanks for the Reznikoff *Testimony*[,] an austere and impressive book. I would like to do a statement for [George] Oppen but wait and let's see if I get inspired. I won't force one. . . .

All the best always,

Cordially in Christ,
TOM

---

149. TLS-1   Nov. 8, 1965

DEAR J.,

You know about Miguel Grinberg, I think. He is doing an anthology of U.S. poets for Losada in Buenos Aires and it might be a good idea to send him the Oppen books and anything else real special you would like him to take note of. Could you also send a review copy of *Chuang Tzu?* He has a magazine, *Eco Contemporaneo,* which printed a couple of things that are to be in *Raids.*

On *Raids* I am doing quite a bit of rewriting and adding so maybe I will only write a very short preface.

Do you by any chance have this new book of Claude Brown, *Manchild in the Promised Land?* I would like to borrow it to read if you do. It sounds good, no? . . .

Thanks again,
All the best,
TOM

/ · /

Claude Brown: New York-born writer who graduated from Howard University in 1965. The best-seller *Manchild in the Promised Land* (1965) is an autobiography of Brown's Harlem youth.

150. TLS-1   Jan. 4, 1966

DEAR J.

I have many things to thank you for. First the copy of the testimony of the Italian priest, from Elizabeth Mann Borgese, I was very glad to have it and was able to make use of an idea that was in it, in a commentary I have written on the [Second Vatican] Council *Constitution on the Church in the [Modern] World.* Please thank her for me. I doubt if I will get to writing her directly just now, as I am buried under Christmas mail most of which will probably remain unanswered.

Thanks for *Manchild in the PL.* It is a pretty sobering book all right. I thought I knew something about Harlem, but one finds that there are always plenty of deaths one has not heard about. What an existence.

The main point of this letter: a Moslem friend found an error in Ibn Abbad. It is the word *Mawlid* for which I have Mawhid. In the note, instead of just Moslem feast, we might put "feast of the nativity of the Prophet Mohammed." Could someone make that correction?

Another thing I have forgotten to tell you about: yes, I am certainly agreed that it would be good to have some of the drawings on exhibition in a bookstore or stores where the book *[Raids on the Unspeakable]* comes out. Meanwhile, I think the nuns up at Manhattanville College, Purchase, New York would probably be very happy to have an exhibition. . . .

After it is all over, we can think of something to do with them. I don't want them back here. Why don't you and

Naomi as my executors take a few of them in custody so to speak and hang them up somewhere. The rest could go to Bellarmine. Or better still we might sell a few of them. Ed Rice is coming down. I can talk to him about it.

Did I tell you Victor was over here in November? He was looking very well. There is a new road to Lexington now, and it saves them a lot of trouble getting over. Avoids all those twists and turns, though I must say I liked the old road and the barns etc.

I have been getting a lot out of the Rilke books, and am still working on him. Never really read him before. I guess I am in a good spot to absorb the *Duino Elegies* now. I gave some talks on him to the monks: still have to give one conference a week.

All the best for the New Year

Cordially as ever,
TOM

/ · /

Elizabeth Mann Borgese: Daughter of the German novelist Thomas Mann, Elizabeth Mann Borgese, a writer and social critic, began teaching political science at Dalhousie University (Halifax, Nova Scotia) in 1979. She was senior fellow at the Center for the Study of Democratic Institutions, specializing in maritime law.

a commentary I have written: "An Open Letter to the American Hierarchy: Schema XIII and the Modern World" first appeared in America in *Worldview,* 8 (September 1956).

Ibn Abbad: "Readings from Ibn Abbad" in *RU,* pp. 141–151.

151. TL-1   January 18, 1966

DEAR TOM:

Many thanks for your good letter of January [4th] which I found on my return from a very pleasant holiday out west. Paul and I stopped off first at the MLA convention in Chicago, which was most interesting. There were about 7,000 professors milling around in the hotel there, among them a great many Catholic sisters. I was so busy watching over the booth, I did not manage to attend many of the speeches, but the ones I heard were pretty lively, and the general tone of them was interesting. William Carlos Williams really seems to have "made it" into the pantheon of the professors, and the person who was worrying them most now is Charles Olson. And then, too, they all like to get in their little digs at [Allen] Ginsberg.

After Chicago, we flew on to Salt Lake and had a week of very fine skiing up at Alta. There were about five feet of snow on the ground, and it was coming down fresh all the time. It took me a few days to get adjusted to the altitude, but after that I had a lot of fun. Then Paul went back to Harvard, and I went on to San Francisco to visit with Kenneth Rexroth for a few days, and also saw the other poets, Ferlinghetti, who is busy writing a new play, and poor old Patchen, who is still pretty sick, but doing a little new work, and a very fine production at Stanford of Jack Hawkes' little play. San Francisco still is the greatest city, I guess. So beautiful, both in the fog, and when the sun is hitting those white buildings on the hills.

I'll let Elisabeth Borgese know that you enjoyed the stuff about the Italian priest, and were able to make use of it.

Thanks also for the correction of "Mawlid" which I believe Jerry [Fried] has already picked up.

I'll follow up on the lead for the exhibition of [your calligraphic] drawings at the Manhattanville [College] later on. First, at the time the book *[Raids on the Unspeakable]* comes out, I think we ought to try for something right in New York. And I note that you are willing to have the drawings sold, which should be welcome to whatever store puts on the exhibition.

As you can imagine, I found a big stack of mail on my

return, so I have not had a chance to read the piece on "Zen Koan" which you were kind enough to send, but I will get to it soon.

> With very best, as ever,
> [UNSIGNED CARBON]

/ · /

Charles Olson: (1910–1970), Poet and teacher at Black Mountain College whose poetics influenced many students, including Robert Creeley, Robert Duncan, and Denise Levertov. ND published the *Selected Writings of Charles Olson* in 1966.

their little digs at Ginsberg: The American poet of the Beat movement, Allen Ginsberg (1926–) had published four volumes of poetry with Lawrence Ferlinghetti's City Lights by the time the MLA professors began arguing over his force and popularity in 1966.

Jack Hawkes: American novelist and Brown University English professor John Hawkes. The Stanford play was collected in *The Innocent Party* (ND, 1966). ND also published several Hawkes novels, including *The Blood Oranges* (1971).

Jerry: Jerome Fried, ND editor.

"Zen Koan": "The Zen Koan"—TM's review of *The Three Pillars of Zen,* by Philip Kapleau, and *The Zen Koan,* by Isshu Miura and Ruth Sasaki— appeared in the *Lugano Review,* 1 (1966) and was later included in TM's *Mystics and Zen Masters* (1967).

152. TLS-1   Feb 17, 1967

DEAR J.

About the remaindering of *Bread [in the Wilderness]* and *Behavior [of Titans].* First of all, I don't mind. I am fortunately in a position where I do not have to worry about making every last possible cent out of my books, and I don't care how they get around as long as they get around somehow.

Could you please send *50 of each* at the remainder

prices? They should be sent to the Bookstore here. I'll use some of them for gifts.

Thanks for the new Rexroth *Collected [Shorter Poems]* which is very nicely done. I will get into it soon and perhaps send along a reaction.

Do you think I could bum the two *Collecteds* of W. C. Williams that you did? I would be most grateful. I never really got into him but am beginning to now. *Paterson* is a marvelous book.

Snow here today. Everything is very peaceful and quiet. Victor has been trying to get over but I know he is going down all the time. I wonder if I will ever see him again. It is so sad to think of losing such a wonderful person. He is weaker all the time and I think his last bout has really got him down. But let's hope he will get back again for a while.

Hope things are better at the office.

I am going to get an operation for my bursitis a week from today. Will be there four or five days I guess, if not more. I guess I mentioned this in my last letter. I hear Ping Ferry is having trouble with bursitis too.

> Take care of yourself.
> All best wishes always,
> T O M

---

153. TLS-1   Feb 25, 1966

DEAR J.

Thanks for looking up the German poets, and send [Günter] Eich along too: "I like Eich." Sorry for the horrible pun, but maybe the 1960 election is by now long forgotten. I will take care of the books and get them back to you. I will not forget to return all the Rilke, but I am still working on him and that is why I have not done so. Have I other books of yours that I should have returned? I hope not.

As to translations [of German poets], if I do any at all I will do them just for your Annual, and thus we can keep everything straight.

By the way talking about the Widow Vallejo: [Clayton] Eshleman who is in Lima has written me that he has looked into the whole thing thoroughly and that in his opinion she has no legal right whatever to Vallejo's stuff, that it is doubtful that he was married to her, and that there is nothing she could do about it if someone published Vallejo in English. That therefore it is not right to just let her prevent the publication of such an important poet. He asked me to urge you to reconsider the project and for the sake of Vallejo to override her. Well, I am telling you what he said. I do think it is a great pity that she should be permitted to simply prevent Vallejo from ever being printed in English. On the other hand, even though she might not have the rights (which would be hard to establish) it would mean a lot of trouble. I do not know what you think about it but in any event since Eshleman wanted me to, I have told you this. He has seen her, and a lot of other people. He is quite sure that one does not need to bother with her. He sounds convinced. That is the best I can do with the question. . . .

I have not seen Ed [Rice]'s television script, I think the show was on the 20th, but of course did not see it. I am a bit tired of all this publicity as a matter of fact. Did the monastery send you by the way the copy of the Louisville Paper, the Sunday magazine [interview] article? I asked for a few to be sent out but apparently none were, because I have got no reaction from anyone to whom they were supposed to have gone. No matter. We just had a lot of them and I thought a few could go to friends. But actually it is silly that there should be TV programs and all that about me. This is just making something out of nothing. A book is a fact and people can read it and like it or not. The rest is hot air. I hope it will all evaporate soon. Not that it bothers me much, as I do not have to see most of it or get involved in any of it.

I will think about Parra: would really like to meet him. I don't know if it is possible in my present situation however. On the other hand I am still able to see you, Naomi etc. Is it true that you are going to be down this way some time in the spring? If so, I hope to see you. . . .

All the best always, keep well. Looks a bit like spring today.

Ever yours in Christ,
TOM

/ · /

Eich: German poet Günter Eich. See the next letter.

Eshleman: Poet, publisher of Caterpillar Press, and translator, Clayton Eshleman shared TM's interest in Latin American poetry. TM's letters to Eshleman are collected in *Courage,* pp. 245–266.

Ed's television script: Edward Rice's "entertainment" would later become *The Man in the Sycamore Tree: The Good Times and Hard Life of Thomas Merton* (1970).

154. TLS-1   March 19, 1966

DEAR J.

Here is a surprise for you. It is the ms. of a Journal that Bob Lax has been keeping on his Greek Island. I know it looks a little mad at first, but if you are patient with it you will see it is really a fine book, and can easily be edited into the kind of shape that will not terrify the reader. It has wonderful stuff in it. I told him I was sending it to you, and I think it is available. Anyway, here it is. I hope you can use it.

Many thanks for the three books, Eich, Char, [Karl] Krolow. Also for the *Contemporary German Poets,* which I already had (thought I had written about that since it was this that got me talking about the poets). All to the good, it is a copy for the library.

One book I really need, before all else, is Paul Klee's Journals, or Notebooks or whatever they are, in English. They ought to be available, no? Also I see in the listing in the poets book that [Jean] Arp has a collection in English, *On My Way[,]* and I'd like this too, please.

Then as to the poets:

P[aul] Celan, *Die Niemandsrose*

F[riedrich Georg] Junger[,]   *Failure of Technology,* Regnery[,] Chicago

M[arie] L[uise] Kaschnitz, *Wohin denn ich*

H. Piontek, everything in sight

As usual, please charge all this to the royalty account, I don't want to burden you with it.

Did I tell you I have to go to the hospital for a back operation? Next Wednesday is when I go and I suppose the operation will be soon after that. It is necessary. I thought of the guy you know who fixes up skiers and who might do it without an operation but there is no way of getting in touch with him, and anyway the back is pretty far gone now, deteriorated disk and two vertebrae rubbing together on the nerves. Guess it has to be operated on. My hands go dead a lot of the time, besides pains in the shoulder, shocks down the arm etc. etc. A mess.

I must get this off now, so no more at present. I saw the TV script but they messed up Ed [Rice]'s original ideas and made the whole thing a bit silly if you ask me. Hence I am all for avoiding that kind of jazz in the future. Let's stay scrupulously away from the popular especially Catholic press. *Jubilee* however did ok in this month's issue. Did you see it?

All the best always. Hope Marie Tadie is not too much of a headache to all of you.

Cordially always,
T O M

/ · /

a Journal Bob Lax has been keeping: The following year, an extract from Robert Lax's *The Kalymnos Journals* appeared in the *ND Annual 31* (1967).

Contemporary German Poets: Contemporary German Poetry: An Anthology, translated and edited by Gertrude Clorius Schwebell (ND, 1962), included selections by Günter Eich and Karl Krolow.

Paul Klee: (1879–1940), German-born abstract painter. TM is referring to *The Diaries of Paul Klee* (University of California Press, 1964).

Arp: Jean [or Hans] Arp (1887–1966), Dadist, whose poems and essays—*On My Way*—were first published in 1948.

155. APCS-1   Friday. 4/66

D E A R J .

The operation worked out fine, I have made a good recovery and am to go home tomorrow. Fr. John Loftus from Bellarmine came down and spoke of your coming. If all goes well and I get back ok there will be no problems about seeing you any time convenient to you after next week.

All the best,
T O M

156. ALS-1   April 20 1966

D E A R J .

Everything is going along well. No pain and no special bother—I can get around fine and go up to the hermitage during the day. Can't do much work yet though. Will see the doctor next week and check on how the whole thing turned out, but as far as I can see all is well and I will look forward to seeing you in early May—also Fr. Abbot gave his ok for me to see Nicanor Parra. Will you let me have his address again? It got lost in the shuffle. Let me know when to expect you.

All the best—
T O M

Thanks for the review of *Chuang Tzu*. Very good. It will help!

157. TLS-1   May 12, 1966

DEAR J.

. . . I very much enjoyed your visit here with Nicanor and especially like him. Hope to see him again some day.

I am going to send this letter from Louisville Saturday, and enclose two poems for the secret archives [the Menendez File]. I think we might as well plan on you having a file of this kind of material that could not yet be in the Bellarmine collection and what Naomi would perhaps not understand—and a fortiori the monastery. I will give [S.] a personal notebook she wants to read and she will send that along to you later too. I hope to see her Saturday. Naturally you realize that your mail to the monastery is opened so be careful not to mention her in any way they would recognize.

I will be glad when the business end of the Bellarmine affair is all straightened out. Is there any likelihood that you might be coming down at that time? I hope so. . . .

Back to the question of the will etc. My own desire in all this has been to make sure that things are not tied up too tight and that people can get at any relevant material if they want to study it. On the other hand there are some Journals they have at Bellarmine and there will be your "secret file" which will have to be somewhat classified for a while. So I suppose this distinction should be kept in mind somehow.

As to [S.] we had a fine time Saturday last, which turned out to be the most beautiful day of all. We continue as usual, and more so. But I think we both realize that it is not something on which one can build unlimited hopes for the future, and I think we both accept the fact that there is really no future for it on this earth, though I am sure we will always continue to love each other, and perhaps keep in contact somehow. I will certainly always welcome any possible chance of seeing her, and I suppose such chances will present themselves though sooner or later I will be through with the doctors, at least for this particular thing.

All the best. I will get busy and write Victor another note soon.

Yours ever,
T O M

{May 13—wrote another poem—"Aubade on a Cloudy Morning" and am enclosing it. The clouds turned to rain and the copy got rained on.}

/ · /

two poems for the secret archives: When TM was in St. Joseph's Hospital for back surgery in late March 1966, he met and fell in love with a young student nurse who cared for him. The story of the relationship, which continued for several months, is told by Michael Mott in *The Seven Mountains of Thomas Merton,* pp. 435–454. During the course of the relationship, TM wrote several love poems which he sent to JL for safekeeping under the code name "Menendez File." Many years later (in 1984), JL explained the origin of the name in a letter to the abbot of Gethsemani: "You'll never guess why we called it the 'Menendez File.' Tom, who always enjoyed his little ploys, wanted a codeword for it. I was out skiing at Alta at the time and chose the name of the chef at the Alta Lodge—Frank Menendez!" The poems were eventually published in a strictly limited edition as *Eighteen Poems* (ND, 1985). The following comment appears on the copyright page: "These poems were written by Thomas Merton in 1966. He entrusted them to a friend, requesting that they be published after his death."

[S.]: "S." is the pseudonym given by Michael Mott for the nurse TM fell in love with. See Letter #165 for "the personal notebook."

some journals: Under the general editorship of Brother Patrick Hart, OCSO, these private journals are being published in seven volumes by Harper San Francisco, beginning with *Run to the Mountain: The Story of a Vocation. The Journals of Thomas Merton. Vol. One, 1939–1941* (1995). See also Letters #165 and #167.

158. TLS-1   June 1, 1966

DEAR J.

Here are some poems for the Menendez file. It looks as if in almost no time at all there might be material for an (impossible) Menendez book. It has been fun dealing with this Peruvian talent and I hope it will continue. The life of Menendez continues as before. I am all for better and more frequent Peruvian inspirations.

Paraclete Book Center sounds good for the drawings. As I said in another note (did you get it?) there was no special charity that the proceeds went to. Give them to CORE [the Council on Racial Equality] if you like or let's figure out some other group. I am a little out of touch at the moment. Don't know any hot new group.

We ended by selling the drawings for $100 but if that is too much it makes no difference to me. They have sold as high as $250 but maybe at a place like the Paraclete they should go a little lower like $75. I leave you all to judge that . . .

Glad to hear *Raids* is coming along. Look forward to seeing it.

All the best always,
TOM

159. TLS-1   June 9 1966

DEAR J.

Another one for the Menendez file ["Evening: Long Distance Call"], you will see it continues part of the series I sent you last time. Cut my finger today and my typing is a bit more erratic than usual. I suppose that if I am rational about it these Menendez poems will have to remain classified for a long time even after I die. But anyway they are there and life cannot always be fully consistent. Just for the record, all the laws and proprieties are being kept faithfully as far as the strict obligations go. The rest is not inhibited. Which does not always make for a perfectly comfortable or safe situation. . . .

All the best always,
TOM

160. TLS-1   June 16, 1966

DEAR J.

First of all I want to let you know that I have received three of the German poets. . . . I have a very special liking for [Heinz] Piontek. I think he is my favorite among the present generation. I don't know if I will get around to any translations, because my German is much slower than my Spanish and I want to get started on other work. But if you need any let me know.

It has been slow getting back to real work and this has been bothering me. The back is about fixed up by now. I will go in for the three month exray checkup in a couple of weeks. I don't expect I will be able to do any hard manual work for a while yet, but I will probably be in the clear for ordinary activities. Don't need the collar much anymore. But I have developed a rather bad case of bursitis in an elbow and that slows me up. Typing is bad for it. Since I need my work and thrive on it, having to do without serious production has been a little frustrating. But I will be able now I think to buckle down to work on a book (for Naomi, it bores me as a matter of fact and so it won't help much). Perhaps after a period of being more or less fallow like this I will get a good inspiration for something new along ND lines. Incidentally I heard a record of Bob Dylan lately and like him very much indeed. Respond extremely to that, very much at home in it.

Now I need to ask for something more: as usual I hope you will charge this to me. Ought to be easy to get Camus anywhere in NY. I need the following:

Albert Camus	*l'Exil et le royaume*	Gallimard 1957
	l'Etat de Siège	Gallimard 1947
	L'Envers et l'endroit	Gallimard 1958
	L'Eté	Gallimard 1954
	Actuelles I, II and III	Gallimard
	Noces	Gallimard 1950
	Le Mythe de Sisyphe	Gallimard 1947

I would be much obliged, as this would help me very much in work I am beginning. Incidentally that Buddhist monk Thich Nhat Hanh was down here, a very fine guy indeed. Buddhist existentialist and likes Camus. You ought to get in touch and get some of his poems (a few were in *NY Review*).

That's all for now. Best wishes always,

As ever,
TOM

/ · /

Piontek: Heinz Piontek, German poet and short story writer whose work has not been translated into English.

Bob Dylan: Born Robert Allen Zimmerman, Bob Dylan (1941–), singer, songwriter, guitarist, has cut thirty-three albums since his debut LP *Bob Dylan* in 1962. The inspirational album TM refers to is Dylan's seminal *Bringing It All Back Home* (1965). Although TM often talked about writing an essay on

Dylan, he never got around to it, although he continued to enjoy Dylan's music in the hermitage.

Camus: (1913–1960), Albert Camus, the French Algerian novelist and existential philosopher. His writing, in particular *The Plague* (1948) and *The Rebel* (1954), greatly influenced TM, who would spend the next two years in a systematic study of Camus that led to several critical essays. See "Seven Essays on Albert Camus," *LE,* pp. 181–301.

Thich Nhat Hanh: Vietnamese poet who visited Gethsemani with John Heidbrink. See TM's letter to Thich Nhat Hanh in *Ground,* pp. 381–382.

161. ALS-1   June 17, 1966

DEAR J.

I finally got to hear something of Bob Dylan's and like his stuff immensely. Can you get me a copy of the *New Yorker* of Oct. 24, 1964 with a profile of B. Dylan by [Nat] Hentoff? . . .

All the best always,
TOM

/ · /

New Yorker . . . profile: Nat Hentoff's "The Crackin', Shakin', Breakin' Sounds," pp. 64–66.

162. TL-2   June 23, 1966

DEAR TOM:

I was so distressed to hear about the bursitis. That really is a shame, on top of all you have had to go through with your back, and I can well understand how frustrating it must be for you not to be able to use the typewriter. Have you tried any cortisone shots for the bursitis? I understand that that often does wonders for it.

Perhaps you should go up to Louisville again and try a course of shots.

Raids came from the bindery yesterday, and I think it is one of the most beautiful paperbacks, physically, that we have ever done. I hope you will be as pleased with it as I am. Your copies are being mailed down to you. The drawings came out wonderfully well, I think. I hope to get up to see the lady at the Paraclete Bookshop with them this week, and that all will go smoothly with the show. I note that you would like us to set the prices here, whatever seems right for the market, and that the contribution can go to anyone of the groups working for the Negroes in the South. I will see which one the lady favors. Actually, some of these groups have gotten extremely militant lately, and have changed their character. But I think that the one which Martin Luther King runs is still peaceful, so perhaps that would be the best.

I agree with you that Bob Dylan is extremely interesting, both as a poet in his own right, and as a social phenomenon. His influence on the young is tremendous. He has a book coming out soon, and I will order two copies, so there will be one for you.

Mrs. [Elsa] Lorch telephoned the French bookshop this morning, and they will be getting the Camus titles for you. She decided, after talking with them, that the best would be to get you the Pleiades collected volume, which is expensive, but very beautiful, and contains a lot of the stuff you want, plus the two early ones that are not in it.

I am glad that the volumes of the German poets have been coming through and that you like them. I agree with you that Piontek is very fine. We could certainly use a little group of translations of him in the next annual, if you do them. However, before you start in on them, I think we ought to write to him or his publisher in Germany. . . . It would be awful to have you do a lot of work on them and then find that they were already placed. . . .

I am glad that the Buddhist monk [Thich Nhat Hanh]

got down there. I saw some of his poems in the *New York Review,* and thought they were good. Maybe we can get something from him, though the trouble would be the timing, as the next annual won't be out for a year or so.

I stupidly left a couple of your letters up in the country when I came down this week, so there may be points I have not covered, but I will check them over on Sunday.

We have ordered a copy of the October 24, 1964 issue of *The New Yorker,* and shall send you the article on Bob Dylan when it comes.

Very best, as ever,
[UNSIGNED CARBON]

/ · /

the one which Martin Luther King runs: The Southern Christian Leadership Conference—see Letters #170 and #173.

Mrs. Lorch: Elsa Lorch, JL's assistant at ND.

163. TLS-1   July 8, 1966

DEAR J.

My authors' copies of *Raids* arrived last week and I am very happy with them. Was able to give Ping Ferry one when he was here for a brief visit. The book turned out very handsome as you said. It is one of my favorites in every respect, though as far as the writing goes it is patchy and uneven. No matter. I like it. . . .

Thanks again and best wishes,

TOM

164. TLS-1   July 25, 1966

DEAR J.

Your letter of the 20th arrived today. I am trying to track down the Camus books. They must have reached here. If they have somehow got lost, that will be a bit sickening I must say. I certainly hope not.

Thanks for sending [The Prospects of] Nostradamus to *Poetry.* I am sure they won't take it though. But I tell you who *will.* Send it to *Ramparts,* and you'll see.

About Lionel Landry, Asia Society and Buddhism: yes, I thoroughly agree that this is a good line to follow. As a matter of fact it has been growing on me lately that this is the kind of work I am really supposed to get into now. The Suzuki set has been after me to write in their magazine published in Japan, and here and there I get requests for or about Buddhists who want to come down here. So I really think this is something that is opening up and it is just about the only work that really interests me thoroughly at the moment. I just can't get into the other more humdrum stuff and it does not seem to me worth while. So let's hope this is opening up a new avenue or something. Father Abbot has approved my having talks with people in this field. Is Lionel Landry someone who would like to come down and discuss all this? He might have good ideas and leads on a few people who should come. I don't however want to get caught up in a lot of chit chat with secondary people. I want to see the real Zen men. Did I tell you about Thich Nhat Hanh being down here? There was a bit about him in the *N'Yorker* which mentioned his visit. I will send the statement I wrote which you probably never saw. If you think Landry should come down let's consider working on it—not right away as I want to space them. I really do want to do a book on Zen. . . .

I'll let you know if I can get the Camus after all.

> All the best and thanks for
> everything,
> T O M

/ · /

Nostradamus: "Prospects of Nostradamus" never appeared in a periodical, but it is included in *Cables to the Ace* (ND, 1968) and in *CP,* p. 437.

Lionel Landry: Director of the Rockefeller-funded Asia Society.

the statement I wrote: "Nhat Hanh Is My Brother," *Jubilee,* 14 (August 1966), among TM's most virulent statements against the war in Vietnam; see also *Passion for Peace,* pp. 260–262.

165. TLS-1   July 27, 1966

D E A R J.

Here is more material for the top secret [Menendez] file. First a poem. Then two other manuscripts, both of which were written for [S.] and are not for publication, at least in my lifetime. To explain—they explain themselves when you get into them—our relationship has been more or less broken up due to the fact that one of the brothers listened in on a phone call of mine and reported it to the Abbot. The Abbot was very upset indeed about the whole thing, and laid down a very strict set of prohibitions which amount to my not having anything whatever to do with her. I have not kept these prohibitions very strictly, but in any case [S.] and I both see that there is no point in trying to go on with it as we have before. It would only mean a great deal of trouble and there is nothing we can do about our love anyway. When she graduates from nursing school in a couple of weeks, she is going back to work in her home city, Cincinnati. We are not able to keep in touch directly, though I have managed to see her a couple of times. Probably we won't see much of each other after this. Naturally I can see that it is the only way, in the circumstances, and there is no point in trying to circumvent authority when there is little or nothing to be gained by it in any case.

Of the two manuscripts, one, *Midsummer Diary,* is a day by day record of what went on in my mind the first week or so after we were separated. This is not so bad, and it might perhaps be published some day after I am dead. At any rate some of it is worth while. It would have to be edited.

The other *Retrospect* is very poorly written and not very interesting I should imagine. I just thought I would write, for her, an account of what the whole thing had looked like. But I did not really manage it very well, and it is a poor piece of writing. Still, I thought it ought to be there with the other stuff as an authentic record. Stories might start getting around and when stories travel they get distorted. For that reason I thought it might be a good thing if this were on record somewhere.

As to the poems, Victor and Carolyn were talking tentatively of printing some of them (anonymously or over a pseudonym) but even this I think is perhaps not advisable. At least not now. Perhaps in a few years. We shall see. But really I do not think there is any point in considering any of this as material for publication, until after my death anyway.

It is obvious that these mss. are both uncorrected carbons and both would need considerable editing if they were ever published.

[S.] has copies of all this. She also has some letters I wrote her. I trust her as a discreet person to keep these confidential and I am sure she will. But in any case they exist.

I suppose all this is really a bit silly and I don't mean to give the impression that I take it all with infinite seriousness. It is just that I am the kind of person that writes everything down, and after all, to fall in love again after twenty five years of isolation was, to me at least, an event.

You don't need to acknowledge this by letter. Will you be coming down after you have seen [Bill] Dwyer, or won't that be necessary? I do look forward to the time when everything is fully straightened out with the people at Bellarmine.

Thanks for taking care of all this stuff—thanks for bothering with it.

All the best always,
TOM

{One thing about even posthumous publication is that the monastery has to be considered and probably would be adverse to publication. As to rights, I think the monastery owns the rights to this material, as far as publication goes. Though I have the right to dispose of it apart from publication.}

/ · /

Dwyer: Bill Dwyer, lawyer, who drafted the indenture setting up the Thomas Merton Legacy Trust.

166. TLS-1   Aug. 11, 1966

DEAR J.

Thanks for the tearsheets from *Playboy.* After being in *Life* last week I certainly can't risk being in another square magazine so fast. No, joking aside, I think it would be most inadvisable for me at this moment to give anyone the impression I was an assiduous reader of *Playboy.* The God-is-dead boys in some sense have something, which is very intricate and dialectical (it all ends up that God is really not dead like you thought) and in the end it is so complex that God alone can unravel what they are talking about. I certainly don't want to get involved with them, and I have already said a bit in the new book which Doubleday is doing. That will have to suffice. But thanks for sending the stuff down. I am interested in anything like that.

Also the Camus books safely arrived, for which many thanks. That Pleiade job is simply superb. Two thousand pages in one volume with every possible kind of good thing, all sorts of obscure articles C[amus] wrote for the paper in Algiers, and so on. It is an enormous help. I am already finishing one article.

Any news on Nostradamus? And how about the [Bill] Dwyer meeting? Naomi has rejected a book of essays on the grounds that another book of bits and pieces would be bad policy now. I agree. Perhaps it would best be post-humous. On the other hand you might want a few bits of it in an annual or something. I will send it along to you when it gets back, and you can use some of it or else just store it away. If I keep it here it would probably get lost.

Things fine in hermitage. Wonderful rainy stormy night last night. Rain makes the solitude much more tangible so to speak. Like it more than ever. Still haven't written to Nicanor [Parra]. I can see where I am going to become a worse and worse letter writer.

All the best and thanks again,
T o m

/ · /

The God-is-dead boys: TM refers to the principal figures of the New Theology movement. TM's six essays on the death-of-God theology are collected in Part Four of *Faith and Violence* (1968).

167. TLS-1   Aug 18, 1966

DEAR J.

Thanks for your letter which got to me just after I mailed one to you at the office this morning. It can wait—about getting another volume of Camus. I thought I would write this more personal one to Wyoming to bring you up to date. . . .

I think I made clear that with me and [S.] there is nothing more going on now. As I always more or less anticipated, it turned out that there was nothing we could do once authority clamped down. That is to say that since my own choice is for this solitary life, and the choice is one I have no reason to go back on, there is no further question of anything else and there is no point in trying to dictate other terms than those which are accepted here. Anyway, I can see now that it is much better for things to be completely simple, and there is no way in which one can successfully mix an erotic love with the kind of life I am trying to live. So that's that. The only thing is that I think it would be more humane if we had at least some contact. We have none, except in very roundabout ways. So, as far as the bare, vast human essentials are concerned, for instance if I die or something, I wish you would let her know. It might or might not be in the papers. You should have her address anyway. . . . But anyway, in case of some important event like my death or sudden transportation to the moon or something, I wish you would tip her off. No one here would.

Then, while we are talking of sweeping events, there is the question of my making a will, isn't there? I think you mentioned that. I would like to know what that involves. And of course I would like to get all that whole trustee thing tied up in a neat package. . . .

Talking about mss.: do you still do any of that little "Modern Classics" series? I thought one on Edwin Muir might be worth while, he is quite extraordinary. I would do it, in time, if you liked. Also I have several essays generally on the question of peace. They were in a larger collection of topical essays which Naomi said "Not right now" about (because she does not want a collection of bits and pieces right now). I wonder if she would let ND do a little paperback of three or four bits on peace? If you were interested I could ask.

Did the Bob Dylan book come out yet? I am perhaps going to write a piece on him for *Jubilee.*

Hope you enjoy the ranch—and good weather.

> All the best always and God bless you,
> T O M

/ · /

Edwin Muir: (1887–1959), Scottish poet, essayist, and translator. See TM's "The True Legendary Sound: The Poetry and Criticism of Edwin Muir," *LE,* pp. 29–36.

168. TLS-1   Sept 13, 1966

DEAR J.

First of all, thanks for the Record of the reading of my poems which someone sent down. I suppose it is fair enough, though the listing of the poems is all fouled up and they have read Raissa Maritain's "Chagall" without any indication that it is a translation from her French poem and not an original poem by me. No mention of her at all. Could someone call them and rectify this in some way? I'd be much obliged.

I think I said that the Char, Gide and Camus volumes arrived and I am busy with them. I take note of what you say about the possibility of complications in translating Char. I would really like to do some one day, but don't want to get tangled up in a lot of red tape.

Main thing: here are two poems of mine. One you recognize is the hospital poem you read when you and Nicanor were here. It sat four months with the *Lugano Review* and now I hear the magazine is bankrupt. I don't know where to think of placing it. Somewhere visible, I sure think. *Poetry* strikes me as awful dull. The other "First Lesson of Man" might conceivably go to *Saturday Review*. I have not sent them anything for a long time and N. Cousins said he would always be delighted to get anything. . . [.] Any news on ["The Prospects of] Nostradamus["]? Sorry to bother you with these things. I might conceivably do my own dirty work in this regard if you could give me a few names and addresses. Most of the magazines floating around seem to me to be very tedious, as far as poetry is concerned. I am by the way doing some reviews for the *Sewanee*. . . .

Have some fine records of Dylan (Bob Dylan) and am working on an article on him for *Jubilee*. Exciting stuff, very real, very good. New horizons in poetry opening up. Still expecting the book.

Did I tell you? Last few weeks I got busy batting out a series of poems, loosely strung together, cryptic, bit wacky, but I think a good series, provisionally called *Edifying Cables*. With this lot I think we have enough for another poetry book, like end of [67 or early] 68. I'll get the whole prospective "book" typed when I can and you can look it all over. When are you planning Nicanor's book for?

Thanks for all. Best of everything.

in the Lord,
TOM

/ · /

Char: French poet René Char (1907–1988).

Gide: French novelist, essayist, critic, and playwright, André Gide (1869–1951) won the Nobel Prize for Literature in 1947.

the hospital poem: "With the World in My Blood Stream," *Florida Quarterly,* 1 (Summer 1967); *CP,* pp. 615–626.

"First Lesson of Man": "First Lesson about Man," *CP,* pp. 624–626.

169. TLS-1   Sept. 22, 1966

DEAR J.

First, thanks for the Cendrars book which is handsome. I have not gone into it yet, though I remember liking him in the past. Have you done anything of Artaud? I must get into him soon. I like Char tremendously. Also Robert Desnos. Do you think they could dig up some Artaud and Desnos for me, or do you want me to send precise titles? As I have nothing, I'll take anything they can find. As usual on royalty acct. Many thanks.

Main purpose of this letter is to send the enclosed for Menendez file and then take up a couple of confidential points on the executor thing.

1) There will probably have to be a secret clause somewhere about the "special" personal stuff that I am entrusting to you. In case you want to speak of this with Bill Dwyer (in a *general* sort of way) here is the way I look at it. This material should be out of the reach of the monks so that some irresponsible person does not decide to destroy it. They don't have that right. But on the other hand they do have a right to prevent its eventual publication, and this should be respected. In other words the material should be kept safe from tampering or destruction by L'Eglise, but should not be published without the consent of same. At least tacit consent of the then Abbot.

In other words they retain a right of veto. In practice I suppose it may amount to putting off publication considerably, which I don't object to, and perhaps for quite a long time. Whatever may seem best. I do not of course mean that this material has to get through the barrage of censors that have been usual up to now. In fact I think that right of [the] Order to censor any of my material should be kept within narrow limits, as narrow as canonically possible, but things are of course changing in this regard anyway. I hope. There is a good censorship, strictly theological, and there is a silly censorship, which I usually get from censors of the Order (except one or two good ones) and this centers on trivial and absurd things they don't like the sound of. Things they are just not accustomed to after having their heads in the sand for thirty years.

2) Other material that is ready for publication but publication of which has been put off for business reasons (too many books of a certain type etc.). This should be stashed away somewhere, preferably not here, with the explicit understanding that they have been earmarked for future publication. This supply of publishable material will then be understood to be available for publication whenever this is considered expedient, either before or after my death. It should be where no one will start wondering if it should or shouldn't be published or "improved" or something. (Publishers can of course edit it as they see fit.)

3) Notes and other material for scholars: it should be clear that students have free access to and use of this material except the special personal stuff which will be kept separate. About their use of this in publication there should be no unnecessary difficulties, provided everything is in order, proper permissions are obtained etc. If any agreement is signed with Fr. Abbot as Superior now, it should be in such a form that a future Superior can't revoke it (unless to widen the permissions and accessibil-

ity of the material). In other words, without taking this stuff entirely out of the control of the monks, we should put it in a situation where they will not be able to close down on it and restrict its use in the future in any way that is not agreed on now.

Those are the things I had on my mind at the moment. If you see Dwyer and discuss all this and it gets to the point where I can sign things, make a will etc., I hope you will come down for this and we can go over it all. Hope it will not be too much trouble for you. End of Oct. or during November would be fine. Or December for that matter.

Thanks again and all the best. Mention of Artaud and Desnos will be enough to let me know you have this letter.

Yrs ever

TOM

/ · /

Cendrars: Blaise Cendrars (1887–1961), prolific French writer, Henry Miller's favorite author.

Artaud: Antonin Artaud (1896–1948), French poet, writer, playwright. In November 1966, TM considered translating Artaud's annotations on Balinese theater, a project he never completed.

Robert Desnos: Surrealist poet translated by Kenneth Rexroth. In the "Notes on Contributors" to *Monks Pond,* 4, TM described Desnos as "a modern French poet of international reputation who died shortly after being liberated from a concentration camp."

170. TLS-2   Sept. 27, 1966

DEAR J.

Thanks for yours of the 21st which I got yesterday. It is all right with me if the SCLC [Southern Christian Leadership Conference] is the one to benefit by the exhibit of drawings, and of course I don't mind when they have the exhibit. Whatever is arranged is ok as far as I am concerned. I only hope that after so much trouble a few pictures will be sold.

About the poems: let me think a little more over *Edifying Cables*. I have more work to do on them, and if they turn out ok then I think we should plan a new book with them and the new poems. In that case we could fill out the new *Selected [Poems]* with material from *Emblems [of a Season of Fury]*. No? I am not yet sure that *Edifying Cables* is going to be what I want it to be. We'll see. . . .

OK about the poems to [John] Ciardi, and of course I accept your judgment on *Poetry*. When I get in town I generally look up the important magazines in the U[niversity] of L[ouisville] Library when I can, and I took a look at a few issues of *Poetry* recently. You are right of course. Yet nevertheless it seems to me a little dull and futile. I am told there have been a couple of issues devoted to [Louis] Zukofsky. Or one anyway printed quite a big chunk of Zukofsky. Have you seen this? If you have it, could I perhaps borrow it? I didn't find it in the library, but this year's were not all there. Was it March or April?

What do you know about Laurie Lee? Lately I ran across a book of his (hers?) that I thought quite exciting.

Having listened a bit to Bob Dylan's records I think that the rock n' roll is rather essential to the poems: it is meant to bring out the shades of irony and all that: and his peculiar way of singing them too is part of it. Now that I am addicted, I think that just reading him on a printed page misses a lot of it, though it is good too. But I can see where one would be so tired of noise out there that this rather blatant singing and playing would be oppressive. . . .

One last thing: I am really interested in translating Miguel Hernandez, some of his poems I mean, Spanish poet died in jail about 20 yrs back. Any ideas about get-

ting in touch with his executors? The book of his that I
have is put out by Losada in B[uenos] A[ires]. Aguilar in
Madrid also did a fairly recent book of his. I have translated two or three already and intend to do about a
dozen, which I will perhaps try out on the *Sewanee
Review.* I am doing some work for them now.

All the best always, and thanks,
T o m

/ • /

Zukofsky: Along with Charles Oppen, the poet and teacher Louis Zukofsky
(1904–1978) is considered a leader of the Objectivist School. TM wrote an
essay in November 1966 on Zukofsky, "Paradise Bugged," and published it
in *The Critic* (February–March 1967). It is collected in *LE* under the title
"Louis Zukofsky—The Paradise Ear" (pp. 128–133). TM selected Zukofsky's
"Preface" to *Thanks to the Dictionary* to lead off *Monks Pond,* 2 (Summer
1968).

Laurie Lee: (1914–), English poet and author of *Cider with Rosie (1959).* JL
replied to TM on 4 October 1966: "Laurie Lee is a 'he.' He isn't young by
any means, has been writing now for quite a long time, began, as I recall, as
part of the John Lehman Group. He must have had half a dozen books out in
England by now. . . . I have always liked his poetry, but never with a great
enthusiasm."

Miguel Hernandez: (1910–1942), "A very good Spanish poet," TM wrote to
Cid Corman, editor of *Origin,* "who died in prison and wrote a lot of very
good lonely prison stuff" (*Courage,* p. 247). TM translated Hernandez's "The
Two Palm Trees" (*CP,* p. 958).

171. TLS-1   Oct. 8, 1966

D E A R J .

. . . Jacques Maritain was here with some other friends
whose judgment I trust, and I read some of the "Cables"
which they all like immensely. They were encouraging
about this sequence. I had also in any case done some new
work on it which was helping it along even in my own
eyes. Now I see that this is a direction to follow for the

moment, so I will keep at the sequence, and this plus the other new poems will make a volumethat will be all right, if not perhaps even better than *Emblems.* So that is a relief.

Thanks also for the subscription to *Poetry.* I will take steps to ensure that the magazine reaches me, it is very kind of you. I do certainly need to read the best in it anyway. I am not surprised that they rejected Nostradamus. . . .

Jacques Maritain and I both agreed that we thought perhaps the most living way to approach theological and philosophical problems now (that theology and philosophy are in such chaos) would be in the form of creative writing and lit. criticism. I am pleased with the idea and it seems to make sense. . . .

Thanks for the info about [Bob] Dylan. Sorry to hear of his [motorcycle] accident but I hope he recovers ok.

Thanks again, and all the best,
Tom

/ · /

"Cables": *Cables to the Ace; Or, Familiar Liturgies of Misunderstanding* (ND, 1968).

172. TLS-1   Oct. 16, 1966

Dear J.

I know one can't judge a poem so soon after writing it but this one ["Fall '66"] seems to me good. Would you like to place it in a weekly so it would have some chance of being fairly topical? Or does that matter? The *New York Review* might conceivably take it (they took one before that Bob Giroux gave them of mine). Or the *Nation.* I leave you to judge.

Thanks for the little Desnos book. It has some attractive things in it and I like him especially. Also Basil Bunting in the January *Poetry*. But the old *Poetry* of last year with all the Zukofsky has not yet come, instead they sent another copy of the new Zukofsky. In any event I am most grateful for the subscription.

Here I am asking for another favor. It is a medicine that we can't seem to get by mail or around here. It would be in any sort of rather esoteric health food store in N.Y. It is a liquid yeast extract with Vitamin B and herbs, called Bio-Strath, and is made in Switzerland by some Dr. and for some reason is good for my gut. I need something to be good for that right at the moment, as I have to go to the hospital again just for some exrays no doubt, but painful. Could someone somewhere there locate some of this Biostrath elixir or anyway liquid and get me either 8 oz or 16 oz and charge it to the royalty acct? And let me know the address of the place where it came from? I would be most grateful.

At the same time in the same store it should be easy to get some Lindenflower tea, which is also soothing and I can use it in any quantity, in bags or anyhow.

I am working along on the "Cables" and things come out well enough I believe. Should have the whole works ready to deliver in a little over a month at this rate, but there is no great rush.

Sometime ago I spoke of a book of essays on topical stuff like peace etc. which Naomi said should probably not be published now as it would be another book of essays and this is bad. I mentioned it to you and you did not want to dispute her judgment in anyway. My feeling is that it is topical and would be wasted if not published right now, and if published in a cheap paperback would not have the bad effect she fears. I am writing to her about it. Maybe it ought to go into something like New American Library, a real cheap paperback and a large edition. Posthumous pub. on this one would be sheer waste.

All the best always,
T O M

/ · /

but this one: "Fall '66," in *CP,* pp. 644–645.

Basil Bunting: British poet, journalist, editor *(Transatlantic Review),* considered a leader of British literary avant-garde whose work was promoted by JL's friend Ezra Pound.

a book of essays: Faith and Violence: Christian Teaching and Christian Practice (University of Notre Dame Press, 1968). TM's collected essays on peace and social justice have since been edited by William H. Shannon and published as *Passion for Peace: The Social Essays* (Crossroad, 1995).

173. TLS-2   October 17, 1966

D E A R T O M :

Enclosed please find John Ciardi's reply about the two poems I sent him for *Saturday Review.* I am so impressed that there are still editors around who care enough about poetry at its best to give this kind of careful study and advice. Are you willing to go along with him on his suggestions? If you disagree strongly about his feeling on the second page of "With the World in my Blood Stream," you could always let him use the part he wants in the magazine, and then run the whole thing yourself in your new book of poetry. Please send back to me his marked copies of the poems with your okay, or disagreement, and I will follow along with him.

I think we are all squared away now for the exhibition of the drawings, to open on November 18 at the Paraclete Book Center. Miss Sullivan was unable to work things out with the Christian Leadership group. I don't know just what the trouble was but I trust her judgment—but she has gotten good co-operation from the local group of the Poor People's Corporation, and so they have been selected as the beneficiary, and I trust you approve. They are the ones who are organizing a co-operative down in Mississippi, and this seems to me like a good effort. Since we had to get the invitations printed immediately, I took the risk of approving for you and we have gone ahead. As soon as the little invitation cards come in, I will mail some down to you so that you can send them out to any people in this area with whom you correspond.

I was so glad to hear that you had a good visit down there from Maritain, and that he liked your new "Cables" poems. I'll be eager to see them. . . .

Enclosed is copy of a letter from [the Spanish publishers] Aguilar, giving the dope on the Hernandez heirs, apparently his widow, and I hope she will be more amenable than was the Widow Vallejo. Do you want to write to her direct? I'll be glad to tackle it for you, if you want, but you may get a better term yourself. Expectations always go up when a letter comes from a publisher. And you could probably write to her in Spanish. And the thing to say, I guess, is that you want to translate a few poems, for placements in magazines and anthologies here, and that you would split any payments with her.

Very best.

As ever,
J. LAUGHLIN

174. TLS-1   Oct. 24, 1966

DEAR J.

Thanks for your letter with the copy of the letter of J Ciardi and the poems. I have changed the ending of "First Lesson about Man" and hope this emendation will strengthen it a bit. As to "World in Bloodstream" I don't know if I can consent to drop the second page, which seems to me essential: after all I am not merely saying that the hospital was annoying. Of course a religious statement on suffering, perhaps too spelled out and too long winded, is against publication in most magazines. I think I will let it go however, and consider perhaps rewriting the last part tighter. But the poem seems to me to have gelled in its present state and I really don't think it would be subjectively wise for me to go over it again now. It is what it is. I may try it on the *Sewanee Review.* Since I am in direct correspondence with them (over reviews I am doing etc.) why not just let me send it? You can cross it off your list. And send Ciardi the enclosed. I have more poems around, have been writing a lot, am still on *Edifying Cables* but I think they are nearly finished and will get the whole book typed up soon. Any chance of you coming down in November or December? Nothing urgent but I would like to get all the Dwyer affair sewed up and give you this book at the same time, and we could talk about it then and there.

In your letter you mentioned enclosing one from Aguilar but it was not enclosed, or at any rate it was not there when the envelope reached me, may have dropped out during censorship. Could you please let me have another copy? Many thanks.

I want to get this off as soon as I get down to the monastery, which will be in a few minutes, so I close now. An important Moslem religious leader is apparently coming here this week. Will let you know more about it after he has been here.

All the best always,
T O M

175. T L S - 1   Nov 15, 1966

D E A R J.

Many good things in the new [ND] annual, for which many thanks. I especially like the Alberti. The translations seem to be excellent (I don't have the originals). The whole thing is very impressive. I don't think I had ever read anything of Alberti's before—perhaps a poem here and there in an anthology. This is a real discovery. I am writing something about him. Is it possible at all to get any of his stuff in Spanish in NY? I know there is no Spanish bookstore that will get service for you like Lipton for the French. If you can get me anything of Alberti in Spanish, anything at all as I have nothing, let me know. Otherwise I will try my friends in Spain. Though with someone like Alberti that puts them on the spot with the Govt maybe.

Where can I get more information about him? Did I gather he was now dead? Seem to have picked that up somewhere but checked through the introduction and couldn't find it again. . . .

No more for the present. Thanks for the leaflets about the [drawings] exhibit. I could use a few if there are some left over after it. Need some more of the cards at present—as I think I said a couple days ago.

All the best always,
T O M

/ · /

Alberti: Rafael Alberti, Spanish poet and painter whose poem "Concerning the Angels" appeared in *ND Annual 19*.

I am writing something about him: "Rafael Alberti and His Angels," *Continuum,* 5 (Spring 1967). Collected in *LE* under the title "Rafael Alberti," pp. 313–317.

176. TLS-1   Dec 10, 1966

DEAR J.

This is just to say that *Edifying Cables* is all typed, though I am adding a few more pieces. It will make a fair sized book. Do you want me to send it as soon as it is all together (after Christmas probably) or would you be thinking of coming down and picking it up, as there are things in it I want to talk about.

Haven't heard from you since the note where you said things were hectic. I hope that my silly requests for this and that haven't finally driven all your office staff out of their minds: I should have been more considerate. This time of year is tough, I know. Why don't you tell me what is and what is not an unbearable nuisance? I would be perfectly willing to handle directly any transaction about the publication of poems in magazines, if you could give me the right names and addresses. The thing I most depend on you for would be books and I would not imagine that would be too complicated a thing. If the cookie remedies and health teas are too absurd, just say so and I can find some other way of tracking them down, and I don't need that much anyway.

Victor [Hammer] has had another heart attack. I never know when I have seen him for the last time. He is hoping to get over again, but I can see he is not long for this world now. He was eighty five yesterday. Carolyn seemed optimistic in the last note she wrote however.

I did a little piece on Zukofsky, and might send it along

after Christmas: it might come in handy for the annual, maybe. Also I want to return some of your Rilke books, but maybe it would be safer to wait until after the Christmas rush too.

Joan Baez was here: we had a fine visit. She is a most impressive person, one of the best.

All my best Christmas wishes,
TOM

/ · /

Joan Baez: Activist, song writer, lyricist, singer, and central figure in the American folk music revival of the 1960s. TM was equally attracted to Baez's pure singing voice and her social justice activism tempered by a commitment to non-violence. He was particularly interested and supportive of her Institute for the Study of Nonviolence (since renamed the Resource Center for Non-violence) in Carmel Valley, California. Accompanied by her then-husband Ira Sandperl, Baez visited TM at the hermitage on December 8; they listened to a few cuts from Baez's recent release "Noel."

177. TLS-1
Dec 27, 1966

DEAR J.

Your letter about your Mother's passing away reached me just before Christmas and I have of course been praying for her in all the liturgical offices and Masses of the season. I will also offer Mass for the repose of her soul after the holidays. Naturally you feel a great loss there and you have all my sympathy. From all you have told me of her I can see she must have been a really wonderful person. We can certainly hope and believe that she has attained to rest and reward in ways that are beyond our understanding. . . .

Best wishes for the New Year,

Cordially always,
TOM

By the way, Amiya Chakravarty was here and spoke of you. I found him a very interesting person.

/ · /

Amiya Chakravarty: Indian poet, philosopher, and scholar who visited TM while teaching at Smith College. Chakravarty assisted JL, Naomi Burton Stone, and Brother Patrick Hart with the formidable task of editing TM's *AJ.* TM's letters to Chakravarty are collected in *Ground,* pp. 112–121.

178. TLS-1   Jan. 18, 1967

DEAR J.

I have not heard from you in an enormous long time: I certainly hope nothing is wrong. Jonathan [Greene] was here yesterday and we had a good visit. With Guy Davenport, a poet, and with that fabulous photographer [Ralph] Gene Meatyard. I would like very much to try some of Gene's pictures as possibilities for covers of the paperbacks of mine you are doing. I am sure he'd have perfect things for both the books of this year—the *Selected [Poems]* and *the Desert Fathers* (or whenever they are coming out).

Did you get the notes on Alberti? They will not be in *Continuum* (a magazine you perhaps do not see, but it is good, not literary so much). As I said, if you can use them in any way you are welcome to them.

I have been in touch with Hernandez's widow and she seems more amiable than widow Vallejo. I hope to get a few translations together for the Annual, or for you to look at anyway.

Have you seen any sign of the *Saturday Review* lately? They were supposed to be running an article of mine called "Prophetic Ambiguities," on Milton and Camus, but I have not seen anything of it. I don't know whether they send you proofs or not. If you happen to have seen it in print could you let me know? Sometimes copies of magazines with my stuff in may reach me and sometimes not. Everything here is pretty capricious, as you know.

Any luck with those poems of mine? I asked you some time ago to let me know whether you would rather I handled that stuff myself: which I will gladly do if I can get hold of a few good addresses: I have no way of finding them out here. Just let me know.

Your announcement of D[ylan] Thomas's letters looks good. And I was interested in the announcement of his notebooks too. Any chance of seeing them? I'd like to very much, if I could.

I have not seen Victor for some time. He had a heart attack before Christmas, I guess around Thanksgiving, and has not been out and around since getting home from the hospital. I hope he will be all right, but at this stage I suppose anything can be expected.

Did I tell you Amiya Chakravarty was here? He spoke of you of course. A very fine chap, I thought.

I am still hoping we can some day get everything sewed up in regard to the Bellarmine [College] thing, my "will" and all that. However if you are pressed for time as I imagine you are we can wait until your usual spring visit (I do hope to see you at least then!). But I hope it won't drag on indefinitely. Naomi may come down when I have finished my next book for her, but I am not working on it right now. I still have work to do on *Emblems* and don't know what to think about it.

Ping got Joan Baez to come here and I was very happy to meet her, a really excellent person: and by the way I was right about Al Capp after all, he has become a fanatical rightist and as far as I am concerned the guy is totally sick.

Well, maybe when I get down to the monastery there will be a letter from you about half these things, or maybe you have written and I just never got it.

All the best always,
TOM

/ · /

Jonathan: In "Notes on Contributors" to *Monks Pond,* 1 (Spring 1968), TM describes Jonathan Greene: "Jonathan Greene is a designer and Assistant Production Manager of the University of Kentucky Press in Lexington. He has been writing prose and verse for about nine years, has one book published (*the reckoning*—Matter Press) and two more due to appear this spring. Since 1965 he has edited Gnomon Press, Lexington, including Gnomon magazine. He says he likes the relative solitude of Kentucky and prefers it to New York, but he hopes some time to go and live in Dublin."

Guy Davenport: A longtime friend of JL's, Guy Davenport—poet, essayist, critic, translator, and editor—taught literature at the University of Kentucky. TM's letters to Davenport, collected in *Courage* (pp. 251–254), follow up on lines of discussion the two had during Davenport's visits to TM's hermitage. Davenport contributed a foreword to JL's most recent volume of poems, *The Man in the Wall* (ND, 1993).

Gene Meatyard: "Ralph Eugene Meatyard," TM wrote in *Monks Pond,* 2 (Summer 1968), "is one of an avant garde group of Lexington photographers who has been working through a kind of lyric and sardonic surrealism to a photographic abstract expressionism. . . ."

an article of mine . . . on Milton and Camus: TM's article did appear in the *Saturday Review,* 50 (15 April 1967) under a different title: "Can We Survive Nihilism?: Satan, Milton, and Camus." See "Prophetic Ambiguities: Milton and Camus" in *LE,* pp. 252–260.

Thomas's letters . . . And . . . notebooks: ND published *The Notebooks of Dylan Thomas* in the fall of 1967, preceded by the summer, 1967, release of the *Selected Letters of Dylan Thomas.*

Al Capp: Alfred Gerald Caplin (1909–1979), cartoonist ("Li'l Abner"), illustrator, columnist (New York Daily News Syndicate, 1960–72), and social satirist who was very critical of political leftists in the 1960s.

179. TLS-1   Jan. 28, 1967

DEAR J.

Many things to thank you for, and I can't remember if I have or not. Certainly thanks for the good long letter and all the addresses of the magazines. When I get some more poems to send out I'll send. *Sewanee Review* is taking a group of seven. I'll tell Ciardi [at *Saturday Review*] to go ahead and do what he wants about "First Lesson On [sic] Man," but if you are in contact with him before

I am could you remember to tell him also? He can omit the stanza he wants to omit, and I'll say the same.

Thanks for the Rosehips tea good as sleeping potion which arrived just with the cold weather and also when I happened to have a cold, so it was a good healing potion to have around.

I haven't done anything on *Edifying Cables* and am not rushing with it, but will see what happens. Sorry to hear about Bill Dwyer['s resignation as executor attorney]. Have you any other ideas? Should we perhaps think of someone in Louisville? I could then inquire around. Though probably NY would be wiser.

Have you seen a marvelous piece by Milton Mayer in the *Progressive* called "Christ the Orphan"? Best satire I have yet seen on this God is dead stupidity. I feel like writing him a letter. If I had his address I would now, and maybe even if you sent it I still would when I got it. If you get a chance, anyway, could you please let me have his address? Or at any rate if you write him about it tell him how much I liked it. I think you should have it in the annual.

I did not get Gene Meatyard's address when he was here, but I expect him to write and send some pictures in February. Jonathan [Greene] has it anyhow, I guess.

Ping Ferry sent an issue of *Agenda* with marvelous stuff on Basil Bunting. What was good of course was Bunting himself in quotes. I have seen his stuff before and like him immensely. I'm going to write to England to get his books.

Also since I am working on Faulkner I have written to Bennet[t] Cerf at Random House to send me the book of F's I don't have and he will call you about charging them to my account. Is that ok? . . .

As ever, with all my best,
T o m

/ · /

Milton Mayer: Milton Sanford Mayer, friend of Robert Hutchins, who worked at the Center for the Study of Democratic Institutions on First Amendment issues. The Center published Mayer's pamphlet *On Liberty: Man v. the State* in 1969.

Faulkner: TM was only able to complete and publish two essays on American novelist William Faulkner (1897–1962): " 'Baptism in the Forest': Wisdom and Initiation in William Faulkner" (*LE,* pp. 92–116) and "Faulkner and His Critics" (*LE,* pp. 117–123). However, two of TM's talks on Faulkner, recorded in 1967, were transcribed and are included in *LE,* pp. 495–536.

Bennet[t] Cerf: (1898–1971), Publisher and founder of Random House in 1925.

180. TLS-1   March 19, 1967

DEAR J.

First, many thanks for the big box of Bill Williams' books. I am delighted to have them and will make good use of them I think. Also all the others. I have already been through the little [Kenneth] Patchen book which is extraordinary. If I ever get an extra moment I might review it for the *Catholic Worker* or someone, but I must admit there is a limit to that. But I'll see. I'd really like to.

Second: I enclosed a copy of a letter to a friend of mine, John Slate, who is one of the best lawyers in New York. I don't know if he would handle the kind of thing connected with my mss. and all that, but I thought I would sound him out in case we do not get anyone else. It would be good to know what he thinks about the proposition. . . .

The other day I saw Victor [Hammer] in Lexington and he was more or less in bed, but looking fairly well and cheerful. It was nice to be there again even though only for a short time. Saw the pictures Gene Meatyard took of me and some of them are fantastic. One especially, which is not an ordinary portrait but a sort of blurred surrealistic effect would make a marvelous cover—(I still wonder if the new selected should not have a different one, much as I like the old wall too). (This picture I speak of would present no problem as the face is not recognizable.)

> Thanks again and all best wishes,
> TOM

{I was particularly impressed by the Robert Duncan booklet of "passages" on the War. A really fine piece of poetry. Who is he? Should I have heard of him? I can't place him.}

/ · /

John Slate: See the next letter.

Robert Duncan: (1919–1988) Another Bay-area poet who taught at Black Mountain College. See JL's comment about Duncan's *Passages: 22–26* (1966) in Letter #182.

181. TLS-1   April 6, 1967

DEAR J.

Some time ago you sent me your final list of the poems from *Emblems* to be included in the new *Selected [Poems]*. I hope I wrote at once approving it, but if I did not do so, I do it now. Go right ahead.

Following through what I wrote the other day about John Slate. He has been here for a couple of days, is very interested in the case [about literary executorship], has made some good suggestions and has some people in his office working on information and so forth. He is very anxious to go ahead with it and for many reasons I would think he is the right man for it: he expresses considerable interest in the affair, can come down frequently, is personally interested in my work, is an old friend, and so on.

I have asked him to get in touch with you after he returns to New York. Naomi is coming down the 19th and I will also speak to her about it. Please let me know your reaction when possible.

The Alberti anthology reached me: thanks very much for it. The weather here is so hot it is like summer. Almost puts one to sleep.

Today I received this request from a French writer who used my piece on Flannery O'Connor ["A Prose Elegy"] in a book done in France: the same book is being done in NY by Viking and he wants my Flannery piece in that too. I don't know if he realizes that it has appeared here in *Raids.* Anyhow he can have the permission as far as I am concerned: I am sending along the request to you so that it can be checked there, and if you have no objection I would be obliged if you sent it back to him with your ok as well as mine.

I don't know if you have been planning to come down this May, but really I have been so overvisited lately that I would prefer not to have to arrange more visits: not that I don't need to see you some time but if you were to come along in the Fall it would probably work out much better for me. I have been so taken up with the people coming here that I have not been able to get any writing done. However, the visits have had and will have (Naomi) their importance too.

But anyway I do need to get back to putting words on paper. Trouble is that the bursitis operation was not a perfect success and the arm still tends to bother me.

Best wishes and thanks for everything,

Cordially always,
T o m

/ · /

Flannery O'Connor: (1925–1964), an American novelist whose work—in particular, *Wise Blood* (1952) and *The Violent Bear It Away* (1960)—reflected her

Southern roots and deep Catholic faith. O'Connor's vision of violent struggle amid the spiritual poverty of the modern world attracted TM and inspired his "Prose Elegy."

182. TLS-3   April 14, 1967

DEAR TOM:

Up at five this morning with the birds—there are still a few left in New York—in a big effort to get caught up somewhat, and have been doing your royalty checking, and the figures seem to be in pretty good order. I'm sorry to have been silent so long, and hope you understand the jam I am in with Jerry [Fried] gone—he hopes to salvage his health in California—and this coming at royalty time, and on top of that the books have been selling like hot-cakes so there have been a lot of reprints for me to put in work. We are talking to two good people to replace Jerry, and hope to have one of them lined up before too long, so things should get better.

Thanks for sending along the letter from Pierre Dom-ergues in Paris asking for permission to include your essay on Flannery O'Connor in his book. I'll turn this over to Bob [MacGregor], who knows more about your French situation than I do. If *Raids* has been taken by someone over there, then he would have to get permis-sion from them. I'm sorry, on looking again, I see that I had misread his letter, and he is asking for permission in the United States, so we'll have to find out who is doing it here, and get a little fee.

I'm glad that John Slate seems right for the lawyer job for you, but can you help to get me off the hook with Julien Cornell? I had made a rather impassioned plea to him to take you on, and now I feel very embarrassed at your turning him down. Could you perhaps write direct to Julien and explain it in the nice way that I know you can? Please send me a copy of the letter, and then I'll follow up from here. Julien spells Julien with an "e," and his address is Central Valley, New York. I don't think he will mind too much, he certainly doesn't need the business, but he might be offended, as he is rather sensitive.

That is bad news that you are still troubled with the bursitis. I hope that you can find something that will help it. I believe there is some kind of shot which may do it some good. Does your doctor know about that?

Yes, I agree, the fall would probably be better for my visit, since things are so tied up here at the moment.

That's a lovely Alberti poem that you translated and I'll write to him in Rome today to see about permission for it to go into a magazine. I wouldn't think there would be any complication, if it is a new one, but we'd better check. There's a rumor that Alberti may be here in June for the big poetry festival as part of the music festival at Lincoln Center, but I understand the State Department is being sticky about letting him in because of his past.

David [McDowell] wants to use one of your root photographs for the cover for the new paperback edition of Jack Hawkes' novel *The Beetle Leg.* It looks beautiful, so I hope you will approve. The usual fee is $25, and let me know if that is all right, and if the check should be made out to the monastery.

Thanks very much for the nice picture of Nicanor taken down there. I'm having one printed in black to see if we can use it all right. I'll get the negatives back to you in due course. Did you hear that Nicanor's sister, Violeta, the painter, killed herself? That must be a terrible blow to him, and perhaps you'll want to write him, as I shall be doing. We have proofs on his book finally, and it looks good. If there aren't any foul-ups, we should have it out in the fall.

Did the William Carlos Williams book reach you safely? I hope you are liking him as much as I do. He is really great, I think.

Yes, the Rilke books got back to me safely, and many thanks. I see from your later letter that the Williams books did reach you all right.

I'm glad that you liked the Robert Duncan pamphlet [*Of the War*]. He is one of the very best of the San Francisco poets, and really coming into his own now, being recognized. He must be in his 40's now, I would say. Gotham Book Mart could supply his books, I'm sure. He has had a lot of special editions, some of which are very expensive, and you wouldn't want those, but the basic texts are in two trade volumes, one with Scribner's and one with Grove, called *The Opening of the Field* and *Roots and Branches*. He was originally part of the Black Mountain group under Olson. By the way, did we send you the Olson *Selected Writings?* That is certainly something you will want to look at. Let me know if it didn't come down.

I must try to get a look at those pictures Meatyard took of you, as soon as I can get to it.

I hope that Victor isn't in bad shape again. I'm worried because I haven't had any answer to a letter I sent down to Carolyn a few weeks ago, and she's usually very prompt. I guess we must be reconciled to losing him soon, but I certainly will miss him, one of the really unique people I've ever known.

Very best,

As ever,

J.

/ · /

Julien Cornell: JL's attorney. JL asked Cornell to draft the indenture setting up the Thomas Merton Legacy Trust. JL recommended Cornell because of the work he had done on behalf of Ezra Pound when he was first arrested. Cornell wrote *The Trial of Ezra Pound: A Documented Account of the Treason Case* (J. Day Co., 1966).

David: David McDowell (1918–1985), editor *(Kenyon Review* and *transition)* who worked as a sales and promotion manager at ND in 1948–50 before taking a job with Random House.

183. TLS-1   April 18, 1967

DEAR J.

Many thanks for your letter of the 14th. I got off a
letter to Julien Cornell this morning and enclose a copy.
I am sure he will not mind since he said in his letter that
he could not possibly get down here until summer, and I
explained Slate can get here any time he wants and is
already planning to come again soon. Meanwhile I suppose Slate will be in touch with you or has been already.

I hope you will soon get someone to replace Jerry
[Fried] and get you out of the tangle in the office. I am
expecting Naomi here tomorrow and it will be good to
see her and go over a few things.

By all means use the root photo: I am delighted that
you should want it. Since we all take pleasure in doing
something we did not think we were good at, I am inor-
dinately happy about my photographs being wanted for
something. Hope the one of Nicanor is also of use,
though the negative may lack depth.

If you can do anything with the translation from
Alberti, fine. I sent the proofs of the poems back yesterday. (For *Selected Poems*).

I am writing a great deal of verse: actually I have
almost two books for you. *Edifying Cables* and then a collection. I want to go over *Cables* once more and will
probably work it over thoroughly as there is no rush.
Then I am starting on yet another series which will be a
little far out maybe. But I am enjoying it and that is the
main thing. We can go into all that later. I do want to see
you later in the year if you can possibly get free.

Terribly sorry about Nicanor's sister. I will write him.
No, you did not send the Olson *Selected [Writings]* and I
would much like to have that. I will get after Gotham
BM for Duncan's stuff.

Have you heard of a Japanese poet called Shi[n]pei

Kusano? I like him very much (is in the recent Cid Corman's *Origin*). They want to get a book of his out here. Are you interested? You could write Corman if you are.

Lovely spring weather here, lots of green and birds.

All the best always,
TOM

/ · /

Shipei Kusano: Cid Corman lived in Japan, where he edited *Origin,* ran a poetry press, and translated many contemporary Japanese poets, including Shinpei Kusano, whose *Frogs and Others: Poems* was published by Grossman in 1969.

184. TLS-1   May 22, 1967

DEAR J.

I was very happy with the cover of Nicanor's book *[Poems and Antipoems],* and glad that the Zengarden [cover] photo came in handy. Did you ever make any blowups of the portrait of Nicanor? If you did I hope I might have one. I am eager to see the book itself.

Thanks too for the Olson. I looked into it and could see that there was work to do there, but have been digging into other things for the moment. Will get back to it later. I am still held up from doing as much work as I would like by having to go to an allergist. This interminable nonsense about minor health problems is a nuisance. I suppose there is some sort of unconscious fight going on somewhere in me, but it is ok. Also, with Dan [Walsh]'s ordination, there has been a lot of social life for me: I went in to the ordination, to the reception that followed and all that. I hope things will calm down now.

Edifying Cables—now being retyped for the last time (I hope) will be sent to you as soon as I have the finished

copy. It ought to be there at least by the end of June. In
a way I think it has turned out well, though still patchy. I
think there is something there. At least it is "new."

Have you got together with Slate yet?

Are you working on another annual? I ought to send
in something for it. Maybe *Day of a Stranger* would be
good for it, (probably I mentioned this). And also I must
type up the poems of Hernandez I have translated.

I have been meaning to send you my copy of *Origin*
with Shimpei' poems. Have you got a copy yet? If not I
can send mine (if I can find it). Let me know about this
and I'll do something about it.

Hope everything is going ok at the office. Thanks for
check for photos and for the royalties. I am glad to be on
a John Hawk[e]s book, that will give me a chance to read
him. First time.

All my best always,
TOM

/ · /

Dan's ordination: TM wrote about Fr. Walsh and his ordination in a circular
letter to his friends ("Pentecost 1967," *Road*, pp. 102–104): "The main news
of this season is the ordination to the priesthood of my old friend Dan Walsh,
formerly my professor of a scholastic philosophy at Columbia. It was he who
first told me that such a place as Gethsemani existed. For the past seven years
he has been living here and teaching at the Abbey and at Bellarmine College
(Louisville)."

185. TLS-1   June 4, 1967

DEAR J.

Here finally is the completed ms. of *Edifying Cables*. I
want to get it off to you now so that you can get a look
at it. It is not too soon if you are thinking of bringing it

out next spring. There may be some things to talk about, perhaps the title is not good enough for instance. It need not be too loudly called "long poem" or series of poems, and really one can read it forwards or backwards or both ways from the middle as far as I am concerned, though it does fit into a free kind of mosaic pattern the way it is. And I do think it is sort of unusual in its own way. It took a lot of pushing around to get it where I think, at least as far as I myself am concerned, feel it mostly comes off right. I hope you will like it when you get into it.

The trouble with food allergies is now clearing up quite a bit and I am better off. This guy studied me with needles and found drop, shot and other treatment that helps. Summer not too hot yet. Hoping to see Ping on his way back from Geneva. And I do hope there will be some chance to see and talk with you quietly in the fall.

I guess that's all for the moment. I want to go out and have a quiet afternoon in the woods. All my best, as ever,

Cordially,
Том

186. TLS-1   June 5, 1967

DEAR J.

It was certainly good to get your letter, and one from Elsa Lorch, when I got back from town today. All the way in and back I was listening to the news from Israel and Egypt, and it was just like 1939 all over again. When I got home, it was good to hear a couple of sane and friendly voices. I don't know where this will lead, but underneath all the double talk one senses this time a kind of frenzy that is not quite under control, in fact not at all under control, and that once again it is one of those awful situations when the big powers don't want the war they have nevertheless caused, but perhaps can no longer keep everything from going over the falls. I hope I am wrong, but anyway that was the kind of feeling one got today. Maybe it can still be averted or at least maybe it can be kept isolated in that one part of the world. At a point like this, you realize that no one can really say what is about to happen, but that the evil we refuse to recognize in ourselves is once again coming out into the open where it cannot be ignored, and where its effects will be felt. A sense of real pestilence: I think that describes it best. The thought comes easy, as I am working on a commentary of Camus's *The Plague.*

As for the rest: [John] Slate can easily fly to Rome or anywhere else, because his specialty, as a lawyer, is airline business and he has a free pass on any plane. I have no doubt there are some real complications in the estate of someone who in the eyes of the Church does not have an estate (though I do preserve the right to say what is to be done with my mss. as physical properties—apart from sale). . . .

Edifying Cables went off to you today. And of course I am grateful that you can handle the business of getting books when necessary, without too much trouble. Glad too that you have help now and that the Annual becomes once again thinkable. I'll send along a few things for it in a week or two.

I enclose the copy of *Origin.* I'd like it back eventually, but no hurry of course. Many thanks.

With all my best, as ever,
T O M

/ · /

the news from Israel and Egypt: The Seven Day War, 5–11 June, 1967, between Israel and Egypt, Syria and Jordan, which resulted in Israel annexing the Sinai peninsula, the West Bank, Gaza, and the Golan Heights.

a commentary of Camus's The Plague: "The Plague of Camus: A Commentary and Introduction" (*LE,* pp. 181–217).

187. TLS-1   July 12, 1967

DEAR J.

Do you know that Victor died on Monday, the 10th?
I heard about it yesterday. He had been in the hospital
mostly in a coma and paralyzed, for about ten days and
no one expected him to live. I had the good fortune to
see him back at the end of June, when he was very weak
but still very much himself, reading a lot, talking about
ideas concerning the classic design of temples and the
consecration of "sacred space." His little book was finished and he showed me the first bound copy, which is
very beautiful, perhaps the most beautiful book he ever
put together. And it is interesting too. The title is
changed from *Pebbles* to *Fragments*. You know, the
thought comes to me that we might do a little commemorative volume, an anthology of some of his best stuff,
with the entire text of *Fragments* and perhaps some statements about him. What do you think?

I occasionally hear from Jonathan Williams and his
company out in Aspen (Ron Johnson['s *A Line of Poetry,
A Row of Trees*] is remarkable). They are getting up a Fest-
schrift for [Edward] Dahlberg as you probably know. I
sent them something for it. And by the way I have been
meaning to get together some material of mine for your
own Annual but haven't got around to it yet, mainly
because I haven't typed my Hernandez translations which
I want to suggest for it. . . .

Have you seen anything of Ping Ferry? I have been
expecting him and have had no news for weeks. Maybe
he is not able to get here.

                                        Best always,
                                        TOM

/ · /

his little book: Victor Hammer, *Some Fragments for C.R.H.* (Stamperia del San-
tuccio, 1967).

Ron Johnson: (1935–) American poet influenced by the Black Mountain
school of poetry and the work of Louis Zukofsky and Charles Olson, who
was poet-in-residence at the University of Kentucky (1970–71). In addition
to *A Line of Poetry, A Row of Trees* (1964), Jonathan Williams's Jargon Press
published two other volumes of Johnson's poetry, including *The Spirit Walks,
The Rocks Will Talk* (1969).

Dahlberg: Novelist Edward Dahlberg (1900–1977), American expatriate
whose novels capture the human pathos of growing up in orphanages and
slums. In May 1967, TM sent Jonathan Williams a draft of an essay on Dahlberg entitled "Ceremony for Edward Dahlberg." See *CP,* pp. 694–696.

188. TLS-1   Aug. 1, 1967

DEAR J.

Thanks for yours of July 25th. Of course I understand
about the volume of Victor's things. Probably the logical
place would be the Press of the U. of Kentucky. There is
one, or was one. I did enjoy reading his little volume of
Fragments, and thought it was very good. But you are
right of course that it would not be logical on the ND
list.

I have not yet had time to get down to typing the
Hernandez poems. Have been with some rush work—
review articles and things like that which I normally
rather enjoy doing for some reason. I will type the Hernandez things and send one or two other bits. I enclose
an offprint of "Day of a Stranger" from the *Hudson
[Review]*—I have been keeping this in mind for your
annual too. So consider this a possibility. . . .

About [Edwin] Honig and [Fernando] Pessoa: I have
rather lost interest in Pessoa, at least I have no intention
of going on and translating any more of his work (unless
I suddenly discover something that is a new revelation).
But if Honig is interested [in doing a book of transla-

tions], then I'd say let him go ahead with it. If he wants to include a couple of my translations, all right, but I don't see that this would be necessary.

I will see if I can cook up something new in the way of a cover for *Emblems*. I will get hold of the camera again, or perhaps a better one this time. In fact I shot some more root stuff with a Leica, but I think it will be too confusing. I may also get out the brush and ink and try a few more drawings. I hope something will turn up—or I can get a photograph from Gene Meatyard: you may not like the ones of me but there are others that are really fantastic, and I am sure one way or another I'll find something. The book—*Cables [to the Ace]*—is ok with the censors of the Order and there is once again absolutely no point sending it to [Cardinal Francis] Spellman's censor. Anyway I am glad the book is moving along and will help out as best I can with editorial queries, blurb, etc.

I also enclose a peace [Fellowship] pamphlet of mine ["Blessed Are the Meek: The Roots of Christian Nonviolence"]. The race situation is certainly ugly and out of hand, and as I see it pretty hopeless. But it was to be expected. Too bad it tends to nullify all the good work and all the sacrifice of Martin Luther King and his followers. But if the country insists on practicing terrorism in Viet Nam then it deserves to get a taste of it at home. Only the ones who get it aren't the ones who deserve it. I hope to see Carolyn soon and we will have lots of things to talk about. I will discuss the collection of Victor's writings.

Best always,
TOM

/ · /

Honig: Edwin Honig, American poet, critic, translator of Fernando Pessoa, and professor of English at Brown University. ND published Honig's critical study *García Lorca* (1947). In 1983, Honig dedicated his longpoem *Gifts of Light* (Turkey Press) to "the life, work, and spirit of Thomas Merton."

189. TLS-1   Aug. 6, 1967

DEAR J.

This is likely to be a nuisance letter, but I will keep the nuisance part down to a minimum.

I have shot a few rolls of film in the hope of getting something that might work out for a cover. However, there are problems. The brother who did such a first rate job of developing and processing has gone off to our place in Chile, and the one who has taken over is not only not interested in this kind of thing, but simply sends stuff along to a shop in Louisville which does a ruinous job. There is no point in having these films simply put through this kind of thing. Do you have anyone around who does a really serious job on the processing of films? I'm no good at it myself. If you have, I'll just send the rolls along. If there is expense involved I'll pay—or the eventual payment for the photos can cover it. If you don't have anyone handy, I'll try through Ed Rice, or someone else.

Second nuisance. I need some books from that French bookstore. As I have forgotten the address, I wonder if Mrs. Lorch could give them a ring and ask them to send me: everything they have by Claude Lévi-Strauss, and also a book by someone called *Entretiens avec Claude Lévi Strauss.*

When this arrives (please charge as usual) I'll make a note of their address and deal with them direct hereafter.

It is Hiroshima Day, and I have been spending it quietly and thoughtfully up at the hermitage. I wonder if we have learned anything at all. Perhaps a few subtle forms of brinkmanship.

I'm hoping to see Carolyn Hammer shortly, and we can talk about the possibility of doing something with Victor's writings.

Ping wrote that he might come through later in the

year. I am hoping you will be able to make it in the Fall too.

Best always,
TOM

/ · /

Claude Lévi-Strauss: Although TM never published anything on Lévi-Strauss (1908–), founder of structural anthropology, his influence can be seen in TM's essay "Cargo Cults of the South Pacific" (*Love and Living,* pp. 80–94) and in the unpublished monograph *Cargo Theology* (1968).

190. TLS-2   August 11, 1967

DEAR TOM:

Thank you so much for your good letters of August 6 and 7, and for the fine sending of possibilities for the Annual, which provided me with some exciting and varied reading. They are all good, and it is hard to choose, but I think the one I like best, in my present state of mind, is the wonderful essay on "symbolism." That is the one I would like to use, and, in fact, I would like to make it the lead-off piece in the Annual, since it says so much, so well and forcefully, that I, myself, believe. If I were to write a personal "platform" for these present times, trying to explain the mess we have all gotten into and how we got there, what you have said would be it, if I could do it. In the face of all the sloppy and downright wrongheaded thinking that is appearing now in the various advance guard magazines, I would love to lead off the annual with this lucid, powerful statement and just hope that it will get a lot of attention and make some of the kids think about where they are being led by the nose.

Can you recall the name of the Indian magazine where

it first appeared, as we should acknowledge to them? There's no copyright problem, their being in India, but we should give them a credit line.

I'll send back the other pieces right away, as you request, in a separate envelope, so they won't get lost in my shuffle here. I wish we could use some of them, too, but I have to cut down the length of the Annual this time because of the constantly rising printing costs. If it's too big, it makes it too expensive for the kids whom I want to reach. So I hope to get into a rhythm of doing it more often, but less pages.

That's good news that you have taken some more pictures, one of which might do for the cover of *Edifying Cables,* but I'm sorry to hear that the brother who did your printing for you has gone. I'm making some inquiries here about whom we could find good to do it, and will let you know in a few days. The outfit David [McDowell] uses for his occasional printing of negatives is just run of the mill, he says. We must find someone who will really take some pains to bring out what is in the pictures. I'm asking around through some friends who know good photographers.

Elsa [Lorch] has queried the French bookstores for books by Lévi-Strauss, and they report four of them available, but two of them, from the "Mythologiques" series, are very expensive, $12.50 each, so I thought I had better ask you before I got those. (Your royalty account can certainly stand the strain, but I just didn't want to order such expensive books for you offhand, without checking.) So just let me know if you want them all, or only the two cheaper ones.

You ask whether we have learned anything from Hiroshima, and the rest of the mess. I think that a lot of the youngest generation has got the message, but, unfortunately, not the politicians who run the show. I enclose a cutting of today's column by Reston in the *Times* which is pretty grim reading.

Do give Carolyn my love. I had a marvelous letter from her about Victor, a really beautiful letter which expressed what their life together had been like, and I can see it is mighty rough for her now, but she is being very brave about it and determined to carry on.

I wrote to Alberti, at the time you first sent me your good translation of the "Roman Nocturnes," asking whether it could be put in a magazine, but never got any answer from him. I sort of hate to badger him, but maybe you would want to drop him a follow-up card? So far as I know he is still at Via Garibaldi 88 in Rome. It's a beautiful poem, and I'd love to see it get published, but I hesitate to send it to a magazine without checking with him to make sure he hasn't promised it elsewhere first.

Very best, as ever,

J.

/ · /

the wonderful essay on "symbolism": "Symbolism: Communication or Communion?" See Love and Living, pp. 54–79.

the Indian magazine: See the next letter.

today's column by Reston: Associate editor of the New York Times, James Reston's column examines contradictory moves then under way in Washington to influence directions of the war in Vietnam. "The pressure," Reston wrote (p. 36), "for adding new bombing targets at this moment only adds to the difficulties of getting anywhere with the peace feelers" tentatively being extended to Hanoi.

your good translation of the "Roman Nocturnes": In CP, pp. 833–836.

191. TLS-1   Aug 15, 1967

DEAR J.

Thanks very much for your letter of the 11th. Glad you can use the "symbolism" piece. I thought you might like it. The magazine in India was The Mountain Path published at the ashram of one of the former great Indian saints of our time, Ramana Maharshi—the place is Tiruvannamalai, S. India.

In connection with this: how are chances of doing some offprints as we did with the Suzuki stuff? Naturally I'd pay for them. In fact I'd take my cut in offprints, if that is feasible. They could be spread around, and a lot of people might want them. What do you think? I hope this would not be a great chore.

The other pieces got back safely[—]many thanks. Of course I understand about the rising costs and the need to keep the annual within limits. I am appalled when I go into the bookstore at the U of Louisville and see how few paperbacks are within my own limits!! That's good though if the annual will come out more often. Meanwhile I'll not rush in getting Hernandez typed.

About the Lévi[-]Strauss books: I guess the simplest thing is to get everything available at the moment. Probably the costly ones have some very good illustrations, so there will be nothing lost there. Meanwhile about my own photos, I'll wait to hear if you find someone good to process them. And will also scout around and see if there is someone in this area. Gene Meatyard is coming over and I'll tell him to bring possible pictures for the cover of *Cables.* Also he suggested doing a joint project, pictures and poems or poetic texts, with me. I'm eager to try it. I think we would probably get some interesting things said. It is good to have someone like that around close, who is stimulating, and I am keen on trying this kind of experiment. In fact it might tie in with some of the new stuff I have been writing just lately.

I'll write to Alberti, then. It always takes a little effort to get wound up to write in Spanish, though. However I just did some answers to an interview for a Marxist in Chile who published a piece on Nicanor. However I did not write in Spanish (except the letter to the interviewer). If I can dig up the piece on Nicanor I'll send it.

But there isn't an awful lot about him precisely in it. Or nothing exciting.

Well, it's hot but I think I'll get out and get some air in the woods before supper.

> Best wishes always, thanks for everything,
> T O M

/ · /

some answers to an interview: TM's "Answers on Art and Freedom" (*RU,* pp. 165–175) is a response to questions originally posed by Miguel Grinberg in a letter to TM, 19 August 1963.

192. TLS-1   Sept 19, 1967

DEAR J.

The proofs of *Cables* have not reached me yet—unless ··.ey are down there when I go down today. I will leave the envelope open until I go down and if the proofs are there I will add a ps to that effect. So if there is nothing added, you'll know they have not yet come. I hope nothing has gone wrong with them. Incidentally, they do NOT need the imprimatur of the New York archdiocese and in place of a nihil obstat of the Order one can put Cum permissu superiorum, or better nothing at all. It would be preferable to omit all these idiot formulas.

One thing is on my mind. The book needs a better title, perhaps. Is there still time to change it? For instance in the last sections the expression "the Ace of Freedoms" occurs and it is in sort of a key spot, the real ending of the poem, before the last flourishes. It is in a way a kind of hint as to what it is all about. Would *Ace of Freedoms* make a better title? I also thought of *Freedom's Little Eye* because I have a root photo with a bright hole of an eye in the middle of the root shadow which could in that case be a good cover. Please let me know what you think right away as I will hold up the blurb and write it according to the decision we arrive at.

Did [the Hawkes novel] *Beetle Leg* ever appear? I never saw it. I guess Nicanor's book *[Poems and Antipoems]* is not out yet either.

Incidentally in a moment of disgust, wanting to get out of this blighted country and renounce citizenship etc., I offered to go to our foundation in Chile, but the Abbot was inexorable in saying "No." I am apparently a lifetime property of this corporation. But was not surprised or upset because I do like the hermitage here and could hardly expect to find anything better anywhere.

I do hope to see you this fall. Lots of new work cooking.

All my best always,
T O M

{Sept. 21 proofs arrived today. I'll get them back pronto.}

193. T L S - 1   Sept 21, 1967

D E A R J.

I have finished the proofs and am getting them off to Fred Martin right away.

Idea came for title. I think it is a good one this time: *Cables to the Ace*. It fits the book better. *Edifying Cables* is altogether too neutral. Also I think it will appeal to the kids, who seem to like *Raids* (I get quite a fair amount of mail on that from colleges and highschools even). I hope it can be *Cables to the Ace*. But I did not work anything about that into the blurb.

Here's the rough for the blurb as I see it. Nothing wrong with fitting William Carlos Williams in there but I don't think there's room the way I've got it cluttered now. The last part may be too facetious, I leave you to judge, but I don't think the reference to Catholics will do any harm, on the contrary. But you will know best what you want, and I leave you to throw it all out and start over if you like.

I have a lot of real good root pictures, I've seen the contact prints but the final prints may be a little while yet. I'll get some to you when I can. The Meatyard one of the highly perplexed guy sitting on the floor of the abandoned house might do with the new title—or is that over mysterious?

Or even my two chairs . . . [sic]?

Hope to hear from you above all about title.

{No need for imprimatur—did I say this?}

Best always,
TOM

I have been putting some of my stuff on tape, and sent one to Ping who is enthusiastic: but I guess we'll have to be careful where those tapes go. I trust Ping and his friends however, and it's ok for him to make a copy. And then send the original back to Bellarmine. I still feel uneasy about not having all the legal strings tied up in the right knots. Guess Slate's too busy with the airplanes.

{My friend Ad Reinhardt died the other day, too!}

/ · /

Fred Martin: Managing editor at ND.

fitting William Carlos Williams in there: "The reference to Williams in the third paragraph" of the blurb, JL wrote TM (13 September 1967), comes from the way Williams, "in the first version of 'Spring and All,' had used prose interludes somewhat the way you do . . . [although] [t]here is no question that you are imitating him in any way. . . ."

Ad Reinhardt: (1913–1967), TM's Columbia University friend and classmate. TM selected Reinhardt's abstract expressionist manifesto "Art-As-Art" to lead off the first issue of *Monks Pond.* TM described Reinhardt in the contributors notes as "an abstract painter who died in August 1967 at the height of his powers, soon after an exhibition of all his most important work at the Jewish Museum in New York. Though he had made common cause with abstract expressionists like Pollock and De Kooning in the fifties he differed entirely from them. A classicist and a rigorous contemplative, he was only just beginning to be recognized as prophetic by a new generation. He was called the 'black monk' of abstract art, a purist who made Mondrian look problematic, who referred to himself as a 'quietist' and said: 'I'm just making the last paintings which anyone can make.' "

194. TLS-1   November 6, 1967

DEAR TOM:

I wonder if the enclosed piece which Gary Snyder has just sent me, "A Passage to More Than India," will interest you, and what you will make of it. Gary is very serious about this idea that parts of our society, in protest or by inclination, may be moving toward a new type of "family organization" so to speak, and it certainly fits in with what the "hippies" are doing.

It occurred to me that it might be interesting to get a few people, such as yourself, Ping, perhaps Allen Ginsberg, and a few others, to "react" to this piece, and we could run it as a kind of little symposium in the next year's Annual. What do you think? Gary gave me permission to make this copy for you.

He is publishing it in some little obscure magazine out on the West Coast, but I think it should have more exposure than that. Not that I want to load work on to you,

you do so much, but if this intrigues you, perhaps it will set something going that you will want to write about.

Very best, as ever,

J.

/ · /

Gary Snyder: San Francisco-born poet Gary Snyder (1930–), currently serving as poet-in-residence at the University of California at Davis, included his essay "Passage to More Than India" in the durable collection *Earth House Hold,* published by ND in 1969. While studying Buddhism in Japan, Snyder had planned on meeting TM for the first time and showing him around Japan, a plan cut short by TM's accidental death in Bangkok in December 1968.

195. TLS-1   Nov 18, 1967

DEAR J.

Thanks for letting me see the piece by Gary Snyder. I agree that it is very good and I think your idea of having a sort of exchange on the subject in ND annual is fine. On the other hand, I have a piece of my own that might fit, and I am sending it along for you to look at. If it appears here it will be in something smaller like the *Catholic Worker.* I think it fits nicely with what Gary is saying. Let me know what you think about it.

I hope the Trust agreement was ok and that everything will be smooth sailing from now on. We are definitely getting loose from [Marie] Tadie, with the aid of a lawyer in Paris.

Best always,
TOM

196. TLS-1   Dec 31, 1967

DEAR J.

This is a quick answer to your letter received yesterday: before the curtain of the year falls with a crash and the imaginary New Year astounds us. Main thing is about the dates when I am free: Jan. 26th I am in the clear and remain so practically to end of February. Only bad day is Jan. 29 when I have to go to Lexington to get my teeth ground down to nothing and replaced with great caps of precious metal. That will take a couple of hours in the morning. If worst came to worse we could drive over early and you could spend that time with Carolyn [Hammer]. But of course I'd rather do it some better way—all the other days are fine. About the book: here is a title that occurred to me: *Zen and the Birds of Appetite.* In order that this might not be pure flimflam I'd have to write another piece (in place of the promised preface perhaps) and might for example compare Zen with the Dark Night of John of the Cross—this needs to be done. But I think it is a good title.

I have also dug out other copies of the ones that you may have in the wrong kind of shape to give to printers. I am not sure what was on both sides and what wasn't. If this takes care of it, let me know: or else tell me the title of any one you still need.

The "magazine" *[Monks Pond]* will be a very simple matter. As I am not selling it I will give it out to those who want it and mostly give copies to the people in it and they can spread them around among their friends. Main problem may be getting all the copyrights straight for people who have already appeared somewhere else. I do have some very good stuff coming in: don't forget to let me have stuff from ND, maybe bits of books that are in the works or something? And I'd like to do a selection of your poems, published or not. Of course it would be

nice to have a fair amount of hitherto unpublished material. I am hoping to get Asian texts, Zen and Sufi pieces
hitherto unseen in English. Maybe I am too optimistic
but I don't think so.

The main thing though is that I hope you can get here
and we can iron everything out with the library folk in
L'ville and with John Ford, and all will be well oiled and
in working trim. Also we can talk about the book, and
you can get some idea of the new verse I am busy with
(none of it typed yet practically).

Happy New Year and all the best of everything,

TOM

/ · /

The "magazine": Partly in response to the underground independent press
movement of the 1960s, TM planned four issues of the fugitive *Monks Pond*
in 1968. "The purpose of this magazine," he wrote in an editorial in the
inaugural number, "is to publish a few issues devoted to poetry and to some
unusual prose and then go out of business." A facsimile edition was compiled
and edited by Robert Daggy: *Monks Pond: Thomas Merton's Little Magazine*
(University Press of Kentucky, 1989).

John Ford: New Trust attorney who replaced John Slate, who had died in
September 1967. Ford drew up the final version of the Thomas Merton Legacy Trust indenture in November 1967.

197. TLS-1   March 10, 1968

DEAR J.

First, thanks for the copies of *Cables [to the Ace]* which
arrived safely. Very happy with it. I think it is after all one
of my less bad books, or one that says something of what I
want to say, though in spots it is a little off. Could I please
have another dozen, charged to my royalty account?

Enclosed, another Zen saying for the title pages (or
front matter) of *Zen and the Birds.*

Unicorn Press wants me to do a very small pamphlet such as they do, of translations from René Char. It would be only about twelve poems with the originals. They will work on the permissions. Have you any special ideas or objections? I plan to pick out the poems I want to do, send the names to them, let them clear the way, then do the translations. I have no way of knowing what has and what hasn't been done of Char (except what was in the Random House collection).

Naomi likes *Journal of my Escape [from the Nazis]* but the acceptance is not yet official at Doubleday. Someone else might not like it. It is not certain yet that Unicorn will do the antiletters. First the edition will have to be subsidized, and then [Robert] Lax would like if possible a commercial publisher—for obvious reasons. I don't know what will eventually happen, but I doubt if a commercial publisher will take it. And don't feel that would be desirable, really. . . .

> Many thanks,
> my best, as ever,
> T O M

/ · /

translations from René Char: TM's eight translations of poems by Char appeared in the *Unicorn Journal,* 3 (1969).

Journal of my Escape: See Letter #7.

the antiletters: TM and Robert Lax, *A Catch of Anti-Letters* (Sheed, Andrews, & McMeel, 1978).

198. TLS-1

Monks Pond
April 10, 1968

DEAR J.

. . . I have been meaning to ask you this: are you likely to be at your Wyoming ranch in early May? I am going to California for a week to help out some nuns with a workshop, talks etc., and will have a couple of days free after. It would be fun to see some good wild Wyoming country and maybe you might have a hut on the place where I could camp out a couple of days—or just some place to sleep: I could explore a little and meditate some the rest of the time. Will you, or anyone, be out there? How would I plan the stopover on the way back from San Francisco to here? Or have you another idea?

This would be around May 14th–16th, around there.

I was glad to see the ad for *Cables* with the others.

Best,
TOM

199. TLS-2

May 6, 1968

DEAR TOM:

I'm sorry not to have written for so long. Things have been really hectic around here. For weeks I was busy checking the royalty figures, and now there is the new catalog to write. But bless you for doing such a wonderful blurb for *Zen and the Birds of Appetite* that I don't have to do anything on it except type it out.

That is wonderful that you will have the trip to San

Francisco to help the nuns. And I do hope you will have a chance to get into the mountains in the Rockies, too. No, we don't usually go out to the ranch until the end of August. And I think that Jackson may now be a bit more civilized than what you really want. I'm sure that the superintendent on the place, a very nice old man, would welcome you cordially, but I fear you would be appalled by the big ski resort which has been built right adjacent, and by the way the old town has become a tourist trap. I really think your best bet on advice on where to go in the mountains would be from Rexroth. As you know, he takes long walking trips in the Sierras, and knows the whole country out there, and could advise you on what would be "open" (the snow melted) in the Sierras. Rexroth lives at 250 Scott Street in San Francisco and his number is in the phone book. Do call him when you get there, and plan to see him.

If you want to see Kenneth Patchen, he is down in Palo Alto at 2340 Sierra Court, but a visit there is pretty grim as he is so sick and depressed.

Robert Duncan lives at 3267 20th Street in San Francisco, but he may still be in London when you get there. He was here last week, and stayed with us, and then went over to London.

Ferlinghetti you reach through his City Lights Book Shop at 261 Columbus Avenue, and that's in the phone book.

You would be most welcome, too, at Alta, but, there again, it's gotten terribly civilized, and the ski lifts will be running until May 19, so it will be full of skiers. If you do decide you want to stop there, let me know, so that I can telephone them. You could use our little one-room apartment in the lift office building, which is very nice. But it just isn't "wild" any more. And, of course, there is still about 6 feet of snow on the ground. Actually, the middle of May really is too early for the Western mountains unless you want to ski. But Rexroth could put you on to some beautiful places in the red wood country north of San Francisco, I'm sure.

I don't think there have been any significant reviews of *Cables* yet—poetry is always slow—except for a good one that was on the radio, of all things, but we haven't been able to track down a written copy of it.

Maybe the best place for you to go would be the Zen Center down near the Big Sur. I enclose a brochure about it, though you may already have it. That's beautiful country down there, and not too hard to reach if you don't mind a bit of hitchhiking below Carmel.

I trust you safely received my return of the copy of *Origin 4* which you kindly lent me, the issue with the Kusano Shi[n]pei stuff in it. What happened on that was we weren't able to work out the necessary arrangements with [Cid] Corman's Japanese printer, who is difficult, and then some publisher in Japan came along who wanted to do the book, in English, so we said just go ahead. I like Kusano's work very much, but one can't do everything.

Paul seems to have gotten his 4F from the army—for the high blood pressure—though, fortunately, he only seems to get it when he goes to the induction center, the Harvard doctors say he is perfectly all right—and now he has taken off for Oregon to push doorbells for McCarthy. We are very pleased about this development as it is about the first time he has gotten out of himself and gotten involved in something "social."

Nicanor is due to arrive here on the 12th. He has readings, over a span of about 3 weeks, at Brown, Wayne State in Detroit, and then at the "Y" and Stony Brook, and after that I don't know what he plans to do, but I do know he wants to see you if he can get down there.

Very best, as ever,
J. LAUGHLIN

/ · /

push doorbells for McCarthy: Eugene J. McCarthy, senator from Minnesota whose opposition to the Vietnam War and electoral challenge to President Johnson in 1968 galvanized the nation's college youth and brought thousands of young people like JL's son Paul into active involvement in Democratic party affairs.

200. APCS

[San Francisco]
May 16, 1968

DEAR J.

Saw Ferlinghetti in SF. last evening and in fact slept at City Lights Pub office. Am flying to New Mexico today. Proofs [of *Zen and the Birds of Appetite*] are at Gethsemani & I won't be able to get them back for another 10 days.

Best,
TOM

201. TLS-1

Monks Pond
Wednesday May 22, 1968

DEAR J.

When I got back here yesterday I found your nice letter with all the addresses of Rexroth etc. As you know—if you got my card—I saw Ferlinghetti and we had a good talk. I also spent the night in the office of City Lights, where he had a mattress. Enjoyed my whole trip very much indeed. Spent a few days in New Mexico on the way back, at a monastery in the Chamas river canyon.

What I want to say is however that I was expecting to

find proofs of *Zen and the Birds* when I got back. They were not here. I inquired about them and the brother who handles the mail doesn't know anything about them. I am sure Fred [Martin] said he was sending them. They may have gone astray. Could he perhaps follow up on it and if necessary send me an extra set? I'd like to get down to the work, as I will be interrupted on and off through June, and can't guarantee to call my time my own every day.

John Ford is suggesting that I send you some sort of token sum as a way of setting up an account for you as Agent for the Trust. I will get down to that as soon as I can, and will send a check for a hundred dollars. I assume that is about right? Let me know if not.

The main thing is the proofs. I hope that can be straightened out. I must hurry on to a few more urgent letters now. Best always—more later when I have time.

As ever,
TOM

202. TLS-1   Monks Pond
                              June 19, 1968

DEAR J.

Finally I got something on paper about M[arvin] Cohen's beautiful book. I haven't had time to do much writing lately. Conferences, visits etc. Bob Lax was here. Lots of concrete poetry. I'm getting busy on the next two issues of *Pond* and will wind it up. People have liked it.

Geography of Lograire is very much in the works now. A first more or less integral draft is being typed. But more work will be done and much added, I hope.

J. could you do something to help a priest [L'Abbé P.

Lucas] in France who is doing good work trying to salvage guys who have left the priesthood and are trying to adjust, get jobs and so on. He has a couple of buildings full of them and is being thrown out because he has no money to pay his rent. The Abbey is sending him $500 today and as I had to write Clare Luce today I tried to urge her to do something. If you feel you can send him anything at all—his case is really desperate now—it would be a good and noble thing. He really needs steady support from someone. I wonder if there is a foundation around that would have funds for that sort of thing. Have you any ideas? . . . I'd be most grateful for any help, suggestions etc.

I know Nicanor is around. I was invited to the YM[C]A readings and also to a reception for him and [Jorge Carrera] Andrade. I would have liked to go! Is he likely to come down? The hayfever season is almost over (but as been extremely severe). I am planning to go into a much needed retreat and cut off visits for July, but if he can come before or after—or even if he badly wants to come during . . . [sic] [.] I'd like much to see him. But I know it might be a drag to get down here too. But do assure him he is most welcome if he wants to come.

Best always,
Tom

/ · /

M Cohen: Marvin Cohen, Brooklyn-born poet and playwright whose book, *The Self Devoted Friend,* was brought out by ND in 1968.

203. TLS-1   June 27 1968

DEAR J.

My translation of Alberti's *Roman Nocturne[s]* has been accepted by *Kayak* and they paid me twenty bucks. Could you please send him ten dollars and charge to my royalty account? Fair enough?

Finally got an offer from Doubleday for *Journal of my Escape.* They let me know quite definitely that a lot of the editors were leery of it and thought it would be better not to publish. But since they knew that if they didn't someone else would they said go ahead. Naomi and another senior editor being v much in favor of the book, I thought it would be ok to go along with them, as you have a book of mine coming out this fall and I'll be along before too long with the *Geography of Lograire.*

However, if you get your annual out before Doubleday comes with *Journal of Escape,* I can let you have one of my favorite bits. The speech to the army of occupation on Literature. I'm enclosing a copy. If you are interested, I could go over it and edit a bit (if it needs that).

Awaiting news about Nicanor.

Best always
TOM

If Nicanor couldn't get here right soon, would he still be around in August or September?

/ · /

Kayak: Poetry magazine edited by poet George Hitchcock. TM's translation of "Roman Nocturnes" appeared in *Kayak,* 15 (1968).

204. TLS-1 Monks Pond
July 23, 1968

DEAR J.

I might as well let you in on the great news—which remains more or less confidential. Don't know if I told you I had been invited to a meeting of Asian Catholic Abbots in Bangkok. Well, it took a long time for my Abbot to get around to deciding, but he said yes. So I am going to go to that, and also to Indonesia to one of our monasteries there. That having opened the door, I have now been invited to a bigger meeting in Darjeeling in October, to all kinds [of] religions, Hindus, Buddhists, Jains, the works. Amiya Chakravarty engineered this one and will be there. Thus I plan to fly out to Calcutta in October, and that will leave me several weeks before the other meeting in Thailand. So I hope to be around in Nepal and the Himalayas, do a little solitary meditating in the mts. and meet some Buddhists and see some monasteries I hope.

I know you have been out there. So I'd appreciate advice and help. As you know I haven't done much traveling these last years, and I need even the simplest mechanics of it. Abbot's secretary is arranging the plane tickets with a friend of the monastery in Pan Am. Abbot has okayed me getting an American Express Credit card. How does one go about that and how does it work? Could you perhaps help me with that one? Can you suggest some other magic I might need just in an ordinary way? I will be on a very flexible schedule and perhaps flying in and out of Asian cities I never heard of, popping into hotels from airports at late hours and the Lord knows what. I don't even have the usual travel folders.

And are there any people out there I should meet?

Meanwhile thanks for sending something to Fr. Lucas

in Paris, who is very appreciative and sent me a little note of thanks to pass on to you. I realize that the article you mention would be the thing to help, but I couldn't really write it merely from hearsay and scraps of printed information. Someday perhaps if I see his place I can do it. What he is really doing is supporting all kinds of priests—in and out of the Church—for in France they are all desperately poor. American Catholics don't seem to understand this.

I am sorry I missed Nicanor this time, but it has been very hot and nasty and I have been trying to catch up on work before going off to Asia, the visit would not have been well timed, I feel. When he gets back, I hope it will be different.

I'm hoping to see Ping in California on the way out.

Am in contact with Lionel Landry too who is out there. I think he may have good leads.

Best always, many thanks,
TOM

205. TL-3   July 25, 1968

DEAR TOM:

Many thanks for your recent letters and sendings.

That is marvelous news that Father Abbot will let you make that great trip. It should be terrific for you. I will try to get together various "contacts" for you when you let me have your complete itinerary.

I called the American Express credit card office and they are sending down the applications, and I will look them over and send them on. They say there are two ways for you to get a credit card. First, if the monastery has a credit rating, it could be in the name of the monastery, but you would have the signing privilege on it, by designation of Father Abbot. By credit rating I suppose they mean Dun & Bradstreet, or some such organization, Father Abbot would doubtless know if you have one. The other way for you to get it would be to have it guaranteed by someone who does have a credit rating, and I suppose I must, since I have had one of their cards for many years, and I would be glad to do so, as long as you don't leave it in some opium den, so that charges for all sort of frivolous living begin to come through under your signature from miscreant Malaysians.

Of course, there are always some things you can't charge, so you ought to have a supply of American Express checks, which can be gotten at any bank. Generally speaking, it is only usually in the larger centers that the credit card works.

Be sure to take Enteroviaform pills with you. They are made by CIBA, but can be gotten here. If you take them whenever hospitality requires that you eat dirty food, you probably won't get too sick. But those bugs that are in the food out there can really flatten you, so be careful. In general, I found that the best places to eat in small towns were the Chinese restaurants. They use to be all over, though maybe they have kicked them out of some countries now.

In India, you certainly don't want to miss Benares—that is one of the great sights to see all of those people bathing in the Ganges at dawn—and some of the old temples like Khajarhao and Konarak. South India is just beautiful, but you will not have time to get down there.

Did I ever send you our edition of P. Lal's translations of Sanskrit classic plays? Let me know, as you'll surely want to meet him in Calcutta, and he will probably want to put you up if you write ahead. He is a Hindu, but teaches at [St.] Xavier['s] College. He also translated the *Baghavad Gita* recently for Bob Giroux.

You can only get a 30-day visa now for Burma, but it is worth it to spend one day in Rangoon, just to see the

Schwadagon. That is the big pagoda, and one of the great sights, to me at least, even though rather ugly, but fascinating. I'm pretty certain that my friend, Daw Khin Myo Chit, who runs a meditation center for laymen, would love to show you around, although I don't think she has a car, but there are taxis, at least there used to be before "socialism" took over.

Angkor Wat is certainly worth seeing if you can arrange it. The best way used to be to fly over from Bangkok, where you can get a tourist visa for Cambodia. If you don't have time for Angkor Wat, the next best substitute for that kind of architecture would be Borabadur, out from Jakarta. I didn't have time to see that, but they say it is pretty good. Although a bit touristy, I found Bali enchanting, if you have time to get down there, and the planes are still running.

I will think of more places and more people when you give me a more detailed itinerary.

Thank you for praying for Dudley Fitts. He was a dear and wonderful person.

That would be great if you could take a quick look at the Mexican poet, [Marco Antonio] Montes de Oca, but if you are all swamped, send the book back, and I'll try it on Charles Guenther.

I'm glad that you are enjoying the Patchen *Collected Poems*. If you want to do a line or two of statement about him, that might be helpful for later on. Poor guy, he is really going through a bad time again, a lot more pain in his back and great depression about his future.

Many thanks for "Rites for the Extrusion of a Leper" and "Plessy vs. Ferguson." I'll hope to study these carefully soon and give you a report. We certainly do want to have some good things from you for the Annual, as usual. The problem about doing Concrete poetry in the Annual is to get it set, unless the author can supply his own paste-up. It costs a fortune now to get tricky word and type

layouts set at a composition house, and the regular printers can't handle it.

Many thanks for the Bob Lax photograph which is a
beauty. And I'm glad to hear that the restrictions on using
your picture have been relaxed.

I think we have now gotten everything pretty well
straightened out with John Ford on the forms for Bellarmine. I hope I didn't drive him crazy with my several sets
of "improvements," but, the deeper I got into the wording of the documents, the more I began to have further
thoughts about intricacies of copyright situations.

I enclose a review of *Cables* from the *Michigan Daily*.
We sent out a whole lot of copies to college papers, but
I haven't been able to track down yet in the publicity
department how much results we got. Actually, most of
them probably wouldn't think to send us checking copies
of the reviews anyway, and I don't think we have a clipping service anymore.

Very best, as ever,
[UNSIGNED CARBON]

/ · /

P. Lal: Poet, translator, professor of English at St Xavier's College (Calcutta),
and visiting professor of Indian literature at Hofstra University (1962, 1970),
Parmanand Lal's *Great Sanskrit Plays* was issued by ND in 1967; in the same
year Farrar, Straus, & Giroux published P. Lal's translation of the *Bhagavad-
Gita*.

Dudley Fitts: JL's beloved former teacher at Choate had just died.

Montes de Oca: "Recently I met a very pleasant young Mexican poet named
Marco Antonio Montes de Oca," JL wrote TM (15 July 1968). "He has
something to do with the Mexican PEN, and he was up here for a PEN
meeting. Now he has sent me his book, 'Delante de la luz cantan los pajaos,'
and as far as my poor Spanish permits, it seems to me interesting. I hope it is
not an imposition if I send it down to you, and perhaps you could read two
or three poems, to see if he's any good, and if he appeals to you. If you think
he is any good, maybe we could translate a few for the Annual."

Charles Guenther: St. Louis-based book reviewer and translator of LaForgue.

206. TLS-1

Monks Pond
Aug 3 1968

DEAR J.

Thanks very much indeed for sending the forms for the credit card etc. I think it would really be best to take it out in my own name and Fr. Abbot seems to prefer it that way. He is now absent but as soon as he is back I'll get him to write that letter about using the royalties if the card gets lost in that opium den you so graphically conjure up! I am very grateful for your support and have sent in the application.

Actually, I think I am going to have to try to raise some money somehow. I won't be able to stay at Catholic monasteries in a lot of places as I have been advised to contact Buddhists and others direct and keep away from the Catholic background, but stay in hotels. I can't do what would be logical—i.e. go around and give some lectures to raise cash. What about foundation money? I am so ignorant of all this. I don't want to borrow on a future book necessarily, but I sure hope to get two or three books out of this trip, especially if I to Nepal!

Certainly I want to meet Lal. Could I please have his address? I hope to land in Calcutta on an evening flight from Bangkok Oct. 18th. If he has contact with the Jesuits at Xavier College that wd be a good thing as I could say Mass there that weekend. Lal might also steer me out to the monastery of my old friend Mahanambrata Bra[h]-machari who is partially responsible for my own vocation. It's in the suburbs of Calcutta somewhere I think. I like Lal's *Dhammapada* best of the lot. I do have the Sanskrit plays—in the library here I believe. I'll look them up.

I'm sending along some more prints of photos as I have

extras and it is so damp down here they just stick together. If you can use any, fine.

> Thanks again for everything
> My very best
> TOM

/ · /

Mahanambrata Bramachari: In *SSM*, TM tells the story of Brahmachari's influence on him during his years at Columbia University. See also *Road*, pp. 122–123.

Lal's Dhammapada: TM must be confusing P. Lal with Irving Babbitt's translation of *The Dhammapada* (ND, 1965).

207. TLS-1   Aug 18 1968

DEAR J.

I am sorry I was so long in forwarding the enclosed to you. Abbé Lucas was very appreciative of your gift, and I am grateful to you for sending it. He sent his reply to me to pass on to you with his apologies for "not writing in English." It got buried in the pile here.

Saw John Ford recently about some business: the forms are getting mimeographed at Bellarmine and I hope everything will soon be rolling. While I am away on the Asian trip Bro. Patrick here will take care of referring requests for permissions and other such routine business to you. He was formerly Dom James's secretary and knows more than anyone else about these affairs, here. If you need a quick answer on anything, he will take care of it. Normal mail from publishers will I guess follow me to specified points on the journey.

The money question is working itself out. Got a good check from the [Committee of] Southern Churchmen outfit I work for occasionally (the ones who let me use their phone credit card). The people sponsoring the meeting in Darjeeling will also cover some of the expenses for that part of the trip.

I might propose to Doubleday that they advance me some money which I would repay by writing a book about the trip. But I am hesitant to get myself tied up too tight in a formal project I would not like. On the other hand, I will definitely keep a spontaneous notebook type of thing which would be much more interesting. Perhaps New Directions might be interested—or perhaps Doubleday will get first chance, I don't know. I haven't told Naomi about the trip yet but will just before I get going.

However I did keep a notebook on the California trip and I am having it typed up. Actually, to me, this informal and sketchy type of thing is more attractive than a book all spelled out and packaged artificially. I'll send you this brief ms. when it is done. It would make a paper back about the size of *Cables*.

The cover of *Zen and the Birds* is very attractive. Thanks too for the catalogue of the Rare Book place in London: fine pix, I can use some in the final issue of *Monks Pond*.

I am a bit miffed to think that perhaps the American Express people don't think me worthy of a credit card: but really I ought to be delighted. It is an appropriate thing, after all, for a hermit to be reminded that he doesn't quite belong in the accustomed structures!

With my best wishes
TOM

/ · /

Bro. Patrick: Brother Patrick Hart, OCSO, monk of Gethsemani who served as TM's secretary. Since TM's death, Brother Hart has represented the abbey on affairs relating to Merton. In addition to serving as general editor of *The Journals of Thomas Merton*, Brother Hart has edited a volume of TM's letters (*The School of Charity*) along with *The Literary Essays of Thomas Merton, Love and Living, The Asian Journal,* and *The Monastic Journey.*

Southern Churchmen: The Committee of Southern Churchmen, Inc., issued *Katallagete: Be Reconciled,* a journal edited by James Holloway and published by Will D. Campbell, which published several TM essays on race and Christian social witness.

a notebook on the California trip: Since published as *Woods, Shore, Desert: A Notebook, May 1968* (Museum of New Mexico Press, 1982).

208. TLS-1   Aug 28 1968

DEAR J.

Here is first of all the ms. of the new collection of poems. I thought I might as well get it to you now that it is typed and I am about to get going on the trip to Asia. Then you could have it when you wanted it. You might check and see the other versions of the same poems you have on file. These are normally the better versions. There is one of which I have no copy, "Lubnan," which was in the most recent *El Corno Emplumado.*

I am adding several photographs which belong with the other short book, sent recently, *Day of a Stranger* or more properly the section of it called "Woods Shore and Desert." I think the photos add a great deal, and I could also get a few others if you are interested.

There is no rush about either of these books, but I thought this would be the best time to submit the mss. as they are complete and I wouldn't want them to lie around here and get lost while I was away.

Bro. Patrick, Dom James's former secretary, will take care of getting them censored and should also be able to answer urgent questions in my absence.

I hope to leave in about three weeks, going first to the coast for a while. I'll write more about plans later.

Best always,
TOM

/ · /

a new collection of poems: Sensation Time at the Home, CP, pp. 611–665.

209. TLS-1
Sept 5 1968

DEAR J.

The American Express card came all right, but I am sure the extra call from the office helped. Many thanks! I have finished my shopping, have all my shots, have at least my visas for India and Nepal and will get the others in San Francisco. Met that marvelous guy Suedjatmoko, the Indonesian ambassador, who has referred me to a whole pile of interesting people in Java. More than that, I have some fabulous contacts developing, Dalai Lama, Tibetan monasteries in Sikkim etc. This seems to be turning into a fabulous project.

I am taking off from here next Tuesday, going to New Mexico to see my friends at that monastery and also to see the Apache fiesta which is quite good I'm told. Then I go to Alaska, where a Bishop wants me to help out with his priests, nuns etc. Best place to write me is care of Ping Ferry. I'm going to see him in California and then go on to our convent out there to conduct a meeting. I fly to India Oct. 15. You can reach me % Ferry until Sept. 30. Until Oct. 15, Redwoods Monastery, Whitehorn, Cal. 95489. Then Oberoi Grand Calcutta for a while. After that I'm not sure, but I'll let you know. Corny to be on the Oberoi circuit I guess, but I'll probably get to some interesting side places, monasteries, Govt rest cottages etc.

I am really excited about all this. All sorts of really dizzying prospects are opening up. Maybe get invited into Bhutan . . . [sic] etc. Wow.

If I just die of amebic dysentery on the banks of the Ganges, that in itself would be superb. Though doubtless unpleasant. I have to get my supply of enterovioform.

Will *Zen and Birds* be out by November? It would be nice to have a copy to hand to the Dalai Lama when I go to see him, which I hope will be in November.

I am enclosing the rest of the pix for *Day of a Stranger, Woods[, Shore,] [D]esert*. Obviously a choice is indicated, but I think a good selection of pix would be nice. Also two more of me for the files, credit Robert Mays, a nice guy in Lexington and a good photographer.

Did you get *M Pond iii?* I think *iii* and *iv* are the best. *V* will be a while yet.

It's getting late. I'll stuff all this into my last big envelope and have it ready to go tomorrow.

Thanks again for help on the Am Ex card, and my

very best in everything,
Tom

{My Am Ex card # is 093-927-795-0. Will holler if it gets lost in the dens.}

210. TLS-1

Monks Pond
Sept 9 1968

DEAR J.

I got your note this morning and hope you will have a good trip to Europe. Here is another ms. for you to read when you get back.

This is the "first draft" of *[The Geography of] Lograire* but actually, glancing over it, I think it is about complete. I will certainly want to read it over carefully and perhaps make a few changes and slight additions, but I think as it stands it is as it should be. Perhaps the Africa part needs smoothing and completing.

Ping tells me the lady who typed it in Santa Barbara

was quite stirred by it. I do feel that it is a much more significant piece of work than most of what I have done before. In a word, more important than the new poems you have. Maybe should precede them? Note some of the stuff here is in the New Poems *[Sensation Time at the Home]* too, but I think it is probably better here.

I'm off tomorrow, not directly to India, I am going to New Mexico to an Indian festival not much attended by whites (obscure Apache reservation) and my attendance has been cleared with the tribal authorities. Then to Alaska. Then to California with Ping. Then Darjeeling and I have wonderful contacts—and hopes—for bits like Sikkim, Bhutan, exiled Tibetan monasteries etc. It is a real joy. If some little Buddhist gal in Thailand grabs me on the way through I don't think she can pull me down from the ecstatic heights. But we'll see. I am unpredictable. My new Abbot just keeps saying he trusts me, and shakes when he says it.

He needs more faith.

You can reach me at Ping's until end of Sept. Then probably the best address is Oberoi Grand in Calcutta, as I think I said before. I go to India Oct. 14 to 15.

Again, all my best,
Tom

{I have not had time to proof the whole thing—but that can be done later.}

211. ALS-1

TWA: IN FLIGHT
Sept 11, 1968

DEAR J.

Off to the races.
Geography of Lograire is on its way to you.

Credit card ok.

I think you have addresses where I can be reached. Now I will be a couple days with Apaches in New Mexico. Later to Alaska, then California. I certainly hope to look up P. Lal in Calcutta. About *Geography:* let me know if you think it is good just as it stands. Monkeying with it (except for a few minor changes and additions) might spoil it now—don't you think?

Tommie [O'Callaghan], Ron Seitz, Jim Wygal etc., send regards.

All my best

T O M

/ · /

Tommie: Mrs. Thomasine O'Callaghan, Louisville resident and member of the Thomas Merton Legacy Trust.

Ron Seitz: Louisville poet who taught English at Bellarmine College.

Jim Wygal: Louisville psychiatrist and friend who saw TM professionally on irregular occasions during 1967–68.

212. TLS-1

Anchorage, Alaska

Sept 26 [1968]

DEAR J.

. . . Out here in Alaska I feel—and am—miles away from everything that has any connection with business, with writing, with anything. This is a really shattering place. Miles and miles of land occupied by nothing but all kinds of wild animals. The mountains are tremendous. Wonderful little fishing towns that can be reached only by boat or plane. Due to the generosity of the local bishop I am flying all over the place in bush planes and meeting people in cabins on lost lakes etc. and by the time I get out of here next week I think I'll know Alaska as well as I know anywhere else in the country. Fr. Flavian is quite willing to let me settle in a lonely spot here if I find one. (This is confidential.) I wd remain a member of the community and all, just as if I were on the hill behind the abbey, but this would be slightly further than ten minutes' walk. And harder for tourists to discover I believe. The number of remote and hidden places here is infinite and there are many which are close enough to some village for supplies etc. In most cases the village itself is so lost and remote that no one would know where to begin looking for it. Local Bishop is enthusiastic about this plan so, though I cannot make any definite commitment before I have returned from Asia, it is quite possible I might settle here at least for a few years. Of course there are problems, long winter, bad weather, earthquakes, bears, but really they don't make much difference to me.

Next week I go down to see Ping and raise a little pocket money with a conference at the Center [for the Study of Democratic Institutions]. Then a meeting with some nuns for same purpose. Hope to get a useful stipend from work here. Off to Asia Oct. 15.

Best always,
T o m

/ · /

in Alaska: See *The Alaskan Journal of Thomas Merton* (Turkey Press, 1987) and *Thomas Merton in Alaska: The Alaskan Conferences, Journals, and Letters* (ND, 1988).

Fr. Flavian: Dom James Fox gave TM permission to live full time as a hermit in Gethsemani's woods, which he began on August 20, 1966. Fr. Flavian Burns was elected abbot in 1968 after Dom James Fox retired from abbatial office to live in solitude.

213. TL-2   September 26, 1968

DEAR TOM:

Many thanks for your various letters and manuscripts which I found in the office on my return from Europe. There was naturally a big accumulation of work, so I haven't been able to get into the scripts very much yet, but they all look exciting, and I trust we will be able to get them onto the schedule in due course. But I think for the spring, 1969, list, we will want to represent you with a paperback of either *Wisdom* or *Chuang Tzu,* which, as you know, have long been on my mind to get into that format. They are both marvelous books that haven't been doing as well recently in hardbound as they should. Or rather, they have been doing recently about what is normal for a hardbound, single orders and library replacements, but not what I'm sure they could do if available to the young in inexpensive paperback format.

The little quick trip to Europe was somewhat depressing for two reasons. First off, I found Ezra sunk deep again into his melancholy, hardly speaking, and then only monosyllables and completely negative about himself and his work when he did speak. However, physically, he is pretty robust, walking a lot, and eating well, and it seems that the television people will bring him over here next month anyway, and try to make a "silent" picture of it. I have not discouraged the trip because the doctors say that the very best thing for him is to keep him constantly active with something and diverted from his brooding. The other depressing thing about Europe was how horribly American it has gotten, millions of little automobiles and terrible traffic snarls, neon signs, too much advertising everywhere, and frightful prices, at least in France. On the other hand, we took the two little boys, and their reactions were extremely interesting. They liked the toy store in Munich best, of course, but they also liked Notre

Dame, and climbed the Eiffel Tower, and to the dome of St. Paul's, and had a great time at Ezra's daughter's castle in Merano.

Zen and the Birds is ready now, and I think it looks very nice indeed, and I sent a copy of it to you, care of Ping. As you go along on your trip you will be meeting people and probably wanting to send them some paperbacks, so just shoot the requests back along to me, and we'll take care of them for you, charging them to your royalties. If you need a few of anything to take in your suitcase, let me know quickly, and I'll hope to be able to get them to you at the Redwoods Monastery before you fly off for India.

Many thanks for *Monk's Pond 3*. It's very good indeed, and the illustrations are most handsome. You certainly have been getting wonderful results from that little offset press down there. By the way, Brother Patrick has just sent up a request from Nannine Joseph, Mark Van Doren's agent, asking for an assignment of copyright for his poem in the magazine. You will have to sign this, I guess, unless you have left a power of attorney with Brother Patrick, or someone down at the monastery, so Elsa [Lorch] has filled out the form, and I enclose it, if you will sign at the bottom, and get it witnessed, and then send it back to me, or Brother Patrick, as he will have to add the copyright certificate number for that issue of the magazine, which I guess he would have down there, I hope so.

Brother Patrick has already sent up quite a number of permissions requests, and we are handling them as seems best. Of course, where the material is from one of your other books, it's really up to the respective publishers, and we'll just forward them along to them. I don't know the wording of your other contracts, but I would assume that they all have the usual provisions for division of permission fees, etc. Where possible, we will try to extract some "revenue," if it is something which has only been in a

magazine, so that the rights are with you. That is, revenue for you and the monastery, as I guess you will be
needing it on account of your trip.

Take care now, but have some fun, and send along a
postcard when you can.

Very best, as ever,
[UNSIGNED CARBON]

214. TLS-1

Center for the Study of Democratic
Institutions
Santa Barbara, California
Oct 3 [19]68

DEAR J.

I am returning the form for copyright on Mark [Van
Doren]'s poem. Actually I shd have sent it to Bro. Patrick
I guess. I just told him to get busy to do what I neglected
and take out copyrights on all four issues of *MP*. If you
can wait I'll have him send you the number.

As to the request about "Hot Summer 67"[—]this is
now in a book published by U of Notre Dame Press,
Notre Dame, Ind. Title of bk—*Faith and Violence.*

Have had good reaction from a writer I trust (Peter
Nabokov, cousin of Vladimir) on *Geog Lograire.* Gave a
talk to the boys here today—have raised some goodly
dough so far. May need more later.

I'm sorry Ezra is down and that the European trip was
not so happy.

In next couple weeks I am at Redwoods Monastery
Whitethorn, Cal. Guess I may have sent you that. Then
off to Calcutta. . . .

In haste. All my best,
TOM

/ · /

a talk to the boys: TM's dialogue with the fellows of the Center for the Study of Democratic Institutions was taped. Transcribed and edited by Walter Capps, it later appeared in *Thomas Merton: Preview of the Asia Journey* (Crossroads, 1989).

215. TLS-1

Redwoods Abbey, Cal.

Oct 9 1968

DEAR J.

I'm writing this partly in order to get familiar with a borrowed Olivetti on which I am belatedly typing up the talk I am supposed to give in Darjeeling and which they expect me to send in advance for mimeographing. Well . . . [sic] We'll see if I have any ideas. . . .

"Plessy [vs.] Ferguson" is supposed to have been in the *Commonweal* but I am not sure whether they ran it or not. You would have to check that out with them.

I appreciate your remarks about solitude in Alaska. There are certainly various angles to be considered. I will not be in a position to decide anything definite in any case until I have seen Asia and what happens there. In any event when I get back I will probably want to settle in some place more isolated than Kentucky and so far Alaska has had most in its favor (enthusiastic reception by bishop and offers of all sorts of tangible assistance etc.). Also Alaska is half way already to Tokyo . . . [sic] But as I say I have no idea what is coming up and I will have to leave everything open until later.

At present I think the best address for me in India generally will be the USIS (% Mrs. T. Flanagan) 7 Chowringhee, Calcutta. But my first stop will be the Oberoi Grand as I mentioned before. I'll be there until {Oct.} 21st, then can go on to Darjeeling. I hope to meet the Dalai Lama early in November and then get back to various Lamas and monastic groups in the Darjeeling area and Sikkim for the rest of that month. Then to Thailand, Indonesia, and back to India for more Lamas and soon as I have finished the work I have to do in those two places.

Had a good drive up the shore with Ping and Jo [Ferry], looking around for solitary spots but in California everything is booming and developing and it would not be the place for me, even though it may still be ok for a year or two.

Ping by the way has an important suggestion about *the Geography of Logaire.* He thinks, and I agree, that I ought to make a recording of the whole thing on tape at the Center (where they have absolutely the best kind of facilities) and the poem might go in that special form {as well as in book form of course. Together or separately.} I agree with this as I think it is much more significant when read on tape and I can bring out what I want to bring out etc. This is a long term proposition, but I thought I'd mention it. I think more and more by the way that *Logaire* is to be regarded as finished, but for some slight changes and additions.

I guess that's about all for the moment. I have to get to work on that paper.

Best always,
TOM

/ • /

"*Plessy Ferguson*": "An Anti-poem: Plessy vs. Ferguson: Theme and Variation" came out in *Commonweal*, 89 (7 February 1969).

216. ALS-2

Connemara Hotel
Madras
Nov 28 1968

DEAR J.

I haven't heard anything from you since I got to Asia six weeks ago, so it seems that American Express in Calcutta did not forward mail that was sent there—if that was where you sent it. Maybe you could let me have some news. . . . I have been wondering about the mss. I sent you back in September—especially *Geography of Lograire, Day of a Stranger,* etc. Hope they are ok. Wonder what plans you might have for the ms.

The Asia trip has been great so far. Fine talks with the Dalai Lama and other Lamas—met lots of Tibetians. Now am in S. India which I like tremendously and am just hopping off to Ceylon this p.m. Lots of good material piling up from observations— . . . get to typewriter when I have a chance—but will be busy in Bangkok at the monastic meeting. Do let me hear from you—maybe send copies of letters I may have missed. B[r]. Patrick is handling business efficiently as you know, but I am not really *au courant* with the books.

Best always,
TOM

217. TLS-2

December 4, 1968

DEAR TOM:

Many thanks for your letter from Madras. It was great to hear from you, and how well I remembered the Hotel Connemara, where I always stayed when I was in Madras, and loved the beach down there, with all the activity on it. I had not realized you were going to South India, and wish I had known, as I have various friends still in Madras who would have interested you.

No, I hadn't sent any letters to Calcutta, there wasn't really much to report, and I doubted whether you would want to be bothered with a lot of mail when you were traveling.

Brother Patrick sent up a copy of your circular letter and I enjoyed that so much, and was glad to know of the fine meetings with the Dalai Lama and various others. It all sounds like a terrific experience.

Perhaps one of my letters written to California did not reach you, because I'm sure I did write there to let you know that the three manuscripts had been safely received. That is, *Geography of Lograire, Day of a Stranger,* and *Sensation Time at the Home.* They are all most interesting in their very different ways, and we can certainly put one of them on in the fall, 1969, list, whichever you think ought to come first. (As I also wrote, but maybe you didn't get the letter, your spot on the spring, 1969, list is occupied by the paperback of *Chuang Tzu.*)

I informed Naomi about these three scripts, because she always likes to keep track of what is happening, she doesn't like to see two books by you scheduled by two different publishers in the same season, but she raises no objection to there being a book of poetry at the same time as a book of prose, which simplifies matters a little. She did, as I recall, have some question about *Day of a Stranger,* whether it duplicated something you had sent to Doubleday, but I don't have her letter handy at this moment, and will have to check into that further.

My own feeling is that the very exciting *Geography of Lograire* would be the thing to do next fall.

I must rush off now to catch the train to Philadelphia for sales meeting, but will write again to your next address, the one in Java, with more details and perhaps some carbons of letters that would interest you.

Things are really falling apart here. There seems to be some new big strike in New York every day, and all the students are rioting all over the country, apparently, and yesterday here the high school students even rioted in the subways. And just this morning, in our quiet street in the Village, two quite nice looking schoolboys attacked an old lady, and snatched her purse. Fortunately, an intrepid sailor caught one of them, and held him for the cops. Kids apparently playing hooky from school and looking for spending money.

Very best, as ever,
J. LAUGHLIN

/ · /

your circular letter: See "Asian Letter—November 9, 1968" in *Road,* pp. 118–121.

EPILOGUE

TLS-2   July 25, 1970

DEAR [S.]:

Thank you so much for your letter of July 8th. I'm
sorry to be so slow in replying. I have been a bit "under
the weather," some mean virus, but I think it is cleared
up now, my strength is coming back. I was so very glad
indeed to hear from you and be in touch again. When
Tom died, I wanted so much to reach you, I hated to
think of your having to read about it in the papers, but
he had never given me your address after you left . . . and
I just didn't know where to begin to search.

His death really knocked me for a loop. I was so upset
I couldn't even make it down to the funeral, but I went
down later and communed with him there where he is
buried beside the church and out at his hermitage, which
they have kept just about the way he left it. I suppose we
have to accept it as "God's will," but I just can't get reconciled to it yet, he was so full of life and his writing, I
thought, especially his poetry, was getting better and better all the time. He had so much to tell the world, really
to help people all over the world in the terrible state it
has gotten into, why did God take him so soon? I think
of him every day as I work over the manuscripts; I am

editing his beautiful *Asian Journal* now, and help the Abbey with his literary business affairs as one of his Trustees. Before he went off to Asia he appointed Naomi Burton Stone, Tommie O'Callaghan and myself to be his Trustees to help the Abbey with the publication arrangements for his books and so forth. I'll send you the one we got out last year, his last long poem, *Geography of Lograire,* and I'll send *Asian Journal* when it comes out next year, and if there are any of his older books which we did that you would like to have, please just let me know and I'll send them, too.

Yes, Tom left with me copies of the poems he wrote for you, and . . . [a short journal] called *A Midsummer Diary for [S]*. I know he would want you to have copies, if yours have been lost, and I will get them xeroxed for you as soon as I can and send them along to you by registered mail for safety. When he entrusted these to me he said that some day he thought they might be published, but they are so personal, they really shouldn't be published yet, I feel, and I trust you agree.

I don't believe you ever met John Howard Griffin, but I'm sure Tom must have told you about him. John was one of Tom's best friends, a wonderful man, and he visited him often at Gethsemani. Now John is writing the biography of Tom, at the request of the Trustees and the Abbey. Tom had, I believe, told John of his friendship with you, of how close you were to him, and I know that John would like to meet you, if that is possible, so that you could tell him your memories of Tom. I think these should form part of the book, but you can trust John, he is devoted to Tom's memory, and would not, I'm sure, put anything in except what you wanted him to. John's address is 3816 West Biddison, Fort Worth, Texas. His telephone number down there is 817-923-8666, but he spends part of his time each month down at Gethsemani, working on the book there. He stays in Tom's hermitage when he is there. I do hope you will want to call John or drop him a line.

[S.], I don't think you should feel, as you say in your letter, that Tom didn't know how devoted you were to him. As I reread the poems and journals, it seems clear to me that he did understand, and that you were as close to him as any mortal person could be. He always spoke to me of you with the deepest affection and gratitude for what you brought to his life. But you know, in one way, Tom didn't belong to this world that you and I live in, that is something we have to understand and accept, and just be grateful and feel blessed that God privileged us to be his friend, and have as much of him as he could give us.

If you ever get East, I hope you will let me know, I would love to see you again. I suppose it would make us both feel sad to talk about Tom, but if there were anything I could tell you about him which would help you, I certainly would want to do that.

Very best,
J. LAUGHLIN

/ · /

when Tom died: From Madras TM went to Ceylon (present-day Sri Lanka) and then traveled to Bangkok, Thailand, where, on the morning of 10 December 1968—the twenty-seventh anniversary of his arrival at Gethsemani—he gave a talk entitled "Marxism and Monastic Perspectives" (*AJ,* pp. 326–343) to a gathering of Catholic and Asian religious. Six Trappist delegates at the conference described the events surrounding TM's sudden death in a letter to Abbot Flavian Burns (*AJ,* p. 345):

On the morning of his death he had delivered to us the paper that he had prepared, and all were eagerly looking forward to the evening session when he was to answer questions on his paper and on matters dealing with monasticism in general.

After lunch he retired to his room, and on his way he commented to one of us that he was looking forward to his meridian [afternoon nap] as he had been unable to have it the day before due to an organizing meeting that he had had to attend.

Not long after he retired a shout was heard by others in his cottage, but after a preliminary check they thought they must have imagined the cry.

He was found at the end of the meridian and when found was lying on the floor. He was on his back with the electric fan lying across his chest. The fan was still switched on, and there was a deep burn and some cuts on his right side and arm. The back of his head was also bleeding slightly.

One of the nuns who had medical experience was quickly at his side, but it was evident that he was already dead.

The next morning the U.S. Army transported TM's body to an army hospital in Bangkok. A week later, it was flown to the United States in a military transport plane, accompanied by the bodies of American soldiers killed in Vietnam. Thomas Merton's remains arrived at Gethsemani the afternoon of 17 December. That evening, under a light snowfall, he was buried in the monastic cemetery next to the church where his fellow monks and friends chanted the funeral liturgy.

the biography of Tom: See Letter #115.

APPENDIX: THOMAS MERTON—A PORTRAIT BY JAMES LAUGHLIN*

He was a wonderful friend. He loved people, and he could bring them out; he enjoyed bringing them out. Thomas Merton transformed many souls with his writing, but he wasn't a man to lecture or proselytize. I felt he was interested in me, as a poet, a publisher, a person— not as a lost sheep. I surely wasn't alone; the files at the Merton Center at Bellarmine College show that he corresponded with several thousand people.

I loved to go down to Gethsemani to visit him at the monastery because, very simply, we had such good times. I would pick up a car at the Louisville Airport and drive down to the monastery. "Pax Intrantibus," (Peace to those who enter) it says over the gate. Father Abbot always gave Tom permission to go off with me for the day. Tom would start out circumspectly—he would go to the storage room for an old bishop's suit and exit from the monastery looking very ecclesiastical, so as not to shock the gate brother. A few miles, and he'd say "Stop

* This portrait first appeared in Paul Wilkes, ed., *Merton By Those Who Knew Him* (San Francisco: Harper & Row, 1984).

here." He would go into the woods, take off his bishop's suit, put on his blue jeans, his old sweater, and his beret, and get back into the car with a sigh of relief. Then we would head east, stopping, I must confess, at a few rural beer parlors along the way; Tom was always very popular with the local farmers. He knew how to talk to all kinds of people; they found him funny and they liked him. Often we'd head on over to Lexington for lunch with his wonderful friends, the great old Austrian painter and printer, Victor Hammer. Carolyn Hammer put on superb gourmet lunches for us, and there was always an excellent bottle (or two) of wine, which Tom and I would down with relish, he never showing any effect. It was curious—he had no allergy whatsoever to alcohol.

Later in his life he became even more relaxed, but right from the beginning of our friendship there was something wonderful and alive in him that even the Trappist life couldn't suppress.

My first contact with Tom, back in the early 1940s, came through Mark Van Doren. Mark was one of the greatest teachers of literature we have ever had in this country. He was Tom's mentor at Columbia.

When Mark, for whom I had published some poems at New Directions, told me he had received thirty poems from a very promising young poet, one with deep spiritual feeling and one whom he thought I would probably not find out about in the normal course of business, I was interested. I liked those early poems very much. There was a freshness there, a liveliness, a verbal spriteliness that was attractive. They were not like anything that any of the other New Directions poets were writing. There was an almost ingenuous character to them, which was appealing.

The Catholic message in those early poems was strong. I mean, there were poems about the night the monastery barn burned up and the portrait of the Virgin in the cloister . . . At first, such subjects didn't interest me too much. What I liked was Merton's imagery and the way he could take a religious subject and carry it into real-life metaphors, so that I, as a heretic, a benighted Calvinist, was able to get some feeling, as I never had before, of what the Catholic faith was about.

At that time this was the only kind of poetry that the abbot wanted Fr. Louis to write. As religious poetry, it didn't come close to George Herbert or Hopkins; yet those poems have passionate, authentic feeling for what he is writing about. The finest of *Thirty Poems* is the poem written in memory of his brother, John Paul, who was killed in the war. This is a very beautiful, very moving poem by anyone's standard. Just to quote a few lines:

> For My Brother:
> Reported Missing in Action, 1943
>
> Sweet brother, if I do not sleep
> My eyes are flowers for your tomb;
> And if I cannot eat my bread,
> My fasts shall live like willows where you died.
> If in the heat I find no water for my thirst,
> My thirst shall turn to springs for you, poor traveller.

As Merton matured in the 1950s and 1960s, becoming more secular in his interests, he began to write a different kind of poetry, which was more concerned with what was happening outside the monastery, and inside himself.

I'll never forget my first trip to Gethsemani. It was after New Directions had published *Thirty Poems*. Tom and I had corresponded, talking about other books that he might write, and the abbot invited me to visit him. This was a very novel experience for me, going to stay in a monastery—which, if I accepted the prejudices of my Presbyterian mother, I would have considered an invention of the devil himself. Of course, it wasn't at all. It turned out to be a place full of happiness and high spirits. I had expected to meet a somber-faced monk, such as you saw in old etchings, pacing silently in the cloister, muttering prayers under his breath. Tom wasn't like that at all! From the moment I was greeted by a smiling gate brother, I saw that I had been completely misinformed about monasteries; this was a joyous place, and Tom Merton was joyous. For me, he had, in the old sense of the word, *gaiety;* he had a wonderful gaiety, about his vocation and about life.

Tom wasn't the handsomest man but he had a wonderful smile, a lovely laugh, and he was smiling most of the time. He was charismatic and empathetic; he put himself immediately in touch with me. Immediately he was asking me all sorts of questions: what was I writing? did I have any new poems with me? what was my family background? what books was New Directions publishing? Tom was interested in everything; there was practically no subject he didn't want to know about. He was bubbling with enthusiasm. One problem, of course, occasionally, was that he bubbled so much, though not in any stupid or foolish way. He would arrive at dawn at the guesthouse, when I was struggling to get my eyes open, with a green sack full of books and notes, things he had thought of during the night—did he sleep at all?—that he wanted to discuss with me. And this would go on all day.

He was a man churning with ideas who constantly asked himself if those ideas stacked up. And that is the sign of a writer and a thinker who is constantly growing. And grow he certainly did, from the early days of *The Seven Storey Mountain* to later writings, which, as the French would say, were *"au point."*

The Seven Storey Mountain was a great best-seller because it had things to say that people—and not just Catholics—were, at that moment in our social history, waiting to hear. It was 1948, and the book presented an answer to spiritual problems that many were confronting—particularly the young, who were upset by the way things were going in the country, by the threat of an atomic holocaust, and all the rest of it. Merton voiced their concerns, so simply and directly. He was responding in his personal terms to a general angst.

One might say that *The Seven Storey Mountain* is in some respects slightly undisciplined, perhaps even preachy at times. But in his later books, particularly in the journals, Tom controlled himself more and held to the track. He also gained greatly in writing style. Merton was a natural, born writer. He understood the possibilities of language. And he got better and better as he went along.

Once you've been bitten by Merton, you will continue to read him, and read everything you can. How he actually did it, who knows? Can any of us really analyze the particular magic of a great? Something was combusting inside Tom, and it came out in fine language, clear thought, persuasive communication. He touched people's minds and hearts.

I think the books (still unpublished) that really give both an insight into his writing and his search are Tom's private journals. He was a prodigious worker, and a very fast writer, and when I visited him I saw that he was working on two sets of journals. One set was the journals that he soon made into books. The other was the private journals, which he kept in big black ledgers. These were his very personal thoughts, like a diary, written just for his own dialogue with himself. The quality of them was very free, very frank; quite often he was talking to God, asking advice from God. Often he was worrying about whether he was a good contemplative, whether he was indulging egotism in writing worldly books; seeking from God enlightenment on why he had never had a major mystical experience. He directed us, his trustees, that these journals should not be published until twenty-five years after his death.

I know Tom sought to lose his identity in the great nothingness, "to drown in the sea of the infinite," as

Leopardi put it. That is what every contemplative seeks. But he was humble; he knew the literature of mysticism and knew that this is something you can't reach out and take. He knew his place, his need for grace.

If you read the end of Merton's *Asian Journal*—when he got to Polonnaruwa in Ceylon—I think you will be convinced, as I was, that he finally had his great mystical experience there. It's ironic that it was Buddhism, and the art of Buddhism, that brought him this long-sought experience, and not something in the monastery or in the Catholic faith. And to me it's appropriate that this vision came to him through his ecumenism. He would never have gone to Ceylon if he had not read Buddhist texts at the monastery. There at Polonnaruwa he looked at those sleeping Buddha figures in their massive tranquility, and knew that he had at last come to the place where time stopped. He was a part of the universal whole that is nothing. There was no more Thomas Merton, there was only the infinite compassion. This is how he reported the event:

I am able to approach the Buddhas barefoot and undisturbed, my feet in wet grass, wet sand. Then the silence of the extraordinary faces. The great smiles. Huge and yet subtle. Filled with every possibility, questioning nothing, the peace not of emotional resignation but of Madhyamika, of sunyata, that has seen through every question without trying to discredit anyone or anything—*without refutation*—without establishing some other argument. For the doctrinaire, the mind that needs well-established positions, such peace, such silence, can be frightening. I was knocked over with a rush of relief and thankfulness at the *obvious* clarity of the figures, the clarity and fluidity of shape and line, the design of the monumental bodies composed into the rock shape and landscape, figure, rock and tree. And the sweep of bare rock sloping away on the other side of the hollow, where you can go back and see different aspects of the figure.

Looking at these figures I was suddenly, almost forcibly,

jerked clean out of the habitual, half-tied vision of things and an inner clearness, clarity, as if exploding from the rocks themselves, became evident and obvious. . . . All problems are resolved and everything is clear, simply because what matters is clear. The rock, all matter, all life, is charged with dharmakaya . . . everything is emptiness and everything is compassion. I don't know when in my life I have ever had such a sense of beauty and spiritual validity running together in one aesthetic illumination. Surely, with Mahabalipuram [near Madras] and Polonnaruwa, my Asian pilgrimage has come clear and purified itself.

I mean, I know and have seen what I was obscurely looking for. I don't know what else remains but I have now seen and have pierced through the surface and have got beyond the shadow and the disguise.★

In the ten or fifteen years before his death, there was a definite change in the inner climate of Merton's life. When he first came to the monastery in 1941, he had all the proper attitudes of a postulant, then those of a novice, then those of a young priest. He was humble, he was obedient, he fully believed that whatever the abbot said was what he should do. But later, as he matured, had his success, and realized his power as a writer, his perception of his role began to change. I think that in the response to *The Seven Storey Mountain* he sensed the element of sensational publicity, perhaps little more. You know. "Wicked young man runs off to monastery to save soul." But, with his other books, he saw what he could do with his writing, and this gave him more confidence to be himself. He grew less willing to accept the restrictions demanded by some bishop writing to the abbot to tell him what Fr. Louis might and might not write. Was this vanity, or arrogance? No, because Tom was always mindful of working for God. He was a monk; he would serve. But he altered his interpretations of what God wanted

★ *The Asian Journal of Thomas Merton* (ND, 1975), pp. 233–236.

him, as a writer, to do. This comes through very clearly in Michael Mott's biography of Merton. With much detail of actual quotations, working from the journals, Mott traces the stages of Merton's revisions of his attitudes toward the Deity, the Church, and the responsibilities of a monk.

There were frequent debates with the abbot when Tom began to write about social conditions, civil rights, and more when he became involved—even became a leader—for liberal Catholics in the movement. Friction with the abbot increased when his opposition to the Vietnam War led to articles attacking the Pentagon or the President. The more conservative Catholic bishops bore down on the abbot: "You must restrain this monk. All he's supposed to do is pray; he has no business concerning himself with social movements and the Vietnam War." Tom often let off steam to me about this repression in his letters, and naturally I sided with him, though I liked and admired Dom James.

On my next visit to Gethsemani, I accosted Dom James as he was coming across the west field. His robes were blowing in the wind and he looked very handsome and beautiful—like a figure in a Winslow Homer painting.

"Father Abbot, can I have a word?"

"Certainly, James."

"Father, I think God wants Father Louis to go on being *slightly* political." (I underscored the *slightly*.)

Dom James said to me, "James, try to understand. Fr. Louis's work and the work of all us monks is to pray; our prayers will rise up to Heaven and God will hear them, and God will solve the problems of the world."

Well, I was polite, and I didn't say the short word that popped into my mind.

I just said "Thank you, Father."

I understood that Dom James was trying to run the monastery by the Rule of St. Benedict and that he honestly believed it was best for Tom's soul to submit to obedience. Tom, with his spirit and his gift with words, was not an easy monk to "handle." When we talked about Dom James, it came through to me that Tom, in a certain way, relished the arguments with his superior and even, in a stranger way, *needed* them. He sounded off to his friends about Dom James in letters, but there was, I'm convinced, deep love and respect between these two strong-willed men who were so different in temperament. Dom James, beyond his abbatial duty, cared for Fr. Louis; he chose him to be his personal confessor.

The bishops kept up the pressure, and Tom finally agreed that he would stop publishing his political writing. But he set up a private publishing system for them; it reminded me of the Russian *samizdat* network. And there are a whole series of polemical writings that Tom called the "Cold War Letters." Tom wrote these pieces, got young friends in the novitiate to mimeograph them, and then (through friends such as "Ping" Ferry) had them sent to an ever-growing mailing list. Thus the "Cold War Letters" had an influential circulation. They were quoted and passed from hand to hand.

We also see a profound change in Merton's poetry about 1963 when his book *Emblems of a Season of Fury* was published. This was the first time he felt he could write secular poetry about social and political themes and get away with it. Here was a superb poem called "Chant to Be Used in Processions Around a Site with Furnaces." This is about the German concentration camps of the Holocaust. It is done with a wonderful kind of ingenuous irony, such as he later uses in "Original Child Bomb," his dead-pan account of the Hiroshima bomb. In "[Chant to Be Used in Processions,"] Merton uses Pound's "persona" mask technique, where he speaks through the mouth of one of the Nazi executioners. The irony is devastating when the SS officer urges the prisoners in the camp to write home to their friends to invite them to come to their "joke." This kind of black humor crops up continually in his later work.

The poetry of Merton that I find the greatest, the most liberated from convention, and the most extraordinary is the first book of his long poem, *The Geography of Lograire.* This was planned to be his "work in progress," his *Cantos,* his "Paterson." He told me he expected to be working on it for the rest of his life.

The "geography" of the poem simply is that of Merton's mind. He intended to make a personal epic of everything that had gone on in the geography of his mind, everything he had read, everything he remembered, but all distilled into compact, almost symbolic short poems. He only completed one volume of *Lograire,* which he left with me before he went to Asia and said, "If anything happens to me, I want you to publish this." I composed the necessary notes on his sources and brought it out about a year after his death.

Tom had read widely in history, in anthropology and in many other areas. Few such books were in the monastery library, but Carolyn Hammer found them for him at the University of Kentucky. But *Lograire* is not simply pastiche or a potpourri. What matters is what he could do with such diverse materials. From history he fashioned myths about the English Ranters and the Dakota Indian "Ghost Dances." From anthropology he made his own myths, such as those about the Cargo Cults in Micronesia. Blending language from ads in the *New Yorker,* with Covarrubras's accounts of the early Mexican Indians, he made delicious parodies of female fashions. Where he got copies of the *New Yorker,* I'll never know, but he did.

Merton had an acute sense of humor, which is seen in his poem "Chee$e." This makes fun of the Trappist cheese business at the monastery, of which Tom was always scornful; it parodies Joyce Kilmer's poem "Trees." There's a nice touch when he spells it *chee$e.*

Chee$e
Joyce Killer-Diller

I think that we should never freeze
Such lively assets as our cheese:

The sucker's hungry mouth is pressed
Against the cheese's caraway breast

A cheese, whose scent like sweet perfume
Pervades the house through every room.

A cheese that may at Christmas wear
A suit of cellophane underwear,

Upon whose bosom is a label,
Whose habitat:—The Tower of Babel.

Poems are nought but warmed-up breeze,
Dollars are made by Trappist Cheese.★

During these years when he was maturing, Tom did grouse a good deal about restrictions at the monastery. He disliked the cheese business and the junky stuff in the shop that sold little crucifixes or rosaries to the tourists. Once I asked, "Well, Tom, why, if it gives you this much pain, why do you stay there? After all, you're a brilliant writer, you could go out in the world. You could still do your spiritual teaching, you'd be a very successful writer. Why do you stay there?" He looked at me incredulously and said, "J., you don't understand. That's where I belong. That's my home."

Until he was given his hermitage up in the woods, he complained about conversation in the monastery. We think that Trappist monks don't talk, but that isn't necessarily so. They may talk as much as they want with their hands, in sign language. This irritated Tom and may have

★ *The Collected Poems of Thomas Merton* (ND, 1980), pp. 799–800.

been a reason why he longed for the life of a hermit. Of course, I found a curious contradiction there, that this man who loved people and was in touch with so many of them all over the world wanted to isolate himself. Yet some of his most beautiful prose is about the solitary life and the concept of solitude. His translations of the writings of the Desert Fathers reflect this concern. It is a theme that recurs in so many of his later books.

At one point he was corresponding with a bishop in Cuernavaca about the possibility of living in a cave and administering to the poor Indians. If he had actually done that, how much would he have missed those interesting intellectual visits from Catholic thinkers such as Jacques Maritain and the writers from everywhere who came to see him. And I don't think he would have stuck it out very long as a hermit in Mexico or Alaska, away from Gethsemani, which was the only home he ever really knew.

SELECTED
BIBLIOGRAPHY

James Laughlin

The River. Norfolk, CT.: New Directions, 1938.
Some Natural Things. New York: New Directions, 1945.
Skiing East and West. New York: Hastings House, 1946.
A Small Book of Poems. Milan and New York: Giovanni Scheiviller and New Directions, 1948.
The Wild Anemone & Other Poems. New York: New Directions, 1957.
Patent Pending. London: Gaberbocchus, 1959.
Confidential Report, and Other Poems. London: Gaberbocchus, 1959.
In Another Country. San Francisco: City Lights Books, 1978.
Stolen and Contaminated Poems. Isla Vista, CA: Turkey Press, 1985.
Selected Poems, 1935–1985. San Francisco: City Lights Books, 1986.
The Master of Those Who Know: Pound the Teacher. San Francisco: City Lights Books, 1986.
The Owl of Minerva. Port Townsend, WA: Copper Canyon Press, 1987.
Pound as Wuz: Essays and Lectures on Ezra Pound. St. Paul: Graywolf Press, 1987.
This Is My Blood. Covelo, CA: Yolla Bolly Press, 1989.
The Bird of Endless Time. Port Towsend, WA: Copper Canyon Press, 1989.
Random Essays. Mt. Kisco, NY: Moyer Bell, 1989.
Random Stanzas. Mt. Kisco, NY: Moyer Bell, 1990.

Collected Poems. Mt. Kisco, NY: Moyer Bell, 1992.
The Man in the Wall: Poems. New York: New Directions, 1993.
The Music of Ideas: New Poems. Waldron Island, WA: Brooding Heron Press, 1993.
Heart Island and Other Epigrams. Isla Vista, CA: Turkey Press, 1995.

Thomas Merton

Thirty Poems. New York: New Directions, 1944.
A Man in the Divided Sea. New York: New Directions, 1946.
Figures for an Apocalypse. New York: New Directions, 1948.
Exile Ends in Glory. Milwaukee: Bruce, 1948.
The Seven Storey Mountain. New York: Harcourt, Brace, 1948.
Seeds of Contemplation. New York: New Directions, 1948.
The Tears of the Blind Lions. New York: New Directions, 1949.
The Waters of Siloe. New York: Harcourt, Brace, 1949.
What Are These Wounds? Milwaukee: Bruce, 1950.
The Ascent to Truth. New York: Harcourt, Brace, 1951.
The Sign of Jonas. New York: Harcourt, Brace, 1953.
Bread in the Wilderness. New York: New Directions, 1953.
The Last of the Fathers. New York: Harcourt, Brace, 1954.
No Man Is an Island. New York: Harcourt, Brace, 1955.
The Living Bread. New York: Farrar, Straus, 1956.
The Silent Life. New York: Farrar, Straus, 1957.
The Strange Islands: Poems. New York: New Directions, 1957.
Thoughts in Solitude. New York: Farrar, Straus, 1958.
The Secular Journal of Thomas Merton. New York: Farrar, Straus, 1959.
Selected Poems. New York: New Directions, 1959.
Disputed Questions. New York: Farrar, Straus, 1960.
The Wisdom of the Desert. New York: New Directions, 1961.
The Behavior of Titans. New York: New Directions, 1961.
The New Man. New York: Farrar, Straus, 1961.
New Seeds of Contemplation. New York: New Directions, 1962.
Original Child Bomb. New York: New Directions, 1962.
A Thomas Merton Reader, ed. Thomas McDonnell. New York: Harcourt, Brace, 1962.
Life and Holiness. New York: Herder, 1963.
Emblems of a Season of Fury. New York: New Directions, 1963.
Seeds of Destruction. New York: Farrar, Straus, 1964.
The Way of Chaung Tzu. New York: New Directions, 1965.
Seasons of Celebration. New York: Farrar, Straus, 1965.
Raids on the Unspeakable. New York: New Directions, 1966.

Conjectures of a Guilty Bystander. Garden City, NY: Doubleday, 1966.

Mystics and Zen Masters. New York: Farrar, Straus, 1967.

Cables to the Ace. New York: New Directions, 1968.

Faith and Violence. Notre Dame, IN: Notre Dame University Press, 1968.

Zen and the Birds of Appetite. New York: New Directions, 1968.

My Argument with the Gestapo. Garden City, NY: Doubleday, 1969.

The Climate of Monastic Prayer. Kalamazoo, MI: Cistercian Publications, 1969.

The Geography of Lograire. New York: New Directions, 1969.

Opening the Bible. Collegeville, MN: Liturgical Press, 1971.

Contemplation in a World of Action. Garden City, NY: Doubleday, 1971.

The Asian Journal of Thomas Merton, ed. Naomi Burton Stone, James Laughlin, and Brother Patrick Hart. New York: New Directions, 1973.

The Collected Poems of Thomas Merton. New York: New Directions, 1977.

The Monastic Journey, ed. Brother Patrick Hart. Kansas City: Sheed, Andrews, 1978.

A Catch of Anti-Letters: Letters by Thomas Merton and Robert Lax. Kansas City: Sheed, Andrews, 1978.

Love and Living, ed. Naomi Burton Stone. New York: Farrar, Straus & Giroux, 1979.

Geography of Holiness: The Photography of Thomas Merton, ed. Deba Prasad Patniak. New York: Pilgrim, 1980.

Thomas Merton on Saint Bernard. Kalamazoo, MI: Cistercian Publications, 1980.

The Non-Violent Alternative, ed. Gordon C. Zahn. New York: Farrar, Straus & Giroux, 1980.

Day of a Stranger, ed. Robert E. Daggy. Salt Lake City: Peregrine Smith, 1981.

The Literary Essays of Thomas Merton, ed. Brother Patrick Hart. New York: New Directions, 1981.

The Hidden Ground of Love: The Letters of Thomas Merton on Religious Experience and Social Concerns, ed. William H. Shannon. New York: Farrar, Straus & Giroux, 1985.

Thomas Merton in Alaska, ed. Robert E. Daggy. New York: New Directions, 1988.

The Alaskan Journal of Thomas Merton, ed. Robert E. Daggy. Isla Vista, CA: Turkey Press, 1988.

Vow of Conversation: Diary, 1964–1965, ed. Naomi Burton Stone. New York: Farrar, Straus & Giroux, 1988.

Thomas Merton: "Honorable Reader"—Reflections on My Work, ed. Robert E. Daggy. New York: Crossroad, 1989.

The Road to Joy: Letters of Thomas Merton to New and Old Friends, ed. Robert E. Daggy. New York: Farrar, Straus & Giroux, 1989.

The School of Charity: Letters of Thomas Merton on Religious Renewal and Spiritual Direction, ed. Brother Patrick Hart. New York: Farrar, Straus & Giroux, 1990.

Thomas Merton: Spiritual Master. The Essential Writings, ed. Lawrence S. Cunningham. New York: Paulist Press, 1992.

The Courage for Truth: Letters to Writers, ed. Christine M. Bochen. New York: Farrar, Straus & Giroux, 1993.

Witness to Freedom: The Letters of Thomas in Times of Crisis, ed. William H. Shannon. New York: Farrar, Straus & Giroux, 1994.

Passion for Peace: The Social Essays, ed. William H. Shannon. New York: Crossroad, 1995.

Run to the Mountain: The Story of a Vocation, ed. Brother Patrick Hart. San Francisco: HarperSanFrancisco, 1995.

INDEX